CRIME AND CRIMINAL JUSTICE IN DISASTER

CRIME AND CRIMINAL JUSTICE IN DISASTER

Edited by

Dee Wood Harper

Kelly Frailing

CAROLINA ACADEMIC PRESS
Durham, North Carolina

Copyright © 2010
Dee Wood Harper
Kelly Frailing
All Rights Reserved

Library of Congress Cataloging-in-Publication Data

Harper, Dee Wood.
  Crime and criminal justice in disaster / Dee Wood Harper, Kelly Frailing.
    p. cm.
  ISBN 978-1-59460-775-2 (alk. paper)
  1. Crime. 2. Disasters--Social aspects. 3. Disasters--Law and legislation. I.
Frailing, Kelly. II. Title.

    .C 75
  HV6190.H37 2010
  364--dc22

                              2009044992

CAROLINA ACADEMIC PRESS
700 Kent Street
Durham, North Carolina 27701
Telephone (919) 489-7486
Fax (919) 493-5668
www.cap-press.com

Printed in the United States of America

CONTENTS

Part 3
The Criminal Justice System Response to Disorder and Disaster

TABLES AND FIGURES

Tables

Figures

Foreword: Toward a Criminology of Disaster

Behavioral scientists have historically been myopic in their quest for understanding of the social enterprise. Sociologists and criminologists seem to have been particularly suspect in this regard. Consider the example of business-related crime. Crime constituent to commerce is as old as civilization. Provisions and regulations such as the establishment of appropriate weights and measurements for commerce were contained in the Code of Hammurabi from the 18th century B.C. and also in the Laws of Manu, written about 2,000 years ago. There have been myriad normative systems that have addressed the practices of business and commerce over the centuries and where there are normative systems, there will be violations and deviations. Even uneducated people were aware of the "butcher's thumb" concept, in which the butcher might add his thumb weight to that of the meat on the scale in order to increase its purchase price. Historians were very much aware of similar deviance, referring to it as "fur collar crime," or that crime committed by nobility. In time, even criminologists turned their attention toward business and commercial crime. In 1939, the eminent criminologist, Edwin H. Sutherland, in his presidential address at the annual convention of the American Sociological Society (now Association), electrified his audience with his "discovery" of white collar crime. Today, of course, white collar crime is a household phrase and a major topic of criminological research and scholarship.

Many other vagaries of criminal behavior essentially went unnoticed by social scientists that could not see the forest for the trees. Over time, however, many insightful criminological scholars have identified configurations of crime that had been hitherto undiscovered or neglected by the criminological community. Examples here might include zoological crime, thanatological crime, marine, maritime or oceanic crime (briny crime, if you will) and military or "khaki collar crime." All three of these previously "undiscovered" forms of crime have been extant for centuries, if not millennia. Livestock theft dates back to the Neolithic Age. Grave robbing was a problem crime in ancient Egypt. Marine crime, in the form of piracy, was rampant even in the Phoenician Era. Military crime predates Alexander the Great. Only in recent years, have astute criminologists recognized that some such criminal acts represent much larger and complex patterns of illegal behavior, with distinctive parameters and unique dynamics, and properly require appropriate conceptual paradigms for analysis and understanding. Other illustrations of recently "discovered" crime might be computer crime, ecological or environmental crime, identity theft and intellectual property crime, to mention but some.

After a fruitful voyage of discovery, Dee Wood Harper and Kelly Frailing have conceptualized a new, intellectually compelling and exciting subfield of criminology—the criminology of disaster. Throughout history, disasters of many varieties have visited havoc and destruction on both humans and the social enterprise. Disasters take their economic, emotional and physical toll and disrupt the normal functioning of society, resulting in social anomie.

Professor Harper and Frailing have recruited an eminently well-qualified and talented team of researchers and assigned them the task of producing penetrating and insightful essays that demonstrate the linkage between disaster and crime. The basic paradigm guiding this book is the simple equation—disaster begets anomie, which begets crime and deviance. The resulting chapters focus on a variety of types of disasters, including floods, hurricanes, riots, earthquakes and terrorists attacks. The book is particularly effective in relaying its message because a number of the chapters focus on specific disasters, such as Hurricane Katrina, the *Exxon Valdez* oil spill, the Los Angeles riot of 1992, the Mumbai terrorist attack and the 9/11 terrorist attack.

The disaster-engendered crime examined includes looting, sexual assaults, fraud, and illegal drug trafficking, among others. Beyond the matter of disaster crime, the book also examines the criminal justice system's response to the disasters and their consequences. The role of response agencies and response policies and the deployment of response and recovery assets are explored. The book additionally examines the matter of possible future disasters and the application of lessons learned from those in the past.

This book is a groundbreaking effort. It builds on the sociological studies of disasters in the past and opens important and exciting research frontiers for the future. Disaster-related crime and deviance is a very much-neglected area of research. This book will certainly precipitate and encourage a robust research initiative in exploring this new field of criminology and its fascinating possibilities.

Dee Harper and Kelly Frailing have pushed the conceptual and theoretical envelope of criminology a step further in recognizing the very significant impact of disasters upon patterns of criminal activities and on the criminal justice system. In documenting the present state of knowledge regarding the influence of disaster on crime, they are inviting their fellow criminological scholars to join them in the quest for better understanding of the critical role of disasters in shaping the context in which crime occurs. I would encourage fellow behavioral scientists to follow them in exploring this new frontier.

Clifton D. Bryant

Professor Emeritus of Sociology at Virginia Tech University
November, 2009

PART 1

HISTORICAL AND THEORETICAL ASPECTS OF DISASTER AND CRIME

1

Introduction

This shortest section of the book begins with a chapter that examines crime during and after a variety of disasters. In *Crime and Disaster in Historical Perspective*, Frailing and Harper provide historical evidence that crime and disaster are closely linked. This chapter surveys the disaster literature over time, examining different types of disaster in different parts of the world and the crime that occurs in conjunction with them. This chapter, of course, is not a comprehensive listing of all disasters that have been inflicted on humanity. Not included, for example, is probably the worst natural disaster that ever occurred. In the middle of the 14th century in Europe, the Black Death left in its wake an estimated 25 million dead. It also engendered its own forms of deviance. Indeed, the point of this book is not to provide comprehensive coverage of disasters. Instead, it is to develop the thesis that crime does occur in the various stages of disaster and that the criminal justice system must be cognizant of this if it hopes to effectively respond.

The chapter begins by taking up the issue of exactly what constitutes a disaster. While there is little agreement, the most influential current research paradigm views disaster as a social phenomenon that reflects the ways in which social changes occur. The chapter continues by reviewing crimes and hurricanes, crimes and earthquakes, crimes and floods and finally, the manmade disaster of the September 11, 2001 attacks, an event in which the disaster itself is the crime. First examined is Hurricane Hugo, which hit St. Croix as a Category 4 storm in 1989. The storm caused the widespread destruction of support systems and physical structures on the island. Massive looting of all types of property occurred after the storm passed. The National Guard was sent in to quell the unrest. It is argued that the social conditions on the island prior to the storm contributed to the high rate of looting, a theme which will appear elsewhere in this volume.

Three earthquakes, that in San Francisco in 1906, that in Kanto, Japan in 1923 and that in Tangshan, China in 1976 are examined next. A first hand account of conditions in San Francisco immediately after the quake reveals that looting, which included people attempting to take jewelry off corpses still laying in the streets occurred, as did property looting in Chinatown. Price gouging immediately after the quake was also problematic for survivors. In Kanto,

Japan, a much different kind of post-quake crime occurred. Rumors of a Korean uprising emerged and were actively spread by the government. Though no such uprising was taking place, Japanese military and civilians killed 6,000 Koreans living in Japan. The Tangshan earthquake in China is the deadliest earthquake of the last four centuries. Data reveal that crime in Tangshan was higher in 1976, the year of the quake, than either the year before or the year after and surveys with survivors revealed that mass looting was the most common crime in the wake of the earthquake. These findings contradict the disaster research notion that looting after a natural disaster (as opposed to during a civil disturbance) is a rare, private event that is condemned by locals.

The first flood of interest in this chapter is the Buffalo Creek flood, which occurred in 1972 in West Virginia when a coal mine dam broke, unleashing millions of gallons of coal waste and water onto 16 small towns. It took two hours for the flood to pass through all of Buffalo Creek's towns. Not only did the flood leave 4,000 homeless, it caused a painful loss of community among survivors, which led to increased drug and alcohol use and theft. That outsiders provided most of the relief exacerbated the loss and led to reports of looting, as well. Also in 1972, the flooding of the Susquehanna River in Pennsylvania to 43 times its normal width flooded Wilkes Barre. Thirty percent of the city was underwater. Data from crime reports and newspapers revealed a significant increase of property crime after the flood as compared to before. Other crimes occurring in the wake of the flood included price gouging, contractor fraud, reselling of damaged automobiles and Small Business Administration fraud. Finally, an earthquake in the Indian Ocean produced the Boxing Day tsunami of 2004, which devastated four countries and killed hundreds of thousands of people. The destruction and death toll were worsened by the lack of a warning system. In the wake of the tsunami, prosocial, helping behavior was evident, but so was antisocial behavior. Corpses were looted for jewelry and money, hotels and supply convoys were also looted, survivors were raped and there were fraudulent claims made on the tsunami relief fund. Moreover, government and military officials were keeping relief supplies for themselves or selling them to those in need and demanding bribes from journalists and relief workers to enter affected areas.

Finally, *Crime and Disaster in Historical Perspective* examines the 9/11 disaster, which itself was a crime. Terrorists were responsible for hijacking and crashing four commercial jets in New York, Washington D.C. and Pennsylvania that resulted in the deaths of almost 3,000 people. However, the terrorist threat began long before 2001 and this chapter delves into some of that history, focusing on other attacks as well as law enforcement and governmental agencies' efforts (or lack thereof) to combat the problem. More specifically, federal law enforcement failed in several areas—imagination, policy, capability and management, not to mention the failure of interagency communication. This section also contains recommendations to avoid similar events in the future.

The second chapter in this section lays out a typology that connects phases of disaster with the types of crime that tend to emerge during those phases. In their chapter titled *Disaster Phase Analysis and Crime Facilitation Patterns*, Thornton and Voigt argue that each phase of disaster facilitates its own unique forms of criminality. Phase models as a framework for conceptualizing the impact of disaster have been used by emergency planners and social scientists alike. This book, and this chapter in particular, represent one of the first attempts to examine the impact of different phases of disaster as it relates to enhanced opportunities for a wide spectrum of crimes to occur. With a few exceptions, criminal behavior throughout the life cycle of disaster has been largely ignored by disaster researchers, criminologists and other social scientists.

Disaster researchers examine disasters in terms of predetermined phases. Looting, for example, tends to take place in the early phases, while contractor fraud occurs later in the disaster, during the recovery and reconstruction phases. Other crimes, such as sexual victimization, may occur throughout. Therefore, the main thrust of the chapter is to discuss how disaster phase analysis may be used as a framework to better understand how different phases of disasters lend themselves to vulnerabilities or opportunities for certain types of crime to occur.

The chapter continues by providing the overall conceptual framework of the book by first defining precisely what a disaster is. This is followed by a thorough examination of the disaster phase literature, which reveals that phases vary with regard to the names or labels associated with them, the number of stages and identifying elements or degree of complexity associated with activities of each phase in the life cycle of a disaster, but that they all attempt to provide a timeline of how a disaster progresses.

Using research on the Katrina Disaster as their primary evidence, Thornton and Voigt show how phase analysis illuminates individual and collective criminality. They provide a detailed account of the crimes known to have occurred in each phase of Katrina. They point out that everyone in the area of impact as well as those who were geographically displaced run the risk of being criminally victimized at any phase during a disaster, but certain populations including the poor, children, women, the elderly and ethnic and minority groups tend to be impacted the most by disasters and are subsequently more vulnerable to crime.

The third chapter in this section looks at disaster as crime. In *When the Disaster is a Crime: Legal Issues and the* Exxon Valdez *Oil Spill*, Gill, Picou and Ritchie examine different types of disasters and the attendant criminal and civil liabilities associated with the *Exxon Valdez* oil spill, as well as the consequences of litigation. Their typology includes natural disasters triggered by natural processes and hazards, technological disasters which are the result of irresponsible and reckless behavior combined with a failure of technology and the breakdown of social organization, natech disasters which are defined as disasters involving the dynamic interaction of natural events with technological systems and terrorism disasters, which involve deliberate targeting of critical infrastructure. They conclude that these disaster types have overlapping qualities, characteristics and impacts.

The authors next turn to a discussion of the *Exxon Valdez* oil spill as an environmental crime. The supertanker *Exxon Valdez* ran aground in 1989 in Alaska spilling tens of millions of gallons of oil. The captain of the ship was known to have a drinking problem and was drunk at the time of the grounding. The spill resulted in the destruction of thousands of animals and their habitats, as well as native and fishing communities along the coast. Damage to these communities continues in large part because of ongoing litigation. The authors conclude that while the award of monetary damages should serve to make individuals and communities whole, the long, drawn-out nature of the litigation often serves instead to re-victimize those initially affected.

These chapters are intended to help readers understand the ubiquity of disaster and crime over place and time, as well as what research has to say about the phases of disaster and the crime that occurs in each and what happens when the disaster itself is a crime. The chapters should also provide opportunities for critical thinking on these issues, about disasters that do not seem to fit the typologies, for example, about what constitutes a disaster and by extension when a disaster can be considered to be finished or about the relevance of a historical perspective on disaster and crime for future events. Moreover, these essays provide the foundation for theorizing about the linkage of crime and disaster.

2

CRIME AND DISASTER IN HISTORICAL PERSPECTIVE

By Kelly Frailing and Dee Wood Harper

Introduction

Why do people take advantage of disruptions in the normal flow of life and do illegal things? Disasters present such disruptions, which while encouraging some people to respond altruistically and help others, some seem to view the disruption as an opportunity to exploit the situation and those affected by it for what they conceive of as their personal benefit. In this chapter, we will examine what scholarly research has revealed about crime and a variety of natural and manmade disasters. It may seem at first glance as though we have left some major disasters out of this chapter, Hurricane Katrina chief among them; but because they will be covered at some length elsewhere in this volume, they are omitted here.

Definition of Disaster

Before we discuss various disasters and crime that occurred in their wakes, it is important to properly define what exactly is a disaster. This is a more difficult task that it might seem. While readers may have their own, implicit definitions, scholars have disagreed on just what constitutes a disaster. In his summary of the literature on attempts to define disaster, Perry (2006) notes that there are at least three dozen published definitions. It was after World War II that one of the most enduring elements of the definition of disaster began to be incorporated, namely that disasters cause the disruption of societal functioning. This element, first noted by Charles Fritz in 1961, is evident in subsequent disaster research, where a cycle of stability followed by disruption followed by adjustment is emphasized. The social disruption caused by disaster is probably most widely associated today with eminent disaster researcher E. L. Quar-antelli,[1] who views disasters through a prism of defining features, which in-clude a sudden onset, disruption of collective routines, undertaking unplanned courses of action in response and danger to valuable social objects. His defi-nition is of an entirely social nature; disasters exploit the vulnerability in so-cial systems. Another venerated disaster researcher, Russell Dynes, defines disaster similarly, as a situation in which norms fail and new ones emerge. These emergent norms are designed to protect valuable social resources. It should be clear by now that the current paradigm of disaster research is firmly rooted in the complimentary ideas that disasters are social phenomena and that they reflect the ways in which social changes occur (Perry 2006).

Even with some consensus about the current research paradigm, there continues to be disagreements about which characteristics should be included in the definition of a disaster. The fact that studies of disasters are produc-ing contradictory findings is all the more reason for coming to a consensus on a definition of disaster. With consensus, researchers can be certain they are studying the same things and not examining disparate phenomena and trying to extrapolate conclusions about disasters from them (Perry 2006). An agreed upon definition of disaster is all the more important because we may be experiencing an increased number of disasters as we become more re-liant on various technologies. Moreover, we are starting to observe new types of events that may also be disasters. These events have been called trans-sys-tem social ruptures (TSSRs) and have several characteristics: first that they transcend international borders, second that they spread very quickly, third that they have no known origin, fourth that there is a potential or actual large number of victims, fifth that typical community-based solutions are not obvious and sixth that there is a great deal of emergent behavior in these events. One example of a TSSR is the spread of the SARS virus in 2003. In addition to an increased number of disasters experienced and to TSSRs, some disasters are taking on new characteristics in addition to retaining some of their traditional ones. These have been dubbed social amplification of crises and disasters (SACD) and are exemplified by recent heat waves, snow and ice storms and blackouts. The novel aspects of TSSRs and SACDs call for in-novative responses, but not to the exclusion of those which have already proven effective in traditional disasters, such as a legitimate early warning system (Quarantelli, Lagadec and Boin 2006).

---

1. Astute readers will notice that Quarantelli's work is referenced numerous times throughout this volume. A student of disasters would do well to become familiar with his many publications.

Though an agreed upon definition of a disaster remains elusive, especially in light of new types of events, it should be clear that the events described in the remainder of the chapter fit within the current disaster research paradigm where the social element is of the utmost importance.

Crime and Hurricanes

Hurricane Hugo

On September 17, 1989, Hurricane Hugo, a Category 4 storm, made landfall on the U.S. Virgin Island of St. Croix. The hurricane destroyed all the support systems the island of 50,000 relied on for water, electricity and fuel. Stored food and water was damaged, as were telephone lines and the vast majority of buildings, many of which completely destroyed (Global Security 2008). The looting that occurred in the wake of the storm was massive. All consumer goods were taken and looters ripped wires, fixtures and carpets out of houses. Only ten percent of businesses in the three largest malls on the island reported that they were not completely looted. Researchers found that the looting was begun by delinquent youth who took consumer goods, followed by people with noncriminal lifestyles who took items from hardware and other stores and finally a third group of people who took survival items from grocery stores and generally did not engage in looting of the type that the first two groups did (Quarantelli 2007). On September 20, 1989, then President George H. W. Bush federalized the National Guard and nearly 1,000 soldiers were sent to the island. Law and order was restored quickly after their arrival (Global Security 2008). Eminent disaster researcher E. L. Quarantelli, who has contended that looting after natural disasters is a rarity, maintains that the social circumstances on St. Croix in advance of the storm facilitated this otherwise unusual phenomenon (1994, 2007). Looting as it follows natural disasters is covered elsewhere and at some length in this volume.

Crime and Earthquakes

The San Francisco Earthquake

On Wednesday, April 18, 1906, at 5:12 in the morning, an 8.3 magnitude earthquake struck the city of San Francisco. The damage caused by the quake included 52 fires, which eventually combined into a number of large fire storms that burned out of control until Sunday, April 21. The best initial account of this disaster was provided by Philadelphia native Charles Morris (2002: x, vii).

San Francisco was no stranger to earthquakes by 1906, having been struck in 1856, 1865, 1872, 1898 and 1900 (25). In just a few seconds, though, the 1906 earthquake brought theretofore untold devastation, destroying and damaging many of the city's buildings and causing dozens of fires (27). Three hundred thousand people were left homeless by the quake and camped around the city, 100,000 in Golden Gate Park alone. Food, water, shelter and sanitation were immediate concerns (106, 105). The estimated death toll at the time was approximately 1,500, with many more injured (117). San Francisco was certainly the most devastated city, but it was not the only one in northern California. Santa Rosa, San Jose, Palo Alto, Berkeley and Salinas were all badly damaged as well (138–142). An outpouring of donations for relief reached $5,000,000 within three days of the quake and came from all over the United States and Canada (143).

Morris notes that though many were stunned by the shock, others immediately began rescuing the trapped and injured. A third group, "those base wretches to whom plunder is always the first thought were as quickly engaged in seeking spoil in edifices laid open to their plundering hands by the shock" (29). He later speaks of other crime, namely, price gouging on the part of grocers and ferry operators, who sought to charge as much as a dollar for a loaf of bread and 50 dollars for a ferry ride out of San Francisco (31).

It is commonly known that firefighters in San Francisco used dynamite in an attempt to quell the fires that raged after the earthquake. This may seem counterintuitive, though it is important to note that the earthquake damaged water mains to the extent that a steady stream was impossible to obtain (39). Dynamite was used to "meet ruin with ruin," to destroy buildings so that the fire could not consume them and continue its path of destruction (57). In addition to fighting the fire, authorities had to concern themselves with those who would steal not only from stores but from the dead. Soldiers and police had orders from the mayor to shoot anyone engaged in looting and these orders were executed (57–58, 77–78). A number of detailed accounts describe the response to attempted looting. Mine workers discovered a man robbing a corpse of its jewelry. The workers hanged the man in a hotel entrance. Another man tried to cut the fingers off a dead woman to obtain her rings. Soldiers shot him dead in the act. A third man convinced troopers a dead woman was in fact his mother. Apparently overcome with grief, he threw himself on top of the corpse but began to chew off her earlobes in an effort to get her diamond earrings. Soldiers took notice and killed him as well (78–80). Looting took on a different form in the devastated Chinatown, where San Franciscans of prominence went rooting through the destruction in search of relics. It took a military intervention to stop this theft (82).

The Kanto Earthquake

Crime of a very different sort took place after the Kanto earthquake that struck Japan in 1923. On September 1 at a couple of minutes after noon, a 7.9 magnitude earthquake hit the Kanto area, which was both heavily populated and industrialized. Over 91,000 deaths were attributed to the quake and fires that followed, as was the devastation of over 381,000 homes. In the most desolate and devastated areas, rumors about an uprising on the part of Koreans living in Japan began to circulate. On September 2, martial law was imposed, but it did little to quell the confusion in the most affected areas, where both the government and the army encouraged the formation of civilian vigilante groups to retaliate against reported violence perpetrated by Koreans. The government actively spread these rumors about the Koreans, especially those of sedition, subversion and violence, including the poisoning of well water. Koreans held a less than esteemed place in Japanese society at the time, at once being encouraged to completely assimilate and treated as an inferior race. In the minds of at least two Japanese public officials intimately involved in the response to the earthquake, Koreans made a convenient scapegoat in the interest of maintaining Japanese public safety (Ishiguro 1998).

Scapegoating led to a horrific scene in the week after the Kanto earthquake. The Japanese police and military, as well as civilians, began to hunt Koreans, killing 2,500 of them with whatever was handy—bamboo, clubs, bare hands. It is estimated that ultimately, about 6,000 Koreans were killed by the Japanese during the aftermath of the earthquake. In great contrast to the events of 1923, Japanese and Koreans worked together as allies to facilitate the region's recovery after the Hanshin earthquake that struck Kobe in 1995 (Ishiguro 1998).

The Tangshan Earthquake

The deadliest earthquake of the last four centuries struck Tangshan, China on July 27, 1976. A 7.5 magnitude quake, it was followed 15 hours later by a severe aftershock. Over 240,000 people perished in the disaster and nearly 800,000 were injured (USGS 2009). A thorough study of crime in the wake of this earthquake was performed by Zhou, who was interested in testing disorganization theory in a disaster situation. He predicted that both property and violent crime would increase rapidly immediately after the disaster, then decrease gradually during the reorganization (1997: 70). Data were collected from official statistics and from a retrospective survey. The survey was done more than 10 years after the earthquake and about 3,000 respondents completed it (72, 77). The disorganization model was composed of the independent variable (intensity of the earthquake as measured in deaths and property damage), three intervening variables (community, family and individual disorganization) and four dependent variables (mass looting, mass violence, individual stealing and individual assault) (79–85). The greatest concentration of deaths occurred in the Lunan district of Tangshan, where over 17 percent of the district's population was killed. Over half of survey respondents reported that their homes had been destroyed by the earthquake (98–99).

The crime rate in Tangshan per 1,000 spiked in 1976, the year of the earthquake (1.10), as compared to both 1975 (.50) and 1977 (.58). Moreover, the crime rate in Tangshan was higher in 1976 than that of either nearby comparison city, Tianjin and Handan. In most other years, however, the crime rate in Tianjin was higher than that in Tangshan (122–23, 197). Having established crime's positive relation to disaster, Zhou turns his attention to testing his model of disorganization. He used the survey to measure his four dependent variables and found the common crime of the four was mass looting during the earthquake, followed by individual theft after the earthquake. Property crimes were much more prevalent than were crimes of violence (172).

In more detail, more mass looting occurred in the areas more directly affected by the earthquake. Possible explanations for this finding include the loss of guardianship of property due to death and exposure of goods due to property damage as well as the weakening of informal organization control, again due to death and destruction. Community disorganization also explains individual theft and to a lesser extent mass violence; individual assault is not well explained by the model (139–41). A path analysis of the same data revealed that the earthquake had a greater effect on and therefore explains more mass looting (.27) than mass violence (.08) or individual theft (.05) (143). Taking all these results together, Zhou concludes that the causes of mass looting are rooted in the earthquake itself, namely in death and destruction, but that the causes of individual theft and mass violence are rooted in the disorganization caused by the quake (145). These findings directly contrast Quarantelli and Dynes (1969), who contend that looting is a type of conforming behavior in the emergent norms that occur during civil disturbances such as riots. Looting in these situations is widespread, collective, public and it has the support of the community. Property appropriation during natural disasters, in contrast, is limited, perpetrated by individuals and done in secret by outsiders. It is strongly condemned by the disaster victims. There is also anecdotal evidence of mass looting also following the Kashmir earthquake that hit Pakistan at a magnitude of 7.6 on October 8, 2005 (Quarantelli 2007).

In contrast to the Tangshan earthquake, China's immediate relief efforts following the Sichuan earthquake, an 8.0 magnitude quake that hit China on May 12, 2008, were impressive and praised in Western media.

Crime and Floods

The Buffalo Creek Flood

Buffalo Creek lies in a hollow in Logan County, West Virginia. Its 16 towns were, like other West Virginian towns in the 1970s, dependent on coal mining and had been for decades. Nearly all of the 5,000 residents of the hollow relied on coal in one way or another to make a living. Typical for this industry, the Buffalo Mining Company had been dumping about 1,000 tons of slag per day on the middle fork of the creek, creating a dam there and a body of water 200 feet deep and 600 feet wide. The massive quantities of water used to prepare coal for shipping, a half a million gallons a day, were added to this lake, which by February 1972, contained 132 million gallons of black water. At 7:59 a.m. on February 26, the dam holding this water back from the towns in Buffalo Creek collapsed, unleashing a flood that included not only water and coal waste, but the material it picked up on its way into the hollow, approximately a million tons' worth. The first town to be hit, Saunders, was completely wiped out by a 20 foot wall of water, "as if a thousand bulldozers had been at work" (Erikson 1976: 21–29). It took two full hours for the flood to pass through Buffalo Creek. Hundreds of homes and buildings were destroyed, becoming piles of unrecognizable debris, and leaving 4,000 homeless. Train tracks had been picked up and bent like coiled wire and 125 were killed, their bodies found in trees, buried under silt or on the creek's banks. Some were unidentifiable (40–41). Within hours, the relief effort had begun, but for the most part it was the work of outsiders. Those who survived the flood were too much in shock to act. The National Guard, Red Cross, Salvation Army and volunteers arrived with meals and coffee and a local school served as a makeshift morgue. This sudden influx of outsiders brought with it reports among the residents of looting (42–43).

Relying on the thousands of pages of transcribed interviews, Erikson contends that what was so devastating to the Buffalo Creek residents was not just the flood but the near absolute loss of the community that theretofore had been so meaningful. Other disaster literature bears out the same conclusion, but also describes a post-disaster euphoria on the part of victims, a sudden and inexplicable feeling that the community is not gone after all. Erikson maintains that nothing of the sort occurred among the residents of Buffalo Creek. Part of this absence of the aforementioned euphoria may have been due to the outsiders who came in to provide relief. In other disaster-stricken communities, residents may have derived a new and reassuring sense of community as they worked together to recover. In Buffalo Creek, the opposite was true, with outsiders cleaning up wreckage and cordoning off homes without consulting residents. This activity likely contributed to the widespread reports among the residents of looting (194, 199–201). Another result of the loss of community was a general increase in crime as people found themselves housed next to new neighbors and subjected to declining moral standards. The use of alcohol and drugs increased in the wake of the flood, as did juvenile delinquency, adultery and theft, a sure indicator of social disorganization in Appalachia (205).

The Wilkes Barre Flood

Probably the most thorough account of crime and the 1972 flood in Wilkes Barre, Pennsylvania is provided by Siman (1977). Hurricane Agnes, the first storm of the hurricane season that year, brought almost daily rain during the first part of June and then a sustained rain pattern to the area by June 21 (11–12). The evacuation from Wilkes Barre began on June 23, with the Susquehanna River surging over dikes and into the valley in the late morning that day at 43 times its normal width. Nearly 30 percent of the city of about 58,000 was underwater by that evening and nearly 13,000 homes had been irreparably destroyed (15–16, 31). Some National Guard members on flood duty described the scene's devastation as rivaling that from the Vietnam War (20).

In his summary of post-disaster behavior, Dynes notes that disaster victims act positively with their welfare and that of their families and others in mind. They undertake rescue operations, for example, and looting, though feared, is very rare (1970: 8). There do exist, however, documented cases of looting following disasters, such as after the tornado that struck Judsonia, Arkansas in 1952 and the Kansas City tornado of 1957 (Siman 1977: 81–82).

Because of cases such as these, the Disaster Research Center at the Ohio State University revised its previous contention on the subject, which held that post-disaster looting was a rarity. The revision acknowledged that looting in fact does occur after disasters and that a major disaster might produce a significant amount of looting (Wright and Quarantelli 1974). Looting occurred after the Wilkes Barre flood, as well. Siman examined Uniform Crime Reports (UCR) data for Wilkes Barre and for the nearby city of Scranton, comparable but unflooded, for the six months before and after the flood. Reported property crimes increased significantly in Wilkes Barre in the six months after the flood as compared to the six months before, from 598 to 805. Offenses related to drinking also increased significantly from 217 before the flood to 309 after the flood (90–91, 100–01, 105). A content analysis of the city's two newspapers in the two months after the flood also revealed several reports of looting, supplementing the conclusions drawn from UCR data (152–53).

In addition to documented looting, Siman discovered instances of fraud committed by a group she calls profiteers. Both interviews with flood victims and news reports revealed price gouging, especially at the grocery stores. A Senate Subcommittee Hearing on Disaster Relief decried the "legal looting" committed by fraudulent contractors, who were increasing prices and doing shoddy work, if any, repairing homes and businesses. Some people, as well as insurance companies, bought flooded cars with the intention of selling the useless vehicles (167–72).

Siman also investigated Small Business Administration (SBA) fraud in the wake of the flood. She notes that the SBA is authorized to provide low rate disaster loans to home and business owners and that by the end of March, 1973, the SBA had approved over $775,000,000 to disaster victims in Pennsylvania (181–82, 188). However, complaints against the SBA abounded, especially those concerning false information provided by loan officers, rule changes that adversely affected applications and an inability to obtain updates on an application's progress (190). The SBA was not only an alleged offender, but also a victim of fraud. Claims of fraudulent behavior, when reported to the SBA or to the Federal Bureau of Investigation (FBI), underwent initial investigation and continued investigation up to prosecution by the U.S. Attorney where warranted (196–98). Of the approximately 44,000 applications made to the SBA loan disaster program, 74 resulted in indictments involving 83 people (198–99). The typical SBA fraudster was a 33-year-old white male with at least a high school education and a skilled job residing in a non-flooded area of Wilkes Barre who attempted a fraud of about $4,500. In the majority of instances, the fraudster was sentenced to 13 to 24 months of incarceration, with one to two years of probation to follow, and ordered to make restitution in the average amount of $2,250 (200).

Siman concludes her investigation of crime and the Wilkes Barre flood of 1972 with these sage words: "Perhaps in times of disaster, law enforcement personnel should concentrate more time and effort on the various types of disaster convergers who doubly victimize the stricken victim, thereby heaping insult upon his injury" (227). Another, similar type of re-victimization is evident in an analysis of two years' worth of Peruvian household surveys. Among other things, the approximately 36,000 respondents were asked about misfortunes, such as crime, job loss, death and natural disaster, as well as their use of public services. Victims of misfortunes, especially crimes but also natural disasters, were more likely to bribe public officials in order to have their cases given attention. These bribes were made out of desperation and with an understanding that Peruvian public officials are amenable to bribery. This amenability—corruption, in other words—serves to re-victimize people at one of the worst points of their lives (Hunt 2007).

The Boxing Day Tsunami

The Boxing Day Tsunami of 2004 was a truly devastating disaster. On December 26, an earthquake in the Indian Ocean produced a wall of water that hit Indonesia, Sri Lanka, India and Thailand with such force that many of the hundreds of thousands of the dead were never recovered. While a number of Western tourists were killed, the tsunami disproportionately affected the poor and disenfranchised. No warning system was in place for the coastal communities most devastated by the tsunami and natural barriers such as coral reefs, sand dunes and mangroves had been removed over time in the interest of commercial enterprise. The military control of the massive relief efforts was also problematic for poor victims. In Indonesia, for example, the military had been engaged in conflict with members of the Acehnese independence movement. With the military in charge of distributing aid to this devastated area, the Acehnese found themselves victimized again. A similar situation was evident in Sri Lanka between the military and Tamil Tigers. In India, aid was distributed by caste so that the untouchables received the least, if any. In fact, they were made to retrieve and bury corpses. The government in Thailand used the tsunami as an opportunity to round up and deport illegal Burmese immigrants. Women faced a particularly dire situation. Many more women than men were killed by the tsunami, as more of them were at home when it struck. Those that survived have been subject to abuse, physical and sexual assault and forced marriages, which can bring a dowry to her family, since the disaster (Keys, Masterman-Smith and Cottle 2006). Remembering that the military leaders in Myanmar were slow to accept aid after Cyclone Nargis hit on May 2, 2008 and killed hundreds of thousands, it is not difficult to see how military control of aid can lead to revictimization after a disaster.

A study of crime after the Boxing Day Tsunami focuses first on the prosocial behavior observed in the wake of the disaster. These behaviors included relief workers and volunteers, as well as political rebels, arriving immediately in affected areas, the creation of online blogs to share information and to direct aid, donations from around the world and the arrival of armed forces from unaffected countries to assist with the relief. However, antisocial behavior, some criminal, was also clearly observed at the individual, organizational, governmental and societal levels (Teh 2008).

Combining two theories of crime, Shaw and McKay's social disorganization (1942) and Cohen and Felson's routine activity theory (1979), Teh maintains that the disorganization created by the tsunami resulted in an increased number of opportunities for crime at all four levels. At the individual level, victims and non-victims of the tsunami stole money and jewelry from corpses. Looters were arrested in the process of taking appliances from hotels. Relief convoys were also looted. Orphans were used by family members and others to obtain aid. Victims of the tsunami who lived in Britain and Sweden had their homes in those countries broken into. Men raped homeless survivors. Fisherman attempted to make fraudulent claims from the tsunami fund. Thieves tried to empty the bank accounts of the dead. At the organization level, a tsunami souvenir industry sprang up in Thailand, producing and selling videos, t-shirts and pictures of victims. At the governmental level, as alluded to above, military and political officials were suspected of pilfering money and goods from relief donations and keeping them for themselves or selling them. There were also reports of soldiers demanding bribes from journalists and relief workers in order to enter a tsunami-affected area. At the societal level and again as alluded to above, those who were viewed as less important, including India's untouchables, received little if any aid. Religious intolerance was also problematic. Muslim extremists in Indonesia, for example, threatened Christian relief organizations who assisted Muslim orphans. Hindus in India disallowed Christian groups' relief under their anti-conversion laws (Teh 2008).

While this examination focuses on antisocial behavior, including crime, that occurred in the immediate aftermath of the Boxing Day Tsunami and this chapter generally focuses on crime in the wake of disasters, Redo (2005) cautions that the study of crime in the months and years that follow disasters is more complex. Situations created by disasters that may persist and contribute to crime include exploitation of vulnerable women, lack of schooling for children, organized crime becoming involved in the rebuilding and fraud throughout the reconstruction process. In fact, at least two researchers have already anticipated the risk of money laundering in the wake of natural disasters. It is possible for sophisticated, organized criminals to launder money through relief organizations, which collect large amounts of money to aid in the disaster relief. Similarly, if bank customers have been separated from identification or account information due to a disaster and banks relax their customer identification standards as a result, it creates an opportunity for identity theft and money laundering, as well as the financing of terrorist operations. Suggestions for preventing these crimes include verifying reported Social Security numbers for credit reports, current and former addresses and previous fraudulent activity, especially when large cash deposits or withdrawals are involved. Charitable organizations should make their finances as transparent as possible and disclose their transactions as they relate to distributing donations. Finally, both the authorities and financial institutions need to exercise vigilance against fake charities established after a disaster for purely criminal purposes (McKenzie and Bryant 2006).

Manmade Disasters

September 11, 2001

The September 11, 2001 terrorist attacks on New York and Washington are examples of those disasters in which the disaster itself is the crime. Of course, crimes were perpetrated in the wake of 9/11 (see for example, the chapter on disaster and fraud in this volume). However, the main criminal incidents in this case were the attacks perpetrated by terrorists on targets in the United States. Moreover, it will become clear that the terrorists engaged in a variety of criminal activity in their preparation for these attacks and afterward, as have other terrorists who perpetrated similar acts. Because of the significance of the September 11 attacks, they are covered in some detail here.[2]

The events of September 11, 2001 will be familiar. On that day, four flights were hijacked and flown into pre-selected targets that symbolized the American economy and government. American Airlines flight 11 left Boston for Los Angeles at 7:59 a.m. The last routine transmission was made 15 minutes later. The plane got as far west as upstate New York before turning south toward New York City. Piloted by Mohammed Atta and with four other hijackers on board, it crashed into the North Tower of the World Trade Center at 8:46 a.m. A short time later, United Airlines flight 175 left Boston for Los Angeles, taking off at 8:14 a.m. The last routine transmission was made about a half hour after takeoff. The plane got as far south as the border between Pennsylvania and New Jersey before turning north toward New York City. Piloted by Marwan al Shehhi and with four other hijackers on board, it crashed into the South Tower of the World Trade Center at 9:03 a.m. Both towers later collapsed as a result of being struck. Meanwhile, American Airlines flight 77 departed Washington, D.C. for Los Angeles. It took off at 8:20 a.m., with the last routine transmission occurring about a half hour later. The plane got as far west as eastern Ohio before turning east and heading toward Washington, D.C. Piloted by

---

2. The literature on September 11 is extensive. Among some of the most important books, in addition to *The 9/11 Commission Report*, are *Out of the Blue* by Richard Bernstein, *Why America Slept* by Gerald Posner and *Ghost Wars* by Steve Coll. There is also a variety of work that challenges the official accounts of that day.

Hani Hanjour and with four other hijackers on board, it crashed into the Pentagon at 9:37 a.m. Finally, United Airlines flight 93 left Newark for San Francisco, taking off at 8:42 a.m. The last routine transmission was made about 45 minutes later. The plane made it as far west as Ohio before turning back east toward Washington and its target, the White House. It is estimated that the famous passenger revolt began at 9:57 a.m. The revolt caused pilot Ziad Jarrah, one of four hijackers on board, to crash the plane into an empty field in Shanksville, Pennsylvania at 10:03 a.m. (9/11 Commission 2004: 32–33, 238–39). Nearly 3,000 people were killed in the attacks.

The events leading up to the attacks in terms of the terrorists' actions are probably less well known, or at least less well remembered. To execute their plans, the terrorists would need trained pilots and so-called "muscle hijackers." Two of the pilots, Atta and al Shehhi, came to the U.S. in the early summer of 2000. They met the third pilot, Jarrah, in Florida and all three trained at flight schools there. A flight school instructor remembers Atta and al Shehhi as aggressive and rude and recalled that they had attempted to take control of the aircraft from him while he was flying during a lesson. In 2000, two men were being considered for the fourth pilot's position, Nawaf al Hazmi and Khalid al Mihdhar. They were living in California at the time and attempted to enroll in flight school in San Diego. Because they spoke no English and had difficulty learning it, they were unsuccessful in flight school. A flight school instructor remembers that Hazmi and Mihdhar had no interest in learning how to take off or land, only in controlling the plane in midair. Because neither Hazmi nor Mihdhar would do as a pilot, they were relegated to muscle hijacker status and Hani Hanjour was chosen as the fourth pilot. He had recently received a commercial pilot certificate from the Federal Aviation Administration (FAA) and returned to Arizona for additional training at a flight school in Mesa, though his work there was deemed below average. Meanwhile, Atta, al Shehhi and Jarrah received their commercial pilot licenses in Florida (221–27). As for the muscle hijackers, 12 of the 13 came from Saudi Arabia and most had undergone al Qaeda basic training, which included learning firearms, explosives and topography. These men were recruited for their extreme views, willingness to participate in this suicide mission and perhaps most importantly, clean records that allowed them to travel internationally without attracting attention (231–34). In the early summer of 2001, three of the four pilots, Atta, al Shehhi and Jarrah, began taking cross country surveillance flights (242).

Though the terrorists took steps to avoid detection as they prepared for their attack, such as the aforementioned selection of muscle hijackers who could travel without detection, there were instances in which the terrorists' behavior could have brought them to the attention of the authorities. In addition to the strange behavior displayed during their flight school training, two of the pilots, Atta and al Shehhi, had difficulty reentering the United States after trips overseas. Neither had a student visa and for that reason, both were detained by the Immigration and Naturalization Service (INS) upon their arrival. They convinced Customs officials that they should be allowed to continue their flight school training and were permitted to enter the U.S. (227–29). Another pilot, Jarrah, received a speeding ticket on the I-95 in Maryland in the early morning hours of September 9, 2001 (253). Finally, Atta, Suqami and the al Shehhi brothers were selected by the Computer Assisted Passenger Prescreening System (CAPPS) for additional screening before boarding American Airlines flight 11 in Boston. The only consequence of being selected by CAPPS was that checked baggage was kept off the plane until it was confirmed that those passengers had passed inspection. Hanjour, Mihdhar and Moqed were selected by CAPPS for additional screening before boarding American Airlines flight 77 in Washington, D.C. The Hazmi brothers were also selected for extra scrutiny there because one had no photo identification, nor did he speak English. Mihdhar and Moqed both set off the metal detector alarm. Mihdhar passed the second metal detector; Moqed did not, though he did pass a wand screening. One hijacker, Haznawi, was selected by CAPPS for additional screening before boarding United Airlines flight 93 in Newark (1–4).

Readers may remember that the first attack on the World Trade Center did not happen in September, 2001. Rather, it occurred on February 26, 1993, when a Ryder truck packed with explosives was detonated, blowing a seven story hole up from the underground parking garage. Six people were killed and over a thousand were injured. This attack signaled a new type of terrorism. The FBI and Justice Department investigated the attack quickly and effectively and three suspects were quickly arrested, Mohammed Salameh, who had rented the Ryder truck, Nidal Ayyad, who procured the necessary chemicals and Mahmoud Abouhalima, who helped mix the chemicals. These arrests led to others, including that of Ramzi Yousef and Omar Abdel Rahman, the so-called "Blind Sheik." The suspects were convicted of the bombing. Although this attack signaled a new type of terrorism, as mentioned above, it was ironically the speed and efficiency of the investigation and prosecution of suspects that blinded the U.S. to the extent of the coming threat (71–73). Readers would do well here to consider that terrorists are criminals and as such, engage in the same behavior, some savvy, some not so much, that ordinary criminals do. For example, Salameh came to the attention of law enforcement after the first attack on the World Trade Center because he reported stolen the truck used in the blast and then attempted to get his $400 deposit back from the rental agency (Hamm 2007: 45–47).

The man deemed responsible for the 9/11 attacks, Osama bin Laden, has yet to be brought to justice. He is presumed to be hiding in either Afghanistan or Pakistan. Bin Laden has been on the United States' radar since 1993, but at that time, only as a financier of terrorist acts. It was not until 1996 that he was understood to be an inspirer and organizer of these acts, as well. By early 1998, as he and al Qaeda became more well known to various government agencies, each developed a strategy for dealing with him. The Central Intelligence Agency (CIA) planned to capture and remove him from Afghanistan, the Justice Department planned to indict him and the State Department was focused more on Indian/Pakistani relations than on bin Laden. The CIA was not able to execute its plan to capture bin Laden as he moved between his residence and the Taliban capital of Kandahar before August 5, 1998. On that day, the U.S. embassies in Nairobi, Kenya and Dar es Salaam, Tanzania were simultaneously bombed. Two hundred thirteen people were killed in Nairobi and 11 were killed in Dar es Salaam. Bin Laden and his associates were quickly deemed responsible for the attacks (9/11 Commission 2004: 108–116). The embassy attack in Nairobi provides another example of criminal incompetence. Mohammed al-Owhali, charged with helping to drive the bomb-laden truck up to the embassy building, forgot his gun on the passenger seat and was unable to subdue an unarmed guard at the gate. The truck's driver parked near the embassy, but not as close as originally intended. Both the initial attacks on the World Trade Center and the embassy bombings demonstrate that people of variable criminal capabilities are involved in terrorist acts. Sophisticated surveillance, financing, communication and bomb making occur alongside incompetent acquisition of travel documents, ineffective getaways and thoughtless discarding of evidence. Moreover, terrorist operatives involved in these attacks all underwent training, but at times were ill utilized, with those specially trained performing some of the most elementary jobs, especially in the case of the embassy bombings (Hamm 2007: 75–77, 81–82).

In an eerie portent, a memo that then President Clinton received in his daily briefing on December 4, 1998, just four months after the embassy attacks, indicated that bin Laden was already preparing to hijack U.S. aircraft and engage in other attacks. Increasingly urgent reports began to follow in May, 2001, culminating in the now infamous August 6, 2001 memo entitled "Bin Laden Determined to Strike in US." Among the highlights of this memo were that bin Laden had been wanting to attack inside the U.S. since 1997, failure of previous plots is no deterrent and that he is capable of planning over the course of years (9/11 Commission 2004: 255–62).

A review of the relevant governmental structure and procedures in place at the time of the 9/11 attacks should be instructive and changes since then should be evident. Though then FBI director Louis Freeh recognized terrorism as an imminent threat, insufficient resources were allocated for the Bureau's counterterrorism operations. The INS, with its 15,500 agents, was more focused on illegal immigration across the southwestern border of the United States than it was on terrorists. The FAA perceived sabotage as a greater threat than hijacking. At the time of 9/11, the so-called "no fly" list contained the name of just 12 terrorist suspects. Knives less than four inches in length were permitted through security checkpoints and onto airplanes and lastly, the security aboard commercial aircraft was not designed to prevent suicide hijackings. Perhaps most importantly, there were misunderstandings about interagency information sharing, especially among the National Security Agency (NSA), the FBI and that holdover from the Cold War, the CIA, and these misunderstandings led to information going unshared. For example, there were at least 10 opportunities for the FBI and CIA to either act on information or share it with one another. Had they taken these opportunities, some of the people responsible for 9/11 would have been under much closer surveillance before the attacks (76–91, 355). Among the principal changes the creation of the Department of Homeland Security (DHS) was supposed to bring about was improved interagency information sharing (DHS is covered at some length elsewhere in this volume).

The 9/11 attacks revealed failures in four areas, the first of which was imagination. Before 9/11, an attack from a stateless terrorist organization on American soil using aircraft as weapons was inconceivable. The second failure area was policy. The pre-9/11 response to al Qaeda was formed in response to the embassy bombings of 1998. The tragedy of those attacks provided an opportunity for the U.S. to examine the full threat that bin Laden posed, but this opportunity was not taken. The third failure area was capability. Though al Qaeda was probably the most dangerous threat to the United States, at no time before 9/11 did the Department of Defense fully engage in countering it. Finally, the fourth failure area was management. The inability to effectively share information was especially symptomatic of the government's broader inability to adapt to changing threats (339–53).

With all that said about what went wrong and what could have been done better, the 9/11 Commission made 28 detailed recommendations on what to do to prevent another attack and to shore up the United States' standing in the world. It made 13 equally detailed recommendations on how to implement them and in so doing, reorganize the government (361–428).

Conclusion

In this chapter, we have summarized some of the debate on the definition of disaster and what is known about crime and a variety of disasters, Hurricane Hugo of 1989, the San Francisco earthquake and fire of 1906, the Kanto earthquake of 1923, the Tangshan earthquake of 1976, the Buffalo Creek flood of 1972, the Wilkes Barre flood of 1972 the Boxing Day Tsunami of 2004 and the September 11, 2001 terrorist attacks. The data presented above especially counter the long held notion that looting only rarely occurs after natural disasters. In fact, crime of different types, from theft to murder, verifiably takes place in the wake of natural disasters. In some manmade instances, the disaster is the principal crime perpetrated. The study of crime and disaster should continue in this fashion in an effort to both better understand the circumstances in which these crimes are likely to occur and to devise protocols that may prove useful in putting a stop to criminal activity that follows disasters and that increases the victimization of those already devastated. Additionally, this approach should lead to the development and testing of some theoretical propositions concerning the complex linkages between disaster and crime.

References

9/11 Commission. 2004. *The 9/11 Commission Report: Final Report of the National Commission on Terrorist Attacks Upon the United States.* Washington, D.C.: U.S. Government Printing Office.

Cohen, L. E. and M. Felson. 1979. Social change and crime rate trends: A routine activity approach. *American Sociological Review* 44: 588–605.

Dynes, R. 1970. *Organized Behavior During Disaster.* Lexington, MA; Heath Lexington Books.

Erikson, K. T. 1976. *Everything In Its Path: Destruction of Community in the Buffalo Creek Flood.* New York: Simon and Schuster.

Global Security. 2008. Operation Hawkeye. Available online at: http://www.globalsecurity.org/military/ops/hawkeye.htm.

Hamm, M. S. 2007. *Terrorism as Crime: From Oklahoma City to Al-Qaeda and Beyond.* New York: New York University Press.

Hunt, J. 2007. How corruption hits people when they are down. *Journal of Development Economics* 84: 574–89.

Ishiguro, Y. 1998. A Japanese national crime: The Korean massacre after the Great Kanto Earthquake of 1923. *Korea Journal* 38(4): 331–55.

Keys, A., H. Masterman-Smith and D. Cottle. 2006. The political economy of a natural disaster: The Boxing Day tsunami, 2004. *Antipode* 38(2): 195–204.

McKenzie, M. and K. L. Bryant. 2006. Natural disasters and money laundering risks. *Journal of Money Laundering Control* 9(2): 198–202.

Morris, C. 2002. *The San Francisco Calamity by Earthquake and Fire.* Urbana, IL: University of Illinois Press.

Perry, R. W. 2006. What is a disaster? In *Handbook of Disaster Research*, eds. H. Rodriguez, E. L. Quarantelli and R. Dynes, New York: Springer: 1–15.

Quarantelli, E. L. 1994. Looting and antisocial behavior in disasters. University of Delaware Disaster Research Center Preliminary Paper #205.

Quarantelli, E. L. 2007. The myth and the realities: Keeping the "looting" myth in perspective. *Natural Hazards Observer* 31(4): 2–3.

Quarantelli, E. L. and R. Dynes. 1969. Property norms and looting: Their patterns in community crisis. *Phylon: The Atlanta University Review of Race and Culture* 31(2): 168–82.

Quarantelli, E. L., P. Lagadec and A. Boin. 2006. A heuristic approach to future disasters and crises: New, old and in-between types. In *Handbook of Disaster Research*, eds. H. Rodriguez, E. L. Quarantelli and R. Dynes, New York: Springer: 16–41.

Redo, S. 2005. Natural disasters and crime prevention: What are we waiting for? In *Current Issues in International Crime Prevention and Criminal Justice: Papers from the Ancillary Meetings Held in the Framework of the United Nations Eleventh Congress on Crime Prevention and Criminal Justice, Bangkok, 18–25 April 2005*, ed. J. Abanese, Milan: International Scientific and Professional Advisory Council of the United Nations Crime Prevention and Criminal Justice Program: 273–81.

Shaw, C. R. and H. D. McKay. 1942. *Juvenile Delinquency and Urban Areas.* Chicago: University of Chicago Press.

Siman, B. A. 1977. *Crime During Disaster.* University of Pennsylvania PhD diss. Ann Arbor, MI: University Microfilms International.

Teh, Y. K. 2008. The abuses and offenses committed during the tsunami crisis. *Asian Criminology* 3: 201–11.

USGS. 2009. Historic Earthquakes: Tangshan, China. Available online at: http://earthquake.usgs.gov/regional/world/events/1976_07_27.php.

Wright J. and E. L. Quarantelli. 1974. Anti-social behavior in disasters: Myth or reality? Disaster Research Center paper, the Ohio State University, 1–10.

Zhou, D. 1997. *Disaster, Disorganization, and Crime.* University of Albany State University of New York PhD diss. Ann Arbor, MI: University Microfilms International.

Discussion Questions

1. Describe the characteristics of the current disaster research paradigm.
2. Summarize the seven disasters described in this chapter, including what types of crime occurred in their wakes.
3. What are some potential problems in studying crime after a disaster? Consider, for example, the ability to report crimes and keep records after a disaster and the use of retrospective surveys.
4. What are some of the theories of crime that seem useful in explaining crime in the wake of disasters? What are the strengths and weaknesses of these theories in this particular context?
5. What are some steps that could be taken to stop various criminal activities that occur after disaster? Consider, for example, effective guardianship by authorities but be mindful of other post-disaster duties these organizations must undertake.

3

Disaster Phase Analysis and Crime Facilitation Patterns

By William E. Thornton and Lydia Voigt

Introduction

Even though there is debate over the conceptual clarity of disaster phase models (e.g, Lewis Killian's (2002) four phase model including *warning, impact, emergency* and *recovery*), disaster researchers and emergency planners continue to apply modeling techniques, such as phase analysis, to formulate disaster risk assessment capabilities, crisis management planning and crisis response and recovery tactics. While social scientists have utilized disaster phase models to study the differential vulnerability of people to disasters based on characteristics, such as social class, gender, race and ethnicity, disability, health and age, as well as to examine the susceptibility of communities to the varying impacts of disasters, relatively few researchers have conducted studies on the impacts of different phases of disasters as they relate to enhanced opportunities for a wide spectrum of crimes to occur. Alice Fothergill (1996, 1999), for example, discusses the connection among gender risks and disasters and the occurrence of domestic violence at different phases of disasters. More recently, William Thornton and Lydia Voigt (2007, this volume) have studied the incidence of sexual assaults during the various phases of the Katrina Disaster, trying to make sense of the nature and circumstances of rape victimizations, which occurred and are still occurring. However, research on the enhanced opportunities for criminal behavior throughout the *life cycle of disasters* has not generally been of much interest to disaster researchers, criminologists or criminal justice practitioners.

One may ask why until recently, with some exceptions, the study of the effects of disasters on the causes or facilitation of crime has not received much attention by social scientists, including criminologists and disaster researchers. Is this a case of too little evidence of the occurrence of crimes in the context of disasters to warrant attention or is this a case of unexplored territory? Or, is this a case of just assuming that there is very little crime based on tiny snippets of disaster-crime incidence accounts, which mostly focus on looting and isolated and random street crimes, therefore missing the larger manifestation of crimes in their various forms (e.g, ranging from interpersonal violence and sexual assaults to cyber fraud, white collar crimes, corporate crimes, political corruption and malfeasance and institutional and structural violations of human rights) and their expression through the different phases of the disaster?

The enormous human, socio-cultural and economic consequences and complexities associated with the World Trade Center Disaster of September 11, 2001 and the Katrina Disaster beginning August 29, 2005 have forever altered the way we all look at disasters. The field of disaster research has been expanding significantly over this decade. Damon Coppola (2007) notes that in addition to the unprecedented disasters in our recent history, which have certainly stimulated interest in disaster research, growing attention may be attributed to changing patterns and trends of disasters. For instance, the number of disasters worldwide has been increasing each year. Moreover, the overall number of people affected by disasters, directly and indirectly, has been rising. There is also evidence that disasters are becoming more costly. Poorer countries probably suffer the greatest impact of disasters including internal civil conflicts that lead to complex humanitarian emergencies, bringing to light the disproportionate physical and social consequences of disasters including the enhancement or facilitation of many possible crimes occurring throughout the life cycle of a disaster (13–24).

Disaster researchers over the years have sought to codify and organize disasters in terms of predetermined phases, what we refer to in this chapter as phase analysis. For example, when crimes such as looting (i.e. theft and intentional and unauthorized entry of a residence or business unprotected because of a disaster) occur, they usually take place in the early stages of the disaster, during the *impact* or *emergency phase*, in the context of relative social disruption and less social control by the police. Other crimes such as contractor fraud (e.g, when unscrupulous builders take disaster victims' money and fail to do the proper work on their damaged homes or businesses) generally occur later in the disaster, during the *recovery* or *reconstruction* phase. While some crimes seem to appear at specific times during a disaster, others, such as rape and other forms of sexual assault, depending on the disaster event, may be found throughout the life cycle of the disaster.

The purpose of this chapter is to discuss how disaster phase analysis may be used as a framework to better understand how different phases of disasters, each with their own unique physical, social, economic and environmental challenges, lend themselves to vulnerabilities or opportunities for certain types of crime to occur. We shall begin with a definition of disaster.

Definition of a Disaster

Surprisingly, there is no commonly agreed upon definition of what constitutes a disaster. The World Health Organization's Emergency and Humanitarian Action Department defines a disaster as "Any occurrence that causes damage, ecological disruption, loss of human life or deterioration of health and human services" (Gender and Health in Disasters 2002). Another definition developed by the National Governors Association (NGA) defines a disaster as an "event that demands substantial crisis response requiring the use of government powers and resources beyond the scope of one line agency or service" (Haddow, Bullock and Coppola 2008: 27). Accordingly, not all hazardous occurrences or events are identified as disasters; rather only those events that cause serious physical or social disruptions, which exceed the ability of an affected locale to cope using its own resources are defined as such (UN 1992). The disaster literature generally makes a distinction between four specific types of disasters:

- *Natural*: Natural disasters include natural phenomenon that occur regardless of the presence of humans, such as hurricanes, floods, earthquakes, storm surges, tornadoes, tsunamis, et cetera. It is possible, however, that humans may exacerbate these natural processes.
- *Technological*: Technological disasters are hazards based on the negative consequences of human innovations, which can damage or destroy life, property or the environment. They range from toxic contamination events (e.g, biological, chemical, radiological and nuclear) to power failures, from computer program bugs to mass transportation accidents.
- *Natural-technological*: A natural-technological disaster is a natural disaster that directly or indirectly releases hazardous materials into the environment (Showalter and Myers 1994). A natural-technological disaster may also refer to the confluence of natural and technological catastrophic events. The Katrina Disaster is an example of the natural-technological type (Picou and Marshall 2007).
- *Terrorism*: Terrorism is defined in the Code of Federal Regulations as "the unlawful use of force and violence against persons or property to intimidate or coerce a government, the civilian population, or any segment thereof, in furtherance of political or social objectives" (28 C.F.R.

Section 0.85: 51). Terrorist acts may employ any number of destructive means including biological and chemical weapons, as well as nuclear weapons and explosives, et cetera. Terrorists engage in their criminal and often disastrous ends by any number of means including weapons of mass destruction (WMD), which include four principle categories often referred to as CBRNE, meaning chemical, biological, radiological/nuclear and explosive (Mahan and Griset 2008: 3, 22).

It is not always easy to classify a disaster since there are often overlapping elements. For instance, terrorists may use combined hazards to achieve what is referred to as a synergistic effect such as using explosives to deliver chemical or biological weapons (Coppola 2007: 103). Many of the new and emerging technologies included in technological disasters no doubt will find their way into future terrorists' arsenals. It is important to note that terrorism does not have to involve an actual attack; even a serious threat can elicit disastrous consequences including physical, social and financial consequences.

Since the September 11, 2001 terrorists attacks, there has been a tendency in the U.S. to assume that future threats of disasters will come in the form of terrorism. At the federal level, planning and resources have indeed been directed toward that belief. Shortly after the events of 9/11, the Federal Emergency Management Agency (FEMA) was subsumed under the new Department of Homeland Security (DHS). In fact, some disaster researchers suggest that the current emphasis on terrorism has created serious conflicts between those with a focus on mitigating social/physical consequences and victim-centered prevention/responses (e.g, the orientation of disaster researchers or disaster crisis managers) versus those who focus on the criminal elements and controlling terrorism (e.g, the orientation of law enforcement officials). As an example, in the 1995 Oklahoma City bombing of the Murrah Federal Building, in which a truck bomb ripped away the front of the building killing 168 people and injuring over 800, there was a clash between different groups of first responders (Clements 2009: 70). Various levels of law enforcement perceived the event as another form of criminal attack, which called for sealing off the area as a crime scene for eventual investigation. Other groups such as emergency managers, who responded to the event as a disaster (not necessarily as a crime event), triggering a "universal" disaster response. This group was more concerned with assessing the impact of the disaster, searching for and rescuing survivors, assessing injuries, examining emerging hazards and hazard effects, et cetera. Six years later, following the World Trade Center catastrophe, similar clashes continued over issues such as controlling the perimeter of the areas and securing the areas versus providing rescue services, handling dead bodies, debris removal and assessing hazardous conditions (Quarantelli, Lagadec and Boin 2006: 23).

Some disasters may by their very nature constitute a crime or what many believe *should* be considered a crime. Criminologists have studied this aspect of disasters including terrorism, which is a federal crime, as well as various corporate crimes, also known as organizational crimes. Corporate crime may be defined as the illegal behavior of individuals or groups of individuals in decision-making positions of business organizations that enhances the profitability, competitive edge or power of the businesses and that, consequently, often increases, directly or indirectly, the wealth or professional status of those directly involved (Voigt et al.. 1994: 352).

Corporate crimes, which frequently spawn technological disasters, are perpetrated against the environment, leaving people at risk of injury and death for the purpose of reducing costs and/or maximizing profits. Corporations often try to define these events as "industrial" accidents over which they have no control. The Union Carbide Disaster in Bhopal, India serves as an illustration of a corporate crime/disaster.

> On December 3, 1984, a Union Carbide (UC) chemical plant in Bhopal, India, leaked cyanide fumes (methyl isocyanine used in pesticide production), exposing thousands of people to the deadly gas. It is estimated that 3,500 people died from the exposure and hundreds of thousands were injured, many enduring the harmful symptoms (e.g, respiratory and nervous system ailments) for their entire lives. In an effort to cover up the disaster, which would jeopardize both the income and employment generated by UC, the local government downplayed the actual safety risks to the community. Despite the abject neglect and the willful contempt for prior warnings by both U.S. and Indian safety engineers, UC was never investigated for negligent homicide in the United States, nor was it fined for the Bhopal disaster. The company settled with the Indian government and paid India $470 million, which resulted in average payments to victims ranging between $1,570 and $2,350 per victim for a lifetime of suffering and health care costs (Voigt et al.. 1994: 358–60).

While most people do not normally think of corporations or their executives as criminals or engaging in corporate violence, there are hundreds of cases of serious injuries and deaths caused by corporations in the U.S. and foreign countries, most of which never achieve disaster status.

Disaster Phases

Social scientists, disaster researchers and more recently, emergency managers, have attempted to study the physical and social aspects of disasters in terms of the "phases of disasters" or "life cycle of disasters" and have devised numerous approaches (Drabek 1986, National Governors Association (NGA) 1979, Powell, Rayner and Finesinger 1953, Carr 1932). Disaster phase analysis has a long history starting with sociologist Lowell Carr's work in 1932 on a method of analysis for social change based on disaster phases.

Carr begins with a preparation stage, which he calls the *preliminary* or *prodromal* period, when "forces that are to cause the ultimate collapse are underway." The next phase is called the *dislocation* or *disorganization* phase, which takes into account the effects of the actual disaster agent including the resulting deaths, injuries and other losses as well as "cultural collapse." Carr labels the third phase as the *readjustment* or *reorganization* phase that depicts the community's initial responses; he describes this as being determined by "its culture, its morale, its leadership, and by the speed, scope, and complexity, and violence of the catastrophe itself." The final stage in Carr's timeline is the *confusion-delay* phase, which is the period when emergency plans begin to be implemented (1932: 211–12). Although Carr was not particularly interested in disasters as an area of study, his sequence-pattern model of typical disasters and his early efforts to differentiate different types of disasters by various factors, such as diffused or focused damage, established a framework for later phase models including those that are currently used by researchers.

In 1979, the National Governors Association (NGA) took the first step in "professionalizing" the emergency management field by assigning four concrete disaster phases, which include *mitigation, preparedness, response* and *recovery* (1979, Neal 1997). The NGA report describes mitigation as the initial phase that occurs earliest before the actual disaster event—a period when efforts are made to lessen or eliminate the effects of the disaster (12). The preparedness phase occurs during the time closest to the disaster event and is present when the mitigation phase efforts are unable to reduce the effects of the catastrophe; planning and warning are included in this stage. The response phase occurs directly after the disaster and usually includes rescue, emergency shelter, damage assessments, et cetera. The final phase, recovery, follows the response period and consists of both short- and long-term physical and social rebuilding (13).

As mentioned above, Lewis Killian's commonly employed phase model identifies four phases: *warning, impact, emergency* and *recovery*. In his model, the warning stage captures the period where there is information available about a hazardous event highly likely to occur "but before the danger has become immediate, personal, and physically perceivable." The impact stage is the "period where the destructive agent is actually at work." The emergency stage "is the post impact period during which rescue, first aid, emergency medical care, and other emergency tasks are performed." Finally, the recovery stage is "the period, which begins roughly as the emergency crisis passes and during which the longer-term activities of reconstruction, rehabilitation and recovery proceed" (2002: 51).

The different phase models proposed by researchers vary somewhat with regard to the names or labels associated with the phases, the number of stages, and identifying elements or degree of complexity associated with activities of each phase used to depict the life cycle of a disaster. They all, however, seek to delineate a *timeline* for disaster events beginning with the period before the disaster event (e.g, warning and preparation), progressing through the event (impact), various emergency responses to the event and culminating in disaster recovery, which may range from a short to long period of time. Certain types of hazards may lack a warning phase, while others may have a relatively long warning period. For example, earthquakes, fires, explosions and crashes generally do not give much (if any) warning, while hurricanes, floods and tidal waves typically offer advance notice and time to react.

Critique of Disaster Phase Models

As has been discussed thoroughly in the disaster literature, there are heuristic, theoretical and methodological problems associated with the use of disaster phase models (Neal 1997). Some scholars have claimed that the phases used to study disasters are not mutually exclusive and that the various schemes are overlapping and arbitrary (Haas, Kates and Bowden 1977). Moreover, it has been argued that the demarcation points of the phases should not rest primarily on time factors, but should also include consideration of spatial distinctions (e.g, impact zone, fringe impact zones or filter zones) and relative degree of damage to a city's infrastructure (i.e. economic, political and social infrastructure).

Researchers also note that recovery rates are not linear. After an emergency crisis is over, the longer-term activities of reconstruction, rehabilitation and recovery often take years, even decades as in the case of most technological disasters. These activities proceed at different rates depending on many factors such as the amount of funds and resources that can be applied to remedying damages, the ability to actually correct the physical and social devastation, relative strength of local governmental infrastructure and general political will to rebuild and whether there is the occurrence of new disasters. Needless to say, it is often hard to pinpoint the pace of recovery and reconstruction. The rates of recovery and restoration or reconstruction will also vary depending on variables such as race, ethnicity and social class of the residential and commercial population (e.g, Neal 1997, Phillips, Garza and Neal 1994). The long-term effects of disasters are very complex and can be difficult to predict.

Sometimes the long-term effects become disconnected from the disaster event and are treated as separate issues. For example, the September 11, 2001 terrorist attacks on America caused the deaths of over 3,000 victims in a single day, but the social, psychological and even various physical manifestations of the disaster have continued for years. For example, immediately following 9/11 there was a backlash of anti-Islamic hate crimes followed by a longer period of lingering or residual hate crime. Chris Dunn (2006) has reported that anti-Islamic hate crimes occurred at an average of 0.1 per day in 2001 prior to 9/11 (N=26). During the remainder of September after the attack, he found that anti-Islamic hate crimes averaged 15.4 per day (N=308). During 2002–2003, anti-Islamic hate crimes averaged 0.4 per day (N=305). Dunn concludes that these residual hate crimes have been directed at Arab-Americans, Muslims and other groups perceived to be Arab-Americans or Muslims, at about 4 times the rate of pre 9/11 levels. A review of the Uniform Crime Reports for the years 2000 and 2001 shows over a 1,500 percent increase in anti-Islamic hate crimes, from 33 offenses in 2000 to 546 offenses in 2001 (Crime in the United States 2000, 2001). The great bulk of the increase of the anti-Islamic hate crimes for 2001 occurred after 9/11.

Another problem that exists with general disaster phase models is that they assume a single, short-term disaster with relatively clear-cut phases. Much of the disaster research has focused on sudden, *single impact* disasters (e.g., flash flood, tornado) as opposed to multiple impact or *serial-impact* disasters like the Katrina Disaster, which had a prolonged impact because of the chain of disasters that followed (i.e. levee breaches and flooding, explosion at a chemical facility and associated fires, Murphy Oil spill and Hurricane Rita) all of which occurred within a one-month span and all representing catastrophic events that would constitute major disasters in and of themselves (Thornton and Voigt 2007, this volume). Serial disasters, which can occur either *sequentially* or *simultaneously*, can exacerbate the physical and social consequences for victims as well as first responders. In the case of the Katrina Disaster, for example, the culmination of the hurricane and the breaching of the levees within a few hours of one another decimated the ability of local law enforcement to maintain order among citizens. Several teams of researchers have reported that the Katrina Disaster was far more than just another traditional natural disaster (Picou and Marshall 2007, Hartman and Squires 2006, Quarantelli 2006). Sociologists J. Steven Picou and Brent Marshall believe that the Katrina Disaster may be conceptualized as a *natech* disaster, which is a natural disaster that releases hazardous material into the environment, either by direct or indirect means (2007).

In contrast to natural disasters that typically exhibit short-term disruptive social consequences and are associated with effecting collective solidarity and community recovery efforts that have therapeutic effects, the natech disasters, such as the Katrina Disaster, with a prolonged and protracted recovery period tend to generate "specific forms of collective pathology ... from which corrosive social cycles may emerge," which include social structural, cultural, interpersonal and personal impacts, some of which may involve the opportunity for criminal activities to occur (Picou and Marshall 2007: 13–15). Obviously, the longer the duration of the impact and emergency phase of the disaster, the greater the potential for criminal activity to occur. Concomitantly, disasters with extended recovery and reconstruction periods provide greater opportunity and facilitation for certain types of criminal activity.

Phase Analysis and Crime Facilitation

In considering the potential for various crimes to occur within the different phases of disasters, it is important to remember that criminologists have reported for decades that crime is not randomly distributed across social space and social groups. Some groups have a higher probability of engaging in certain criminal activity and some groups have a greater probability of being victimized. This variation in the likelihood of victimization is called *differential vulnerability*, or the relative risk of being a victim. While the spectrum of crimes, which can and do occur during times of natural and human-made disasters, cut across all social economic groups, disaster research suggests that certain individuals, particularly the poor, irrespective of race or ethnicity, are generally affected the most by disasters (e.g, by loss of income, loss of households, loss of health, loss of life and family disruption). They also run the greatest propensity of being victimized by crime of all varieties, including property crimes (e.g, thefts, burglaries), violent crimes (e.g, domestic violence and sexual assaults including rape) and white collar crimes (e.g, fraud, and corporate crimes). Other risk factors connected with disaster victimization, particularly criminal victimization from disasters, include race and ethnicity, gender, age, disability and family status. These are obviously exacerbated by poverty.

Perhaps more than any modern day disaster, the Katrina Disaster lends itself to a phase analysis study of individual and collective or group criminal activity during various phases of the disaster. At each stage of the disaster, various breakdowns in infrastructure, such as the physical (e.g, devastation of commercial buildings, homes and neighborhoods), social (e.g, lack of social support systems such as safe havens or advocacy support groups) and structural (e.g, breakdown in governmental leadership and operation of the criminal justice system) worked together to create increased criminal opportunities or otherwise facilitated conditions for crimes to occur, including interpersonal violent crimes, property crimes, drug crimes and white collar crimes. We turn now to an examination of crimes occurring during each phase of disaster.

Warning Phase

According to the report entitled "A Failure of Initiative," by the Select Bipartisan Committee to Investigate the Preparation for and Response to Hurricane Katina: "It remains difficult to understand how government could respond so ineffectively to a disaster that was anticipated for years, and for which specific dire warnings had been issued for days. This crisis was not only predictable, it was predicted. If this is what happens when we have advance warning, we shudder to imagine the consequences when we do not" (2006 xi). In this statement, the Bipartisan Committee is referring to two types of warnings with respect to the Katrina Disaster before it hit New Orleans and the Gulf Coast. One warning came from a hurricane simulation report issued in August, 2004 regarding the hypothetical Hurricane Pam, a Category 3 storm with sustained winds of 120 mph, which strikes southeastern Louisiana, including the city of New Orleans, with dire consequences, most of which became reality when Katrina struck a year later (Southeastern Louisiana Catastrophic Hurricane Functional Plan 2004). This type of warning is generally included in what emergency managers refer to as *mitigation*, which involves long-term planning measures to make a hazard less likely to occur (e.g, reinforce levees) or to reduce the negative consequences (e.g, implementation of evacuation plan or provide shelters) if it were to occur. These include all those things that take place *before* a disaster ever occurs. The other warning, of course, refers to a more immediate type of warning from the National Weather Service and others regarding an impending disaster.

The warning phase of a disaster is the "period during which information is available about a probable danger, but before the danger has become immediate, personal and physically perceivable" (Killian 2002: 51). As mentioned above, not all disasters have a clear warning stage. In the case of Hurricane Katrina, local, state and federal governmental response teams had 56 hours before landfall on August 29, 2005, more than adequate time to order a mandatory evacuation.

Depending on the type of disaster, when there is a period of warning, there may be enhanced opportunities for certain crimes to occur. In hurricane areas, especially in urban areas, citizens often begin evacuating during the warning phase, leaving their homes and businesses susceptible to highly motivated offenders who may take the opportunity to commit residential and business burglaries. During certain disasters, there may be a lack of capable guardianship in the form of law enforcement. In cases of highly eminent disasters, law enforcement officials are gearing up for possible emergency responses and not fully deploying routine crime-oriented patrols as they would during normal times. Some natural disaster researchers have examined the subject of people disregarding evacuation warnings for a number of reasons; principal among these reasons are lack of understanding, lack of access to information, disbelief (Trainor, Aquirre and Barnshaw 2008) and fear of crime to their property during their absence, including burglary, looting and thefts from their residences or businesses (Tobin and Whiteford 2002, Haque and Blair 1992, Lindell and Perry 1992).

Evacuation from an impending disaster is the most critical part of emergency preparation and such preparation includes not just warning citizens of impending danger but also detailed planning and implementation of an evacuation plan. While close to 500,000 citizens evacuated from New Orleans during the approach of Katrina, thousands of people were relocated to shelters in the city where there were enhanced risks for criminal victimization. Disaster researchers have shown that women are less likely than men to have the necessary resources and mobility to leave before a disaster strikes (Barnshaw 2006, Marshall 2005, Fothergill 1996). Also, because of their relative lack of status, power, money and access to motor vehicles, minority women are usually at a greater disadvantage in terms of leaving an area when warning of an impending disaster is announced and they often suffer as a consequence of their inability to evacuate.

Crimes against Women, Children and the Elderly[1]

The best documented research, nationally and internationally, on the relationship of disasters to crime vulnerability comes from those studies documenting that women and girls are victims of violent crimes, including rape and other sexual assaults, during all phases of a wide-spectrum of disasters,

---

1. As noted, sexual victimization of women throughout the phases of disaster is covered at some length elsewhere in this volume.

which are accompanied by cultural dislocation and anomie (Phillips, Jenkins and Enarson 2010, Thornton and Voigt 2007 and this volume, United Nations High Commission for Refugees (UNHCR) 1999, Lentin 1997). Much of this research reports that women are the most vulnerable to sexual assaults in shelters and other "places of haven" when they are evacuated or otherwise relocated as in the case of women placed in refugee camps. An early study conducted by the National Sexual Violence Resource Center in Louisiana reported that evacuation sites including shelters, accounted for about one third of all locations for sexual assaults against women reported to them by victims six months after the storm (2006). Thornton and Voigt (2007, this volume) have uncovered cases of women raped in shelters in New Orleans and in other states. They found that the environments in these facilities were overcrowded, with no screening of evacuees, and little security making conditions ripe for rapes and other sexual assaults to occur. Based on reports of sexual assaults occurring in New Orleans and the surrounding region and in places where women evacuated during the Katrina Disaster, the Louisiana Foundation Against Sexual Assault and the National Sexual Violence Resource Center, in a joint report called "Sexual Violence in Disasters: A Planning Guide for Prevention and Response" (Klein 2006), recommend a range of policy changes and safety standards to mitigate these types of crimes from occurring in future disasters.

Young children are particularly at risk of criminal victimization during evacuation and in shelters and other places of haven. Instances of the Red Cross setting up secured and supervised "Safe Spaces" in evacuation centers after disasters are indicators of the concern shown for children's safety and the potential for child predators to be among the evacuees (Smith 2008). During Katrina, over 2,000 registered sex offenders were evacuated and their whereabouts unknown; obviously some were housed in shelters in New Orleans as well as shelters in other cities. With 60,000 evacuees housed in the Superdome and another 25,000 in the Convention Center, untold numbers of children were exposed to potential dangers including sexual abuse, especially if separated from their parents. In fact, there were many instances of children being separated from their parents during the evacuation process. While procedures to unite children with their legal guardians to reduce the potential for child abductions and sexual abuse were instituted post-Katrina, it has been urged that better planning take place in the future (Brandenburg et al.. 2007, National Center for Missing and Exploited Children 2006).

Although victimization research indicates that elderly people are statistically the least criminally victimized group in general, their diminished economic, social, psychological and physical attributes make them particularly vulnerable to disasters, particularly during evacuations (Garrett et al. 2007, Perry 1990). Those elderly living in nursing homes or assisted living facilities may run a higher risk of injury or death during disasters even though these facilities are required to have disaster and evacuation plans. As was discovered during Katrina, these plans do not ensure the safety of the elderly when disasters strike. Negligent homicide charges have been brought against the owners of St. Rita's Nursing Home in St. Bernard Parish for the drowning deaths of 35 elderly residents when the owners made the decision not to evacuate. While the owners were eventually acquitted of the charges, the case has raised serious questions about the care of elderly during disasters. The Louisiana Nursing Home Association reported that 32 of the 74 nursing homes in New Orleans did not evacuate (*Times Picayune* 2007). The Louisiana Attorney General's office has investigated a large number of patient deaths at nursing homes and hospitals, including 22 people who died at Lafon Nursing Home, run by nuns of the Holy Cross order in eastern New Orleans (Foster 2007).

Geographical Crime Displacement

While there is evidence of evacuees fleeing from a disaster during the warning phase that find themselves in shelters and houses in less than desirable environments and running the risk of crime victimization (Thornton and Voigt 2007, this volume), there is relatively little research on the phenomenon of evacuees perpetrating crimes in towns and cities where they are temporarily housed. Results of a survey conducted with 52 Texas law enforcement agencies document increased demand for police services by Katrina evacuees. These police agencies have reported that some evacuees in towns and cities across Texas had criminal records and were on probation or parole for property, drug or violent criminal offenses. Some of the evacuees committed crimes or otherwise engaged in public disorder activities, which required law enforcement intervention. The city of Houston, for example, which had the largest number of Katrina evacuees (153,000), spent $4,732,529 by May 2006 on additional law enforcement costs to handle calls for service involving Katrina evacuees. The Houston Police Department made 482 arrests for a variety of offense categories including violent and property offenses. Other states that have tracked crime statistics and performed background checks on Katrina evacuees including Massachusetts, South Carolina and West Virginia likewise reported relatively large numbers of evacuees with criminal histories and an increased demand for law enforcement services (Pullin 2006).

Impact Phase and Emergency Phase

While the *impact* phase usually refers to the actual disaster event, the *emergency* phase generally refers to post-impact relief efforts including activities such as rescuing and conducting the emergency evacuation of people (e.g, infants, young children, pregnant women, the elderly and the sick), administering first aid and emergency medical care, supplying food, water and other life sustaining resources, performing public health functions (e.g, removal of dead bodies) and other emergency management tasks and restoring law and order. Unpreparedness on the part of local, state and federal agencies and continued disruptions of an already distressed locale from multiple disaster impacts, as in the case of the Katrina Disaster, no doubt serve to enhance the opportunity for criminal activity to occur. The severe storm conditions and storm surges of Hurricane Katrina were hardly over before the breaches of the levees occurred. Within 12 hours of the first effects of Katrina, 80 percent of New Orleans was flooded. It was at this point that social disorder in the absence of police protection ensued and that crimes began taking place in the city including looting, armed robberies and shootings, despite dismissal of early exaggerations and rumors of crime, many of which were unsubstantiated. Given that the New Orleans Police Department (NOPD) virtually ceased all normal operations (i.e. making arrests, answering regular "calls for service" and reporting or officially documenting crimes, which occurred during the early phases of the Katrina Disaster), debate among disaster researchers continues regarding the existence of crimes during this disaster. Lack of official police reports not withstanding, Thornton and Voigt (2007, this volume) provide evidence of crimes based on extensive interviews with first responders, including former and current police officers, as well as on victim interviews.

Looting[2]

Even though there is debate in the disaster literature over the question of whether looting occurs in the wake of natural disasters (Quarantelli 2007), reports of looting, usually of businesses as opposed to residences, immediately after natural disasters such as hurricanes (Frailing 2007, Frailing and Harper 2007, Siman 1977), floods (Erikson 1976) and earthquakes (Morris 2002, Zhou 1997) are common. However, it is difficult to discern how prevalent looting is during the *actual* occurrence of a disaster. Media accounts based on unofficial

---

2. The subject of looting is covered at some length elsewhere in this volume.

reports from law enforcement agents suggest that substantial looting occurred during the elongated impact phase of the Katrina Disaster. Reports of looting began as early as the first day of the storm after two levees failed and continued for the next several days when conditions worsened including the almost complete breakdown of law and order infrastructure (e.g, Frailing and Harper 2007). Media reports document a broad spectrum of looting, which include thefts of merchandise other than drinking water, food and other survival items. Some disaster researchers have argued that while looting may occur during civil disturbances such as riots, chiefly as a form of protest, it is relatively infrequent in natural disasters because people are stealing mainly for survival as opposed to sending a message of protest (Dynes and Quarantelli 1968). Some clarification of this stance, however, can be found indicating that looting after major disasters may take place (Wright and Quarantelli 1974).

Cyber-Looting

The ability of criminals to adapt their skills to new opportunities is always amazing. Almost within hours after landfall of Katrina, what some term as "online looting" began with scam artists registering Katina-related web domains such as katrinahelp.com and katrinafamilies.com, which were used to solicit money to bogus relief organizations. Legitimate relief organizations feared that these scams, falling under the broader category of charity fraud, could seriously hurt the collection of funds for various relief efforts for storm victims (Roberts 2005). The Hurricane Katrina Fraud Task Force reports have documented numerous instances of fraud involving illegal solicitations of donations from victims throughout the life cycle of the disaster (United States Department of Justice 2005–2007). Frauds of this type are also common in other types of disasters.[3]

Drug and Alcohol Use[4]

There is research evidence in the disaster literature that drug and alcohol use generally increase during impact and emergency phases. Various stresses associated with the effects of such events which seem to lead to increased alcohol consumption and drug use, especially for males, have been connected to domestic violence. Research has shown that sexual assaults against women were perpetrated by men who had consumed large amounts of alcohol (Thorn-

---

3. The subject of fraud is covered at some length elsewhere in this volume.

4. The subject of drugs in the context of drug markets is covered at some length elsewhere in this volume.

ton and Voigt 2007, this volume). During the impact and the aftermath of Katrina, reports depicted looting of grocery stores, drug stores and convenience stores involving thefts of beer, wine, hard liquor, cigarettes and drugs.

There has been limited research on the impact of disasters on drug-related crimes including drug usage and dealing. Research conducted by the Office of National Drug Control Policy examined the effects of the terrorist attacks' impact on short- and long-term drug abuse and generally found that 9/11 affected the local illegal drug trade in New York in terms of drug availability, pricing, selling and use. According to researchers, almost immediately after the attacks, drug dealers operated openly in the streets and availability of illegal drugs, particularly heroin, declined in New York. Drug trafficking routes also shifted and there were signs of increased drug use, such as demand for treatment in New York (2002: 9–10). An ethnographic study by Dunlap, Johnson and Morse (2007) interviewed 100 New Orleans evacuees regarding their patterns of drug use before, during and one month after evacuation. Respondents were asked about their participation in drug markets during the week of August 30 to September 5 when New Orleans was flooded. One drug dealer reported that he did not evacuate for fear someone would break in and steal his drug supply; others reported that they had purchased drugs as the storm approached and then used them during the week of flooding. Some did report that they purchased drugs during that week or obtained supplies by burglary or theft from drug dealers who had evacuated and left drugs in their residences. One respondent reported that crack was being sold in the Superdome. The researchers noted that "the overall impression is that illicit drug markets were consistently suppressed during the hurricane and flooding of New Orleans, but were not entirely eliminated" (14). Recent research such as that conducted by Patrick Walsh (in this volume) indicates that while there may have been a lull in the drug market in New Orleans and the region because of Katrina, new drug markets emerged very early in the recovery period that included new drug use populations and new and returning drug dealers, who were often in violent conflict with one another over changing drug territory because of the damage inflicted by the disaster.

Sexual Assaults

As several disaster researchers have documented, in the early stages of a disaster, many women have care-taking obligations for children and elderly parents and relatives, which make it difficult for them to evacuate. Many of these women are often young, poor, minority and are heads-of-households (Marshall 2005, Fothergill 1996, Morrow and Enarson 1996). Thornton and Voigt

(2007, this volume) interviewed rape victims in the impact and emergency stages of Katrina who indicated that they were on the streets or in convenience stores looking for groceries and other things for themselves and their children when their assaults took place. Other reports of sexual assaults occurring early in the disaster can be found (Klein 2006: 39). Most of these crimes are never reported to the police.

Peek (2010) reports on several studies which indicate that in the aftermath of disasters, there may be increased rates of children's vulnerability to physical and sexual abuse (164). In the aftermath of Hurricane Hugo and the Loma Prieta earthquake, researchers found significant increases in child abuse reports (Curtis, Miller and Berry 2000). After the Indian Ocean Boxing Day Tsunami in 2004, incidents of human trafficking of children and other sexual violence in refugee camps in Sri Lanka were reported (Enarson, Fothergill and Peek 2006) and interviews with individuals from advocacy organizations have documented instances of sexual assault and physical abuse against women and young girls (Fisher 2005).

Recovery and Reconstruction Phases

Recovery can be divided into two phases, short-term and long-term. Short-term recovery immediately follows the emergency phase of a disaster. There is still likely to be disorder and confusion in the short term recovery process. Long-term recovery, on the other hand, refers to rebuilding and rehabilitation of all aspects of a community including economic renewal. During short-term recovery, some people may still be displaced from their homes and many businesses remain closed. Progress may be made toward restoring essential infrastructures, such as inter-organizational communication, electrical service, potable water supplies, public transportation, homes, businesses and city services—things that will allow individuals to reoccupy a disaster area to begin eventual longer-term reconstruction. The pace of reopening schools in a community has a significant impact on population growth in the city from new and previously displaced citizens. The re-establishment of health facilities and services, including mental health services, is also among the critical factors of recovery.

Some communities "recover" from disasters sooner than others based on such things as the degree of physical destruction, the degree of social disruption and the degree of financial assistance needed to repopulate commercial and residential areas of the city, et cetera (Drabek 1986: 234–42). In the case of New Orleans, it may take many years for long-term recovery and reconstruction to be fully realized and the footprint of the city may be much different than pre-Katrina New Orleans in terms of population and geographical livable areas. Because of physical damage, loss of clients and customers, high commercial insurance rates, lack of affordable housing for remaining employees and future employees and fear of future storms, many small and large businesses will not rebuild in the area thus making long term recovery all the more difficult. Also, the loss of thousands of residences including physical neighborhoods as well as cultural milieus may never be replaced because of lack of resources, the inability to obtain or afford homeowners insurance and displacement of individuals who are established in other cities and do not wish to return. In the city, there still remains considerable social inequality in terms of socioeconomic status, particularly within ethnic and racial minority groups, a fact which has not changed since before Katrina. Mental health care professionals including domestic abuse centers and psychiatric facilities are in short supply, which has, at a minimum, an indirect effect on the increase of violent crimes in the city including domestic violence.

Another factor impeding recovery in New Orleans, possibly unique in the annals of disaster research in the United States, is the return of a serious crime problem during this early recovery stage. Many citizens in the city were living in FEMA trailers or makeshift homes in varying degrees of repair in areas with reduced police protection. Violent and property crime rates have been creeping up in Orleans Parish and adjoining parishes since Katrina. In 2008, the city had the highest murder rate in the country. Widespread crimes including armed robberies, robbery-murders and home invasions against Latino workers have been taking place in the city and region since 2006. The NOPD, which was severely broken by Katrina, still has a shortage of police officers and serious infrastructure problems. In addition, the criminal justice system has been facing serious challenges during the reconstruction period.

Violent Crimes against Migrant Latino Workers and Katrina Volunteers

As the floodwaters receded in New Orleans after Katrina in 2005, thousands of laborers from Central and South America, as well as migrant workers from other regions of the United States, came to the devastated city and surrounding metropolitan areas to engage in a variety of jobs including tearing down houses, hauling away debris and working in the construction industry. A large number of these workers, almost exclusively males, were undocumented illegal aliens who were living in the city on a temporary basis, often packed into makeshift housing structures or "work camps." Estimates indicate that the metropolitan area's Latino population has tripled since the storm, from about

60,000 to about 180,000. The illegal status of many of these laborers has necessitated keeping their hard-earned cash on their persons until such time that money could be sent to their families. Being associated with carrying large amounts of cash or not trusting banks (or being unable to initially use banks) has made many migrant workers targets of armed robberies, including home invasions, and robbery/murders. In the local vernacular, these individuals are often referred to as "walking ATMs." Thornton, Voigt and Walsh have analyzed official data on Latino workers from 2005 through 2009 as well as conducted interviews with select victims. They report that the unique post-recovery environment of New Orleans, with the influx of highly vulnerable Latino workers, coupled with the absence of capable guardianship in the form of lack of police concern for illegal workers, has created this new victim pool (Walsh, Thornton and Voigt 2009). In addition to armed robberies and robbery/murders, other violent crimes such as aggravated assaults at day labor camps and hate crimes have been more prevalent in the region during the past four years since Katrina. And in addition to violent crimes, there have been numerous reports of wage thefts of Latino workers in the New Orleans area where laborers, especially those who are undocumented, are not paid for their labors by the various contractors, often under threats of violence if they try to collect their pay. A report by the Southern Poverty Law Center indicates that as many as 80 percent of these Latino workers have been ripped off by their employers while working in the New Orleans region (Bauer 2009). Until recently, many of the crimes committed against migrant workers have either not been reported for fear of discovery of their illegal status or have not been given a high priority by law enforcement in terms of classification of the crimes or investigation of the crimes.

In their study of Latino workers, Thornton, Voigt and Walsh (2009) have also found cases of sexual assaults against female "migrant" workers (i.e. those of Latina heritage) who have come to the region because of a shortage of labor and higher paying jobs in various industries. Similarly, Enarson and Morrow (1998) in their studies of Hurricane Andrew, have reported that poor and marginalized women with limited English skills including migrant workers "[felt] at risk of male violence during the lengthy reconstruction period in disrupted neighborhoods and temporary camps" (6).

Although there is sparse research in the disaster literature devoted to the criminal victimization of disaster volunteers who work in various recovery projects in devastated areas, evidence in New Orleans shows that crimes such as rapes, armed robberies, burglaries and minor thefts have been perpetrated against volunteers, including both younger and older victims, during their extended stays in New Orleans during the recovery phase. For example, Thornton and Voigt (2007, this volume) have uncovered a number of cases of sexual assaults against volunteers who have been working in blackout zones, which still remain without electricity and relatively poor law enforcement protection.

Violent Crimes in Temporary Housing

In the recovery period, conditions in the city and region remain particularly ripe for sexual assaults to occur under a variety of circumstances and in a variety of environments. Rapes of women and other crimes, including murder, in FEMA trailer parks in New Orleans and in the region have been documented (e.g, Anastario, Shehab and Lawry 2009, *Times Picayune* 2007a, Maggi 2007). These trailer parks were notorious for the poor security supplied by FEMA and they were not patrolled by the local police on a routine basis because of a shortage of manpower. A recent study conducted from 2006 to 2007, which surveyed 420 women living in FEMA trailer parks in Mississippi after Katrina has found that these women were three times more likely to become victims of domestic and sexual violence than they were before the storm (Anastario, Shehab and Lawry 2009). Other disaster researchers such as Enarson have pointed out that the risk of sexual assault is greater in temporary housing sites such as trailer camps/parks, which are often located in remote and isolated areas of devastated communities without adequate access control, physical security and lighting (1999a and 1999b). In addition to fearing for their personal safety, women in trailer camps in Miami after Hurricane Andrew "were often isolated, lacked mental and reproductive health services and reliable transportation and were unable to access needed community services" (Enarson 1999b: 48). In another example, during the aftermath of Hurricane Charley in 1992, residents of FEMA trailer parks located in Punta Gorda, Florida reported concern over "security, especially safety for their children from a child molester, incidences of theft, and wariness of their neighbors" (Tobin, Bell, Whiteford and Montz 2006: 94–95).

Violent Crimes in Abandoned Housing Projects

Abandoned properties in New Orleans, which create any number of criminal opportunities, including havens for drug addicts, drug dealers and street prostitutes, abound in the city since Katrina. As of August 2009, an estimated 66,000 unoccupied residential properties, 30 percent of the housing in New Orleans, remain blighted (Kirkham and Krupa 2009). Since Katrina, there has been an extreme shortage of affordable rental housing for residents The Iberville housing development, a 1,000 unit complex, which is obsolete and in disrepair with over 200 vacant and abandoned apartments, had seven murders in a three month period in 2008; the murder count continues to climb in 2009. The 630 families living in Iberville have complained to the New Orleans Housing Authority (HANO) and have demanded that the apartments be rehabilitated so that they can provide much needed housing for the working classes. The police department has been unable to provide routine patrols in the housing development because of a shortage of officers (Reckdahl 2009).

Architectural Looting

Reports of thefts of historical architectural items such as doors, mantels, shutters, windows, wrought iron fences from old houses and other structures in New Orleans neighborhoods throughout the city in the aftermath of Katrina have been rampant. Although there is a state law governing antique dealers and their documentation of used building components that they acquire, the law is not very well enforced. Concern over the piece by piece dismantling of hundreds of historical homes has prompted organizations such as the New Orleans Preservation Resource Center and other neighborhood associations to seek prevention methods for the problem (Thevenot 2006, Bonnette 2005/2006, Cooper 2005).

Scrappers

Extending well into the recovery phase, thefts of copper (e.g, wire, pipes, condenser coils and transformers) from abandoned homes and businesses, new residential and commercial building sites as well as occupied homes and buildings have become a problem both to the people who have their property stolen and destroyed, and to the police who cannot keep up with the new crime. These crimes became so numerous that in 2007 the New Orleans City Council "passed an ordinance making it unlawful for any purchaser of certain types of scrap metal to buy from persons or scrap metal businesses, who do not have specific licenses, requiring all purchasers to record very detailed information on the seller and making that information available for police inspection" (Preventing Copper Theft 2007).

Fraud in Its Many Manifestations

Many opportunities for fraud, including government relief procurement, contractor fraud and insurance fraud abound in the recovery phase of disasters (Preventing and Detecting Bid Rigging 2009, Leeson and Sobel 2008, United States Department of Justice 2005–2007, Frailing and Harper 2007).

Although certain types of fraud can take place in the early phases of disasters, most cases of fraud occurs in the period of recovery. In the case of Katrina, 36 individuals had been criminally charged with fraud related to obtaining emergency relief money from FEMA and the American Red Cross as early as October, 2005 (Frailing and Harper 2007: 53). Over 141 cases of this type of fraud have been reported since 2005 (McCarthy 2009: B-2/3). Some of the more recent federal fraud cases have involved payments from the Louisiana state-run, federally financed Road Home Rebuild program.

During the recovery period of disasters, especially in the rebuilding and reconstruction stage, fraud involving public corruption such as public officials engaging in bid-rigging conspiracies, soliciting and receiving bribes in return for the award of contracts, commission of wire fraud and conspiring to launder money can be found in many different types of disasters (Preventing and Detecting Bid Rigging 2009, United States Department of Justice 2005–2007). Recently in neighboring St. Tammany Parish, former Councilman Joe Impastato was sentenced to federal prison for soliciting and receiving kickbacks for a hurricane debris removal contract that he arranged for a local businessman. He also brokered other contracts for which he was indicted (Harvey 2009: A-4). However, most damaging to victims, and, perhaps one of the most prevalent types of Katrina fraud, are cases of contractor fraud wherein individuals are ripped off by alleged "contractors," many who came from other states and took peoples' money for work that was partially completed, poorly done or not done at all. One such case is that of Georgia contractor Terry Ferguson, who took checks totaling about half a million dollars from 17 families, never did the jobs and then left the state. His victims handed over their insurance settlements, savings or government aid and were left with no funds to rebuild (Filosa 2009). Most recently, the ex-chief financial officer of the New Orleans Housing Authority (HANO), Elios Castellanos, has been charged with embezzlement of about $900,000 for his alleged fraud associated with payments to contractors for work that was either not performed or overcharged for in public housing developments (Hammer 2009).

Intimate and Domestic Violence

As is the case of domestic violence in general, which includes many offenses such as intimate partner assault, child abuse, child sexual assault, elderly violence and rape, there is gross underreporting of the crime to the police even during times of normalcy. There is no doubt that domestic violence incidents during times of disasters are likewise underreported, which has certainly been the case with the Katrina Disaster. As we have noted, the very nature of some disasters even in the recovery periods places family members under extreme stress caused by crowded living conditions, loss of jobs, financial problems, destruction of social networks and increased use of alcohol and drugs, which sets the stage for domestic violence. Disaster researchers who study domestic violence indicate that "it is not clear whether rates of domestic violence increase after a disaster, but some data and anecdotal evidence suggest that such is the case" (Phillips, Jenkins and Enarson 2010: 288, Enarson 1999). A study conduced by Mechanic, Griffin and Resick (2001) examined a sample of 225 women, either married or cohabiting with men, after the Midwestern flood of 1993. During a nine month period after the disaster, "14 percent reported at least one violent act of physical aggression from their partners, 26 percent reported emotional abuse, 70 percent verbal abuse and 86 percent partner anger" (Norris no date). Other early studies identify cases of domestic violence after disasters, with some reporting life threatening or physical injuries (Norris and Uhl 1993); however, most of these studies report non-physical instances of domestic violence in the form of verbal conflicts or "troubled interpersonal relationships" (Shariat et al. 1999, Norris et al. 1999). Very few studies offer empirical documentation of increases of domestic violence after disasters. Adams and Adams (1984) have discovered that official police reports of domestic violence increased 46 percent after the eruption of Mount St. Helens volcano in Washington. As noted above, Curtis, Miller and Berry (2000) reported increases in child abuse cases in the periods following Hurricane Hugo and the Loma Prieta earthquake as compared with the same periods before these two disasters. Reports of increases in domestic violence in the form of intimate partner abuse, elder abuse, child abuse/neglect, child sexual abuse and rape were also reported after the *Exxon Valdez* oil spill. Research from international disasters claims increased domestic violence for women and children (UNHCR 1999). While official reports are plagued by underreporting and reliability problems, possible "proxy" indicators of increases in domestic violence post-disaster can be found from various reports from domestic violence shelter providers during many disasters, including Katrina. These reports indicate increased calls and overrun shelter facilities after disasters, as well as the inability of law enforcement agencies to respond to domestic violence calls for service (Jenkins and Phillips 2008). Likewise, there have been reported increases in calls for help for intimate partner abuse to telephone hotlines after some disasters, as well as an increase in the need for counseling for domestic violence victims (Phillips, Jenkins and Enarson 2010).

Violent Crime, Stress and Mental Illness

The link between mental disorders, in all their manifestations, and criminality has been studied extensively by social scientists suggesting that the connection is often tenuous, depending on the specific classification scheme utilized, type of diagnosis and many other factors. If findings regarding the linkage between the psychological stress of disasters to aggression and hostility can be generalized to Katrina, some individuals, particularly males, who have experienced lasting psychological effects, may manifest violent behavior in any number of ways such as homicide, assaults and sexual assault including domestic/intimate partner violence. While there is some debate regarding the long-term psychological effects of disasters, such as chronic psychopathology, there is evidence suggesting that disaster victims who have experienced life-threatening situations suffer certain symptoms of post traumatic stress disorder (PTSD), including suicide, depression, anxiety and hostility for relatively long periods after the events (e.g, Kessler et al. 2008, Norris and Uhl 1993). There have been many criminal incidents in post-Katrina New Orleans apparently linked to mental distress facilitated by the storm, including the 2008 murder of a young female police officer, Nicola Cotton, shot 15 times by a man suffering from a psychotic mental illness who had been released from a mental facility days before due to a shortage of space there (McCarthy and Maggi 2008). In July, 2007, Stacy Youngblood, suffering from hallucinations, shot a man in her FEMA trailer. In March, 2006, a National Guardsman patrolling the city shot a 53-year-old mentally disturbed man who aimed a rusted metal BB gun at him inside his 9th Ward storm-shattered residence (Filosa and McCarthy 2007). In May, 2006, a 46-year-old man with a history of mental problems was fatally shot by police in a standoff and gunfight at his home. In December, 2005, a knife-wielding mental patient was shot to death by police in a standoff on Saint Charles Avenue (Maggi and McCarthy 2008: A-1/6, Waller 2007).

In post-Katrina New Orleans and the surrounding region, there is a well documented shortage of mental health care facilities, including psychiatric beds for people with chronic mental illness. Since closure of the Charity Hospital in the city, which prior to Katrina provided 100 psychiatric beds, people with psychiatric disorders have to be taken to emergency rooms in neighboring Jefferson Parish. Additionally, there are substantially fewer practicing psychiatrists in the city since Katrina. Dr. Jim Arey, former commander of the New Orleans Police Negotiation Team, which deals with psychiatric patients, reported that when officers escort patients to emergency rooms, they must often wait for hours before the hospital can accept them. The closure of Charity Hospital, which in the past provided psychiatric treatment, has severely limited the choices for the city's poor who cannot afford private treatment (Moran 2007). Very little improvement in mental health care and facilities has taken place in 2009, especially with recent state cuts in funding for health care, which include a decline in inpatient and outpatient mental health services for adolescents and adults (Abramson 2009).

Prostitution

As part of a larger study on crime in post-Katrina, New Orleans, Voigt and Thornton (2008) have examined official reports of vice crimes in New Orleans and also interviewed police officers working in the vice unit regarding the effects of the disaster on crimes such as prostitution and crimes against nature. In Louisiana, only females can be charged with prostitution, which encompasses vaginal sex for compensation; crime against nature deals with anal and oral sex for compensation. While there is some evidence to suggest that the New Orleans Police Department (NOPD) has made more arrests for prostitution in the early recovery period of Katrina as opposed to pre-Katrina, the volume of prostitution has not gone up significantly post-Katrina. About a year after Katrina, during the early recovery period, when there was a large influx of mostly male construction workers, street level prostitution in the city shifted from a relatively broad geographical area in the city and was concentrated almost exclusively in the French Quarter and on nearby Esplanade Avenue. As parts of the city have been reopened, street level prostitution has returned to the other parts of the city and has appeared to decline. However, as the recovery period progresses, there seems to be a significant growth of escort services (a higher income level form of prostitution) advertised on the Internet and in local news publications using false names. Internet advertisements for escorts usually include a picture, a brief description and a phone number.

Conclusion

In this chapter, we have discussed how phase analysis may be used as a framework to understand how the different phases of disaster—warning, impact, emergency and recovery—may be used to explain the vulnerabilities or opportunities related to disasters that serve to facilitate certain types of crimes. Each phase of a disaster has its own unique physical, social, economic and environmental challenges, which can influence or facilitate the commission of a multitude of different crimes including property crimes, violent crimes, white collar crimes and political crimes. While some crimes seem to appear at specific times during a disaster, other crimes, depending on the type of disaster, may be found throughout its life cycle.

There are four types of disasters: natural, technological, natural-technological (or natech) and terrorism. Phase analysis can be used with any of these disaster types to study the facilitation of crime. In some instances, actual crimes such as terrorism or corporate crimes may be the cause of a specific type of disaster. Factors that influence criminal activity occurring in a specific phase of a disaster can include whether the disaster is a single-impact or multiple-impact disaster and the subsequent length of time of each phase. There is obviously a greater potential for criminal activity to occur the longer the duration of a phase. All people run the risk of being criminally victimized at any phase during a disaster, but certain populations including the poor, children, women, the elderly and ethnic and minority groups tend to be impacted the most by disasters and are subsequently more vulnerable to crime. Probably more than any modern disaster, the Katrina Disaster lends itself to a phase analysis of individual and collective criminality.

References

A Failure of Initiative: Final report of the select bipartisan committee to investigate the preparation for and response to Hurricane Katrina. 2006. Washington, D.C.: U.S. Government Printing Office. Available online at: http://www.gpoaccess.gov/congress/index.

Abramson , N. 2009. Jindal slashes mental health. *The Times Picayune*, July 2: B-7.

Adams, P. and G. Adams. 1984. Mount Saint Helen's ashfall. *American Psychologist* 39: 252–60.

Anastario, M., N. Shehab and L. Lawry. 2009. Increased gender-based violence among women internally displaced in Mississippi 2 years post Katrina. *Disaster Medicine and Public Health Preparedness* 3: 18–26.

Barnshaw, J. 2006. Beyond disaster: Locating Hurricane Katrina within an inequality context. In *Learning from Catastrophe: Quick Response Research in the Wake of Hurricane Katrina*. Boulder, CO: Natural Hazards Center: 47–70.

Bauer, M. 2009. *Under Siege: Life for Low-Income Latinos in the South*. Montgomery, AL: Southern Poverty Law Center.

Bonnette, S. G. December 2005/January 2006. Architectural looting on the rise after Katrina. *Preservation in Print*.

Brandenburg, M. A., S. M. Watkins, K. L. Brandenburg and C. Schieche. 2007. Operation Child-ID: Reunifying children with their legal guardians after Hurricane Katrina. *Disasters* 31(3): 277–87.

Bushman, B. J. and H. M. Cooper. 1998. The effects of alcohol on human aggression: An integrative research review. *Psychological Bulletin* 107(3): 341–54.

Carr, L. 1932. Disaster and the sequence-pattern concept of social change. *American Journal of Sociology* 38: 207–18.

Clements, B. S. 2009. *Disasters and Public Health*. Burlington, MA: Butterworth-Heinemann.

Code of Federal Regulations. 2008. 28 C.F.R. Section 0.85. Available online at: http://frwebgate.access.gpo.gov/cgi-bin/get-cfr.cgi.

Cooper, C. 2005. Architectural theft adds insult to injury in old New Orleans. *The Wall Street Journal*.

Coppola, D. P. 2007. *Introduction to International Disaster Management*. Burlington, MA: Butterworth-Heinemann.

Crime in the United States. 2000. Uniform Crime Reports, Federal Bureau of Investigation. Washington, D.C.: U.S. Department of Justice.

Crime in the United States. 2001. Uniform Crime Reports, Federal Bureau of Investigation Washington, D.C.: U.S. Department of Justice.

Curtis, T., B. C. Miller and E. H. Berry. 2000. Changes in reports and incidence of child abuse following natural disasters. *Child Abuse and Neglect* 24: 1151–62.

Dunn, C. 2006. Towers of rage, echoes of hate: Patterns of post 9/11 anti-Islamic hate crime. Paper presented at the annual meeting of the American Society of Criminology, Los Angeles, CA. Available online at: http://www.allacademic.com/meta/p_mla_apa_research_citation/1/2/5/0/0/p125 006_index.html.

Drabek, T. E. 1986. *Human System Responses to Disaster*. New York: Springer-Verlag.

Dunlap, E., B. Johnson and E. Morse. 2007. Illicit drug markets among New Orleans evacuees before and soon after Hurricane Katrina. *Journal of Drug Issues* 37(4): 981–1006.

Dynes, R. and E. L. Quarantelli. 1968. What Looting in Civil Disturbances Really Means. *Trans-action* 5(6): 71–73.

Enarson, E. and B. H. Morrow. 1998. Why gender? Why women? An introduction to women and disaster. In *The Gendered Terrain of Disaster: Through Women's Eyes*, eds. E. Enarson and B. H. Morrow, Westport, CT: Praeger.

Enarson, E. 1999. Violence against women in disasters. *Violence against Women* 5: 742–68.

Enarson, E. 1999a. Emergency preparedness in British Columbia: Mitigating violence against Women in Disasters. An Issues and Action Report for Provincial Emergency Management Authorities and Women's Services. Victoria, British Columbia, B.C.: Association of Specialized Victim Assistance and Counseling Programs.

Enarson, E. 1999b. Women and housing issues in two U.S. disasters: Hurricane Andrew and the Red River Valley Flood. *International Journal of Mass Emergencies and Disasters* 17: 39–63.

Enarson, E., A. Fothergill and L. Peek. 2006. Gender and disaster: Foundations and directions. In *Handbook of Disaster Research*, eds. H. Rodriguez, E. L. Quarantelli and R. Dynes, New York: Springer: 130–36.

Erikson, K. T. 1976. *Everything in Its Path: Destruction of Community in the Buffalo Creek Flood*. New York: Simon and Schuster.

Federal Bureau of Investigation. 2002. Press Release February 13. Available online at: http://www.fbi.gov/pressrel/pressrel02/director021302.htm.

Filosa, G. 2009. Contractor pleads guilty to rash of fraud. *The Times Picayune*, July 10: B-2.

Filosa, G. and B. McCarthy. 2007. Guard kills man in lower 9th Ward. *The Times Picayune*, March 9: B-1/2.

Fisher, S. 2005. *Gender Based Violence in Sri Lanka in the Aftermath of the 2004 Tsunami Crisis: The Role of International Organizations and International NGOs in the Prevention and Response to Gender Based Violence*. University of Leeds PhD diss.

Fothergill, A. 1996. Gender, risk and disaster. *International Journal of Mass Emergencies and Disasters* 14: 33–56.

Fothergill, A. 1999. An exploratory study of women battering in the Grand Forks flood disaster: Implications for community responses and policies. *International Journal of Mass Emergencies and Disasters* 17: 79–98.

Foster, M. 2007. Louisiana nursing home owners acquitted. *The Dispatch* (Davidson County, NC).

Frailing, K. 2007. The myth of a disaster myth: Potential looting should be part of disaster plans. *Natural Hazards Observer* 31(4): 3–4: Available online at: http://www.colorado.edu/hazards/o/archives/2007/Mar07/index-.html.

Frailing, K. and D. W. Harper. 2007. Crime and hurricanes in New Orleans. In *The Sociology of Katrina: Perspectives on a Modern Catastrophe*, eds. D. L. Brunsma, D. Overfelt and J. S. Picou, Lantham, MD: Rowman & Littlefield: 51–68.

Garrett, A. L., R. Grant, P. Madrid, A. Brito, D. Abramson and I. Redlener. 2007. Children and mega disasters: Lessons leaned in the new millennium. *Advances in Pediatrics* 54: 189–214.

Gavazzi, J. M., T. Julian and P. C. Henry. 1996. Utilization of the brief symptom inventory to discriminate between violent and non-violent male relationship partners. *Psychological Reports* 7(3): 1047–56.

Gender and Health in Disasters. 2002. Geneva, Switzerland: World Health Organization.

Haas, J. D., R. W. Kates, and M. J. Bowden, eds. 1977. *Reconstruction Following Disaster.* Cambridge, MA: MIT Press.

Haddow, G. D., J. A. Bullock and D. P. Copolla. 2008. *Emergency Management.* Burlington, MA: Butterworth-Heinemann.

Hammer, D. 2009. HANO ex-worker accused of theft. *The Times Picayune,* Sept 1: B-1/2.

Haque, E. E. and D. Blair. 1992. Vulnerability to tropical cyclones: Evidence from the April, 1991 cyclone in coastal Bangladesh. *Disasters* 16(3): 217–29.

Hartman, C. and G. D. Squires. 2006. *There is No Such Thing as a Natural Disaster: Race, Class and Hurricane Katrina.* New York: Routledge.

Harvey, C. 2009. Former council member enters prison: He sought kickbacks on Katrina contract. *The Times Picayune,* August 14: A-4.

Jenkins, P. and B. Phillips. 2008. Battered women, catastrophe, and the context of safety after Hurricane Katrina. *NWSA Journal* 20(3): 49–68.

Kessler, R. C., S. Galea, M. J. Gruber, N. A. Sampson, R. J. Ursano and S. Wessely.2008. Trends in mental illness and suicidality after Hurricane Katrina. *Molecular Psychiatry* 13: 374–84.

Killian, L. M. 2002. An introduction to methodological problems of field studies in disasters. In *Methods of Disaster Research,* ed. R. A. Stallings, Xlibris Corporation: 49–93.

Kirkham, C. and K. M. Krupa. 2009. While St. Bernard razes, New Orleans holds back, creating contrasting landscapes. *The Times Picayune,* August 29: B-1/12.

Klein, A. 2006. Sexual violence in disasters: A planning guide for prevention and response. Louisiana Foundation against Sexual Assault and National Sexual Violence Resource Center.

Leeson, P. T. and R. S. Sobel. 2008. Weathering corruption. *The Journal of Law and Economics.* 51: 667–81.

Lentin, R. 1997. *Gender and Catastrophe.* New York: Zed Books.

Lindell, M. K. and R. W. Perry. 1992. *Behavioral Foundations of Community Emergency Planning.* Washington, D.C.: Hemisphere Publishing.

Maggi, L. 2007. Guard shot inside his hut at FEMA trailer lot. *The Times Picayune,* March 6: B-2.

Maggi, L. and B. McCarthy. 2008. Profile of a murder. *The Times Picayune,* January 30: B1/6.

Mahan, S. and P. L. Griset. 2008. *Terrorism in Perspective.* Thousand Oaks, CA: Sage.

Marshall, L. 2005. Were women raped in New Orleans? Addressing the human rights of women in times of crisis. *Dissident Voice.*

McCarthy, B. 2009. 18 face Katrina fraud charges: More complex cases appearing, Letten says. *The Times Picayune,* August 29: B-2/3.

McCarthy, B. and L. Maggi. 2008. N.O. cop killed with own gun. *The Times Picayune*, January 29: A-1/8.

Mechanic, M., M. Griffin, and P. Resick. 2001. The effects of intimate partner abuse on women's psychological adjustment to a major disaster. Manuscript submitted for publication. (Cited in Norris, no date. Available online at: http://www.ptsd.va.gov/professional/pages/disasters-domestic-violence.asp.).

Moran, K. 2007. Mental health care hospital planned. *The Times Picayune*, February 14: B-1/2.

Morris, C. 2002. *The San Francisco Calamity by Earthquake and Fire*. Urbana, IL: University of Illinois Press.

Morrow, B. H. and E. Enarson. 1996. Hurricane Andrew through women's eyes: Issues and recommendations. *International Journal of Mass Emergencies and Disasters* 14: 5–22.

National Center for Missing and Exploited Children. 2006. National Center for Missing and Exploited Children reunites last missing child separated by Hurricanes Katrina and Rita. Alexandria, VA: National Center for Missing and Exploited Children.

National Governors Association. 1979. Emergency Preparedness Project Final Report. Washington, D.C.: U.S. Government Printing Office.

National Sexual Violence Resource Center. 2006. Hurricanes Katrina/Rita and sexual violence: Report on database of sexual violence prevalence and incidence related to hurricanes Katrina and Rita. Available online at: http://www.nsvrc.org/sites/default/files/Publications_NSVRC_Reports_Report-on-Database-of-Sexual-Violence-Prevalence-and-Incidence-Related-to-Hurricane-Katrina-and-Rita.pdf.

Neal, D. M. 1997. Reconsidering the Phases of Disasters. *International Journal of Mass Emergencies and Disasters* 15: 239–64.

Norris, F. H. No date. Disasters and domestic Violence: prevalence and impact of domestic violence in the wake of disasters. Department of Veterans Affairs. Available online at: http://NWN.pted.VA.gov/professional/pages/disasters-comeestic-violence.asp.

Norris, F. H. and G. A. Uhl. 1993. Chronic stress as a mediator of acute stress: The case of Hurricane Hugo. *Journal of Applied Social Psychology*, 23: 1263–284.

Norris, F. H., J. L. Perilla, J. K. Riad, K. Kaniasty and E. A. Lavizzo. 1999. Stability and change in stress, resources and psychological stress following natural disaster: Findings from Hurricane Andrew. *Anxiety, Stress and Coping* 12: 363–96.

Office of National Drug Control Policy. 2002. Pulse check: Trends in drug abuse, April 2002, Special topic: The impact of September 11. Available online at: http://www.ncjrs.gov/ondcppubs/publications/drugfact/pulse-chk/impact_of_sept11.pdf.

Peek, L. 2010. Age. In *Social Vulnerability to Disasters*, eds. B. Phillips, D. Thomas, A. Fothergill and L. Blinn-Pike. New York: CRC Press.

Perry, R. W. 1990. Evacuation decision making in natural disasters. *Mass Emergencies* 4: 25–38.

Phillips, B., L. Garza, and D. Neal. 1994. Issues of cultural diversity in times of disaster: The case of Hurricane Andrew. *Journal of Intergroup Relations* 21: 18–27.

Phillips, B. D., P. Jenkins and E. Enarson. 2010. Violence and disaster vulnerability. In *Social Vulnerability to Disasters*, eds. B. Phillips, D. Thomas, A. Fothergill and L. Blinn-Pike, New York: CRC Press.

Picou, J. S. and B. K. Marshall. 2007. Katrina as paradigm shift: Reflections on disaster research in the twenty-first century. In *The Sociology of Katrina: Perspectives on a Modern Catastrophe*, eds. D. L. Brunsma, D. Overfelt, and J. S. Picou, Lantham, MD: Rowman & Littlefield: 1–22.

Powell, J., J. Rayner and J. Finesinger. 1953. Responses to disaster in American cultural groups. Paper presented at the Symposium on Stress, Army Medical Graduate School, Washington, D.C.

Preventing and Detecting Bid Rigging. 2009. Preventing and detecting bid rigging, price fixing and market al.location in post disaster rebuilding projects. Available online at: http://www.usdoj.gov/atr/public/guidelines/disaster_primer.htm.

Preventing Copper Theft. 2007. Arnie Fielkow Council at Large. Available online at: http://www.fielkowcitycouncil.com/newsletters/2007_oct9.php.

Pullin, M. 2006. Impact of Katrina evacuees upon law enforcement. Texas Law Enforcement Management and Administrative Statistics Program 13(5).

Quarantelli, E. L. 2006. Catastrophes are different from disasters: Some implications for crisis planning and management drawn from Katrina. In *Understanding Katrina: Perspectives from the Social Sciences*. Available online at: http://understandingkatrina.ssrc.org/Quarantelli/.

Quarantelli, E. L., P. Lagadec and A. Boin. 2006. A heuristic approach to future disasters and crises: New, old and in between types. In *Handbook of Disaster Research*, eds. H. Rodriguez, E. L. Quarantelli and R. Dynes, New York: Springer: 16–41.

Quarantelli, E. L. 2007. The myth and the realities: Keeping the "looting" myth in perspective. *Natural Hazards Observer* 31(4): 2–3. Available online at: http://www.colorado.edu/hazards/o/archives/2007/Mar07/index.html.

Reckdahl, K. 2009. HANO is neglecting Iberville, some say. *The Times Picayune*, March 23: A-4.

Roberts, F. F. 2005. Cyber-looters capitalize on Katrina. *eWeek* 22 (36): 11–12.

Shariat, S., S. Mallonee, E. Kruger, K. Farmer and C. North. 1999. A prospective study of long-term health outcomes among Oklahoma City bombing survivors. *Journal of the Oklahoma State Medical Association* 92: 178–86.

Showalter, P. S. and M. F. Myers. 1994. Natural disasters in the United States as release agents of oil, chemicals or radiologic materials between 1980 and 1989: Analysis and recommendations, *Risk Analysis* 14: 169–82.

Siman, B. A. 1977. *Crime During Disaster*. University of Pennsylvania PhD diss. Ann Arbor, MI: University Microfilms International.

Smith, F. 2008. The smallest victims of California wildfires are often forgotten. *Crisis and Emergency Management Newsletter* 14(1). Available online at: http://www.seas.gwu.edu/~emse232/february2008_7.html.

Southeastern Louisiana Catastrophic Hurricane Functional Plan. 2004. Baton Rouge, LA: Innovative Emergency Management, August 6.

Thevenot, B. 2006. Adding insult to injury, thieves are stealing pieces of the city's soul: Irreplaceable architectural thefts. *The Times Picayune,* June 6: A-1.

Thornton, W. E. and L. Voigt. 2007. Disaster Rape: Vulnerability of women to sexual assaults during Hurricane Katrina. *Journal of Public Management and Social Policy* 13(2): 23–49.

Thornton, W. E., L. Voigt and P. D. Walsh. 2009. Migrant workers and criminal victimization in post-Katrina New Orleans. Paper Presented at the Southern Sociological Association Meetings, New Orleans, LA.

The Times Picayune. 2007. St. Rita's nursing home trial on hold, September 4. Available online at: http://blog.nola.com/times-picayune/2007/09/st_ritas_nursing_home_trial_on.html.

The Times Picayune. 2007a. Gunshot victim found in trailer on Touro Street, April 2: B-3.

Tobin, G. A. and L. M. Whiteford. 2002. Community resilience and volcano eruption of Tungurahua and evacuation of the Faldas in Ecuador. *Disasters* 26(1): 28–48.

Tobin, G. A., H. M. Bell, L. M. Whiteford and B. E. Montz. 2006. Vulnerability of displaced persons: Relocation park residents in the wake of Hurricane Charley. *International Journal of Mass Emergencies and Disasters* 24(1): 77–109.

Trainor, J., B. D. Aquirre and J. Barnshaw. 2008. Social scientific insights on preparedness for public health emergencies, Miscellaneous Report #59. University of Delaware: Disaster Research Center.

UN. 1992. United Nations Department of Humanitarian Affairs. Internationally agreed glossary of basic terms related to disaster management, DNA/93/36. Geneva: United Nations.

United Nations High Commission for Refugees (UNHCR). 1999. Reproductive health in refugee situations: An inter-agency field manual. Geneva: UNHCR. Available online at: http://unfpa.org/emergencies/manual/4.htm.

United States Department of Justice. 2005–2007. Hurricane Katrina fraud task force report. Links to HKFTF Progress and Annual Reports available online at: www.usdoj/katrina/Katrina_Fraud/.

Voigt, L., W. E. Thornton, L. Barrile and J. Seaman. 1994. *Criminology and Justice*. New York: McGraw Hill, Inc.

Voigt, L. and W. E. Thornton. 2008. Sex and vice crimes in post-Katrina New Orleans. Unpublished manuscript.

Walsh, P. D., W. E. Thornton and L. Voigt. 2009. Homicide trends and drastic population shifts: Latino migrant worker homicides in post-Katrina New Orleans. Paper presented at Homicide Research Working Group, Amherst, MA.

Waller, M. 2007. Psychiatric bed shortage jams jails. *The Times Picayune*, March 13: A-1/4.

Wright, J. and E. L. Quarantelli. 1974. Anti-social behavior in disasters: Myth or reality? Disaster Research Center paper, the Ohio State University, 1–10.

Yelvington, K. A. 1997. Coping in a temporary way: The tent cities. In *Hurricane Andrew: Ethnicity, Gender and the Sociology of Disasters*, eds. W. G. Peacock, B. H. Morrow and H. Gladwin, London: Routledge.

Zhou, D. 1997. *Disaster, Disorganization, and Crime*. University of Albany State University of New York PhD diss. Ann Arbor, MI: University Microfilms International.

Discussion Questions

1. List and briefly explain the four general phases of a disaster. Describe how the various events and subsequent activities of each stage may be associated with enhanced opportunities for criminal activities to occur.

2. What are the strengths and weaknesses associated with disaster phase analysis? How do single-impact versus serial-impact disasters affect the various phases with respect to the commission of various types of crimes?

3. Explain how some disasters by their very nature constitute a crime or crimes. Give an example and speculate on whether you think these types of disasters are different in their consequences for communities and individual victims.

4. Describe the broad categories of crimes that often occur during the recovery phase of disasters. Why do you think that most types of crimes, personal and property, seem to be more prevalent in this phase of a disaster?

5. One category of crimes, sexual assaults including intimate partner violence, seems to occur throughout all the phases of disasters. Discuss the possible reasons for this, noting physical and social factors connected with each phase, which might help explain the phenomena.

6. While all individuals run the risk of being criminally victimized at any phase during a disaster, certain populations appear to be more vulnerable than others. Describe these populations and explain the circumstances that may facilitate their criminal victimizations. What recommendations would you offer to disaster/crisis managers to help prevent these types of crimes from occurring?

When the Disaster is a Crime: Legal Issues and the *Exxon Valdez* Oil Spill[1]

By Duane A. Gill, J. Steven Picou and Liesel A. Ritchie

Introduction

Disasters disrupt social relationships and cause extreme trauma and stress for survivors. Accordingly, social systems are seriously impacted and as the chapters in this volume illustrate, the resulting social disorganization is a context for different forms of crime and criminal behavior. In this chapter, we suggest a conceptual framework that distinguishes different types of disasters and provides a basis for understanding criminal and civil liabilities that characterize human-caused catastrophes. Next, we review the criminal and civil litigation associated with the largest and most ecologically damaging oil spill in the history of North America—the *Exxon Valdez* oil spill (EVOS). We conclude by briefly noting consequences of the litigation associated with the EVOS for survivors of the spill and for future disasters.

A Typology of Disasters

Over the last decade, a variety of disasters have increasingly impacted communities and regions around the world. The concept of disaster brings to mind a sudden event that results in loss of life, the destruction of property, and diminished social well-being. The word "disaster" literally means "bad star" and

1. Major funding for the collection of data reviewed in this chapter was provided by the National Science Foundation (Grants DDP-910109, OPP-0082405, OPP-002572 and OPP-0852932). The opinions and contents of this chapter remain the responsibility of the authors and do not reflect the policy or position of the National Science Foundation.

the scope of modern disasters may seriously disrupt the day-to-day activities of regions, communities, groups and families. In fact, disasters significantly change human communities and in their most catastrophic forms actually destroy them.

Given the complexity of disasters, it is useful to consider these events in terms of a typology that includes natural, technological, natural disaster-triggered technological (natech) disasters and terrorism. We begin this section with a discussion of natural and technological disasters, and then examine how natech and terrorism events can be incorporated into this framework using Hurricane Katrina and the 9/11 terrorist attacks as examples.

In general, researchers, emergency management personnel, politicians and survivors have identified two primary types of disasters—natural and technological. Natural disasters are triggered by natural processes and hazards that threaten human life and damage the "built" and "modified" environments. The built environment includes residential homes and commercial buildings, while the modified environment includes roads, bridges and utilities. Some natural disasters, such as earthquakes, occur suddenly and are unanticipated. Others, such as hurricanes and floods, can be predicted and anticipated, allowing warnings and evacuation notices to be issued. Natural disasters tend to follow a sequence of warning, threat, impact, inventory, rescue, remedy, recovery and rehabilitation (Drabek 1986). These features facilitate development of emergency response organizations and plans for mitigating and preventing losses. Often, a therapeutic community emerges as survivors and others come together to offer support and reaffirm social networks (Barton 1969). Given the predictability, general sequence of events and therapeutic community characteristic of natural disasters, individual trauma and social disruption tends to be acute, but relatively short-lived for most survivors.

On the other hand, technological disasters involve irresponsible and reckless behavior on the part of individuals, groups, corporations or institutions, which result in the failure of technology and subsequent breakdown in organizations designed to control technological processes. In recent history, we find technological disasters such as Buffalo Creek (West Virginia, 1972), Three-Mile Island (Pennsylvania, 1979), Bhopal (India, 1986), Chernobyl (Ukraine, 1986), Love Canal (New York, 1978) and the *Exxon Valdez* oil spill (Alaska, 1989). This type of disaster tends to damage a bioregion. A bioregion is "part of the earth's surface whose rough boundaries are determined by natural rather than human dictates, distinguishable from other areas by attributes of flora, fauna, water, climate, soils and landforms and the human settlements and cultures those attributes have given rise to" (Sale 1991: 78). More often than not, technological disasters damage the "natural" environment or ecosystem through toxic contamination and resource loss. The natural environment includes all naturally occurring biotic (living organisms) and abiotic (chemical and physical factors) components and processes. When ecosystems are contaminated, impacts on components and processes may persist for decades, even generations. Similarly, natural resource losses resulting from a technological disaster can also persist and injure individuals and communities that rely on them for sociocultural purposes. For example, human exposure to toxins can result in illness, miscarriages, deformities and loss of life—conditions that are often difficult to trace back to the source (Vyner 1988).

Unlike the visible physical damages inflicted by natural disasters, contamination associated with technological disasters tends to be invisible and difficult to detect, a condition that leads to an "ambiguity of harm" and competing "definitions of the situation." As a result, instead of progressing through phases leading to recovery and rehabilitation, social processes in the aftermath of technological disasters tend to become mired in a series of "secondary traumas." Secondary trauma "can be defined as a blow to the social fabric caused by ... events, occasions, or public perceptions that inhibit timely community recovery and prolong stress and disruption" (Gill 2007: 625). Litigation, conflicting information regarding contamination and prolonged uncertainty arising after the original event are typical examples. The uncertainty and contested meanings associated with technological disasters lead to a "corrosive" rather than a therapeutic community (Freudenburg and Jones 1991). Corrosive communities are characterized by conflict, the loss of social capital, prolonged individual trauma and social disruption (Picou, Marshall and Gill 2004, Ritchie and Gill 2007). Furthermore, beliefs that recreancy—"the failure of experts or specialized organizations to execute properly responsibilities to the broader collectivity with which they have been implicitly or explicitly entrusted" (Freudenburg 2000: 116)—was a primary cause of the technological disaster also leads to anger and litigation. In sum, environmental degradation and human culpability associated with technological disasters tend to affect social and ecological elements of bioregions at multiple levels.

Two recent events in the U.S. demonstrate that not all disasters fit neatly into the categories of natural or technological. Hurricane Katrina and the 9/11 terrorist attacks raise questions that highlight a need to expand how disasters are classified. Although Hurricane Katrina was triggered by a natural meteorological event, much of the damage in New Orleans was a result of a breakdown in human engineered systems (e.g., the levee system) and subsequent releases of toxic substances into the flood waters. Terrorism disasters like the 9/11 attacks are human-caused acts of violence and destruction motivated by a combination of political, social and cultural reasons, directed to frighten and influence more people than the immediate victims (see Waugh 2006). As will be discussed below, two additional categories—natech and terrorism—can be integrated into our typology of disasters.

Hurricane Katrina struck the coasts of Louisiana and Mississippi on August 29, 2005, unleashing one of the deadliest and most expensive disasters in U.S. history (Brinkley 2006). Coastal communities in both states were heavily damaged by 135 mph sustained winds and a 20 to 32 foot storm surge. New Orleans survived the Category 3 hurricane winds, but the failure of its levees resulted in a massive flood which covered 80 percent of the city with up to 12 feet of water (Johnson 2006). Along the Mississippi Gulf Coast and parts of coastal Louisiana, survivors attributed the disaster to "nature" or an "act of God"—something beyond human control. In New Orleans, however, Katrina was portrayed as a product of political incompetence and system failure, a "government-induced disaster" created by the U.S. Army Corps of Engineers and their poorly designed, constructed and maintained levee/floodgate system. This situation was aggravated by a breakdown of emergency response organizations such as FEMA, the state of Louisiana and the city of New Orleans. Although the storm was caused by natural meteorological events, the ensuing New Orleans flood and disaster arguably reflected failures in technology and human organizations.

For decades, experts across a wide variety of disciplines predicted that in the event of a large hurricane, the levees would not protect the city, much of which is below sea level (van Heerden and Bryan 2006, Laska 2008, Tierney 2008). These predictions went unheeded as part of the government's institutional neglect, bureaucratic inefficiency and internal conflicts. Combined with poverty, racial segregation, crime, an aging population and a crumbling urban infrastructure, "Katrina the disaster" was both predictable and inevitable (Brinkley 2006, Glantz 2005).

A variety of household, commercial and industrial toxins were released into the air, water and soil during the Katrina disaster. For example, according to EPA (Environmental Protection Agency) estimates, more than 8 million gallons of oil were released in the New Orleans area and throughout south Louisiana (Picou and Marshall 2007). Post-Katrina ecological damage in New Orleans included contamination of the air (mold spores), soil (arsenic, lead, hydrocarbons and diesel fuel) and water. The concentration, spread and persistence of this "toxic gumbo" are not known, nor are the health effects of exposure to these contaminants.

Within this context, Hurricane Katrina exemplifies a third type of disaster—the natech disaster. This concept, introduced by Erikson (1994) and Showalter and Myers (1994), can be defined as a dynamic interaction of natural events with engineering, production and technological systems of industry and government. This type of disaster is a combination of natural, technological and organizational forces, displaying elements of both natural and technological disasters. Natech disasters affect the built, modified, natural and social environments. There is relative certainty about physical damage impacts and, at the same time, *uncertainty* about contamination and health risks. Survivors experience therapeutic community benefits after the disaster accompanied by some of the corrosive elements of conflict, recreancy and loss of trust. Although natech disasters may go through phases resembling those of a natural disaster, recovery and rehabilitation may take longer. In terms of psychological trauma, acute, short-lived stress is experienced by many survivors, but trauma may be prolonged by delays in recovery and become chronic when there are perceived injustices and a lack of restitution. The components of technological failure and organizational breakdown associated with a natech disaster mean there are individuals and organizations to blame; holding these responsible parties accountable will likely involve criminal charges and civil litigation (Picou 2009).

Terrorism disasters became visible and more widely recognized when the events of September 11, 2001 unfolded (Clarke 2003). The collapse of the twin towers of the World Trade Center, damage to the Pentagon and crash of another plane in rural Pennsylvania tragically revealed societal vulnerabilities to intentional acts of destruction. Acts of terrorism share similarities with disasters in that they damage the built, modified and natural environments, disrupt social structures and relationships, activate emergency responses and challenge community response, recovery and resilience. Like technological disasters, terrorism disasters have identifiable responsible parties (individuals and organizations), involve perceptions of recreancy, fall outside normal emergency response operations, create unusual health threats and cause long-term social and psychological trauma (Marshall, Picou and Gill 2003).

Terrorism disasters often target the engineered environment—critical infrastructure and lifelines such as electric power grids, cyberspace, computer networks, information technology, telecommunications and transportation systems—to maximize social disruption and terror. They occur with very little warning and reveal a lack of social preparedness and mitigation. Terrorism disaster phases are similar to those of a natech disaster, with a combination of progression to recovery and rehabilitation mixed with secondary traumas such as uncertainty, contested meanings and efforts to collect for loss of life and property. Likewise, terrorism disasters are followed by elements of both therapeutic and corrosive communities—therapeutic in the "rally effect" whereby people from all over the country offer support and corrosive if citizens perceive issues of recreancy that may have prevented the disaster or diminished its impacts. Furthermore, recovery from terrorism disasters may be delayed and justice prolonged, leading to long-term social and psychological trauma (Natural Hazards Research and Applications Information Center 2003).

A summary of the four types of disasters we have discussed is presented in Table 4.1. The hazard origin or cause is significant because disasters with human origins are characterized by high levels of social and psychological trauma. Technological, natech, and terrorism disasters affect more than the built and modified environments. They usually involve toxic contaminants or pathogens that cause long-term damage to natural resources and pose long-term health effects to those exposed. Natural disasters have been a part of human development and history but human-caused disasters are a "new species of trouble" that "contaminate rather than merely damage; they pollute, befoul, and taint rather than just create wreckage" (Erikson 1994: 144). In the context of this chapter, perhaps the most salient characteristic of human-caused disasters—whether they are technological, natech or terrorism—is that criminal charges and civil litigation usually result from these disaster types.

In addition to identifying various types of disasters, it is also useful to consider them on a continuum, with overlapping qualities, characteristics and social impacts (Gill and Ritchie 2006). On such a continuum, our typologies represent "markers" along a "continuum of deliberateness" of action (see Green 1996 and Ritchie 2004). Criminal charges and civil litigation associated with human-caused disasters are part of this continuum. As shown in Figure 4.1, natural disasters are situated at one end of the continuum where causes are attributed to acts of nature or deities rather than purposive human actions. Natech and technological disasters involve more purposive action and are caused by negligence, recreancy, recklessness and/or intent. At the other end of the continuum is terrorism, which represents premeditated, purposive acts designed to achieve political or ideological goals. As the level of deliberateness increases, so does the likelihood that the events will involve criminal and civil legal processes.

Human-caused disasters involve "principle responsible parties," that is, people and organizations are identified as being accountable for the disaster. Perceptions of recreancy are more likely to emerge after human-caused disasters than natural disasters. The question arises, "Who is responsible for the contamination and loss of resources?" The pursuit of accountability often involves *criminal litigation* for violation of laws and regulations, as well as *civil litigation*, seeking restitution for damages caused by the disaster. Intertwined with issues of accountability is the need for recovery and restoration on the part of individuals, groups and communities. There are typically three ways to accomplish this: (1) self help or grassroots efforts—a sort of "civil" defense which involves drawing on social capital (2) state, federal and other not-for-profit

Table 4.1 A Summary of Disaster Types

Disaster Type	Hazard Origin	Example Event	Primary Affected Environments	Basic Consequences	Commentary
Natural Disaster	Meteorological and geological systems	2004 Indian Ocean earthquake and tsunami	Built and modified	Immediate and acute threats to life and destruction of community resources.	In Ideal form viewed as "acts of God." Results in amplified rebound, with improved building codes and engineering designs.
Natech Disaster	Interaction of natural and technological systems	Hurricane Katrina	Built, modified and natural	Large-scale destruction, including loss of life and contamination. Both acute and long-term impacts occur.	In Ideal form a natural disaster causes techno-logical break-downs and loss of control of toxins. Civil litigation is part of restitution.
Techno-logical Disaster	Industrial production/ engineered systems	*Exxon Valdez* oil spill	Natural	Contamination of natural resources that create long-term exposure threats to ecosystems and people.	In Ideal form these disasters could have been prevented and reveal human-error. Criminal behavior and civil litigation ensues.
Terrorism Disaster	Political/ ideological groups	9/11 terrorist attacks	Built, modified, natural and engineered	Large-scale destruction including loss of life and toxic/pathogen contamination. Long-term damage to ecosystems and people.	In Ideal form these are politically motivated acts designed to intimidate and symbolically threaten identified political units. Criminal behavior and civil litigation ensues.

Figure 4.1 Continuum of Deliberateness for Various Types of Disasters

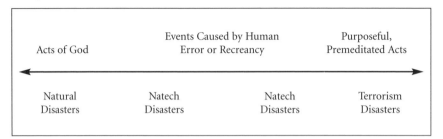

emergency response/support systems (e.g., FEMA, the Red Cross, et cetera) and (3) litigation. If the first and second approaches are not sufficient, accountability and resources for recovery and restoration are often addressed through the court system.

Given the adversarial nature of the U.S. legal system, contested meanings become intensified, facts are disputed and court decisions are appealed for years. In some cases, the social and psychological impacts associated with litigation are more intense than for the actual disaster (Picou, Marshall and Gill 2004). Within this context, beliefs about how recovery and rehabilitation occur are influenced by notions of restitution, justice and transformation. That is, the litigation process becomes a substitute for recovery and has potential to fundamentally alter how survivors view the world. For some survivors, "closure" may never occur. This is evident in the case of the *Exxon Valdez* oil spill, a technological disaster that occurred over 20 years ago and continues to be litigated in Federal Court.

The EVOS: A Disaster and Environmental Crime

At four minutes past midnight on Friday, March 24, 1989, the supertanker *Exxon Valdez* ran aground on a well-marked reef in Prince William Sound, Alaska. The vessel spilled between 11 and 33 million gallons of oil into one of the most pristine ecosystems in the world (Ott 2005). The primary responsible parties for the spill were Exxon and the tanker's captain. According to court records, "The accident occurred after the tanker's captain, Joseph Hazelwood— who had a history of alcohol abuse and whose blood still had a high alcohol level 11 hours after the spill—inexplicably exited the bridge, leaving a tricky course correction to unlicensed subordinates" (*Exxon* v. *Baker*, 554 U.S. __ 2008: Syllabus). Records also revealed that Exxon knew of the captain's alcohol issues but failed to supervise or reassign him. Other documents suggested the tanker had faulty radar equipment in need of repair for almost a year and that, in working order, this system might have averted the accident. Once the tanker grounded, however, a technological disaster ensued.

Local, regional and state oil spill contingency plans were inadequate and the Alyeska Pipeline Service Company, the corporation responsible for oil spill response, was completely unprepared. After two calm days during which the spill could have been contained, a powerful storm spread the oil beyond control. As a result, more than 44,000 square kilometers, including 1,900 kilometers of Alaskan coastline, were oiled. The destruction of habitat, fish, marine mammals and birds was beyond that for any spill in the history of oil transportation. Initial estimates suggested more than 250,000 birds, 4,400 sea otters, 300 harbor seals, 250 bald eagles, 22 orca whales and countless numbers of fish perished in the immediate aftermath of the spill (Spies et al.. 1996). However, the ability to accurately document the damage caused by the spill suggests these are conservative estimates.

The EVOS was also devastating to residents of the small Alaska Native villages and commercial fishing communities that were negatively affected by the spill. These "renewable resource communities" (RRCs) derive their "cultural, social and economic existence" from "the harvest and use of renewable natural resources" (Picou and Gill 1997: 213). For example, cultural subsistence practices of Alaska Natives include harvesting and gathering fish, animals, birds and berries, as well as the development of exchange relationships, family solidarity and cultural identity (Gill and Picou 1997). Initially, the spill severely reduced subsistence harvests because of concern for the health consequences of consuming contaminated resources.

Initial social impacts within these communities included elevated levels of family conflict, domestic violence, increased consumption of alcohol and drugs, collective trauma, social disruption, economic uncertainty, community strain and psychological stress. As key commercial and subsistence resources such as herring failed to recover, many area residents, particularly those most closely tied to the resources (e.g., Alaska Natives and commercial fishermen), experienced long-term psychological stress, social disruption and collective trauma.

Alaska Natives and commercial fishermen were the two social groups most negatively affected by initial and long-term impacts of the EVOS. These groups were the most vulnerable to ecological contamination and resource loss inflicted by the spill. Thus, their values, attitudes and behaviors were highly disrupted. The resulting social pathology included the breakdown of social relationships, losses of economic and personal resources, severe psychological stress and depression and the emergence of conflict-prone corrosive communities (Picou, Marshall and Gill 2004). In sum, impacts of the EVOS severely diminished the economic, social and cultural capital of oiled communities dependent on commercial fishing and the harvest of renewable natural resources (Ritchie and Gill 2007).

Social capital refers to the nature and extent of people's participation in social networks and civic organizations in their communities (Putnam 2000). Strong social relationships and having trust in others, including institutions such as the legal system and government, are also important elements of social capital. The overall well-being of a given community depends on the extent to which social capital exists in that community. In other words, the more social capital in a community—exhibited as trust, fellowship, associations, connections, networks, social interactions, good will, sympathy and norms of reciprocity—the "healthier" the community. Arguably, the health of communities affected by the EVOS has deteriorated as a consequence of this disaster. The most important secondary trauma perpetuating a lack of timely community recovery was the chronic pattern of adversarial litigation that has continued to the present. The litigation produced many changes in these communities, including an emergence of litigants as a new vulnerable group who experienced ongoing exposure to this secondary trauma—namely, adversarial litigation.

Tragically, the chronic ecological impacts of the EVOS continue to unfold as volatile oil remains in the subsurface of many beaches, leaches into salmon streams and continues to poison exposed fish and wildlife (Short et al. 2007). The most recent figures indicate only 10 of 26 resources/species have recovered from the oil spill (*Exxon Valdez* Oil Spill Trustee Council [EVOSTC] 2006: 6). This lasting ecological contamination will continue to disrupt the local habitat and produce serious problems for the small communities in the spill area. Because RRCs are intimately linked to the local ecology, community recovery is inextricably connected to ecological recovery.

EVOS Crime and Punishment[2]

In searching for causes of the *Exxon Valdez* disaster, there is almost as much blame to spread around as there was oil on Alaska's shoreline. Alyeska was responsible for initial spill response and containment but it lacked trained personnel, equipment, supplies and vessels. The state of Alaska had responsibilities for oversight of Alyeska through the Department of Environmental Conser-

---

2. A version of this section was published in the November, 2008 issue of the *Natural Hazards Observer* (Gill 2008).

vation, but its most effective inspector had been reassigned because of industry complaints against him. The U.S. Coast Guard had responsibilities for monitoring tanker traffic in and out of the area but funds for state-of-the-art radar equipment had not been authorized by the Federal Government as promised in legislation authorizing the pipeline. Oil companies in the 1980s were in an economic downturn that led to cost-cutting measures such as reducing the number of tanker crewmembers, extending working hours and encouraging more risk taking in an effort to reduce travel time from terminal to refinery and back. In retrospect, a complacent culture characterized oil transportation in this area. This, combined with our nation's high demand for oil, helped set the stage for this disaster. Against that backdrop, however, the primary responsible parties for the EVOS were Exxon and the tanker's captain.

In the months following the spill, criminal charges were filed against Exxon for violations of the Clean Water Act, the Refuse Act and the Migratory Bird Treaty Act. In 1991, the State of Alaska and the U.S. Government collaborated to negotiate a settlement with Exxon for approximately $900 million in criminal and civil fines. The agreement established the EVOSTC to administer the funds and monitor recovery of resources damaged by the spill. Paid out over a 10 year period, these funds were used in recovery and restoration efforts in coastal areas heavily impacted by the spill. Some of the money was used to conduct scientific research on injured species. However, the bulk of the funds were used to purchase, preserve and protect more than 650,000 acres of land directly adjacent to the most heavily oiled shorelines. This was a controversial move, given that much of this land was owned by Native corporations put in the position of balancing a need for money with maintaining their cultural heritage. Critics of the sale claimed, "We have sold our children's birthright" (Gill and Picou 2001).

The EVOS Civil Litigation

Civil litigation has been a significant feature of the *Exxon Valdez* disaster. The numerous civil cases filed against Exxon in the wake of the oil spill were eventually consolidated into a "class" consisting of almost 33,000 plaintiffs. The class included Alaska Natives, commercial fishermen, deckhands, cannery workers, business owners, land owners, local governments and others financially harmed by the spill. A 1994 jury trial in Federal District Court in Anchorage, with the Honorable H. Russel Holland presiding, found Exxon reckless and liable for $287 million in compensatory damages and $5 billion in punitive damages. Exxon waited three years to appeal the verdict and the amount of punitive damages became a major point of contention.

The class action EVOS litigation took a series of unanticipated twists and turns that delayed resolution for almost 14 years. First, the case languished in the Ninth Circuit Court of Appeals more than four years until a 2001 decision ruled against Exxon[3] on all points except the amount of punitive damages, which was deemed excessive. The case was returned to Federal Court where Judge Holland reduced the award to $4 billion in 2002. ExxonMobil appealed and in 2003, the Appeals Court sent the case back to Federal Court with guidelines for reducing punitive damages. Judge Holland revised the punitive award upward to $4.5 billion in 2004 and ExxonMobil appealed again. The Ninth Circuit Court of Appeals cut the award to $2.5 billion in 2006 prompting another appeal by ExxonMobil—this time to the Supreme Court.

While the legal saga unfolded, disastrous impacts continued to be experienced among communities and groups closely tied to the damaged resources. Commercial fishing was slow to recover, not only in quantity but also with respect to prices and marketing. Attention to legal issues and efforts to restore damaged natural resources effectively diverted efforts to market local fish products. In addition, fish prices plummeted against changes in global fish markets and the influx of farm-raised salmon. The national economic boom of the 1990s skipped these communities and instead, bankruptcies, business closings, out-migration and low tax revenues became the norm. Uncertainty over recovery of ecosystem resources and delayed justice from prolonged litigation contributed to a chronic social-psychological malaise that drained communities of social capital, people and groups were increasingly fragmented and frustrated. Each appeal and court delay seemed to deflate the morale of disaster survivors a little bit more. Moreover, almost 20 percent of the plaintiffs died during this time. They never saw resolution of the lawsuit or deliverance of justice.

Exxon v. *Baker*: The Supreme Court Decision

The U.S. Supreme Court heard oral arguments in the EVOS case on February 27, 2008. Exxon argued that punitive damages were not permitted under maritime law and the Clean Water Act. The corporation also contended that punitive damages were unnecessary because it had already spent more than $3.4 billion in cleanup costs, compensatory damages, criminal and civil fines and other expenses. The plaintiffs argued that corporations like ExxonMobil should be held accountable for reckless actions and punitive damages serve to deter sim-

---

3. Exxon Corporation merged with Mobil to become ExxonMobil in 1999.

ilar actions and wrongs. They argued the spill caused extensive damage to the environment and the lives of area residents, much of which occurred or became apparent *after* the case went to trial in 1994. For example, the commercial herring fishery collapsed in 1994 and has yet to recover. Prior to the spill, this fishery accounted for a significant portion of fishing revenues in Prince William Sound and no compensation for this loss was ever received by commercial fishermen.

On June 25, 2008, the Supreme Court issued a ruling that upheld the plaintiff's assertion that Exxon was responsible for the spill and punitive damages were allowed in this case. However, the court voted five to three to reduce the $2.5 billion punitive damage award to $507 million—a "one-to-one ratio" of punitive damages to actual damages and one-tenth of the original punitive damage award. Justices Kennedy, Roberts, Scalia, Souter and Thomas were in the majority and Justices Ginsberg, Stevens and Breyer dissented.

Writing for the majority, Justice Souter argued that the punitive damage award was excessive, noting that, "American punitive damages have been the target of audible criticism in recent decades," particularly regarding "the stark unpredictability of punitive awards." He wrote, "In many instances a high ratio of punitive to compensatory damages is greater than necessary to punish or deter" (554 U.S. __ 2008: VI, D). In establishing a one-to-one ratio of punitive to compensatory damages, Justice Souter acknowledged that the decision may appear that the Supreme Court was engaging in policy (legislation), but deemed it justifiable in the narrow context of maritime law.

In dissent, Justice Stevens wrote, "In light of Exxon's decision to permit a lapsed alcoholic to command a supertanker carrying tens of millions of gallons of crude oil through the treacherous waters of Prince William Sound, thereby endangering all of the individuals who depend upon the sound for their livelihoods, the jury could reasonably have given expression to its moral condemnation of Exxon's conduct in the form of this award" (554 U.S. __ 2008: II). Justice Ginsberg's dissent took issue with Court setting the one-to-one ratio on a matter where "Congress is the better equipped decisionmaker." Further, she wrote, "I question whether there is an urgent need in maritime law to break away from the 'traditional common-law approach' under which punitive damages are determined by a properly instructed jury, followed by trial-court, and then appellate-court review, to ensure that the award is reasonable" (554 U.S. __ 2008). Justice Breyer noted, "The jury thought the facts here justified punitive damages of $5 billion ... based in large part on the fact that Exxon's conduct was highly reprehensible" (554 U.S. __ 2008).

Although the Court ruled in favor of the plaintiffs, holding Exxon liable, many considered the decision to dramatically reduce the punitive damage award to favor the oil company. Responses to the decision in oiled Native villages and fishing communities reflected what had been predicted had the Court rendered a decision entirely in favor of Exxon. Feelings of betrayal, shock, injustice, anger, depression, resignation, defeat, sadness and hurt characterized the reactions of many plaintiffs and their communities. Many expressed a lost faith in the justice system and felt helpless, invisible and insignificant compared to corporation citizens. One fisherman stated, "It kind of sends the message that big corporations that have the right money and political power can throw safety and responsibility to the wind." Another characterized the Court as being "part of owned-and-operated corporate America." A third fisherman observed, "It gives big business the formula they need to calculate the cost of their actions when they destroy the environment. This gives them the formula to calculate their risks." Another quipped, "I found out what the true meaning of punitive damages is—puny." A fisherman summed up the decision: " … it's amazing how money can purchase justice in this country. A jury of your peers apparently doesn't stand for much because they [the courts] can change it whenever they want."

Plaintiffs finally began receiving checks for their share of punitive damages in December 2008, continuing into 2009. For most, the amount did not begin to cover EVOS losses they had incurred since 1989.

Problems with Punitive Damages

Punitive damages are often referred to as one of the flashpoints of tort law in the United States. Perceptions fostered by the general media and special interest groups are that juries tend to award exorbitant amounts of money for punitive damages. The 1994 McDonald's coffee case stands as what ABC News referred to as the "poster child of excessive lawsuits" (2007). In this case, a jury awarded $2.86 million in punitive damages and $200,000 in compensatory damages to a woman who was severely burned by coffee she purchased at a McDonald's restaurant. Reports tend to leave out that McDonald's had been unresponsive to thousands of similar complaints filed in previous years and that ultimately, the 79-year-old woman received a lesser, undisclosed amount *after* the judge reduced the award to $640,000. However, and most important, the media also failed to report that the victim spent two years recovering from skin grafts required after suffering third-degree burns over six percent of her body and that she initially tried to settle out of court in the amount of $20,000 to offset her $11,000 in medical bills. In response to her settlement request, McDonald's offered her a mere $800. This case is just one example of a highly visible punitive damage award that led to the mass media misinforming the general public.

Similarly, there has been general confusion and misunderstanding about the awarding of punitive damages in the case of the Exxon spill. Empirical research summarized by Eisenberg, Heise and Wells (2009) reveals:

> After decades of misinformation about the U.S. legal system fostered by groups such as the American Tort Reform Association, it is now generally accepted that the mass of punitive damages awards have been reasonably sober, modest in size, and without significant increases over time (1).

In his opinion on the case, Justice Stevens noted that "discretion to award punitive damages has not mass-produced runaway awards" (554 U.S. __ 2008: II). Moreover, the Court also noted that claims of punitive damages awards increasing over time are not supported by legal records and that, typically, the median ratio of punitive to compensatory awards has actually remained *less* than one to one.

Indeed, there seems to be a considerable disconnect between what the United States Supreme Court acknowledged in its *Exxon* v. *Baker* verdict as the "general sobriety of punitive awards" (Eisenberg, Heise and Wells 2009: 2) and its ultimate decision to reduce the ratio of compensatory to punitive damages to one to one. Essentially, in writing about this decision, the Court expressed concern about what it perceived to be a high mean and standard deviation in the punitive compensatory damages ratio and suggested a rampant unpredictability in awarding punitive damages. However, the authors of the very research on which the Supreme Court based its decision believe the Court misinterpreted the findings and failed to appropriately interpret the data. As summarized by Eisenberg, Heise and Wells, " … the Court relied on our data for a finding somewhat at odds with the above conclusions about the reality of punitive damages awards" (8). In their conclusion, they state, "The danger is that the Court's statements will be unthinkingly applied to compensatory award cases notably smaller than *Exxon Shipping* and contribute to an inability to tailor punitive awards to the facts and circumstances of particular cases" (22).

Beyond purely legal matters, punitive damages are related to basic issues of vulnerability and resilience. Broadly speaking, punitive damages are intended to help reduce vulnerability by punishing egregious behavior and serving as a deterrent to future negligent and reckless behavior. If punitive damages can be calculated as simply a cost of doing business, communities and individuals are at a greater risk and become more vulnerable to actions that might lead to disastrous consequences. Specifically, in the Exxon case, the $507 million punitive damage judgment pales in comparison to the $40.6 billion in profits the company made in 2007. What is even more disconcerting is the fact that Exxon-Mobil, itself, received the largest portion of the award because of a private agreement it made with seven Seattle fish processors. In this context, it is "worth it" to large companies to continue business as usual. More broadly, communities throughout the nation may be more vulnerable to a legal system that is perceived to favor corporate wealth and power. In the aftermath of the Supreme Court decision in *Exxon* v. *Baker*, there is a need to re-establish an adequate level of deterrence.

Similarly, the Court decision is related to issues of resiliency. Resiliency is based on sustainability, a healthy social-ecological system and community survival. The precedent established by *Exxon* v. *Baker* comes at a time when we should be strengthening our protection of the natural environment rather than weakening it through judicial activism. Weakened deterrence, particularly in an era of increasingly scarce natural resources and economic crisis, invites risk behaviors that will inevitably result in more technological disasters. Given the EVOS ruling and the current Supreme Court's inclination to favor business, legislation may be the best way to restore a meaningful level of deterrence.

Conclusion

The *Exxon Valdez* oil spill is a technological disaster that continues to unfold 20 years after the tanker ran aground. As our typology of disasters suggests, the disaster's origins were human caused and the natural environment received the brunt of the devastation. These damaged ecosystems and natural resources negatively affected the bioregion, particularly Alaska Native villages and commercial fishing communities whose existence is based on renewable natural resources. These oiled communities experienced economic, social and cultural losses and individual and collective trauma that, although less intense, continues two decades after the grounding. Elements of a corrosive community were evident, first because of disputes about whether or not to work on the cleanup and later, because of uncertainty in resource damages and recovery. As expected in a technological disaster, uncertainty was perpetuated by contested meanings about the extent of ecological damages, how persistent and long-term damages were and to what extent damages were attributable to the oil spill. Moreover, issues of recreancy initially directed at Exxon, Alyeska and the Coast Guard shifted to the state and federal government and the judicial system as local communities and plaintiffs felt abandoned, betrayed and powerless. Finally, the EVOS civil litigation process proved to be a secondary trauma that combined with persistent ecological damages and economic, social and cultural losses to inhibit community recovery and rehabilitation.

Just when it appeared the EVOS litigation was concluded, a new twist appeared. The 1994 decision included an interest penalty on damage awards not paid within four years of the verdict. Applying interest to the reduced punitive damage award would almost double the amount, but the Supreme Court did not rule on the interest issue. Instead, it was remanded to the Ninth Circuit Court, which ruled in favor of the plaintiffs in June 2009. Later that month, Exxon-Mobil decided not to appeal the decision. However, civil litigation cases continue to be heard in Federal Court and new legal arguments have been initiated as to whether or not ExxonMobil should pay more for clean-up of oil still lingering in streams and beaches heavily oiled in the 1989 spill.

The *Exxon Valdez* disaster involved serious violations of criminal and civil law. Subsequent settlements for these crimes involved payments that served as "punishment" but many survivors believe justice was not served. Survivors were repeatedly re-victimized by the chronic adversarial litigation that emerged. In-depth interviews in several fishing communities clearly reveal this situation. For example, approximately 14 years after the spill, a commercial fisherman stated:

> I can't get anything from the attorneys anymore at the post office without actually almost having an anxiety attack. It has gotten to the point where their paperwork is almost as stressful as the actual spill.... was (Ritchie 2004: 354).

A resident of a commercial fishing community lamented that:

> Every time you think you are finished with something [about the litigation] ... there would be something else. You have done all this and what for? To me the most valuable thing a person has is their time. For somebody [Exxon] to use the system then there should be some kind of standard that works across the board.... [Exxon] put a known drunk on an oil tanker trying to thread his way through icebergs and rocks and mountains on both sides of the boat. [They knew] he was a drunk. He's got a long history of it. It's well documented and [Exxon kept] letting him drive the boat ... It doesn't seem fair and it's not consistent (Ritchie 2004: 408).

Revealing the trauma of the litigation process, an oil spill survivor stated:

> I don't even think about [the oil spill] anymore to tell you the truth. It's kind of like a dull ache in the background. Now we are not being

traumatized by the spill, we are being traumatized by the litigation. [That] ... has been traumatic off and on to people, depending on how seriously they took it. Some people took it a lot more seriously than others. I just kind of kept working. I still don't think we are going to get any [money]. There was a point when I thought we were going to get some money but at this point I have no idea (Ritchie 2004: 418).

Furthermore, many EVOS survivors have loss trust in the criminal justice system and understand they were helpless because of the power and influence of the defendant—ExxonMobil. Approximately 15 years after the spill, a fisherman noted:

Court judgments don't necessarily have to do with fairness. They have to do with power. Corporations can get away with a hell of a lot of stuff and don't get reined in. The oil companies are very, very powerful and have lots of friends in Washington ... The justice system is not necessarily about justice. It is about gain and money (Ritchie 2004: 409).

As recently as March, 2009, we interviewed a commercial fisherman who said:

I was really disappointed with the opinion. I couldn't believe it. I thought the $2.5 billion was a lock.... The vote was equal except for Souter's asinine attempt to create new law in an area of maritime law that had no prior decisions and they just out of thin air pulled this bullshit one to one [ratio]. [The case was] 13 years in appeals and that issue had never come up. It was never in debate.... I think it just indicates how well lubed Exxon had made the system to get what they wanted. They [Exxon] were no doubt disappointed you know, a one to one [ratio] is twice as much as they wanted to pay.

Another fisherman we interviewed stated:

I mean, I can't even say the Pledge of [Allegiance to] the flag anymore because at the very end it says 'with liberty and justice for all.' What the [bleep] are you talking about, you know? It's [a] political rip-off. I mean that's, that's why I am as angry as I am about it. It isn't like we lost because of something that was basically legal. We just got [screwed].

These statements by people directly impacted by the spill demonstrate that technological disasters such as the EVOS pose serious problems for modern society. Because litigation is often the only avenue for victims to receive compensation for damages caused by toxic contamination of their local ecology, many survivors face the risk of re-victimization through long term adversarial litigation. Ironically and sadly, litigation, the very mechanism used to obtain disaster relief, reduce vulnerability and enhance resiliency in this type of disaster can become a secondary trauma prolonging collective and individual stress. Over the past 20 years, this has been the outcome for survivors of the EVOS.

References

ABC News. 2007. I'm being sued for what? *ABC News*, May 2. Available online at: http://abcnews.go.com/TheLaw/story?id=3121086&page=1.

Barton, A. 1969. *Communities in Disaster: A Sociological Analysis of Collective Stress Situations.* Garden City, NJ: Doubleday.

Brinkley, D. 2006. *The Great Deluge: Hurricane Katrina, New Orleans, and the Mississippi Gulf Coast.* New York: William Morrow.

Clarke, L., ed. 2003. *Terrorism and Disaster: New Threats, New Ideas.* New York: Elsevier.

Drabek, T. 1986. *Human System Responses to Disaster: An Inventory of Sociological Findings.* New York: Springer-Verlag.

Eisenberg, T., M. Heise and M. Wells. 2009. Variability in punitive damages: An empirical assessment of the U.S. Supreme Court's decision in *Exxon Shipping Co. v. Baker.* Kloster Eberbach, Germany: Seminar on the New Institutional Economics.

Erikson, K. 1994. *A New Species of Trouble: Explorations in Disasters, Trauma, and Community.* New York: W.W. Norton.

Exxon Valdez Oil Spill Trustee Council (EVOSTC). 2006. Update on injured resources and services, November, 2006. Anchorage, AK: *Exxon Valdez* Oil Spill Trustee Council. Available online at: http://www.evostc.state.ak.us/Universal/Documents/Publications/2006IRSUpdate.pdf.

Exxon v. Baker 554 U.S. __ (2008).

Freudenburg, W. R. 2000. The 'risk society' reconsidered: Recreancy, the division of labor, and risks to the social fabric. In *Risk in the Modern Age: Social Theory, Science and Environmental Decision-Making*, ed. M. J. Cohen, New York: St. Martin's Press: 107–22.

Freudenburg, W. R. and T. Jones. 1991. Attitudes and stress in the presence of technological risk: A test of the Supreme Court hypothesis. *Social Forces* 69(4): 1143–68.

Gill, D. A. 2007. Secondary trauma or secondary disaster? Insights from Hurricane Katrina. *Sociological Spectrum* 27(6): 613–32.

Gill, D. A. 2008. *Exxon Valdez* oil spill, litigation and community resilience. *Natural Hazards Observer.* 33(2): 1, 4–6. Available online at: http://www. colorado.edu/hazards/o/archives/2008/nov08/nov08_observerweb.pdf.

Gill, D. A. and J. S. Picou. 1997. The day the water died: Cultural impacts of the *Exxon Valdez* oil spill. In *The Exxon Valdez Disaster: Readings on a Modern Social Problem*, eds. J. S. Picou, D. A. Gill and M. Cohen, Dubuque, IA: Kendall-Hunt: 167–91.

Gill, D. A. and J. S. Picou. 2001. The day the water died: The *Exxon Valdez* disaster and indigenous culture. In S. Biel ed. *Modern American Disasters*, New York: New York University Press: 277–301.

Gill, D. A. and L. A. Ritchie. 2007. The big payout: Anticipated community consequences of the *Exxon Valdez* litigation settlement. Presentation made at the annual meeting of the Arctic Science Conference, Anchorage, AK.

Gill, D. A. and L. A. Ritchie. 2006. Community responses to oil spills: Lessons to be learned from technological disaster research. In *The Selendang Ayu Oil Spill: Lessons Learned*, R. Brewer, ed. Alaska Sea Grant College Program (AK-SG-06-02): University of Alaska Fairbanks.: 77–96.

Glantz, M. H. 2005. Hurricane Katrina rekindles thoughts about fallacies of a so-called 'natural' disaster. *Sustainability: Science, Practice, & Policy* 1(2): 1–4.

Green, B. L. 1996. Traumatic stress and disaster: Mental health effects and factors influencing adaptation. *International Review of Psychiatry* 2: 177–210.

Johnson, D. L. 2006. Service assessment, Hurricane Katrina August 23–31, 2005. U.S. Department of Commerce, National Oceanic and Atmospheric Administration, National Weather Service. Silver Spring, MD

Laska, S. 2008. What if Hurricane Ivan had not missed New Orleans? *Sociological Inquiry* 78 (2): 174–78.

Marshall, B. K., J. S Picou and D. A. Gill. 2003. Terrorism as disaster: Selected communalities and long-term recovery for 9/11 survivors. *Research in Social Problems and Public Policy* 11: 73–96.

Natural Hazards Research and Applications Information Center, Public Entity Risk Institute, and Institute for Civil Infrastructure Systems. 2003. Beyond September 11th: An account of post-disaster research. Special Publication No. 39, Boulder, CO: University of Colorado Natural Hazards Research and Applications Information Center.

Ott, R. 2005. *Sound Truth and Corporate Myths.* Cordova, AK: Dragonfly Sisters Press.

Picou, J. S. 2009. Katrina as a natech disaster: Toxic contamination and long-term risks for residents of New Orleans. *Journal of Applied Social Science* 3(2): 39–55.

Picou, J. S. and B. K. Marshall. 2007. Katrina as paradigm shift: Reflections on disaster research in the twenty-first century. In *The Sociology of Katrina: Perspectives on a Modern Catastrophe*, eds D. Brunsma, D. Overfelt and J. S. Picou, Lanham, MD: Rowman & Littlefield: 1–20.

Picou, J. S. and D. A. Gill. 1997. Commercial fishers and stress: Psychological impacts of the *Exxon Valdez* oil spill. In *The Exxon Valdez Disaster: Readings on a Modern Social Problem*, eds. J. S. Picou, D. A. Gill and M. Cohen, Dubuque, IA: Kendall-Hunt: 211–36.

Picou, J. S., B. K. Marshall and D. A. Gill. 2004. Disaster, litigation and the corrosive community. *Social Forces* 82(4): 1448–82.

Putnam, R. D. 2000. *Bowling Alone: The Collapse and Revival of American Community*. New York: Touchstone.

Ritchie, L. A. 2004. *Voices of Cordova: Social Capital in the Wake of the Exxon Valdez Oil Spill*. Department of Sociology, Anthropology, and Social Work, Mississippi State University PhD diss.

Ritchie, L. A. and D. A. Gill. 2007. Social capital theory as an integrating framework for technological disaster research. *Sociological Spectrum* 27: 1–26.

Sale, K. 1991. Bioregionalism. In *The Green Reader: Essays Toward a Sustainable Society*, ed. A. Dobson, San Francisco, CA: Mercury House, Incorporated: 77–83.

Short, J. W., G. V. Irvine, D. H, Mann, J. M. Maselko, J. J. Pella, M. R. Lindberg, J. R. Payne, W. B. Drisckell and S. D. Rice. 2007. Slightly weathered *Exxon Valdez* oil persists in Gulf of Alaska beach sediments after 16 years. *Environmental Science and Technology* 41: 1245–1250.

Showalter, P. S. and M. F. Myers. 1994. Natural disasters in the United States as release agents of oil, chemicals, or radiological materials between 1980–1989: Analysis and recommendations. *Risk Analysis* 14(2): 169–82.

Spies, R. B., S. D. Rice, D. A. Wolfe and B. A. Wright. 1996. The effects of the *Exxon Valdez* oil spill on the Alaskan coastal environment. *American Fisheries Society Symposium* 18: 1–16.

Tierney, K. 2008. Hurricane in New Orleans? Who knew? Anticipating Katrina and its devastation. *Sociological Inquiry* 78(2): 179–83.

van Heerden, I. and M. Bryan. 2006. *The Storm: What Went Wrong and Why during Hurricane Katrina*. New York: Viking.

Vyner, H. 1988. *Invisible Trauma: The Psychological Effects of Invisible Environmental Contaminants*. Lexington, MA: Heath.

Waugh, W. L. 2006. Terrorism as disaster. In *Handbook of Disaster Research*, eds. H. Rodriquez, E. L. Quarantelli and R. R. Dynes, New York: Springer: 388–404.

Discussion Questions

1. What are the types of disasters?
2. How does each type of disaster proceed through the phases of disaster and recovery?
3. What is meant by therapeutic and corrosive communities? Elaborate on the term recreancy.
4. What are the consequences for disaster survivors when litigation becomes a part of recovery?
5. What kind of disaster was the *Exxon Valdez* oil spill?
6. Describe the *Exxon Valdez* oil spill and the disruption it caused. What two social groups were most seriously impacted by the impact of the EVOS and why?
7. Describe the litigation that occurred in the wake of the EVOS. What were the effects of this litigation on those impacted by the spill?
8. What was the Supreme Court's decision in *Exxon* v. *Baker*? Which judges held which opinions in the case?
9. What was the final ratio of punitive to compensatory damages awarded in *Exxon* v. *Baker* and in what amounts?
10. What two functions are punitive damages designed to serve and how did they do so (or not do so) in the case of the EVOS?
11. What impact can an adversarial litigation process have on disaster survivors?

PART 2

NATURAL DISASTERS, DISORDER AND CRIME

5

Introduction

The chapters that form this part of the book raise the issue of the connections between property and personal crime in the context of disaster and disorder. Following the typologies developed in Part 1 of the book, these selections address examples of the types of crime that are most evident in the various phases of disaster and recovery. Again, this is not a comprehensive treatment of all the forms of crime that can occur as a result of the disruption caused by a disaster. For example, the number of assaults in Louisiana since Hurricane Katrina has increased 15 percent between 2004 and 2007 while the population of the state declined by over 200,000 (Disaster Center 2007). This perhaps suggests that a linkage may exist between the frustrations with the storm experience and interpersonal violence.

In *Fear, Prosocial Behavior and Looting: The Katrina Experience*, the authors explore the connections between fear, prosocial behavior and looting using Hurricane Katrina for illustrative purposes. They review the social scientific literature that links fear and crime and fear and disaster from a conceptual perspective. This is followed by an attempt to understand how and why prosocial behavior emerges in the context of disaster. There is widespread documentation and agreement among researchers that prosocial behavior does occur in disaster situations.

There is however, disagreement over the phenomenon of looting. While disaster researchers have long argued that looting is confined to civil disturbances and rare in natural disasters, evidence from Katrina thoroughly debunked the notion that looting after natural disasters is rare. Social and economic decline in New Orleans over a four-decade period, including the loss of population and high wage jobs and the latter's replacement with low wage employment, created conditions that led to widespread looting. The chapter concludes with a comparison of how state and local government in general and the criminal justice system in particular responded to Hurricane Gustav as compared to Hurricane Katrina. The chapter concludes with a discussion of the complex social conditions that facilitate looting and the necessity of taking this crime into account in disaster planning.

In *Disaster Rape: Vulnerability of Women to Sexual Assaults During Hurricane Katrina*, Thornton and Voigt examine the different stages of disaster and some of the rapes that have occurred at each. Using primarily victim and victim advocate reports, the authors reveal the vulnerabilities that women can face at each stage of a disaster. Because women are more likely to have to stay and care for children and elderly relatives, they are more likely to be at risk of sexual victimization during the warning and impact phases. During the emergency phase, when people are being rescued and their immediate needs are being met, women who were raped during the earlier phases in New Orleans were not permitted to report those rapes once evacuated to another city. They were told they had to report them in New Orleans. Cloistered into FEMA trailer parks during the recovery phase also increased their risk of victimization, as did the influx of construction workers and contractors in the reconstruction phase.

The authors conclude with five policy recommendations for reducing violence against women during disasters. The first recommendation is to identify abused and victimized women as a special needs population during disasters. The second is to educate emergency responders that violence against women is problematic during disaster. The third and fourth recommendations are to integrate transitional housing for women specifically and anti-violence services in general into emergency preparedness planning. Finally, anti-violence service providers need to have their own emergency plans so that they can resume their work and reduce women's risk of sexual violence as quickly as possible after the disaster.

In *Fraud Following the September 11, 2001 and Hurricane Katrina Disasters*, Frailing convincingly demonstrates that disasters as different as 9/11 and Katrina each have characteristics that produce similar outcomes in terms of fraud in their aftermaths. The literature review in this chapter examines the variety of white collar crimes including insurance fraud, benefit fraud, and personal fraud victimization. Each type of victimization is discussed in detail followed by a discussion of some theories of crime that can explain fraud in particular.

Next and most importantly, the author turns to a discussion of fraud in the wake of the 9/11 attacks and in the wake of Hurricane Katrina. In her examination of fraud against the Victim Compensation Fund, established in 2001 for families of victims of the 9/11 attacks, she finds that the many detailed steps through which claimants had to go to receive compensation, which included obtaining official documentation and a lengthy review by Fund staff, deterred fraud. In the case of Katrina, on the other hand, FEMA benefit fraud was very easy to perpetrate, requiring only a working phone and some patience. Finally, the chapter contains an evaluation of three theories of crime in the wake of disaster: social disorganization, routine activities and rational choice theory, especially as they relate to fraud and concludes that the evidence suggests that fraud is best explained by rational choice theory, which by implication suggests methods by which to prevent the crime.

The final chapter in this section, *Changes in the Illegal Drug Market in New Orleans After Hurricane Katrina,* focuses on how certain criminal activities make adjustments to the disruption caused by disaster and often emerge as an even more energetic enterprise after the disaster. Walsh traces the realignment of drug markets in the region following the impact of Katrina on the southeastern region of the United States in general and New Orleans in particular. After explaining the connection between drugs and crime that has long plagued New Orleans, the literature on drug use in the aftermath of disaster is examined.

Then relying on interview data, Walsh explores how the drug markets reorganized in response to new supply connections, new dealers, dealers reestablishing themselves in areas of the city that were not badly damaged and new and returning customers, giving the reader a detailed picture of the post-Katrina drug market in New Orleans. Using several measures of drug use, including a very novel one of legal items regularly used in illegal drug consumption, the author concludes that the drug markets reorganized and flourished in the wake of the storm.

Readers of these chapters should come away with a better understanding of the scope of crime that has and can occur in the wake of disaster. Readers should also be mindful of the different theoretical perspectives and research methodologies authors in this section have employed, considering the inherent difficulty in gathering data in the wake of a disaster. Their creativity and variety in this regard should spark readers to think of similarly novel ways in which they might conduct research in a disordered climate.

References

Disaster Center. 2007. Louisiana crime rates, 1960–2007. Available online at: http://www.disastercenter.com/crime/lacrime.htm.

6

FEAR, PROSOCIAL BEHAVIOR AND LOOTING: THE KATRINA EXPERIENCE

By Kelly Frailing and Dee Wood Harper

Introduction

This chapter examines the linkages between fear of crime, the controversy surrounding whether disasters produce prosocial behavior almost to the exclusion of antisocial behavior, and looting in the wake of disaster. In this chapter, we will focus on New Orleans following the impact of Hurricane Katrina in 2005 and measures taken prior to landfall of Hurricane Gustav in 2008. We begin by defining and examining some research on each of this chapter's key ideas, with particular reference to their complex interplay in the context of disaster.

Fear of Crime

The thesis of a recent opinion column by Nicholas Kristof (2009) has relevance to the issue of fear of crime. Kristof argues that because of our evolutionary makeup, we systematically misjudge certain kinds of risks and react or overreact to them while hardly reacting to other threats at all. For example, even a harmless snake is likely to elicit a fearful response. The reaction to the threat of global warming, which in the long run is more dangerous, may not even elicit a yawn. We react the same way to crime. The violation of personal property by marauding bands of looters elicits a dramatically different reaction than, for example, FEMA benefit fraud.

Quoting Daniel Gilbert, a Harvard psychologist, Kristof (2009) says that threats that get our attention have four features. First, they are personalized and intentional. "We are instinctively and obsessively on the lookout for predators and enemies." Second, we respond to disgusting or immoral threats, third, threats get our attention when imminent and fourth, we are far more concerned with instantaneous rather than gradual changes. Thus, especially in the context of disaster and its aftermath, fear of crime and criminals is palpable because it is experienced in a more visceral and less cerebral way. In this context, our sense of helplessness is heightened, our fear of having property and personal space violated is enhanced and we become perhaps overly defensive and vigilant.

Fear of crime is a relatively new concept. It was not until the 19th century industrialization of many Western societies and the new city dynamics that it created did anxiety about crime, especially that perpetrated by the so-called "dangerous classes" receive attention (Lee 2007: 37). The specific term "fear of crime" had its first recorded use many years later, in a headline in the *New York Times* in 1934. The term began to be widely if unsystematically used in the 1960s (51). It was around this same time that research into victimization and fear of crime began with the use of surveys. The results of these surveys, widely disseminated with increasing frequency, informed the population that it was indeed afraid of crime. This fear allowed law enforcement, courts and corrections to take a tougher approach to crime (76–77). As such, fear of crime operates not only as a problem to be reduced or eliminated, but also as a tactic to encourage people to take more responsibility for their safety (134–35). Taking steps to improve personal safety, as is alluded to below, can actually be fear inducing (149).

All that said about creation of the concept of fear of crime, it remains an area of intense study. Much related to the fear of crime is its cost. Certainly, crime has its direct and fairly straightforward costs in lives lost, injuries sustained and property stolen or damaged. It also has indirect costs, such as the cost of operating the criminal justice system and the effects of crime on peoples' behaviors and attitudes. These behaviors include avoiding certain parts of town and taking home security measures in an effort to prevent victimization. The precautions people take seem to indicate they are more fearful of personal victimization than of loss of property, even though property crimes are much more commonplace than violent ones (Conklin 1975: 3–7). A variety of things contribute to fear of crime, including media portrayals of crime, which are "immediate, dramatic and free of historical perspective" (22) and perceptions of ex-convicts as being dangerous as evidenced by public resistance to halfway houses (39, 41). Fear of crime results in a general suspicion of strangers and an unraveling of the community's social fabric (50). One of the impacts of crime is not, as Durkheim contended, to bring people together. Instead, Conklin argues, it makes people insecure and distrustful of one another, in effect disorganizing the community and robbing informal social control of its power against crime (99). The public reaction to crime, then—where certain parts of town are avoided and thereby deprived of natural guardianship, where strangers are distrusted, where the police are deemed ineffectual, where the bonds of the community are stricken and informal control is diminished—can actually serve to worsen the crime problem (248–49).

Though its meaning may seem obvious and taken for granted in the above paragraph, fear of crime is notoriously difficult to define and study. When Ferraro (1995) first began his inquiry into this field, he discovered that the majority of previous studies examined how certain characteristics such as sex and age affected fear of crime and that they neglected to measure perceived risk of crime as well as fear or neglected to distinguish the concepts from one another (7). Seeing this as a major flaw, Ferraro applied a theoretical approach that combined symbolic interactionism and routine activity theories so that ecological forces which shape opportunities for crime and the interpretive process people use to estimate risk form a risk interpretation model (17). To test the model, Ferraro devised a telephone survey that asked about demographic information, fear of ten different crimes (fear) and how likely respondents felt they would fall victim to each of the same ten crimes in the coming year (perceived risk) on a scale from one to ten. Sixty one percent of the final representative sample of 1,101 responded (33–35). In general, perceived risk of being victimized by these crimes roughly corresponded with official statistics on prevalence of the ten crimes in the areas covered by the survey. The single most important predictor of perception of risk was neighborhood incivility. Indicators of incivility, such as unruly neighbors, neglected lawns and vacant houses were associated with higher perceived risk of crime victimization, as were being a woman and member of a minority group (49, 51–52). Perceived risk substantially affects fear in an indirect way, namely through the constraint of behavior. Constrained behavior includes actions such as avoiding parts of town that seem unsafe, improving home security with locks and lights and carrying a weapon for self-defense. The higher someone's perceived risk of crime victimization, the more he or she will constrain behavior and the more fearful of crime he or she will be. Women, minorities and the young experience the most fear of crime. Taken together, Ferraro argues these results support his risk interpretation model (56, 63–64).

Related to fear of crime is the fear of disasters. It is not only the threat to the community but the way community members are able to make sense of this threat that influences fear. The way they make sense of the threat, in turn, is shaped by previous experience as well as a cultural narrative that influences expectations and sensitizes people to problems. The question of causality is bound up with the ability to make sense of misfortune, such as a disaster. A strong sense of shared meaning allows for a consensus of causality. In the case of Western societies, however, shared meaning is weak and attributions of cause of a disaster are continually contested. Continual contestation breeds speculation and mistrust, which can lead to a feeling of being out of control. Loss of control means that fear is able to run rampant through the community, such as it did after the September 11, 2001 terrorist attacks on New York and Washington, D.C. It also diminishes the ability for the community to respond to the disaster resiliently. The fear market thrives in this sort of environment, where nearly everything is a potential threat to safety. Again, those who further their own agendas by playing on fears actually serve to make the public more fearful and therefore less able to cope with disasters (Furedi 2006).

Anecdotally, fear of crime, especially property crime, is one of the reasons people choose not to evacuate as a hurricane approaches their city. They assume their homes and possessions are very vulnerable after a storm, when the police and other authorities are occupied with search, rescue and caring for the physical needs of those who remained, and they may perceive a high risk of victimization, thereby making them fearful of looting. The criminal opportunities for looting after Hurricane Katrina were many. The botched rescue response meant that there was very little guardianship at retail stores and unoccupied homes were easy targets. It will be easy when reading the remainder of the chapter to imagine how fear of crime can impact perceptions of looting and thereby impact the decision to evacuate in advance of or even after a hurricane, as well as how pervasive the fear of disasters can be.

Prosocial Behavior

We believe it is useful to begin our discussion of prosocial behavior in the context of disaster by first exploring the literature that addresses the underlying reasons why people help others and why they are sometimes reluctant to do so. Why people help or not and who they help or do not is exceedingly more complex than it might first appear. The common sense idea that people help because they are basically good was not scrutinized by researchers until the 1960s.

Interest in helping behavior was spurred by a horrifying incident when people did not help. In the early morning hours of March 13, 1964, Kitty Genovese was attacked by a knife wielding assailant over the course of 45 minutes, eventually dying in a residential area of New York City. The attack was seen and/or heard by 38 witnesses, none of whom took direct action (Rosenthal 1964). The event received extensive media coverage and editorializing, with many wondering whether the society emerging in the 1960s was something less than utopian and instead a society that was callous and desensitized to violence and the welfare of others. Two social psychologists at New York University, Darley and Latané (1968), began their research with the simple observation that there must have been something about the situation that made witnesses reluctant to intervene. Onlookers did not respond because they accepted little responsibility for dealing with the emergency, assuming that others were responding. They hypothesized that as the number of bystanders increases, the likelihood of a prosocial intervention decreases. Their experimental results supported the hypotheses and their research spawned the emergence of a major investigative area in social psychology, namely, prosocial behavior.

Another important line of research that has helped us to understand why people help focuses on peoples' emotional state or their capacity for empathy.[1] Empathy is a complex idea that incorporates both emotional and ideational components that together, make a person responsive to another's distress. Empathy is the ability to put one's self in the place of another, to feel sympathy and to attempt to solve the problem. Empathy gains even greater salience when the person experiencing it has had the same distressful experience themselves. For example, people who have experienced a hurricane have been found to be especially responsive to hurricane victims (Sattler, Adams and Watts 1995). Therefore, empathy may account for the presence of large numbers of volunteers using privately owned boats in rescue efforts in the immediate aftermath of the flooding caused by the levee failures in New Orleans following Hurricane Katrina.

Given the title and some of the content of this book, it may seem as though we want to make the argument that looting and antisocial behaviors are the only types of behavior that follow natural disasters. Other material in this volume might seem to imply as much. This is simply not the case. Prosocial behavior, such as rescuing and otherwise aiding victims as pointed out above, commonly follows natural disasters. This phenomenon has been repeatedly observed and documented. Allusions to prosocial behavior following natural disasters appear elsewhere in this volume, after the San Francisco earthquake of 1906 and after the Boxing Day Tsunami of 2004. In addition, bystanders and uninjured victims engaged in rescue after the Tangshan earthquake hit China in 1976, after the Irpinia earthquake hit southern Italy in 1980, after the Guadalajara gas explosions of 1992 and after the London public transport terrorist bombings

---

1. There are myriad reasons why people help that go beyond the scope of this chapter. See for example Baron and Byrne. 2004. *Social Psychology*. New York: Allyn & Bacon: Ch. 10.

of 2005, to name just four other instances (Poteyeva, Denver, Barsky and Aguirre 2006).

Prosocial behavior also emerged after Hurricane Katrina. Sixty-four semi-structured interviews were conducted three weeks after Katrina's landfall as part of a quick response report on the storm. Individuals and organizational actors were interviewed and asked about looting, as well as prosocial behavior. Respondents were not in agreement on what constituted looting and what constituted appropriating behavior. Put another way, people could not agree on whether the majority of looting that had taken place was opportunistic or survival in nature. Respondents attributed whatever looting did occur to an already criminal element. Many respondents pointed out the prosocial behavior they had observed and their belief that the majority of those in the city had acted prosocially as well (Barsky, Trainor and Torres 2006).

In a more extensive response study of Katrina, Rodriguez, Trainor and Quarantelli (2006) begin by noting that media, especially television, coverage of Katrina's aftermath focused almost exclusively on antisocial and criminal behavior. The authors argue that most of the behavior displayed was actually prosocial. They take care to categorize Katrina as a catastrophe instead of as a natural disaster, noting that Katrina had the six characteristics of a catastrophe: a massive physical impact, it prevented local officials from executing routine duties, assistance came from outside the community, it disrupted most community functioning, national media served to construct the situation and high-level federal officials became involved.

Using interviews and participant observation in a variety of locations including Houston, Texas, a number of cities in Mississippi, New Orleans and Baton Rouge, Louisiana, as well as a review of documents about three weeks after Katrina made landfall, the researchers examined five contexts in which prosocial behavior emerged. These five situations were hotels, hospitals, local neighborhoods, search and rescue teams and Joint Field Offices (JFOs). Hotels housed tourists who could not leave the city in advance of or immediately after the storm and then provided lodging for federal employees and evacuees. In hospitals, staff attempted to evacuate patients and cared for those whom they could not, often unable to use state of the art medical devices or access records. One neighborhood group, comprised of those who had not evacuated in advance of the storm, commandeered boats and searched for both survivors and food and water in abandoned homes. Another took refuge in a school, expelling those who brought in weapons. Search and rescue agencies such as police and firefighters worked together, determining which would search for survivors where. The JFO's headquarters in Baton Rouge were set up in an abandoned mall, where staff ate and slept. In short, prosocial behavior emerged across a wide range of groups and it was largely improvised. It also, according to the authors, far outweighed looting behavior, which they argue may have been confined to the taking of survival items and not consumer goods.

Looting

As noted by Stuart Green (2007), three characteristics, namely, unauthorized entry, the taking or damaging of property and the absence of normal security, are common to all types of looting. The moral content of looting, however, ranges along a continuum. At the one end are predatory acts of theft of property that have little or nothing to do with surviving the disaster, such as liquor, narcotics, television sets, et cetera. In fact, nearly all drug and liquor stores in the city were looted (Riley 2007). Another example of "bad" looting (Green 2007: 1147) is the wanton destruction of the property of others. The Oakwood Shopping Center in New Orleans was looted and set ablaze in the wake of the storm (Woltering 2005). At the other end is behavior dictated by the immediate need for survival such as the appropriation of food and water — "less bad" looting (Green 2007: 1151). Those in the first category seem to deserve harsher legal punishment, while those in the second seem to deserve exoneration. In between is a range of behaviors that are illegal but understandable when they are engaged in by the impoverished and alienated, of whom New Orleans lacked no shortage at the time of Katrina's impact.

Because of its inherent ambiguity, Green argues that a specialized looting statute is needed in the interest of fair application. In his formulation, this new statute would require that normal security of property was absent due to a disaster and that at least some property was damaged or stolen but would eliminate the unauthorized entry requirement of the current statute. Green also identifies 12 factors that can serve to aggravate or mitigate the charge. Eight of these, including extent of need, nature and quantity of property taken, criminal history, et cetera, involve the offender's circumstances and the other four, including nature of the premises involved, harm to the victim, et cetera, involve the effects of the offense. The punishment for looting should be less severe in cases with more mitigating circumstances and more severe in cases with more aggravating circumstances.

All that said, it is a long-held notion in disaster research that looting occurs after civil disturbances such as riots but is a rarity following natural disasters such as hurricanes and earthquakes. Dynes and Quarantelli (1968) maintain that while there are many reports of looting following natural disasters, few, if any, of these reports can be verified. The reasons for these reports are fourfold: misinterpretation of behavior, misunderstandings about property ownership, increased reporting of looting and sensationalization of these reports by the media. In more detail, local officials are prone to misinterpret the behavior of those converging on the scene of a disaster, especially homeowners who return to sift through their contents. This behavior may be mistaken as looting, as might the reception of goods that are being freely given away. Overestimations of what has been lost can result in the reporting of looting when little, if any, has taken place. Finally, media coverage tends to focus on the most negative aspects of the disaster, including the physical destruction caused and any behavior which appears to be looting. While infrequent after disasters, widespread looting certainly does follow civil disturbances. It is selective, focused on goods that have some value, symbolic or otherwise, it is carried out by community members and it has the support of the community. Dynes and Quarantelli (1968) conclude that the widespread looting that follows civil disturbances can be thought of as a kind of mass protest against the present distribution of property.

Taking this argument further, Quarantelli and Dynes (1970) reject the notion of the looter as a poorly socialized individual. They instead see looting as a response to an emergent social norm which follows the disorganization of the community caused by a disaster. They reiterate that looting after civil disturbances is widespread, done by locals and is public in nature, whereas after natural disasters, looting is infrequent, done by outsiders and a private enterprise. To explain these differences, Quarantelli and Dynes turn to an examination of the nature of property. After a natural disaster, consensus holds that all private property temporarily becomes community property to use for the common good. Thus, a new group norm emerges, one in which the personal use of goods while the community is in need is not tolerated. In civil disturbances, a breakdown of the understanding of property rights takes place and what was known to be public or private property is no longer viewed as such. Instead of being deviant, then, in these situations looting becomes normative behavior. Thinking of looting during civil disturbances in this way imbues the behavior with instrumental characteristics, such as sending a message to society at large about property rights.

We take no umbrage with the authors' contention that looting occurs during civil disturbances and that it serves a function beyond the appropriation of property, nor do we disagree with the contention that prosocial behavior follows natural disasters. What we do disagree with is the notion that looting is a rarity following natural disasters and that the looting behavior which occurred after Katrina was confined to survival items. We turn now to detailed evidence from Hurricane Katrina that supports our arguments.

Hurricane Katrina and Looting

We have seen elsewhere in this volume that looting does indeed occur after natural disasters. Looting also occurred in the wake of Hurricane Katrina, a Category 3 storm which hit New Orleans on August 29, 2005. The tidal surge of the storm caused three major levee failures, flooding 80 percent of the metropolitan area. New Orleans remained underwater for two weeks and though hundreds of thousands evacuated the city in advance of the storm, tens of thousands remained, either unable to leave or choosing to stay. It was not until September 3, five days after the storm's initial landfall, that those who remained in the city were evacuated elsewhere.[2] Lawlessness reigned during these five days. People took what they needed, such as food, water, medicine and items for infants, from stores, some of which left their doors unlocked. Others took advantage of the situation and appropriated items unnecessary for survival. Researchers curious about the actual extent of looting after Katrina and other, powerful storms that hit the New Orleans area over time investigated burglary rates in the month before and the month after the unnamed storm of 1947, Hurricane Betsy in 1965 and Katrina. Burglary rate was used as a proxy for looting for a number of reasons. First, the looting statute did not exist in Louisiana criminal law until 1993. Using burglary as a proxy allowed for comparisons over time. Second, they believe it is unlikely that home and business owners would make a report to the police when only items that become necessary after a disaster such as food and water were missing. As such, an examination of the burglary rate is an examination of opportunistic looting.

The burglary rate in the month before Katrina was more than three times that of the burglary rate in the month before either other storm. Researchers found a 94.2 percent increase in the burglary rate in the month after the unnamed storm of 1947, a 15.4 percent increase in the burglary rate in the month after Hurricane Betsy and an astronomical 402.9 percent increase in the burglary rate in the month after Katrina, all as compared to the month before. An important note about the post-Katrina burglary rate: only those losses that could definitely be determined to be burglaries were included in the calcula-

---

2. There are a variety of fine books that describe Katrina and its aftermath in a more general and detailed way than we do here. Among them: *The Great Deluge* by Douglas Brinkley, *Breach of Faith* by Jed Horne, *1 Dead in Attic* by Chris Rose, *Holding Out and Hanging On* by Thomas Neff and *Come Hell or High Water* by Michael Eric Dyson, *Path of Destruction* by John McQuaid and Mark Schleifstein, *Lost in Katrina* by Mikel Schaefer, *Eye of the Storm* by Sally Forman, *Heart Like Water* by Joshua Clark and *Down in New Orleans* by Billy Sothern.

tion. After the storm, the police coded the majority of losses as 21K, meaning those which could not be definitely determined to be due to the storm or to theft. As such, the post-Katrina burglary rate may be higher than what is reported here (Frailing and Harper 2007).

Wanting to explain these differences, researchers examined a variety of sociodemographic variables in New Orleans from 1960 to 2000 to delineate changes in the city. By way of description, New Orleans became a majority black city by the time of the 1980 census. Since then, blacks have earned about half of whites have and have been unemployed at least two times the rate of whites. While nearly 77 percent of high wage manufacturing jobs were lost during this period, there was an almost 197 percent increase in low wage food and hotel service jobs. Variables analyzed included changes in total population, population by race, number of high wage manufacturing jobs and number of low wage food and hotel service jobs. A number of interrelated trends were revealed by the analysis, including that the decrease in manufacturing jobs and the increase in food and hotel service jobs were associated with total population loss and white population loss and that the increase in food and hotel service jobs was associated with black population growth. Unlike the conditions that preceded the other two storms, the majority of New Orleans residents were trapped in abject poverty before Katrina hit. The researchers contend that the socioeconomic conditions in New Orleans set the stage for the looting that occurred in its wake (Frailing and Harper 2007).

Taking their argument further, the same researchers examined the specific roles of school desegregation and the oil bust in the creation of the pre-Katrina socioeconomic conditions in New Orleans that they argue are associated with high burglary rates both before and after the storm. New Orleans had a difficult relationship with school desegregation. Its first attempt at integration took place in 1960. Two schools that wanted to integrate were not chosen. The two that were chosen were very resistant to integration and within a week of the first black students' admission, a white mob had descended on the school board. Mob members stoned black citizens, who then retaliated. Harassment of those attending desegregated schools continued for the rest of the semester. The second attempt at desegregation in 1961 went much more smoothly and was successful, thanks to a supportive new mayor and city business leaders. By 1970, 70 percent of New Orleans public school students were black and the percentage steadily increased from there. In the early 1980s, the oil industry in New Orleans had nearly 15,000 jobs, many of which were well paying. The oil bust occurred in the late 1980s. The most notable oil company to leave town in favor of Houston at that time was Amoco. The loss of 840 of its employees in 1989 resulted in a $43 million loss for the local economy. In 1998, the last of Amoco's employees left the city, leaving none of the major oil companies head-quartered in the city. As of 2005, there were just 2,600 employees in the oil in-dustry in New Orleans (Frailing and Harper in press).

An analysis of relevant school desegregation, oil bust and socioeconomic variables revealed that as manufacturing jobs decreased, the black populations of the parishes contiguous with New Orleans (Orleans Parish) rose, that as the number of white students in Orleans Parish decreased, the black population increased, that as the population as a whole decreased, so did the number of white students in Orleans Parish, that as the number of oil industry employ-ees decreased, the number of low wage food and hotel service jobs increased and that as the percentage of female headed households increased, the white population of contiguous parishes increased. These significant results led the researchers to conclude that school desegregation contributed to white flight from the parish, that the oil bust was deleterious for the New Orleans economy and that those who could leave the parish, black and white, did so, leaving be-hind a group of primarily black residents who were faced with few and only low wage job opportunities. Katrina intensified and worsened the deprivation al-ready faced by its residents (Frailing and Harper in press).

Finally, the same researchers examined the city since Katrina and compared the aftermath of Katrina to that of Hurricane Gustav in terms of looting. Hur-ricane Gustav, a Category 2 storm, made landfall in Cocodrie, Louisiana, south-west of New Orleans, on September 1, 2008. There was great concern that Gustav would be a much stronger storm than it was and that it would hit New Orleans directly, nearly three years to the day after Katrina did. Because of this concern, nearly two million people evacuated south Louisiana, about 200,000 of whom left the New Orleans area (Anderson 2008). The city's levees held and residents were permitted to return on September 4, 2008 (CNN 2008). The researchers examined the conditions in the city between Hurricanes Kat-rina and Gustav and found them to be quite similar to those preceding Katrina, with a majority black population, the black unemployment rate at least three times that of whites, the black percent in poverty at least three times that of whites and the white median income at least double that of blacks. However, they found that the burglary rate in the month after Gustav had increased 91.8 per-cent, as opposed to the month after Katrina, in which the burglary rate in-creased by 198.8 percent.[3] The majority of burglaries that occurred after Gustav were of residential dwellings (Frailing and Harper 2009). With conditions in

---

3. Astute readers may have noticed that the percent change in burglary rates pre- and post-Katrina is lower here than the 402.9 percent increase reported above. Data recently released by the New Orleans Police Department allowed for an accurate and upward revi-

the city being similar prior to Katrina and prior to Gustav, the researchers pos-tulated that what accounted for the difference in burglary rates after Katrina and after Gustav was the improved guardianship in the city, in accordance with Cohen and Felson's (1979) routine activity theory.[4]

The Governor mobilized the National Guard several days before Gustav's land-fall (Gray 2008). In more detail, Governor Jindal declared a state of emergency and the 7,000 person Louisiana National Guard was mobilized and about 1,500 additional troops and equipment were requested from nearby states. About 500 troops assisted with evacuations (Purpura 2008). On Sunday, the day before Gus-tav hit, 1,800 soldiers were patrolling the city (Filosa 2008). Part of the impetus for the early mobilization of the Guard was to avoid another lawless situation such as that which followed Hurricane Katrina. Jindal wanted city residents to know their homes would be safe and that they should feel secure evacuating (Pur-pura 2008a). Guardianship similar to that observed during Gustav was also pres-ent during the 1947 storm and during Hurricane Betsy in 1965, with the National Guard on the ground in New Orleans the day after the storm's landfall in both cases (*Times Picayune* archives September, 1947 and September, 1965). As is widely known, this guardianship was absent for nearly a week after Katrina's landfall.

In the week after Gustav, the calls for service resulted in 119 immediate ar-rests of perpetrators in or leaving properties. Seventy one were arrested in or leaving residences, seven were arrested in or leaving businesses and 35 were arrested for trespassing in or around properties. The Chief of the New Orleans Police Department (NOPD), Warren Riley, credited the ability to make arrests in the immediate aftermath of the storm to the large presence of National Guard troops, who "blanketed" the city. For example, there were two National Guard troops at every pharmacy and drug store in the city, hospitals generally having their own security, to keep those seeking drugs from burglarizing those businesses (Riley 2008). Katrina revealed the need for the guardianship dis-played after Gustav. Another study found that guardianship was important in keeping the crime rate low after Hurricane Andrew. Andrew made landfall in

---

sion of the pre-Katrina burglary rate, thereby reducing the percent increase in burglary rate by about half.

4. Routine activity theory postulates that three components are essential for crimes to occur, suitable targets, motivated offenders and a lack of guardianship. When people evac-uated for Katrina, they assumed they would only be gone a few days and as such, made minimal effort to protect their property from looting. As a result, suitable targets for loot-ing were plentiful. For at least the first five days after Katrina's landfall, there was no for-mal guardianship outside the French Quarter and Central Business District because, as is made clear elsewhere in this volume, the police were exclusively engaged in search and res-cue.

South Dade County in southern Florida on August 24, 1992. Over 65,000 homes were destroyed, as were thousands of businesses and cars. Over a million people were without electricity, telephone and water services. Researchers performed semi-structured interviews with 101 survivors, 60 police officers and 10 people arrested for hurricane-related offenses between two and five months after the storm. They found that local people, especially juveniles, committed the majority of crimes in the first few days after the storm. Then outsiders came to the area and committed contractor fraud, taking money for shoddy or unperformed roof and home repair work. The storm itself created many suitable targets, laying open homes and businesses and displaying their contents. Formal guardianship in the form of law enforcement was absent immediately after the storm, handling only emergency calls. However, informal guardianship in the form of neighbors working together to meet each other's needs and begin the long work of recovering from the devastation was present. All three groups interviewed agreed that the informal guardianship displayed by neighbors served as a deterrent against crime. Indeed, with the increase in motivated offenders and suitable targets, it was the only element that did (Cromwell, Dunham, Akers and Lanza-Kaduce 1995). A second study examining guardianship as it relates to crime and disaster rates in Florida found a reduction in index, property and violent crimes in the Uniform Crime Reports after disasters. This reduction is indicative of the formation of a therapeutic community, disaster survivors who engage in prosocial behavior, which includes informal guardianship against crime. However, this guardianship did not extend into the domestic sphere, as an increase in crimes of domestic violence was observed following disasters (Zahran et al. 2009).

Conclusion

In this chapter, we have covered fear of crime and disasters, prosocial and looting behaviors in the wake of disasters. Perception of risk of victimization directly affects fear of crime, which is one of crime's many indirect costs to society. Moreover, when a community has a weak sense of shared meaning, it is more likely to feel a loss of control, instead of resilience, after a disaster and remain fearful as a result. Some researchers maintain that widespread, public and community-supported looting engaged in by locals occurs after civil disturbances, while what little occurs after natural disasters is done in secret by outsiders and condemned by the community. Prosocial behavior is the type that most often follows natural disasters, just as law abiding behavior under normal circumstances far outweighs the prevalence of lawlessness. We agree that prosocial behavior follows natural disasters, but data on New Orleans supports our contention that looting, and not just survival looting, occurs after natural disasters and that in the case of Hurricane Katrina, it was not rare. Moreover, in comparing Katrina to Hurricane Gustav, we found that a component of routine activity theory, namely guardianship, was important in the disparate post-storm burglary rates between these two hurricanes and concluded that Katrina revealed an important lesson about the necessity of post-disaster guardianship.

Quarantelli (2007) makes an important point when speaking about Katrina, noting the existence of "atypical instances of mass lootings that only emerge if a complex set of prior social conditions exist." In the case of New Orleans, a large proportion of the population was living in poverty without any real hope for economic security, let alone prosperity. What we have described above indicates that New Orleans may have had just the combination of social conditions that facilitate looting. Understanding that there is a connection between a city's social conditions and the likelihood of looting in the wake of a disaster is instructive and useful. It allows for community leadership, law enforcement and business interests to anticipate the potential for looting and other antisocial behavior and incorporate this into their emergency plans. When the anticipation of looting is part of a comprehensive disaster response plan that is properly executed, looting becomes less of an issue and allows for a smoother transition to the recovery phase.

Readers may still be asking themselves what the explicit connection between fear of crime and disaster, prosocial behavior and looting is. It is our contention that prosocial behavior for those engaged in it serves as a prophylaxis against fear of crime. Helping others, an activity that increases one's sense of well being and contributes to a sense of return to normalcy and solidarity with others, would decrease fear. Fear of being a victim of looting in the context of Katrina was quite real. There is no question that the media called attention to the looting, perhaps at the expense of prosocial behavior. The media attention that is routinely paid to bad behavior may have exaggerated the extent of the problem.

Exaggerated or not, looting was a substantial problem that did not dissipate in the weeks following Katrina. In fact, a new form emerged. After residents began to return to their damaged homes, theft of rebuilding materials and items, including copper tubing, air conditioning compressors and water heaters became the *loot de jour*. During the day, volunteers from all over the United States assisted residents with rebuilding their properties. At night, construction sites that were left unguarded became the target of looting. Anecdotal evidence indicates that this type of looting is a persistent problem. We believe that makes the consideration of looting in the disaster response and rebuilding plans all the more important, as anticipation will surely aid in prevention.

References

Anderson, E. 2008. 1.9 million evacuate south Louisiana. *The Times Picayune,* August 31. Available online at: http://www.nola.com/hurricane/index.ssf/2008/08/11_million_people_evacuate_sou.html.

Barsky, L. J. Trainor and M. Torres. 2006. Disaster realities in the aftermath of Hurricane Katrina: Revisiting the looting myth. UCB Natural Hazards Center Quick Response Report 184.

CNN. 2008. Louisianans can return to powerless homes. Available online at: http://www.cnn.com/2008/US/weather/09/02/gustav/index.html.

Cohen, L. E. and Felson, M. 1979. Social change and crime rate trends: A routine activity approach. *American Sociological Review* 44: 588–608.

Conklin, J. E. 1975. *The Impact of Crime.* New York: MacMillan.

Cromwell, P., R. Dunham, R. Akers and L. Lanza-Kaduce. 1995. Routine activities and social control in the aftermath of a natural catastrophe. *European Journal on Criminal Policy and Research* 3(3): 56–69.

Darley, J. M. and B. Latané. 1968. Bystander intervention in emergencies: Diffusion of responsibility. *Journal of Personality and Social Psychology* 8: 377–83.

Dynes, R. and E. L. Quarantelli. 1968. What looting in civil disturbances really means. *Trans-action* 5(6): 9–14.

Ferraro, K. E. 1995. *Fear of Crime: Interpreting Victimization Risk.* Albany: State University of New York Press.

Filosa, G. 2008. Locals might fear storm, but not looters. *The Times Picayune,* September 1. Available online at: http://www.nola.com/timespic/stories/index.ssf?/base/news-0/1220246490171980.xml&coll=1&thispage=1.

Frailing, K. and D. H. Harper. In press. School kids and oil rigs: Two more pieces of the post-Katrina puzzle in New Orleans. *American Journal of Economics and Sociology.*

Frailing, K. and D. H. Harper. 2007. Crime and hurricanes in New Orleans. In *The Sociology of Katrina: Perspectives on a Modern Catastrophe,* eds. D. L. Brunsma, D. Overfelt and J. S. Picou, Lanham, MD: Rowman and Littlefield: 51–68.

Frailing, K. and D. H. Harper. 2009. Hurricanes and crime: Socioeconomic conditions, guardianship and criminal opportunity. Presentation given at the Southern Sociological Society meeting in New Orleans, LA in April.

Furedi, F. 2006. The growth of a market in fear. In *Handbook of Disaster Research,* eds. H. Rodriguez, E. L. Quarantelli and R. Dynes, New York: Springer: 508–520.

Gray, S. 2008. Hurricane alert puts New Orleans on evacuation footing. *The Guardian*, August 28. Available online at: http://www.guardian.co.uk/world/2008/aug/28/naturaldisasters.usa?gusrc=rss&feed=networkfront.

Green, S. P. 2007. Looting, law, and lawlessness. *Tulane Law Review* 81: 1129–74.

Kristof, N. D. 2009. When our brains short-circuit. *The New York Times*, July 1. Available online at: http://www.nytimes.com/2009/07/02/opinion/02kristof.html.

Lee, M. 2207. *Inventing Fear of Crime: Criminology and the Politics of Anxiety.* Portland, OR: Willan Publishing.

Poteyeva, M., M. Denver, L. E. Barsky and B. E. Aguirre. 2006. Search and rescue activities in disasters. In *Handbook of Disaster Research*, eds. H. Rodriguez, E. L. Quarantelli and R. Dynes, New York: Springer: 200–216.

Purpura, P. 2008. Guardsmen on alert, roll into N. O. area. *The Times Picayune*, August 31. Available online at: http://www.nola.com/timespic/stories/index.ssf?/base/library-154/1220161353139690.xml&coll=1.

Purpura, P. 2008a. Guard to help protect homes. *The Times Picayune*, August 29. Available online at: http://www.nola.com/timespic/stories/index.ssf?/base/news-11/121998804956200.xml&coll=1.

Quarantelli, E. L. 2007. The myth and the realities: Keeping the "looting" myth in perspective. *Natural Hazards Observer* 31(4): 2–3.

Quarantelli, E. L. and R. Dynes. 1970. Property norms in looting: Their patter in community crises. *Phylon: The Atlanta University Review of Race and Culture* 31(2): 168–182.

Riley, W. 2007. Personal communication with author Harper.

Riley, W. 2008. Interview with NOPD Chief Warren Riley on WWL 870AM radio, September 18.

Rodriguez, H., J. Trainor and E. L. Quarantelli. 2006. Rising to the challenges of a catastrophe: The emergent and prosocial behavior following Hurricane Katrina. *Annals of the American Academy of Political and Social Science* 604: 82–101.

Rosenthal, A. M. 1964. *Thirty-Eight Witnesses: The Kitty Genovese Case.* New York: McGraw Hill.

Sattler, D. N., M. G. Adams and B. Watts. 1995. Effects of personal experience on judgments about natural disasters. *Journal of Social Behavior and Personality* 10: 891–898.

Times Picayune archives. September 19–23, 1947 and September 10–14, 1965.

Woltering, D. 2005. Post-Katrina fire at Oakwood mall damaged one-third of stores. *WWLTV*, October 25. Available online at: http://www.wwltv.com/local/stories/wwl102505oakwood.4b53da8.html.

Zahran, S., T. O'Connor Shelly, L. Peek and S. D. Brody. 2009. Natural disasters and social order: Modeling crime outcomes in Florida. *International Journal of Mass Emergencies and Disasters* 27(1): 26–52.

Discussion Questions

1. Describe the origination of the concept of the fear of crime. What are some of the direct and indirect costs of crime? What is a main difficulty in measuring fear of crime? What has research shown impacts people's fear of crime? Describe the mechanisms by which a community can become and remain fearful of disasters.

2. Give examples of the prosocial behavior that occurs in the wake of natural disasters, going into some detail about that which followed Katrina. Can you think of any difficulties that might arise in measuring post-storm prosocial behavior?

3. Describe the looting that occurs after both civil disturbances and natural disasters. What are the characteristics of each?

4. What have some researchers determined to be the burglary rates before and after Katrina? What factors do they think contribute to these high rates as compared to other storms? Describe some potential difficulties in measuring burglary after a natural disaster.

5. What aspect of routine activity theory do some researchers think is responsible for the lower burglary rate after Gustav as compared to Katrina? Give examples of this aspect in action.

6. Importantly, Quarantelli (2007) urges us to consider what when anticipating looting after a natural disaster? How is this a useful suggestion in terms of prevention?

Disaster Rape: Vulnerability of Women to Sexual Assaults During Hurricane Katrina

By William E. Thornton and Lydia Voigt[1]

Introduction

Singer and songwriter, Charmaine Neville, daughter of Charles Neville of the famous Neville Brothers rock and soul band, describes how she and others from New Orleans' Ninth Ward sought shelter on the roof of a school after the waters started rising on the night of August 31, 2005, two days after Hurricane Katrina struck New Orleans. An obviously distraught Neville tells her story of being raped in an impromptu meeting in an interview with Archbishop Alfred Hughes of the Archdiocese of New Orleans on a local television station (Worrall 2005, Lauer 2005):

> I had lain down and gone to sleep and somebody woke me up. They put their hand over my mouth, and a knife to my throat, and said... 'If you don't do what I want, I'm gonna kill you and then I'll do what I want to you anyway and throw your body over the side of the building.'
> I found some police officers. I told them that a lot of us had been raped down there by guys who had come [into] ... the neighborhood, where we were, that were helping us to save people. But the other men, they came and they started raping women ... and they started killing them. And I don't know who these people were. I'm not going to tell you I know who they were because I don't. But what I want people to understand is that if we had not been left down there like the animals that they were treating us like, all of those things wouldn't have happened.

---

1. This chapter originally appeared as an article by the same name in the *Journal of Public Management and Social Policy*, Volume 13, Issue 2, 2007.

Neville's willingness to discuss her rape publicly has served several purposes. It shows that despite early dismissals of initial violent crime reports, including sexual assaults, taking place during the hurricane, which were later found to be exaggerated, such offenses did indeed occur. Neville's self-report of rape has encouraged other disaster rape victims to report their sexual assaults to various self-help or counseling and rape crisis groups in the region. This at a minimum has produced some victimization statistics in the absence of early and even later official reports from law enforcement agencies. Neville also made several public service announcements in March and April, 2006 in Louisiana and Texas, urging rape victims to report their rapes to victim advocates. As self-reports and official reports of rapes of women emerge from Katrina, researchers will be in a better position to understand women's heightened exposure to risk at each phase of the catastrophe.

The purpose of the present research is to examine qualitative accounts of women who have been reporting their sexual assaults, which have taken place during various phases of Katrina and related events. We cast these accounts within the framework of well-developed social research and literature, which emphasizes the "gendered nature" of disasters and the exposure of risks that some women experience as a result of factors such as gender inequality, lack of resources, lack of mobility and loss of social support structures (Fothergill 1996). Although we utilize some victim narratives from official police reports of disaster-related rapes in this study, much of our data comes from rape victims' self-reports obtained from victim advocate groups, faith-based counseling groups, domestic violence and other grass-roots community programs that arose in response to the storm to help rape victims.

Our intent in this research is not to try to provide some specific number, volume or rate of storm-facilitated rapes that occurred (and are still occurring). This may be challenging, even under the best circumstances, because rape is a grossly underreported crime (Rennison 2002). Rather, we seek to gain insight into the circumstances and situations that led to the sexual victimization of women who reported their rapes at some time during the disaster.

Due to the damage inflicted by the hurricane and other events that followed, and the subsequent non-operation and/or disruption of regular public health and safety services and emergency channels through which crimes are reported, statistics on all crimes, including rapes, are not available, especially in the early stages of the disaster. In many cases, after a rape occurred there was simply no one for the victim to report the incident to. In a number of instances, as we have found, when a rape was reported to a first responder such as a police officer, an official statement was not taken because of other life-threatening priorities. Some women tried reporting their rapes to various volunteers but, of course, these individuals were in no position to document the offense or otherwise offer help. We have also uncovered cases of women who were raped in the New Orleans area and later attempted to report their victimizations to law enforcement agencies in the towns and cities where they evacuated and were told that "courtesy reports" were not being taken. They were instructed to report their rapes to the respective law enforcement agencies where the assaults took place. Of course, for a substantial period of time, especially during the early phases of the disaster, this was impossible. Many of these evacuees have never returned to New Orleans. We also found that in some cases, female evacuees experienced their sexual assaults after evacuating to other cities in Louisiana or other states.

Preliminary results (based on the first six months) of a recently established Internet survey of sexual violence in the aftermath of Hurricanes Katrina and Rita conducted by the National Sexual Violence Resource Center indicate that 47 cases of sexual assault were reported. Findings show that 93 percent of the perpetrators were male with the remainder unspecified. Close to 40 percent of the perpetrators were strangers to the victims/survivors, 9 percent were family members, 9 percent were current or former intimate partners, 25 percent were acquaintances and about 30 percent were unspecified or other. About 60 percent of the sexual assaults were reported to law enforcement agencies. Approximately 93 percent of the victims were female. The victims' ages ranged as follows: 14 percent were age 14 and below, 36 percent were age 15 to 24, 30 percent were age 25 to 44 and 20 percent were age 45 and over. Ninety-five percent of the victims were "disaster victims," 3 percent were members of host family households, with the remainder unspecified. About 45 percent of the victims/survivors were Caucasian, 33 percent African American, 11 percent Hispanic, 7 percent Native American and the remainder unspecified. The location of the sexual assaults included evacuation sites or shelters (31 percent), victims' homes (10 percent), hosts' homes (13 percent), streets/open areas (13 percent), public buildings other than shelters (10 percent) and other places such as hotels, perpetrators' homes or cars (23 percent) (National Sexual Violence Resource Center 2006).

The crime of rape, perhaps more than any other violent offense, avails itself of the vast human vulnerabilities associated with natural and human-made disasters. Obviously the type of disaster, the degree of disaster preparedness and emergency planning, the efficiency level of social control agents' operations, as well as the extent of communities' disorganization and destruction and relative length of recovery time all have an influence on the nature of criminal opportunities associated with a specific disaster. What made the Katrina Disaster unique was the fact that it actually represented a multi-impact series of catastrophic events, comprised of the impact of Hurricane Katrina, the breach of several levees in the city and subsequent flooding, a major oil spill, a chemical storage facility explosion, a complete breakdown of law and order for several days, the impact of Hurricane Rita followed by more flooding in the city and nearly 100 tornadoes across the region. It may be that conditions that were conducive for crimes such as rape have not existed to this magnitude in modern times in America.

Disaster Rape Literature Review

An extensive literature search on disaster-related rape or sexual assaults suggests that few studies in the United States have empirically examined rape during periods of disasters, thus making it difficult to speculate about the prevalence of this crime in relation to other disasters. One exception to this is a study in which researchers examined pre- and post-event rates of rape in a 1994 Northridge, California earthquake (Siegel, Bourque and Shoaf 1999). Their findings suggest that there may be an increased risk of rape after an earthquake; however, their results have been subjected to other interpretations because of the small number of rapes reported. It has even been difficult to find media accounts of rapes taking place during or after event-specific disasters in the United States. Other than anecdotal references or occasional mention in historical or documentary accounts of disasters such as hurricanes prior to Katrina, rape has largely not been the focus of discussion in disaster literature. Domestic/intimate violence (e.g., battering and verbal "loss of control"), which purportedly increases after natural disasters in the U.S. and Canada (Norris 2006, Clemens and Hietala 1999, Godino and Coble 1995, Laudisio 1993, Centers for Disease Control 1992), has been treated by some scholars. However, empirical studies of disaster-related domestic/intimate battering are minimal (Fothergill 1999, Morrow and Enarson 1996). In her book, *Emergency Preparedness in British Columbia: Mitigating Violence Against Women in Disasters*, Elaine Enarson claims, "Violence against women has only very recently been examined in North American contexts. Social impact studies often consider such factors as alcohol abuse, looting, truancy, interpersonal conflict, and post traumatic stress, but they rarely investigate the incidence of gender violence after disasters" (1999a: 13).

An international literature search on disaster-related rape suggests there is documented evidence that women (and children) are victims of violent crimes, including rape and other sexual assaults, in countries around the world during times of natural and human-made disasters and catastrophes (United Nations High Commissioner for Refugees (UNHCR) 1999: 37, Lentin 1997, Rozario 1997). As Lin Chew and Kavita Ramdas of the Global Fund for Women observe, "In the chaos and social breakdown that accompany natural disasters, women become uniquely vulnerable to sexual abuse, including rape and gang rape" (2005: 2). Refugee emergencies stemming from disasters in particular are documented internationally as situations where there are increased opportunities for the rape of women and girls (UNHCR 2003, Vann 2002, Delaney and Shrader 2000: 27–28, UNHCR 1995). Several causes or circumstances, which contribute to sexual violence perpetrated against females by males in refugee facilities or displaced person situations have been reported: (1) male perpetrators' power and domination over their female victims (2) psychological strains of refugee life (3) absence of communal support systems for the protection of vulnerable individuals (4) crowded facilities—camps, shelters, etc (5) lack of physical protection (6) general lawlessness in camps and shelters (7) alcohol and drug use and abuse (8) politically motivated violence against displaced persons and (9) single females separated from male family members (New York City Alliance Against Sexual Assault 2006, UNHCR 1995). Many of these phenomena are not unlike those associated with the conditions and circumstances that thousands of Katrina female evacuees faced in the various phases of the disaster, which, as we will discuss, resulted in numerous sexual assaults.

Several disaster researchers have argued that much disaster research has taken a gender-neutral stance or otherwise treated female and male differential responses and behaviors to disasters as "dichotomous survey variables in disaster research" (Enarson and Meyreles 2004, Fothergill 1998, Fothergill 1996: 33). Early critiques of gender bias in disaster studies have focused on the clear omission of women's special disaster-associated vulnerabilities (e.g., crime victimization patterns, domestic violence, obligations related to the care of children and elderly family members, evacuation and geographical displacement, economic, racial and age disadvantages, psychological strain and male dominance of law enforcement and other disaster management officials at upper and lower levels, et cetera). Recent works have sought to remedy this problem. The issue of disaster-related vulnerabilities of women to violence has also stimulated interest in the more general field of social science research, which treats women not just as helpless victims of natural and human-made disasters, but rather as individuals who are at risk because of factors such as economic and political powerlessness, cultural gender discrimination and other cultural perceptions of inferiority and superiority (Enarson and Meyreles 2004: 50, Enarson 1999, Wiest, Mocellin and Motsisi 1994).

Research Methodology

This study is part of a larger ongoing research project, which began in September 2005 in New Orleans while the city and region were still dealing with the immediate impact of Hurricane Katrina. We embarked upon this research seeking to examine the media's role in the social construction of reality regarding perceptions of crime, crime control and public safety during and immediately following Katrina's landfall. Initially we content-analyzed over 2,500 newspaper articles on crime during and after Katrina's strike. We considered several research questions: (1) what are the sources of information regarding crimes during and after Katrina? (2) How do media accounts compare with official accounts of crime and (3) how do official accounts of crime compare with unofficial (e.g., victim) accounts of crime (Thornton and Voigt 2006)?

Our interest in rape arose mainly because of the immense amount of false information that was initially disseminated about crimes reported in the media (some of the misinformation coming from public officials) and the general scarcity of empirical research on disaster-related rape.

Several sources of crime data inform this analysis, including: (1) over 300 mass media reports of rapes and sexual assaults using major search engines (2) 25 daily journals of law enforcement officers working in New Orleans during the preparedness and impact stages of the disaster (3) five victim advocates' narratives of their views regarding the vulnerability of women and opportunities for rape during the disaster, which are based on their cases (4) 22 victim self-reports of victimization (rape and other crimes) during various phases of the disaster (5) over 120 official reports of criminal victimizations from law enforcement agencies, which involve disaster-related rapes (although it is noteworthy that official reports of crimes from local/regional law enforcement agencies are obviously not available in the earliest stages of Katrina) and (6) 40 completed surveys of attendees at a neighborhood meeting of concerned citizens.

In trying to capture the "voices of Katrina" for this chapter, we chiefly employ the qualitative aspects of our initial research methodology, utilizing narratives and other accounts given to us by rape victims (i.e. taken from self-report narratives and official victim reports), first-responders' daily logs, and interviews with law enforcement officers and victim advocates.

One of the advantages of this type of qualitative data is that the accounts given by respondents "are grounded in people's actual experiences ... [and] ... the possibility of identifying new, relevant questions becomes more likely" (Phillips 2002: 203). An obvious methodological problem with the technique is the lack of generalizability of the findings to larger disaster rape populations in the U.S.

or even rape populations in New Orleans. Given the unique nature of the Katrina Disaster and the surrounding complexities, generalizability may be impossible, even under the most rigorous sampling circumstances.

Vulnerability of Women during Various Phases of the Katrina Disaster

For over 75 years, disaster researchers have attempted to study physical and social aspects of disasters in terms of the "phases of disasters" and have devised numerous approaches (Lystad 1995, Drabek 1986, National Governor's Association 1979, Powell, Rayner and Finesinger 1953, Carr 1932). For instance, Lewis Killian (2002) identifies four phases: warning, impact, emergency and recovery, which are mainly determined by time factors. Some scholars, such as David Neal (1997) have argued that the demarcation points of the phases should not rest primarily on time factors, but should also include consideration for spatial distinctions (e.g., impact zone, fringe impact zones or filter zone) and relative degree of damage to the city's infrastructure (i.e., economic, political and social systems). Neal notes that the phases are not mutually exclusive and that recovery rates are not linear. It is often hard to pinpoint the pace of recovery and reconstruction. The rates of recovery and restoration or reconstruction will vary depending on variables such as race, ethnicity and social class of the residential and commercial populations (Neal 1997, Phillips, Garza and Neal 1994). Despite continued controversy over the conceptual and theoretical clarification of these various categories (Richardson 2005, Neal 1997, Neal 1984, Haas, Kates and Bowden 1977), the employment of functional time phases and spatial zones for the study of disasters has been extremely useful in understanding individual and group behavior during the "life cycle" of a disaster (Stoddard 1968). Alice Fothergill, for example, has proposed a modified nine-stage typology to organize and discuss her research on gender risks and disasters, including the occurrence of domestic violence (1996).

The main problem that we see with the general disaster phase models is that they assume a single, short-term disaster with relatively clear-cut phases. As stated above, when we speak of the Katrina Disaster, we are actually referring to a multi- (and prolonged) impact disaster in which any one of the catastrophic components would constitute a major disaster in its own right (i.e. Impact I: Hurricane Katrina, Impact II: Levee Breaches and Flooding, Impact III: Explosion of Chemical Storage Facility, Impact IV: Murphy Oil Spill, Impact V: Hurricane Rita, all of which successively occurring within a relatively short time period). The outline below offers a brief summary of the main stages of the

Katrina Disaster (with only general estimates of time), which serves to demonstrate the complexities of its multi-impact nature:

- Warning (August 24–28, 2005)
- Impact I: Hurricane Katrina (August 29, 6:00 a.m.)
- Impact II: Levee Breaches (August 29, 8:00 a.m.–4:00 p.m.)
- Emergency: Official and non-official "save and rescue missions" (August 30–September 25)
- Waiting for federal rescue response: Anomie, breakdown of social order (August 30–31)
- Emergency: Restoration of law and order (September 2–3), evacuation (September 1–6)
- Impact III: Explosion of chemical storage facility (September 2, 4:35 a.m.)
- Impact IV: Murphy Oil Spill (September 4)
- Emergency: Levee repair and restoration of water pumps (September 4–30), city closed except to official personnel
- Impact V: Hurricane Rita (September 23)
- Pre-Recovery: Clean-up (September 4–30)
- Recovery: Clean-up and restoration of basic services, populations in designated areas permitted to enter city for limited duration to inspect and assess property damage, informal voluntary assistance
- Organized formal voluntary organizations and official relief efforts
- Restoration/Normalization: Restoration of physical, political and social infrastructure, populations begin to return (city officially opened on September 29), formal and informal voluntary relief efforts continue
- Reconstruction on all levels depending on nature of damage
- Longer-term reconstruction, planning and initiatives

The overlapping consequences of the series of catastrophic events have produced many complexities associated with emergency responses as well as short and long-term recovery and rebuilding efforts. For example, the combined impacts of the various disasters along with the non-existent or minimally adequate disaster management plan created a situation in which the impact phase of the event(s) was extended for a relatively long period of time. With water rising at different levels throughout New Orleans and with thousands of people left in the city without adequate shelter, food or water, the emergency phase of the disaster did not begin for almost a week. Likewise, the recovery phase has been difficult to identify with various areas responding very differently. Certain areas of the city have recovered significantly faster than others, whereas the pace of recovery and reconstruction of some other communities will probably extend for years.

Our study of individual and collective or group criminal activity, including the incidence of sexual assaults during various phases of this multi-disaster event, has lent itself to a phase analysis, which helps to make sense of the nature and circumstances of the rapes that occurred and are still occurring. At each stage of the Katrina Disaster, the deficiencies or failures of the infrastructure, whether physical (e.g., devastation of commercial buildings, homes and neighborhoods), social (e.g., lack of social support systems such as safe havens or advocacy support groups) or structural (e.g., breakdown in governmental leadership and operation of the criminal justice system) worked together to create increased criminal opportunities or otherwise facilitated conditions for the sexual assaults of women to occur.

Our case studies and data on rape victimizations suggest interesting differences in both the perpetrator and victim perspectives with respect to time sequences, spatial/geographical impacts of the Katrina Disaster, and social/structural conditions. Preliminary findings indicate, for example, that rapes appeared to be more brutal, often involving multiple offenders, during the disasters' earlier phases, whereas a year later, in the recovery stages, rapes seemed to resemble more typical fact patterns that are not specifically disaster-related. These different patterns of rapes during the various phases are, of course, speculative due to the inherent sampling limitations of our data. Despite their limitations, however, our data demonstrate that the vulnerability of women to sexual assaults may be associated with particular conditions, which prevailed during the different phases of this multi-disaster event.

Warning Phase

This is the "period during which information is available about a probable danger, but before the danger has become immediate, personally and physically perceivable" (Killan 2002: 51). By 8:00 a.m. on Sunday, August 28, 2005, the National Hurricane Center (NHC) in Miami had upgraded Hurricane Katrina to a Category 5 storm, "the highest rating on the Saffir-Simpson scale" (Hurricane Katrina 2005: 37). By 9:00 a.m., President George W. Bush had urged Louisiana Governor Kathleen Blanco to begin evacuation of New Orleans and by 9:30 a.m., Mayor Ray Nagin and Governor Blanco had put the word out that citizens of New Orleans should leave the city. Nagin emphatically stated, "We're facing the storm most of us feared" (37). By 11:00 a.m., NHC officials warned that "Katrina's storm surge could overtop New Orleans' levees" (37). Close to 80 percent of New Orleans' 484,000 citizens evacuated from the city, but many others, particularly elderly, low-income African American residents, could not leave and, thus, remained in the city. Over 140,000 residents were estimated not to have cars. The Regional Transit Authority of New Orleans began transporting people from 12 locations to the Superdome, the largest of the city's 10 designated shelters. The Louisiana National Guard was stationed at the Superdome to provide security. By 9:00 p.m., food and water were distributed. Approximately 20,000 people were housed in a facility that was prepared to care for less than half that number and for only a three-day period (37).

Some disaster research shows that women are less likely than men to have the necessary resources and mobility to leave before a disaster strikes (Marshall 2005, Fothergill 1996). Disaster researchers also argue that because of a lack of status, power, money and motor vehicles, minority women are usually at a greater disadvantage in leaving an area when warning of an impending disaster is announced and they suffer accordingly. This was certainly the case in New Orleans where large numbers of poor African-American women with their children, parents and other family members were unable to leave the city and remained stranded. It is important to remember that African-Americans comprised over 67 percent of the city's pre-Katrina population (U.S. Census 2000) with a substantial proportion living below the poverty line.

However, the stranded also included out-of-state students and visitors who, for various reasons, could not get out of the city. A victim advocate's case summary illustrates the vulnerability of some of these women, like the woman raped by strangers trying to get out of the city during the warning phase described below:

> A twenty five year old Caucasian woman was raped when she accepted a ride to get out of town on Sunday, August 28, 2005 by two males who inferred that they were college students headed to Baton Rouge. The young woman reported that she was from Indiana and was visiting "friends of friends" who left her stranded in their apartment. The friends just took off when they heard that the storm was headed for New Orleans. The woman constructed a cardboard sign stating that she "needed a ride" and walked to Jefferson Highway where she was picked up [by] two Caucasian males in their twenties, who told her that they would take her to Baton Rouge where it would be safe. In route, the men pulled off of the interstate at a rest stop and forcibly raped her one at a time after they parked their Ford van in the parking area designated for commercial trucks ... One punched her so she lost consciousness and then they threw her out of the vehicle. When she regained consciousness, she tried to get help. After being ignored by many motorists trying to evacuate and not wanting to get involved with someone who looked visibly disheveled, she finally obtained an-

other ride to Baton Rouge, where she was taken to a hospital emergency room and later ended up in a shelter. She tried to report the rape in Baton Rouge, but was told it needed to be reported to police in New Orleans or to the state police....

Impact Phase

This stage usually refers to the specific catastrophic event, which is often a single, short-termed disaster with relatively clear-cut phases. As mentioned above, when we refer to the Katrina Disaster, we are actually referring to a multi- or serial- (and prolonged) impact. On Monday, August 29 at the last minute, Hurricane Katrina made a sharp turn to the east, its winds reduced to 145 mph, and the storm made landfall in Buras, Louisiana, a small town southeast of New Orleans. The town was completely destroyed. With approximately 20,000–30,000 residents who could or did not evacuate sheltered in the Superdome, and with countless other residents who, for whatever reasons, also did not evacuate scattered citywide at other shelters and places, including their residences, it now appeared that New Orleans may have escaped the worst of Hurricane Katrina since the storm did not hit the city directly. However, by 8:14 a.m. on Monday, August 29, the resulting storm surges and high water breached the Industrial Canal levee protecting the Ninth Ward and St. Bernard Parish on the city's east side from Lake Pontchartrain, and by 1:00 p.m. an estimated 40,000 homes were flooded with eight to 10 feet of water (Hurricane Katrina 2005: 39). Shortly after, by 2:00 p.m., a 200-foot stretch of the 17th Street Canal on the northwest side of New Orleans failed and other parts of the city began filling up with water. At 4:00 p.m., two more levees along the London Avenue Canal failed, and within 12 hours, 80 percent of New Orleans was under water (37–39). In reality, it is probably the breaches in the various levees and subsequent flooding of the city that most people think of when they refer to the "impact" stage of Katrina, and it is during this period that civil law and order began to break down. During the very first day of the storm, crimes were already taking place in parts of the city, including looting, armed robberies and shootings, despite dismissals of early exaggerations and rumors of crime. By the second day, anarchy existed in parts of the city with a skeleton force of police officers trying to maintain order. The main police headquarters, district stations and cars had been flooded, and there was a complete breakdown of their central communications system.

Below, a personal narrative from a veteran police officer in New Orleans details what he and his partner saw beginning at about 11:00 a.m. on the first day of the storm, August 29. It was still possible for some officers to patrol various areas of New Orleans and they were still receiving dispatches of "calls for service" until severe flooding knocked out all the police department's intra-agency communication. The officer's descriptions suggest that almost immediately aspects of the storm during the impact phase facilitated the opportunities for property and violent crimes, including sexual assaults to occur:

> Billy and I patrolled _____ Street and _____ Street where I observed my first band of looters attempting to get into a corner store. They were trying to take down heavy security doors with crowbars and shovels and any household items they could find. Remember, this is the day of the storm, nobody had been without food or water yet and no one starting to feel the pains of hunger or starvation. These people were attempting to loot only to get "free" liquor and cigarettes ... The next scene we went to was at _____ and _____ Streets. A female had expired in the middle of the intersection from what first appeared to be a gunshot wound to the back of her head. It was later found out that an object had been pushed into her cranium during the storm and had killed her instantly. At approximately two o'clock in the afternoon Billy and I stopped a car at _____ Street. We had to fight the driver of the vehicle so we placed him under arrest. We were in route to central lockup ... and for the first time we saw it, water. The whole northern side of the city had started to flood. We couldn't bring [the suspect] to central lockup because it was under water. We brought the suspect to _____ Street and let him go ... As we headed back to the district, we were dispatched with a signal for an aggravated battery by shooting that occurred at [a clothing store on _____ Street.] We immediately headed in that direction. Once we arrived we observed approximately 1,000 people running for their lives exiting the clothing store. We went in right after them and observed a handful of people around a black male ... who was shot several times, at least twice in the neck.

As several disaster researchers have noted, in the early stages of a disaster, many women have caretaking responsibilities for children, elderly parents and relatives, which make it difficult for them to evacuate. Many of these women are young, poor, minority and heads-of-households (Marshall 2005, Fothergill 1996, Morrow and Enarson 1996).

The self-reported incident of rape described below involves a young minority woman looking for food, water and medicine for her sick elderly mother and her two children in a convenience store that was being looted by a group of young men. The case, which takes place in the same general area the police officer described above, accentuates similar conditions of lawlessness. We met the victim in a domestic violence group session for evacuees living in a shelter in Baton Rouge, Louisiana as she described her sexual assault to the group. She indicated that she did not try to report the crime to the police and probably never would:

> I was in a [convenience store] with maybe fifty other people looking for medicine for my mama and for water or cokes or anything to drink and candy bars to take to my kids. There was almost nothing left in the store when I got there and I was kind of worried cause there was a lot of drunk young guys starting to tear the place up. They was working on a bank machine [ATM] but couldn't get in it and was getting madder and madder. Two of the older ones grabbed me and pulled me in the back of the store and tore my clothes off and raped me one at a time. One held me down in the cooler while the other went at it and then the other took his turn. When they finished the younger one kicked me in the stomach and said fuck you bitch.

The rape victim above expressed a sense of fate and resignation with respect to her sexual assault and a belief that reporting the offense to any official agents would serve no purpose. This, unfortunately, appears to be a common feeling among many rape victims even during non-disaster periods (Voigt et al. 1994: 299).

Emergency Phase

This period generally refers to post-impact emergency relief efforts, including activities such as rescuing and conducting the emergency evacuation of people (e.g., infants, young children, pregnant women, the elderly and the sick), administering first aid and emergency medical care, supplying food, water and other life sustaining resources, performing other public health functions (e.g., removal of dead bodies) and other emergency management tasks and restoring law and order. During the emergency phase of the Katrina Disaster, many "first-responders" including official (e.g., law enforcement agents and National Guard personnel) and unofficial workers (e.g., lay volunteers from all walks of life) engaged in various rescue operations (e.g., plucking people from rooftops, et cetera) and continued evacuation. Even as late as Thursday, September 1, approximately 25,000 people were still stranded in the Morial Convention Center. Chaos and general anomie were pervasive. New Orleans Police Department Superintendent Eddie Compass ordered 88 officers to the Convention Center, but they were unable to control the enormous crowds.

Earlier, he had called his available police officers off the "search and rescue missions" in order to control looting and fires in the city. As a response to Department of Homeland Security Director Michael Chertoff, who claimed that the city was secure and under control, Mayor Ray Nagin, retorted live on CNN: "I keep hearing [help] is coming. This is coming. That is coming. My answer to that today is, b.s.! Where's the beef? They're spinning and people are dying down here" (Hurricane Katrina 2005: 45). Despite a series of explosions in the early morning hours at a chemical storage facility downriver, emergency efforts seemed to improve on Friday, September 2, when 1,000 National Guard troops arrived in the city to help restore control and to assist in the evacuation of 8,000–10,000 people from the Superdome. Evacuees were bused to the Astrodome and the Reliant Center, an indoor convention center, in Houston, Texas (47). On Saturday, September 3, buses began the evacuation of the more than 25,000 people at the Morial Center. President Bush agreed to send 7,000 military troops to the Gulf Coast and promised that 10,000 more National Guard troops would be sent to the city (49). By Sunday, September 4, it was estimated that approximately 250,000 Katrina evacuees were in Texas, and the Army Corps of Engineers had closed the 17th Street Canal breach. On Monday, September 5, Mayor Nagin called for mandatory evacuation of the flooded city and blamed all levels of government for the poor response and handling of the victims (51–53). The city was put under Marshall Order and subsequently closed until officials could declare that it was safe for residents to begin returning. On September 23, Hurricane Rita struck the coastal areas of Texas and western Louisiana. Once again, water surges overpowered New Orleans levees and parts of the city flooded for the second time (51–53).

Largely due to these multiple impacts, the Katrina Disaster's emergency phase extended for a relatively long time in the city (and region). As a result, it is difficult to distinguish between the impact stage and emergency stage as precisely as in a single-impact disaster. However, despite the influx of large numbers of first-responders and various troops into the city, the social milieu of New Orleans, described by some as a "wild west" environment comprised largely of a male population, facilitated many opportunities for crimes, especially rapes, to occur. In addition, the dislocation and evacuation of over 200,000 citizens throughout 48 states across the country further increased the opportunities for women to be raped in other, sometimes "less than desirable" locations. While a relative lack of status, power, resources and options particularly place minority women at risk of endangerment during disasters, all women, representing all classes and backgrounds, are vulnerable to sexual assaults and other violent crimes during periods of uncertainty and anomie (Morrow and Enarson 1994).

A victim advocate from a local law enforcement agency discusses the conditions in general of some women in New Orleans during the emergency phase. Her observations are based on several rape cases that were later officially reported. She describes in particular a sadistic rape that occurred during the emergency phase, which was later reported to a law enforcement agency:

> By the time people realized the magnitude of the storm, it was either too late to get out or you simply did not have the means to do so. Many women did not have the economic means to evacuate, considering that about 40 percent of all female-headed households with children in New Orleans were living below the poverty line and had no cars. Keep in mind we are talking about August in New Orleans. It is hot and muggy 24 hours a day in the summer. So you have no electricity, water or phone service. The city is completely dark as you sit alone with your flashlight waiting for the morning sun to offer some light. You consider that as usual, the storm passed and the extent of the damage may be a few tree limbs down, which caused the electricity to go out. You know something is different though because you have no service on your cell phone. At this point you start to worry because your children have left with other family members and you can't get in touch with anyone because there is no phone service. As the daylight appears, you go outside of your apartment only to find your street is filling at a rapid pace with water. You now have no option but to stay in your apartment, which is slowly heating up to a high temperature. By noon, the heat is unbearable. You check outside again and now your street is completely under water. Your street is completely deserted of any form of life. By nightfall, you are panicked because you have no way to leave your apartment, no communication, and the heat is unbearable. But late that night you leave your apartment in an attempt to get some fresh air. A stairwell is your only refuge as you sit, drenched with sweat in the silence. At this point of desperation, you feel a knife to your throat with a man telling you not to scream. The man brutally rapes you, and leaves you for dead. What do you do now? There is no one to tell and no place to go for help. Your main fear is that the rapist will return and find you again. This was a legitimate fear considering that all traditional societal social support mechanisms had collapsed in New Orleans. Women who stayed in the city during Katrina were vulnerable due to being alone with no form of civilized protection such as law enforcement. It was a period of "anything goes," which predators took advantage of.

Other victim advocates have further observed that despite many good and kind people giving help during the storm, many opportunistic or lawless males took advantage of the social disorganization and this, coupled with the increased vulnerability of many women, especially poor and minority women, heightened the risk of sexual assaults as the following statement of a rape investigator in a local law enforcement agency attests:

> Rapes most definitely did occur during and after Katrina. If rapes did not take place during Katrina then why was I contacted day after day to locate rape kits for hospitals? With New Orleans evacuees spread across the nation, it is next to impossible to ever investigate the rapes that occurred due to the lack of evidence. Another factor to consider is that evidence in rape cases can be collected up to 72 hours after a rape. The majority of women that were raped were still left abandoned in New Orleans days after the rapes occurred. For the few that possibly did make it out of the city within the 72-hour window to collect evidence, they were told they would have to report the crime in New Orleans, where the crime took place. The problem is that for weeks, the city of New Orleans did not exist.

Thousands of women were relocated during the emergency phase of the Katrina Disaster and found themselves in other cities around the United States where they were temporarily housed in public and private shelters, good and bad, as well as an assortment of other places, including motels, hotels, low rent apartments, et cetera. While many of these women may have escaped the dangers of New Orleans during the disaster, they were sometimes thrust into environments that were nonetheless dangerous. Disaster researchers have noted that there are similarities between disaster relocation and refugee situations with respect to the circumstances and conditions facilitating sexual violence against women (e.g., Vann 2002, Wiest, Mocellin and Motsisi 1994). For instance, according to an online reporting survey, of the 47 sexual assault cases reported during Hurricanes Katrina and Rita, nearly a third (31 percent) of sexual assaults occurred at evacuation sites or other shelters, which represents more cases than in any other type of place (National Sexual Violence Resource Center 2006).

While there is relatively scant data on the vulnerability of evacuees of hurricanes or other disasters to sexual assaults in the United States, there is an extensive literature pointing to the vulnerability of women, especially to sexual violence, in refugee situations around the world. The UNHCR released a report in May 2003 entitled Sexual Violence Against Refugees: Guidelines on Prevention and Response, which highlights different causes and conditions that provide the opportunity for rape and sexual assaults to occur in refugee camps, shelters and other places of refuge for asylum seekers and other displaced persons. While sexual and other gender based violence can occur at any phase of the "refugee cycle"—prior to flight, during flight, at the point of asylum, during "repatriation," and during reintegration, there appears to be enhanced vulnerability for victimization in refugee camps. In particular, the destruction of common support, loss of security, disrespectful attitudes of men towards women, psychological strain, alcohol and drug abuse, crowded living conditions and general lawlessness in camps are factors which facilitate sexual attacks (20–22). Likewise, in many refugee situations where men are in charge of basic necessities, they can use these things to subject women to sexual exploitation. An earlier UN report emphasized, "Experience shows that unaccompanied women and lone female heads of households are at the greatest risk of being subjected to sexual violence" (UNHCR 1995: Chapter 1, 1.1). Many of our cases reflect similar conditions in the post-Katrina evacuation centers and emergency situations, which led to women's increased vulnerability to sexual assaults. The following victim's account of rape in a hurricane relief shelter illustrates this problem:

> I was staying in a hurricane relief shelter because of the loss of my family's home. I became separated from my husband and so I was alone. [She was 18 years old.] I awoke in bed to find a male in bed with his pants and underwear down. My pants and underwear were also down. He said that he would suffocate me if I made even a slight noise. He then raped me multiple times. He said that he would kill me if I said anything to anyone. I did not report the rape to the police until much later when I left the shelter.

Evidence from disaster research also indicates that women are more likely than men to seek assistance following natural disasters, and that "women are more likely than men to receive help from strangers" (Fothergill 1996: 44). During an emergency state, when communal support is lacking, women who may find themselves helpless and isolated in certain situations often have to rely on others for emergency assistance. Unfortunately, an offer of help from some men during disasters can be used as a pretense for sexual victimization. We have identified numerous cases of sexual assaults, especially during the emergency phase, by men offering assistance to women seeking or accepting aid, in the form of giving rides, or offering of things such as food, furniture and refuge. Rapes occurred at various times during the "aid" encounter.

The following is an account of a rape victim who was seeking help. The victim, left homeless by the storm and living in her car, was offered a place to stay by a male co-worker. The young woman had known the perpetrator for some time and accepted his offer; however, he used the situation to take advantage of her vulnerable state:

> I was raped in the early morning hours. I had been living with this guy that I knew from work for two days. He came into the den, where I was sleeping. He came in without clothes on, at which point he forced me to have sex with him. He left me in kitchen area after the rape. My whole family lost everything in the storm—houses, cars, clothes, and jobs. Because of Katrina, I was homeless, living in my car. If Hurricane Katrina did not hit the area, I would not have been put in the situation of living out of my car and I would not have had to accept an invitation to stay with this guy who raped me.

Recovery Phase

This is the phase that begins after the crisis or emergency period has passed and progress is made toward restoring essential infrastructures, such as inter-organizational communication, electrical service, potable water supplies, public transportation, homes, businesses and city services—things that will allow individuals to reoccupy a disaster area and eventually begin eventual longer term reconstruction. Likewise, the pace of reopening public (and private) schools in the city has a significant impact on population growth in the city from new and previously displaced citizens. The re-establishment of health facilities and services, including mental health services, is also among the critical factors of recovery.

Different communities "recover" from disasters sooner than others based on variables such as the degree of physical destruction, the degree of social disruption and the degree of financial assistance needed to repopulate commercial and residential areas of the city (Drabek 1986: 234–42). In the case of New Orleans, it may take many years for recovery/reconstruction to be fully realized, and the footprint of the city may be much different than before Katrina. Physical damage, loss of clients and customers, high commercial insurance rates, lack of affordable housing for remaining and future employees and fear of future storms, may prevent many small and large businesses from rebuilding in the area, thus making recovery all the more difficult. Additionally, thousands of lost residences that comprised physical neighborhoods as well as cultural milieus may never be replaced because of lack of resources, residents' inability to obtain or afford homeowners insurance and the displacement of individuals who established themselves in other cities and do not wish to return.

Another factor impeding recovery in New Orleans, possibly unique in the annals of disaster research in the United States, is the return of a serious crime problem during this stage when many citizens are living in FEMA trailers or makeshift homes in varying degrees of repair in areas with reduced police protection. Slowly but surely violent crime and property crime volumes and rates have been creeping up in Orleans and adjoining parishes since June 2006, when a series of teenage shootings attracted national attention. Because of low numbers of officers in the New Orleans Police Department (NOPD), Louisiana State Police and the National Guard returned to the city in that summer to aid in crime prevention and control, particularly in outlying areas of the city. In defense of the NOPD, the department experienced a significant reduction in personnel post-Katrina, and its main headquarters and several district stations, still unrepaired since the storm, forced many officers to operate out of trailers. Officers were thinly spread over the city and, despite record numbers of arrests, a broken criminal justice system simply cannot process and house that many perpetrators. Even nine months following the storm, the criminal courts were shut down, and by June 2006, there was a backlog of 5,000 cases.

Elaine Enarson, who has written extensively on the gendered effects of disasters, noted that, "Because violence against women is endemic to disasters, it is not unlikely to be present in any community before and after disaster. But does violence increase because of the effects of disasters? Barriers to reporting complicate the investigation of personal violence and other law enforcement issues ... Lack of transportation or communication, closed courtrooms and police stations, non-functional crisis lines, and other factors may deter women from reporting violence or seeking protection" (1999a, 13). Enarson further elaborates that, "Disasters are multi-dimensional and long lasting social events with diverse and complex effects on such factors as local employment rates, various types of criminal behavior, divorce, mental and physical health, school achievement, business decisions, labor migration and household mobility" (13). Enarson also points out that the risk of sexual assault may be greater in temporary housing sites such as trailer camps/parks, which are often located in remote and isolated areas of devastated communities without adequate access control, physical security and lighting (1999a, 1999b). For example, in addition to fearing for their personal safety, women in trailer camps in Miami after Hurricane Andrew "were often isolated, lacked mental and reproductive health services and reliable transportation and were unable to access needed community services" (Enarson 1999b: 48). In another example, during the aftermath of Hurricane Charley in 1992, residents of FEMA trailer parks located in Punta Gorda, Florida reported concern over "security, especially safety for their children from a child molester, incidences of theft and wariness of their neighbors" (Tobin, Bell, Whiteford and Montz 2006: 94–95).

As the recovery period in New Orleans continues, conditions in the city and region remain particularly susceptible for sexual assaults to occur under a variety of circumstances and in various environments, for example, FEMA trailer parks. Women have self-reported several attempted rapes in these trailer parks in New Orleans. In the case below, a woman and her two children had waited several months for a FEMA trailer, and since the neighborhood where her flooded house was located did not have water and electricity, she could not park her trailer on her home-site. She was also afraid of remaining in the abandoned area because of roving groups of men seen during the day and night stripping materials off of abandoned houses. In subsequent temporary housing in a FEMA trailer parker, the woman experienced an attempted rape and gave the following account:

> We are all squeezed in these tiny trailers and the trailers are all squeezed into a field off the side of road. It was okay during the day, but when it got dark, me and my kids were afraid to go out at night even though we have some good friends living in other trailers. It was really pitch-black dark even though there were some lights on poles around the grounds. One night in February my kids were staying at a friend's house and I was coming back to the trailer after work. When I drove in I looked all around like I always do—there are always strangers hanging around visiting I guess. I got my key ready, looked around again and went up the steps to the door. Almost from nowhere a guy grabbed me from behind, put one hand over my mouth and the other on my private parts and said something like, "Don't fight me bitch, I don't want your purse, I want you." I bit his hand hard enough to make it bleed and yelled at the top of my lungs. People on both sides of my trailer came out and the man took off.

Although there is evidence suggesting that women and children tend to suffer more emotional problems than men following a disaster, it has been found that men are more likely to abuse alcohol and drugs (Enarson 1998). Men are also more apt to use relief funds on alcohol, airplane tickets and entertainment, leaving little or no money for their wives and children (Morrow and Enarson 1994). In several of our self-reported cases taken from sexual assault groups, particularly during the recovery stage of the Katrina Disaster, women described abusive husbands and boyfriends who spent what money they had on excessive drinking and gambling in casinos, especially as these establishments began to reopen in New Orleans and along the Mississippi Gulf Coast.

Several cases of domestic/intimate partner rape surfaced from our interviews. The interview notes below are from a case history of a 33-year-old Caucasian female who sought help from a faith-based domestic violence group associated with a church. She and her boyfriend lost their apartment in the storm and lived in Arkansas with relatives before moving back to the New Orleans region in January 2006. The following account attests to the role of alcohol and gambling in intimate partner rape:

> Tom and I have been living together for six years in an "on again and off again" relationship. We lost everything in the storm. We lived for a while with my relatives, which was very hard because they were barely making it. So we found a place of our own. But things have been tough. Tom has a good heart and I love him, but when he drinks his whole personality changes and he hits me and forces sex on me whether I want it or not. He is a welder and makes good money whenever he needs a job. Since the storm, Tom has been drinking a lot more than usual and has also started gambling, something he never used to do. There never seems to be enough money now and everything I make from my little job pays for gas, lights, and rent. It's so unfair. He uses all of his money mostly on liquor and to gamble. He is also much more demanding now about sex and he forces me to have sex with him no matter whether I'm tired from work or whatever ... which I could deal with but I'm tired of being hurt. But I don't want to be alone either ... I don't know what to do. I needed help and was told about these wonderful people at church ...

While there is some debate regarding the long-term psychological effects of disasters, there is evidence suggesting that disaster victims who experience life-threatening situations frequently suffer certain symptoms of post traumatic stress disorder (PTSD) including depression, anxiety and hostility for relatively long periods after the events (Norris, Perilla, Riad, Kaniasty, Kand and Lavizzo 1999, Norris and Uhl 1993). The victim advocate's account below indicates a case of stress-related intimate partner sexual assault:

> The victim reported that she and her boyfriend had not been getting along very well since the storm. He was very depressed and often woke up shaking saying that he had nightmares of the storm. He lost his job and was having trouble finding another job and the bills were piling up. They were arguing one night and the boyfriend started hitting, punching, and kicking her and she told him that she had had enough and that she was going to leave him. He indicated to her that

he "was going to have it one more time." She was subsequently sexually assaulted multiple times and held against her will until the next morning. The next morning after he left, her friend came and she left the house and reported the incident to the police.

Although we did not uncover any discussions in the disaster literature regarding the sexual victimization of volunteers who have aided in various recovery projects in disaster areas, our case studies include several cases of volunteers, both younger and older women, who were raped during their extended stays in New Orleans during the recovery phase. We also have cases of sexual assaults against female "migrant" workers (many of Hispanic heritage) who came to the region because of a shortage of labor and higher paying jobs in various industries. Similarly, Enarson and Morrow (1997), in their studies of Hurricane Andrew, reported that poor and marginalized women with limited English skills, including migrant workers "[felt] at risk of male violence during the lengthy reconstruction period in disrupted neighborhoods and temporary camps" (Enarson and Morrow 1998: 6). The following is victim advocate's account of a volunteer worker who was raped in abandoned housing site:

> The young woman was a college student from out-of-state, who was volunteering in the city with a group that was engaged in Katrina-related community services. Her companions went to various work sites from a central location early in the morning and she was assigned to a house gutting site deep in one of the severely flooded areas of the city. She worked later than usual at the site and did not ride back to her motel with her regular crew of volunteers that she knew. Instead, she accepted a ride with two males who she assumed were volunteer workers based on how they were dressed and their general appearance. Once in the car, the males took the woman to an abandoned public housing site where she was raped in her vagina and anus.

Below is a summary of a case involving a migrant worker who was raped by a stranger:

> The victim was a migrant worker from _____ working to make some money for her family. She had several cleaning jobs. Late one night after she finished cleaning she took out the trash to a dumpster out in the street. She spotted a man coming toward her and she began to run, but he caught up and grabbed her and pulled her back around the side of the dumpster. He proceeded to orally and vaginally assault her. She began to choke and then threw up, which made him mad, so he got up and kicked her in the face.

Reconstruction Phase

This phase involves long-term recovery planning and activities, including massive rebuilding projects (e.g., commercial and government buildings and planned communities of single and multi-dwelling housing, which meet respective disaster building standards), stabilization of the ecological components of the built and natural environment to mitigate certain future disasters (e.g., the construction of New Orleans' levee and floodgate system and the enhancement of buffer space between natural bodies of water and human occupied spaces) and the stabilization and augmentation of economic (business and industrial) and governmental infrastructures. In addition to re-engineering the built environment, this period also focuses on key aspects of the social infrastructure, ensuring that less represented citizens, like those previously living in pre-disaster public-assisted housing, are included in reconstruction policies and plans (USAID 2006).

However, as Fothergill notes, low-income women in disaster regions often "fare poorly in the reconstruction phase. The poor, of which women are the majority, have less insurance, less savings, and thus less likelihood of a full, long-term recovery" (1996: 47, also see Bolin and Bolton 1986). Morrow and Enarson report, for example, that even two years after Hurricane Andrew struck Miami in 1992, thousands of families were still living in crowded and substandard temporary housing and many of the inhabitants were poor minority women (1994: 8).

Unfortunately, the establishment of temporary residences after the destruction of thousands of homes is associated with enhanced opportunities for sexual assaults to occur in the affected region. Many people are living in less than ideal environments. In an effort to rebuild residences and commercial establishments in the later recovery and reconstruction phases, large numbers of outside laborers are brought into the disaster area to live and work. Most of these construction workers are male, often young men, who appreciably increase the population of the area. While most of them are no doubt honest, hard workers, some disaster research has reported the exploitation of women, particularly poor women, by contractors and laborers in the reconstruction of their homes (Enarson and Morrow 1997). In addition, groups of individuals, often disguised as work crews and reconstruction contractors (popularly referred to as "scrappers"), come to disaster sites with the specific intent to pilfer vacant homes and otherwise victimize—including sexually assaulting—vulnerable residents. Large areas of vacant and abandoned residences become refuges for various criminals, drug dealers and juvenile gangs, a situation which creates unprecedented challenges for law enforcement officials.

Some of our cases involve construction workers or other itinerant groups of men who have sexually exploited or assaulted women. The following cases offer illustrations of such incidents. The first is a victim advocate's general description of rapes committed by construction workers:

> Another unfortunate fact is that women continue to deal with societal changes due to Hurricane Katrina. The fortunate women that still have a home in New Orleans now live in a "different world" as we now call it. Due to the influx of construction workers, women are now being intimidated by workers staring, following, stalking, attacking, and, unfortunately, raping. One of our victims was threatened with a sheetrock knife, another went back after the storm to check on her house and a man offered to assist her with renovations. After a brief exchange, he raped her.

This second case is a victim's account of rape after a group of men in a truck followed her car and caused an accident:

> I was driving home when a truck began to follow me and beeping its horn. Then the truck came up beside my car. The guys were yelling things to me and throwing kisses with their hands. I think there were three, maybe four men. They were drinking and having a time for themselves. I tried to turn off to another street hoping to lose them, but it turned out to be the dark side of town. There were still no streetlights or traffic lights, or any sign of life in the houses—most were still abandoned. I was really scared driving in the total darkness, except the dim lights of the car behind me. Then all of a sudden (and I don't know if this was an accident or on purpose) the truck hit the side of my car. I lost control and ran up the sidewalk into the steps of an abandoned building. The guys came running; I thought for a minute to check on me, but that was not it. They pulled me out and dragged me into the empty building and gang raped me. At some point I guess I passed out. When I woke up there was blood all around. I found some of my clothes and luckily remembered my cell phone in my car. I called a friend who came and got me and took me to a hospital.

The feeling of intimidation created by some construction workers' sexually explicit behavior has been a common theme expressed by female respondents to a survey randomly administered to attendees of a concerned citizens meeting in a relatively affluent neighborhood where major reconstruction of homes has been taking place. The following quotations capture surveyed residents' commonly expressed views:

- I no longer feel safe in my own neighborhood. When I leave to bring my kids to school in the morning, construction workers stare and make comments at me. I tell my children to ignore them, but it is difficult. It is scary for me to come home alone after bringing my kids to school.
- It is getting so bad with construction workers. I live alone, so I now put a pair of men's boots at my door so they will think a man lives here.
- A few weeks ago, I went to Home Depot. There were several workers that followed me around and would not leave me alone. Every department that I walked to, they would follow me. One kept asking me if I needed help with anything. I ignored them and finally left my basket and walked out. When I got to my car, they were directly behind me. I was petrified. I took off as fast as I could. I now carry a Glock 17, which I recently received training on using.
- New Orleans is now an entirely different world for women in our city. Ask any woman what is the main difference that they notice post-Katrina? Most women will answer that it is the hundreds of construction workers. Every neighborhood has damaged homes, so every neighborhood has workers.

Conclusion and Policy Recommendations

The Katrina Disaster is uniquely different when compared to other disasters in the United States in modern times. It is actually a multi-impact catastrophe which destroyed over 500,000 houses and displaced more than half of New Orleans' population, far surpassing any other recent disasters (see Brinkley 2006). Additionally, because of poor leadership and inadequate disaster response planning and implementation at the local, state and federal levels, the Katrina Disaster turned the city into a vast refugee camp for thousands of citizens, including a disproportionate number of poor and minority populations. Large numbers of individuals, including women and their children, the sick and the elderly, were virtually stranded in a submerged city without food, water, shelter or protection for several days before emergency relief efforts arrived.

Each phase of the Katrina Disaster, ranging from the warning phase to the reconstruction phase, created conditions and opportunities for the victimization, particularly the sexual assaults, of women. In the earlier phases of the Katrina Disaster, certain unique aspects of the disaster, such as the breakdown of social control agencies, loss of power, anonymity of collective groups of males and dangerousness of disaster shelters and other temporary housing, facilitated assaults on women, many of whom were left alone with their children. While later phases lent themselves to more typical patterns of sexual assaults, earlier phases nonetheless possessed disaster–related characteristics associated with sexual assaults. Even in the more recent recovery/reconstruction phases, there is evidence of disaster-related opportunities for rape. For instance, there are still women living in vulnerable conditions such as FEMA trailer camps or other isolated residences and there are still large numbers of male construction workers operating throughout the city. We have uncovered cases that embody different types of women's vulnerability present through each of the disaster phases. Although there are a number of conceptual and methodological problems associated with phase analysis of disasters, we believe that the phases provide an excellent framework for examining the violent and non-violent crimes that occur during disasters.

At this juncture, the sociology of disaster literature (including works by criminologists and disaster researchers) generally offers little empirical evidence on the sexual victimization of women during catastrophes. The dearth of evidence on this phenomenon impedes the development of key policies related to emergency preparedness and planning, which recognize women's vulnerabilities and serve to protect them against violence and sexual assaults. For example, Elaine Enarson's report on emergency preparedness in British Columbia to mitigate disaster-related violence against women concludes that, "[W]omen experiencing violence are not identified as a special-needs population with life safety concerns" (1999a: 4). Although Enarson's report addresses the needs of women in Canada, her critique certainly applies to the victimization of women in the U.S. She discusses five critical service gaps suggesting strategic changes that are necessary to mitigate violence against women during disasters. These are:

- *Lack of a mandate for addressing violence against women as a risk factor in disasters.* Existing emergency statutes, regulations, and procedures and guidelines do not identify abused and sexually assaulted women as a highly vulnerable population with special needs during emergencies … Key planning groups … and key responders … are not mandated to identify risks in existing systems, which endanger the life safety of women.
- *Lack of knowledge about the link between violence against women and emergency preparedness.* Violence against women as a concern in disasters has not been integrated into the training of emergency responders or women's services staff. Violence against women is also not communicated to the public as a health concern in disasters …
- *Lack of priority attention to the emergency needs of transition homes and related women's services.* No provisions are currently in place to support the role of women's services, such as residential shelters or critical care facilities, in emergencies.

- *Lack of an integrated emergency preparedness system fully engaging women's services and emergency managers.* The ability of anti-violence women's services to continue functioning or quickly recover from the effects of a major community disaster must be enhanced on a priority basis.
- *Lack of emergency planning in anti-violence women's services.* The critical services provided by women's anti-violence agencies to women whose safety and well-being is at heightened risk during emergencies make effective organization disaster planning essential. Yet, few concrete measures have been taken serving highly vulnerable populations located in or near known hazards (Enarson 1999a: 3–7).

In conclusion, perhaps one of the most overlooked aspects regarding needed policy changes in the protection of women from criminal victimization during disasters is to include women in pre- and post-disaster planning at the local, state, national and international levels and to bring them into all decision-making processes for short and long-term reconstruction plans (Chew and Ramdas 2005: 4).

References

Bolin, R. C. and P. A. Bolton. 1986. *Race, Religion, and Ethnicity in Disaster Recovery.* Boulder, CO: Institute of Behavioral Science, University of Colorado.

Brinkley, D. 2006. *The Great Deluge.* New York: Harper Collins.

Carr, L. 1932. Disaster and the sequence-pattern concept of social change. *American Journal of Sociology* 38: 207–18.

Centers for Disease Control. 1992. Post-Hurricane Andrew assessment of health care needs and access to health care in Dade County, Florida. EPI-AID 93-09. Miami, FL: Department of Health and Rehabilitative Services.

Chew, L. and K. Ramdas. 2005. *Caught in the Storm: The Impact of Natural Disasters on Women.* San Francisco, CA: Global Fund for Women.

Clemens, P. and J. Hietala. 1999. Risk of domestic violence after flood impact: Effects of social support, age, and history of domestic violence. *Applied Behavioral Science Review* 7: 199–208.

Delaney, P. I. and E. Shrader. 2000. Gender and post-disaster reconstruction: The case of Hurricane Mitch in Honduras and Nicaragua, LCSPG/LAC Gender Team: The World Bank. Available online at: www.gdnonline.org/resources/reviewdraft.doc.

Drabek, T. E. 1986. *Human System Responses to Disaster.* New York: Springer-Verlag.

Enarson, E. and B. H. Morrow. 1997. A gendered perspective: The voices of women. In *Hurricane Andrew: Ethnicity, Gender and the Sociology of Disasters*, eds. W. Peacock, B. H. Morrow and H. Gladwin, London: Routledge: 116–40.

Enarson, E. and B. H. Morrow. 1998. Why gender? Why women? An introduction to women and disaster. In *The Gendered Terrain of Disaster: Through Women's Eyes*, eds. E. Enarson and B. H. Morrow, Westport, CT: Praeger: 1–8.

Enarson, E. 1998. Surviving domestic violence and disasters. Paper presented at the

FREDA Centre for Research on Violence against Women and Children, British Colombia.

Enarson, E. 1999. Violence against women in disasters. *Violence Against Women* 5: 742–68.

Enarson, E. 1999a. *Emergency Preparedness in British Columbia: Mitigating Violence Against Women in Disasters: An Issues and Action Report for Provincial Emergency Management Authorities and Women's Services.* Victoria, British Columbia: B.C. Association of Specialized Victim Assistance and Counseling Programs.

Enarson, E. 1999b. Women and housing issues in two U.S. disasters: Hurricane Andrew and the Red River Valley Flood. *International Journal of Mass Emergencies and Disasters* 17: 39–63.

Enarson, E. and L. Meyreles. 2004. International perspectives on gender and disaster: Differences and possibilities. *The International Journal of Sociology and Social Policy* 24: 49–76.

Fothergill, A. 1996. Gender, Risk and Disaster. *International Journal of Mass Emergencies and Disasters* 14: 33–56.

Fothergill, A. 1998. The neglect of gender in disaster work: An overview of the literature. In *The Gendered Terrain of Disaster: Through Women's Eyes*, eds. E. Enarson and B. H. Morrow, Westport, CT: Praeger: 11–26.

Fothergill, A. 1999. An exploratory study of women battering in the Grand Forks flood disaster: Implications for community responses and policies. *International Journal of Mass Emergencies and Disasters* 17: 79–98.

Godino, V. and C. Coble. 1995. The Missouri model: The efficacy of funding domestic violence programs as long-term recovery. *Final Evaluation Report.* December 1995. Jefferson City, MS: The Missouri Coalition Against Domestic Violence.

Haas, J. D., R. W. Kates and M. J. Bowden. 1997. *Reconstruction Following Disaster.* Cambridge, MA: MIT Press.

Hurricane Katrina: The Storm that Changed America. 2005. New York: Time Books.

Killian, L. M. 2002. An introduction to methodological problems of field studies in disasters. In *Methods of Disaster Research*, ed. R. Stallings, Philadelphia, PA: Xlibris Corporation, 49–93.

Laudisio, G. 1993. Disaster aftermath: Redefining response—Hurricane Andrew's impact on I & R. *Alliance of Information and Referral Systems* 15: 13–32.

Lauer, N. C. 2005. Rape-reporting procedure missing after hurricane. *Women's E News*.

Lentin, R. 1997. *Gender and Catastrophe*. New York: Zed Books.

Lystad, M. 1995. *Phases of Disaster: The Missouri Model*. Rockville, MD: Center for Mental Health Services, U.S. Department of Health and Human Resources.

Marshall, L. 2005. Were women raped in New Orleans? Addressing the human rights of women in times of crisis. *Dissident Voice*, September 14.

Morrow, B. H. and E. Enarson. 1994. Making the case for gendered disaster research. Paper presented to the XIIIth World Congress of Sociology. Bielefeld, Germany.

Morrow, B. H. and E. Enarson. 1996. Hurricane Andrew through women's eyes: Issues and recommendations. *International Journal of Mass Emergencies and Disasters* 14: 5–22.

Morrow, B. H. 1997. Stretching the bonds: The families of Andrew. In *Hurricane Andrew: Ethnicity, Gender and the Sociology of Disasters*, eds. W. Peacock, B. H. Morrow and H. Gladwin, London: Routledge.

National Governor's Association. 1979. *Emergency Preparedness Project Final Report*. Washington, D.C.: Government Printing Office.

National Sexual Violence Resource Center. 2006. Hurricanes Katrina/Rita and sexual violence: Report on database of sexual violence prevalence and incidence related to hurricanes Katrina and Rita. Available online at: http://www.nsvrc.org/sites/default/files/Publications_NSVRC_Reports_Report-on-Database-of-Sexual-Violence-Prevalence-and-Incidence-Related-to-Hurricane-Katrina-and-Rita.pdf.

New York City Alliance Against Sexual Assault. 2006. Katrina, natural disasters and sexual violence. Available online at: http://www.nycagainstrape.org/research_factsheet_111.html.

Neal, D. M. 1984. Blame assignment in a diffuse disaster situation. *International Journal of Mass Emergencies and Disasters* 2: 251–66.

Neal, D. M. 1997. Reconsidering the Phases of Disaster. *International Journal of Mass Emergencies and Disasters* 15: 239–64.

Norris, F. 2006. Disasters and domestic violence: prevalence and impact of domestic violence in the wake of disasters. United States Department of Veterans Affairs.

Norris, F. and G. Uhl. 1993. Chronic stress as a mediator of acute stress: The case of Hurricane Hugo. *Journal of Applied Social Psychology* 23: 1263–84.

Norris, F., J. Perilla, J. Riad, K. Kaniasty, L. Kand and E. Lavizzo. 1999. Stability and Change in Stress, Resources and Psychological Distress Following Natural Disaster: Findings from Hurricane Andrew. *Anxiety, Stress & Coping* 12: 363–427.

Phillips, B., L. Garza and D. Neal. 1994. Issues of cultural diversity in time of disaster: The case of Hurricane Andrew. *Journal of Intergroup Relations* 21: 18–27.

Phillips, B. 2002. Qualitative Methods and Disaster Research. In *Methods of Disaster Research*, ed., R. Stallings, Philadelphia, PA: Xlibris Corporation, 194–211.

Powell, J., J. Rayner and J. Finesinger. 1953. Responses to disaster in American cultural groups. Paper presented at the Symposium on Stress, Army Medical Graduate School, Washington, D.C.

Rennison, C. M. 2002. Rape and sexual assault: Reporting to police and medical attention, 1992–2000. U.S. Department of Justice, Bureau of Justice Statistics.

Richardson, B. K. 2005. The phases of disaster as a relationship between structure and meaning: A narrative analysis of the 1947 Texas City explosion. *International Journal of Mass Emergencies and Disasters* 3: 27–54.

Rozario, S. 1997. Disasters and Bangladeshi women. In *Gender and Catastrophe*, ed. R. Lentin, New York: Zed Books.

Siegel, J. M., L. B. Bourque and K. I. Shoaf. 1999. Victimization after a natural disaster: Social disorganization or community cohesion. *International Journal of Mass Emergencies and Disasters* 17: 265–94.

Stoddard, E. R. 1968. *Conceptual Models of Human Behavior in Disaster*. El Paso, TX: Western Press.

Thornton, W. E. and L. Voigt. 2006. Media construction of crime in New Orleans: Hurricane Katrina and beyond. Paper Presented at Southern Sociological Society Meetings, March, New Orleans, LA.

Tobin, G. A., H. M. Bell, L. M. Whiteford and B. E. Montz. 2006. Vulnerability of displaced persons: Relocation park residents in the wake of Hurricane Charley. *International Journal of Mass Emergencies and Disasters* 24: 77–109.

United Nations High Commissioner for Refugees (UNHCR). 2003. Sexual and gender-based violence against refugees, returnees and internally displaced persons: Guidelines for prevention and response. Geneva, UNHCR. Available online at: http://www.unhcr.org/refworld/pdfid/3edcd0661.pdf.

United Nations High Commissioner for Refugees (UNHCR). 1999. Reproductive health in refugee situations: An inter-agency field manual. Chapter 4: Sexual and gender-based violence) Geneva, UNHCR. Available online at: http://www.unfpa.org/emergencies/manual/4.htm.

United Nations High Commissioner for Refugees (UNHCR). 1995. Sexual violence against refugees: Guidelines on prevention and response. Geneva, UNHCR. Available online at: http://www.forcedmigration.org/sphere/pdf/shelter/unhcr/sexual-violence.pdf.

U.S. Census Bureau. 2000. American community survey. Washington, D.C.: U.S. Government Printing Office.

USAID. 2006. Making cities work. Reconstruction and post-disaster mitigation. Available online at: http://www.makingcitieswork.org/.

Vann, B. 2002. Gender-based violence: Emerging issues in programs serving displaced populations. In Reproductive Health for Refugees Consortium. Arlington, VA: JSI Research and Training Institute. Available online at: http://www.rhrc.org/resources/gbv/EI_Intro.pdf.

Voigt, L., W. E. Thornton, L. Barrile and J. Seaman. 1994. *Criminology and Justice.* New York: McGraw Hill.

Wiest, R. E., J. S. P. Mocellin and D. T. Motsisi. 1994. *The Needs of Women in Disasters and Emergencies.* Winnipeg, Manitoba: University of Manitoba Disaster Research Institute Disaster Research Institute.

Worrall, S. 2005. Hell and high water. *The Times,* October 29.

Discussion Questions

1. Describe what happens during each of the phases of disaster.
2. How does the distinction of the Katrina Disaster as a multi-catastrophe event change how it moves through the phases?
3. What are the data sources used in this chapter? What are some of the difficulties in measuring the incidence of rape?
4. At what stages of disaster does rape occur?
5. What increases women's vulnerability for sexual violence at each stage of disaster?
6. What are the five policy areas that need to be addressed if sexual violence against women during disaster is to be reduced?

8

FRAUD FOLLOWING THE SEPTEMBER 11, 2001 AND HURRICANE KATRINA DISASTERS

By Kelly Frailing

Introduction

Fraud is a complex crime that has defied consistent definition and agreement on an explanatory theory. It seems even more difficult to explain fraud in unique situations and perhaps no two situations are more unique than that in New York following the September 11, 2001 terrorist attacks and in Louisiana following the devastation wreaked by Hurricane Katrina beginning on August 29, 2005. Following a literature review on typologies of fraud, this chapter will examine disaster relief fraud that occurred after the 9/11 terrorist attacks and after Hurricane Katrina, posit an explanatory theory for these crimes and discuss the recognition and prevention of fraud after manmade and natural disasters.

The specific types of fraud to be examined here are first, that against the September 11 Victim Compensation Fund (VCF) of 2001, defined as obtaining or attempting to obtain monetary assistance from the fund despite having no entitlement to do so, e.g., not having been injured or not having a family member killed in the attacks and second, FEMA benefit fraud, defined as obtaining or attempting to obtain various types of monetary assistance from the Federal Emergency Management Agency (FEMA) after Hurricane Katrina, despite having no entitlement to do so, e.g., never living in or not currently living in the area affected by the storm. Information on the VCF and fraud against it is available from the Department of Justice and in media reports and information on FEMA benefit fraud is available from a variety of sources including the Department of Justice, the Federal Bureau of Investigation and the U.S. Attorney's Offices in each of the three districts in Louisiana. The tenets of a possible explanatory theory will be considered in conjunction with the information available on each of these types of fraud.

Literature Review of Fraud

White Collar Crime

Perhaps the greatest concentration of fraud research has taken place within the broad topic of white collar crime. The term "white collar crime" was introduced in the first half of the twentieth century by Sutherland, who held it to mean crime committed by respectable, high-status people in the course of their employment (1949). Numerous attempts to further define and classify white collar crime have been undertaken since then, many in the last 20 years. One such attempt examined organizational characteristics that were correlated with fraud and found that within the savings and loan industry, the organizations most likely to have committed fraud were those that departed from traditional activities and made higher risk investments. The authors maintain that the organization is used as a weapon when this type of fraud occurs and hold that fraud in these contexts is difficult if not impossible to reduce to the individual level (Tillman and Pontell 1995). Another study examined both individual and organizational characteristics to find out which ones were associated with any of three types of fraud. Those employees who made fraudulent statements, i.e. deliberately falsifying company records, were more likely to be older, male and either managers or executives, but those who committed asset misappropriation or corruption (using one's position in the company for self-serving benefits), were more likely to be younger and either male or female. Similarly, different types of organizations were more susceptible to different types of fraud. Large, publicly traded companies were most open to corruption, smaller companies suffered most from asset misappropriation and fraudulent statements affected both small and large companies, with the exception of nonprofit organizations (Holtfreter 2005).

Other research has focused on the role of the state in white collar crime. One study argued that the crackdown on white collar crime following the savings and loan scandal of the 1980s was in response to the danger the savings and loan industry's insolvency posed to the economic system and was not a result of a desire to punish the people who commit white collar crime. This much is reflected in the lenient way those who do not follow regulations enacted by the state, especially those in the manufacturing industry, are treated by the law (Calavita and Pontell 1994).[1] Narrowing their focus to individuals, the same re-

---

1. It remains to be seen what punishment, if any, those who facilitated the 2008 global recession largely by involving themselves with high risk mortgages and mortgage packages will receive and from whom.

searchers argued that collective embezzlement, when people working within corporations commit fraud for personal and not organizational gain, have a unique position that allows them to stave off interference from the state by engaging in creative, self-serving lobbying. The researchers maintain that the ability of people with money to participate in the political process by lobbying may take even more of a toll on financial stability in the future than it already has (Calavita, Tillman and Pontell 1997).

Finally, in an attempt to classify white collar crime by the motives behind it, one study contended that corporate crime is committed by employees on behalf of their organizations while organized crime is committed by people for personal gain. Either type of crime is possible within the organizational setting and this categorization of crime by motive has implications for fraud research beyond organizations, as well as for public policy (Calavita and Pontell 1993).

Insurance Fraud

Insurance fraud can occur in settings in which insurance is compulsory or recommended. The literature on insurance fraud has principally focused on individuals who submit fraudulent claims for exaggerated or non-existent services or losses to insurance companies. One industry in which insurance fraud has received attention is the long term medical care industry. Medical error that is considered fraud can fall under the auspices of the Civil False Claims Act (the FCA). Private citizens can bring suit for medical fraud under the FCA without government intervention. Fraud can be difficult to determine, though, because the measurement of quality care is not standardized throughout the industry. The best way to regulate fraud in the long term care industry is likely to standardize and then measure quality of care (Krause 2001).

Non-medical insurance fraud has also received attention in the literature. Fraud perpetrated by individuals against the travel, automotive, household and business contents and fire insurance industries is estimated to occur in one to five percent of claims. Insurers have been reluctant in the past to vigorously investigate dubious claims in large part because their business is based on service. They are selling a protection that may never be claimed, and not goods, so they have an incentive to act in good faith to recruit and retain customers (Clarke 1989).

With a fraudulent claim made approximately one out of every ten times, the United States has the longest and most extensive history of insurance fraud and insurance fraud control among Western nations. There are six nation wide institutions designed to combat insurance fraud in addition to the techniques each company might employ to do so (Clarke 1990). Company techniques that have dominated insurance fraud investigation to date include focusing on individual fraud indicators, but these indicators are merely anecdotal or intuitive and have not been shown to correlate with fraudulent claims. This focus on individual fraud indicators usually occurs in conjunction with inexperience among claims adjusters and the transfer of cases among adjusters within a company. Efficiently targeting fraudulent claims and acting on them will take an improvement in training for staff, ownership of claims cases and improvement in software that can recognize the dynamic nature of potentially fraudulent claims (Morley, Ball and Ormerod 2006).

The attitudes of consumers about insurance fraud are formed in part in relation to their attitudes about the insurance industry. People with negative attitudes about the insurance industry are more likely to commit insurance fraud than those without negative attitudes. Similarly, people who are tolerant of dishonesty across situations are more likely to commit insurance fraud than those who are not tolerant of dishonesty in general. To decrease the likelihood that insurance fraud will be committed, companies can try to improve their images among consumers, though there is probably little they can do to change tolerance of dishonesty (Tennyson 1997).

Benefit Fraud

Benefit fraud is generally defined as the reception of government benefits by people who have no entitlement to them or who do not meet the requirements to receive them. In Great Britain, social security fraud was estimated to compromise nearly 10 percent of the system's 90 billion pound budget. New social security benefit legislation was passed in 1997 in an effort to reduce fraudulent claims. With these new requirements, each applicant was assumed to be committing benefit fraud, despite the fact that the social security benefit requirements are very complicated. Frauds may have actually been errors based on a lack of understanding the requirement rules or a reluctance to report changes, especially temporary changes, that might alter benefits. The recent social security legislation, then, probably increased the problem of benefit fraud instead of combating it (McKeever 1999). One key reason postulated for the failure of enacted legislation to effectively combat fraud in Great Britain is the perception that truly needy people are denied benefits or are underbenefited, which creates apathy among the public about social security fraud. Addressing the possible reasons for claims suspected to be fraudulent, including the complicated paperwork and the afore-mentioned reluctance to report temporary changes in income for fear that they will permanently alter benefits is the first step the social security adminis-tration can take to combat fraud and change public perception about the permissibility of benefit fraud (McKeever 1999a).

The administration seemed to fail on that recommendation, however. After a review of the techniques used by the administration to combat fraud, which included data matching across government benefit agencies, tougher sanctions for those who commit benefit fraud and public education about the problem of benefit fraud, data matching received by far the most monetary resources for its implementation. The author argues that even a significant reduction in the estimated two billion pounds lost to fraud cannot justify the eradication of benefit claimants' rights of privacy and confidentiality, es-pecially because the majority of claimants do not act fraudulently (McKeever 2003).

Personal Fraud Victimization

Research on the victims of fraud has focused on individuals who have had fraud perpetrated against them by other individuals. Defining fraud as delib-erate intent to deceive with the promise of goods, services or financial bene-fits with no intention of providing them, researchers surveyed over 1,000 adults in the United States and found the prevalence of personal fraud victimization to be approximately 15 percent. The researchers note that the only character-istics that made any difference in the success of a fraud attempt were age and education. Curiously, it was younger and more educated people who were more likely to be victims of personal fraud, perhaps because they tend to have a variety of interests and activities in which they are involved (Titus, Heinzel-mann and Boyle 1995). In a follow up paper, the principal author noted that there are five types of personal fraud most likely to lead to victimization and that there are four different types of personal fraud that lead to the largest fi-nancial losses for victims. Although this paper does not examine personal fraud perpetrated via the Internet, it makes recommendations about fraud preven-tion based on the types most likely to result in victimization at all and those most likely to result in high financial loss (Titus 1999).

The types of fraud reviewed to this point have included those perpetuated by organizations for their gain, by individuals against organizations or agen-cies and by individuals against one another. Fraud has been studied in multi-ple contexts and it should come as little surprise that there are a number of different theories of crime that researchers believe explain fraud.

Theories of Fraud

Gottfredson and Hirschi (1990) maintain that their general theory of crime can explain fraud as well as it can other types of crime, contending that the likelihood of both increases when people have low self control. One study of white collar crime cited above refutes this contention, suggesting that fraud is embedded in the arrangement of the organization and cannot be reduced to individuals and their characteristics (Tillman and Pontell 1995). Other research more focused on explicitly testing Gottfredson and Hirschi's theory found that the opportunity to commit crime explained the commission of crime to a higher degree than did the level of self-control (Grasmick, Tittle, Bursik and Arneklev 1993). Other research suggests that the two broad types of crime the general theory is purported to explain, force and fraud, are distinct manifestations that cannot be explained by one underlying construct of low self control. The authors also suggest that the opportunities for fraud in particular may better explain its commission than the characteristic of low self-control (Rebellon and Waldman 2003).

Personal fraud victimization can be explained by a combination of risk heterogeneity, i.e. individual characteristics and circumstance as well as state dependence, i.e. previous victimization (Titus and Grover 2001). Other research on personal fraud suggests that people choose to become involved in fraudulent schemes, a Ponzi scheme in the case of this study, because of their desire to achieve the American Dream of monetary and material success (Trahan, Marquart and Mullings 2005). At least one author has attempted to create a theory for profit-driven crimes that focuses not on who commits profit-driven crimes or why they do, but instead on what is criminally obtained and how it is obtained. Profit-driven crimes that are predatory in nature can involve anything from purse snatching to extortion. Market-based profit crimes involve vices currently deemed illegal such as street drugs and commercial crimes involve profit crimes committed by employees against their employer (Naylor 2003). This is an exciting recent attempt at new categorization of profit-driven crimes, which would include fraud. However, testing of the theory is needed to determine its value and possible need for reorganization and clearer definition of concepts. More research is likely forthcoming in the area of personal fraud victimization, as the massive financial crimes of Bernard Madoff and Allen Stanford are examined in more detail and hopefully more fully understood in an effort to prevent their repetition.[2]

---

2. On June 29, 2009, Bernard Madoff was sentenced to 150 year in prison for his theft of billions of dollars from hundreds of investors. The judge who sentenced him, Denny Chin, called his crimes "extraordinarily evil" (Neuman 2009).

Disasters and Crime

Thus far, this chapter has examined fraud in a number of contexts and the theories that have attempted to explain this crime in those different settings. One thing the settings already examined have in common is their regular place in everyday life. They are almost unremarkable, especially when compared to the unique, sometimes unprecedented circumstances that follow a disaster. Unfortunately, crime of several kinds is almost always a part of those circumstances. An earthquake estimated to measure 7.9 on the Richter scale hit Japan's Kanto region in September, 1923. In the week that followed, rumors about Korean uprisings started in the most isolated and devastated areas and spread quickly among the Japanese. The end result was the torture and murder of about 6,000 Koreans living in Japan at the time (Ishiguro 1998).

Looting may be the most common crime to occur in the wake of natural disasters. It followed the earthquake that struck San Francisco in 1906 (Morris 2002), the flood caused by Hurricane Agnes in Wilkes Barre, Pennsylvania in 1972 (Siman 1977), the flood that devastated Buffalo Creek, West Virginia in 1972 (Erikson 1976) and the earthquake that struck Tangshan, China in 1976 (Zhou 1997). These disasters are covered at greater length elsewhere in this volume. Looting also occurred in the wake of the devastation of New Orleans, Louisiana by Hurricane Katrina. The extent of the looting may never be clear, as a majority of the complaints made to the police regarding lost or stolen items in the months following Hurricane Katrina have been recorded as 21K. The code signifies either lost or stolen property and implies that a definite case cannot be made for either circumstance. Of the 2,682 burglary complaints made to the New Orleans Police Department between October, 2005 and January, 2006, 1,652 (61.6 percent) were coded as 21K. The remainder, 1,030 (38.4 percent), were determined to be either residential or commercial burglaries (*Times Picayune* archives 2006). Using just the police reports that could be determined to be burglaries and using those as a proxy for post-storm looting, one study found that the burglary rate per 100,000 in Orleans Parish increased over 400 percent in the month after Katrina as compared to the month before (Frailing and Harper 2007); this topic is examined more fully elsewhere in this volume.

Finally, contractor fraud, in which contractors accept money up front for home or property repair they do not start, do not finish or do shoddy work, happened to 5.6 percent of people with damaged property following a tropical storm in Houston, Texas in 2001 and to 3.4 percent of people with damaged property following flooding in the San Antonio, Texas area in 2002. The victims of contractor fraud from both cities were more likely to be female, older and college educated (Davila, Marquart and Mullings 2005). With the relevant literature on fraud and disasters and crime now reviewed, this chapter turns to a discussion of the fraud that followed the September 11 and Katrina disasters.

Victim Compensation Fund Fraud after September 11, 2001

On the morning of September 11, 2001, 19 members of the terrorist group al Qaeda boarded four separate commercial flights departing from cities on the east coast of the United States. Using box cutters they had smuggled aboard, the al Qaeda members hijacked three of the planes and attempted to commandeer the fourth as well. The hijackers flew each of the first three planes into pre-selected targets — the north tower of the World Trade Center in Manhattan, New York, the south tower of the World Trade Center and the Pentagon building in Washington, D.C. Passengers on the fourth flight forced hijackers to crash the plane in a field in Shanksville, Pennsylvania instead of its intended target, the White House. From the initial moments after the first plane struck the first tower, television stations began incessant coverage of the attack on New York. Many people were watching this coverage as the second plane hit the second tower and still more watched as the structurally damaged buildings fell to the ground some time later. The biggest, most unprecedented terrorist attack on American soil resulted in approximately 3,000 deaths in New York City alone. The attacks are covered at greater length elsewhere in this volume.

America's response to this attack was swift and multifaceted. One aspect of that response was the creation of the September 11 Victim Compensation Fund of 2001. The VCF was part of the Air Transportation Safety and Stabilization Act passed by Congress on September 22, 2001. The VCF was allotted $5.12 billion to compensate those injured and the families of those killed. The Special Master of the VCF, an administrator appointed by the then Attorney General John Ashcroft, expected to receive about 6,000 claims for funds between the VCF's inception and its sunset date of December 22, 2003. The presumptive awarding scheme was based on categories of claimants, ranging from military personnel, to New York City police and fire department personnel, to federal employees, to civil federal employees to everyone else. In general, the awards were calculated based on what the decedent would have earned through the rest of his/her lifetime, minus assets such as life insurance and plus a pain and suffering payment, presumptively set at $250,000. As of June, 2003, the average death award was $1.44 million and personal injury awards ranged from $500 to $6.8 million (USDOJ 2003: i–iv).

Potential claimants had to follow a number of steps in order to receive these awards. For those submitting a claim on behalf of a deceased family member, the required paperwork included an original death certificate, a document confirming the victim's presence at one of the designated sites e.g., the north and south towers of the World Trade Center, a court document designating a personal representative to receive funds on the victim's behalf and proof that all relevant parties had been notified that the claim had been filed. The required paperwork was similar for those making a personal injury claim. Additional documentation that had to be submitted and then verified by the VCF included income verification for the previous four years and collateral asset verification. Collateral assets could include pensions, social security, life insurance, workmen's compensation and death benefits paid by employers (USDOJ 2003: 3–6). Once the VCF had received and verified the above documentation, it set to work on making an award determination using the general calculation outlined above. The average time from the submission of all required paperwork to the receipt of the reward was 35 days and ranged from 10 to 116 days (USDOJ 2003: 9).

By August 22, 2002, 11 months after creation of the fund, nine of the first 25 claims for awards from the VCF had been paid, totaling about $1.3 million (USDOJ 2002). As mentioned above the Special Master of the VCF was expecting about 6,000 claims for death and personal injury. Upon the passing of the sunset date, December 22, 2003, over 7,300 claims had been received, about 3,000 of which were for those killed during the attacks. The total awarded by the fund was more than $2.6 billion of the $5.12 billion allotted (USDOJ 2004).

As staff at VCF processed claims, they checked for fraudulent ones. Upon receiving documentation from claimants, staff looked for names of claimants on terrorist lists, as well as checked for involvement with suspicious September 11 charities. Next, staff verified the authenticity of the original documents required, namely, death certificates, verification of location on the morning of September 11, 2001 and court documents designating a representative to receive the compensation. VCF staff called the required court documents the program's most important safeguard against fraud. Each representative designated to receive money underwent an FBI background check before receiving the award. Finally, the aforementioned additional information from claimants, that on income and collateral assets, was also examined and verified by VCF staff before awards were disbursed (USDOJ 2003: iv).

Even with this complex and lengthy award process, fraud against the VCF did occur. During the Office of Inspector General's (OIG) audit of the VCF program in 2003, 17 of the 792 claims under review were suspected of being fraudulent, eight of which had been passed along to the OIG's Fraud Detection Office for further investigation and legal action. Two of the eight had pled guilty to making false statements and mail fraud and four others were in ongoing judicial proceedings at the time of the audit (USDOJ 2003: v, vii). Later reports in the media revealed other instances of VCF fraud, such as the Mercer County man who admitted to defrauding the fund of over $1 million by claiming he was permanently disabled in the attacks (Heininger 2008), the woman who was sentenced to nearly two years in prison after inventing a brother victim and fraudulently collecting about $64,000 from the fund (Associated Press 2007) and the Navy officer charged with fraud for exaggerating the injuries he sustained during the attack on the Pentagon and collecting $330,000 from the fund (MarketWatch 2008).

Even with the 17 suspected fraudulent claims VCF staff found and even with the high profile cases reported by the media taken into account, the OIG audit of the VCF found that the procedures in place to review and award claims were sufficient guards against fraud. VCF staff cited the multiple documents required to meet eligibility for the awards as particularly important. As alluded to above, both a death certificate and proof that the victim was at the site of the attack on September 11 were required and had to be verified before a claim could be paid. Both W-2 forms and Social Security Administration documentation were required to verify employment and partially determine award amount. Obituaries and tax returns were used in tandem to determine the number of dependents, also important to the award amount. The principal area of concern to VCF staff about fraud was underreporting of privately held assets, such as life insurance. This underreporting would not affect receipt of an award, but could affect the amount in the claimant's favor. Staff felt threat of prosecution was sufficient to prevent this particular type of fraud (USDOJ 2003: 12).

FEMA Benefit Fraud after Hurricane Katrina

Hurricane Katrina, the third strongest hurricane of all time, hit New Orleans on August 29, 2005. Its storm surge breached three levees, which resulted in approximately 80 percent of the city flooding and remaining underwater for two weeks. Hundreds of thousands of people evacuated in advance of the storm, but many remained in the city. Over 1,300 people died in Louisiana alone because of the storm (*USA Today* 2006). The Department of Justice started a Hurricane Katrina Fraud Task Force (HKFTF) shortly after the storm to combat all types of fraud, not only in the areas most affected, but throughout the nation. One such type of fraud, and the focus of this section, is that committed against the Federal Emergency Management Agency (FEMA) in the wake of Katrina. People who wished to receive the benefits FEMA was distributing in the wake of the storm for a variety of needs, including but not limited to general emergency assistance, renter's and homeowner's assistance and vehicle replacement assistance could register with FEMA. Provided people registered properly and resided in the affected area at the time of the storm, they generally would receive emergency assistance in the amount of $2,000 at minimum. More assistance was possible depending on extent of losses due to Hurricane Katrina. Over 990,000 people registered with FEMA during September 2005 in Louisiana alone and a total of $1.2 billion was distributed among FEMA registrants in Louisiana during that time (DHS OIG 2006).

Obtaining benefits from FEMA after Katrina was very easy. All one needed was a phone or an Internet connection and some patience. Upon making contact with FEMA, claimants were required to give their names, Social Security numbers, names and Social Security numbers of dependents, addresses, evacuation addresses, assessments of damage to their property, estimations of their employment situations and bank account information. A few days after receiving that information, FEMA directly deposited emergency funds in the amount of $2,000 into the accounts of those with addresses in the government-designated affected area. Receiving the emergency funds from FEMA made one eligible for future assistance, some of which was provided without a second request for it.

There are two main sources of data on the commission of FEMA benefit fraud, the Hurricane Katrina Fraud Task Force and the United States Attorney's Offices in Louisiana, each of which will be examined in turn following some background on the HKFTF. The Task Force was established on September 8, 2005 by then Attorney General Alberto Gonzales. The Task Force's 14 members, which include the FBI, the Department of Justice and the Postal Service among others, are committed to deterring, detecting and prosecuting all types of hurricane-related fraud, not just that against FEMA. The HKFTF has released four reports since its inception, all detailing the number of hurricane-related fraud cases that had come to its attention. In October 2005 HKFTF had prosecuted 36 people, 212 people by February 2006, 412 people by September 2006 and 768 people by September 2007. The majority of the cases HKFTF has prosecuted are those of FEMA benefit fraud and fraud of the American Red Cross (USDOJ 2007). Fraud is not limited to the area directly affected by Hurricane Katrina. Figure 8.1 makes this abundantly clear.

One of HKFTF's members, the FBI, provides more detail about the stage of processing for a fraction of the 768 hurricane-related fraud cases around the country. Between January 2007 and November 2008, 240 cases were at the following stages of the judicial process: 12 arrested, 105 indicted, 50 pled guilty,

**Figure 8.1 HKFTF Federal Criminal Prosecutions for Fraud,
September 1, 2005–August 30, 2007**

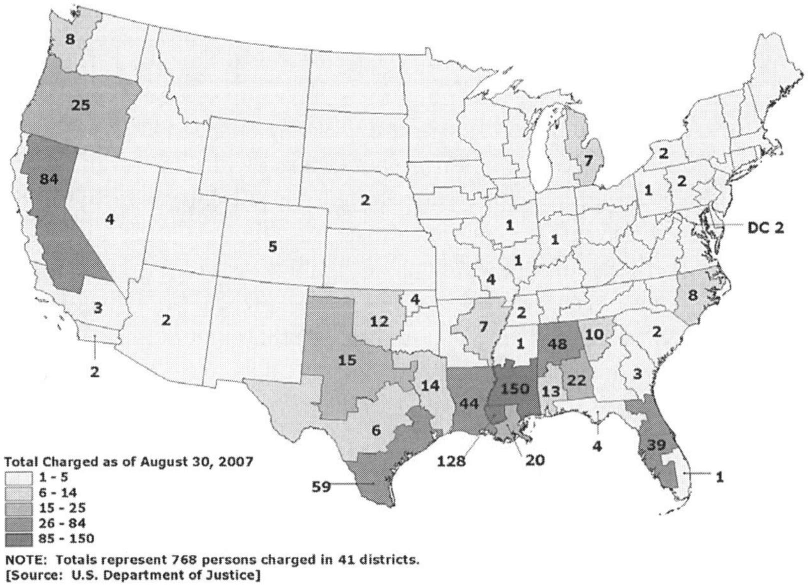

Total Charged as of August 30, 2007
1 - 5
6 - 14
15 - 25
26 - 84
85 - 150
NOTE: Totals represent 768 persons charged in 41 districts.
[Source: U.S. Department of Justice]

Source: USDOJ Hurricane Katrina Fraud Task Force Second Year Report to the Attorney General, September, 2007. Available online at: http://www.usdoj.gov/katrina/Katrina_Fraud/docs/09-04-07AG2ndyrprogrpt.pdf: 3.

7 found guilty and 66 sentenced (FBI 2008). That these data are confined to 2007 and 2008 and do not extend back to Katrina's immediate aftermath indicate that the HKFTF was continuing to detect and prosecute hurricane-related fraud more than three years after the storm's landfall.

The second source of information on FEMA benefit fraud is the United States Attorney's Offices in Louisiana, especially the middle district of the state. It can be seen in Figure 1 that in this particular district, 128 people have been charged with hurricane-related fraud. The middle district of Louisiana is a nine parish region that includes Ascension, East Baton Rouge, East Feliciana, Iberville, Livingston, Point Coupee, St. Helena, West Baton Rouge and West Feliciana. The major city in the Middle District is the state capitol Baton Rouge, with a population of 227,920 (USAO/LAM 2009; U.S. Census Bureau 2000). The attorney's office keeps detailed records of those who are charged with committing this fraud in the form of press releases. Between October 2005 and January 2009, 131 people had been charged with at least one count of FEMA benefit fraud. Of those charged, 89 were women and 42 were men, the average age was 24.6 years, the majority resided in Baton Rouge and their cases had proceeded through the legal process as follows: 26 indicted, 31 pled guilty, 2 found guilty and 72 sentenced. While the most serious charges faced by those charged with FEMA benefit fraud included at least 5 years in prison and a $250,000 fine per count, jail time was a rare sentence. Much more often, those guilty of FEMA benefit fraud were sentenced to a combination of probation, community service and restitution. It is important to reiterate that this tally of fraud only includes that committed against FEMA. It does not include that committed against the American Red Cross, Disaster Unemployment Assistance, the Small Business Administration or the Road Home program, nor does it include fraud committed by FEMA employees. Adding those cases brings the total charged in the middle district of Louisiana with violations related to hurricane disaster relief funds to 170 (USAO/LAM 2009a).

As mentioned above, this chapter deals exclusively with federal benefit fraud in the wake of two disasters. Also deserving of consideration here are the related crimes of price gouging and contractor fraud. In 2006, the Federal Trade Commission (FTC) provided a report to Congress on gasoline price gouging in the wake of Hurricanes Katrina and Rita. The storms, of course, reduced the oil supply and refining abilities and gasoline priced increased as a result. The FTC examined the size and duration of gasoline price increases to determine whether price gouging had occurred. The 16.7 percent increase in average gasoline price from August 2005 to September 2005 was smaller than the FTC was expecting, as was the 9.1 percent increase in average price from August to October 2005. The price increases that did occur were short lived. The main reason for the increase in gasoline price at the pump was the increase in the wholesale price that retailers, uncertain about future supply, were paying after the storms. Despite complaints from consumers and the media about $4 and $5 per gallon gasoline, the FTC found only six gas stations were overcharging for gasoline relative to their usual prices and relative to the other stations in the city and of those six, only one was doing so substantially (FTC 2006).

In the wake of Katrina, the Bush administration allotted billions of dollars for recovery-related goods and services, promising that the money would not be wasted. However, a review of over 550 reports presented to members of Congress indicates waste did occur as this money was allotted through contracts. Some of the more notable contracts in which waste, fraud and abuse were present included those for debris removal, the blue roof contract and manufacture of homes and trailers. The 19 suspect contracts in the report were estimated to have wasted almost $9 billion by 2006. Contract mismanagement was a multifaceted problem. First, 70 percent of contracts awarded by the government in the wake of Katrina were no-bid contracts. Second, both FEMA and the Army Corps of Engineers had insufficient contract contingency plans in place before Katrina, which contributed to ineffective contractor oversight once the contracts were awarded. Third, an excessive reliance on subcontractors resulted in wasted funds. One study found the cost to the taxpayer under the tiered contract system was sometimes 1,700 percent higher than the cost of the job itself. Fourth, while federal employees' ability to use credit cards could expedite relief, the cards were abused after Katrina in the amount of tens of thousands of dollars. Finally, general corruption aggravated contract mismanagement (U.S. House of Representatives 2006).

Theories of Crime in the Wake of Disasters

A number of theories have been put forth in an attempt to explain different types of crime in the wake of natural disasters. In the case of contractor fraud, researchers believe that it can be explained by the social disorganization created by a storm wherein protective institutions and relationships are absent or are altered, resulting in increased likelihood of this specific type of fraud (Davila, Marquart and Mullings 2005). Social disorganization, particularly the disruption of neighborhoods, is also the explanatory theory for mass looting following a devastating earthquake in China (Zhou 1997). Other researchers believe that routine activity theory's component of guardianship is the strongest predictor of crime and that increased formal and informal guardianship accounted for the assumed decrease in crime immediately following Hurricane Andrew's landfall in the Miami, Florida area in 1992, despite an increase in both motivated offenders and vulnerable targets (Cromwell, Dunham, Akers and Lanza-Kaduce 1995). The two types of fraud detailed above do not seem on their faces to be well explained by either of the theories put forth here. Instead, a good explanatory theory for VCF and FEMA benefit fraud is that of rational choice. After a brief explanation of the theory and mention of some supporting literature, a case will be made for its ability to explain both VCF and FEMA benefit fraud.

Rational Choice Theory

Rational choice theory, as conceived of by Cornish and Clarke, is characterized by both the cost-benefit analysis associated with a specific crime and the opportunities to commit that crime (1986). Once people have made up their minds to engage in criminal behavior, they choose their crimes based on the opportunities to commit them and if the benefits of doing so are estimated to outweigh the costs. The choice to commit crime in the first place is based on a number of factors, including temperament, upbringing, self-perception and previous experience with crime (1986: 279). Benefits of a crime that increase its likelihood of being selected by an offender can include low effort, little skill, available targets, high expected yield, confrontation or lack of with victim and low risk of apprehension while costs can be thought of as the opposites (i.e. high effort, high skill, et cetera). Rational choice is considered a crime specific theory because different crimes meet different needs for the offender and because the context in which the rational choice (i.e. the cost benefit analysis) is made will be different for different offenses. Cornish and Clarke later elaborated on rational choice theory, noting that it was developed with crime prevention in mind (1987). Their critics suggested that whatever methods are implemented to prevent crime (target hardening, for example, where a person or a place is made more secure and the cost of offending becomes higher) will result in crime displacement, where another crime is substituted for that which was initially considered. Cornish and Clarke maintain that crime is only displaced when the original and substitute crimes share characteristics and that understanding choice structuring properties for each type of crime will help minimize crime displacement. Choice structuring properties differ somewhat from crime to crime, but they do share commonalities across crimes, including availability, awareness of method, social cachet and moral evaluation (1987: 940).

Rational choice theory has received support in the literature. A study of people on probation across the United States using logistic regression techniques revealed that ongoing offending is done to fulfill offender needs, as rational choice theory would predict (Guerette, Stenius and McGloin 2005). In a study of 699 student responses to scenarios of drunk driving, theft and sexual assault, researchers found that the accessibility and vulnerability of the target and the perceived costs and benefits of offending were significantly related to decisions to offend. This was especially true among the students who were found to have low self control (Nagin and Paternoster 1993). Among high risk youth, the perceived risks of committing theft and violence were updated based on perception of prior risks, experience with crime and arrest and observation of peers. Factors most associated with the commission of theft and violence were perceived risk of arrest, psychological rewards and perceived opportunities (Matsueda, Kreager and Huizinga 2006). In a study conducted with serious offenders on six types of crimes, the choice to commit another or substitute crime of most types was based on the likelihood of arrest in comparison to the number of times they had been able to commit the same crime in the past without being apprehended. This study replicated the oft-observed inverse relationship between experience and risk perception (Horney and Marshall 1992). A longitudinal study on 1,002 people in New Zealand found that for people who were criminally prone, perceptions of deterrence had the greatest impact on their choice whether or not to offend (Wright, Caspi, Moffitt and Paternoster 2004). Finally, in a study of corporate crime, researchers found that personal moral code was an important inhibition against crime. In the absence of that moral code, however, compliance with laws was based on perceived costs and benefits. People were deterred by threats of formal and informal sanctions and the researchers argue for both moral education and evident legal repercussions to control corporate crime (Paternoster and Simpson 1996).

One of the strengths rational choice has as an explanatory theory is that it contains prescriptions for reducing crime, most importantly target hardening and increasing perceived risks of committing the crime. First, target hardening: Compare the number of frauds suspected of being committed and committed against the VCF, 20, to those committed against FEMA after Katrina, 768. To obtain a VCF award was a lengthy and complex process requiring claimants to go through a variety of channels involving face to face contact with a number of individuals. The first VCF awards were not distributed until almost a year after the program's inception. Obtaining FEMA benefits after Katrina, however, was much easier. One phone call or about half an hour on the Internet with no face to face contact had a potential minimum yield of $2,000. FEMA began distributing money just days after it announced it would do so. In short, VCF awards were a much more well protected target than were FEMA benefits. The costs of engaging in VCF fraud was therefore higher than the costs of engaging in FEMA fraud. That FEMA quickly developed a nationwide reputation as a large, inept bureaucracy did nothing to help its status as a hard target.

A second preventive feature of rational choice theory, increasing the perceived risks of crime is something the HKFTF did attempt to employ. The possible sentence for commission of FEMA benefit fraud ranged upward from five years in prison, a $250,000 fine or both per count. While sentences of this magnitude were rarely handed down for those convicted of the crime, these cases were and are still being prosecuted, which is indicative of authorities' attempts to make the costs of FEMA benefit fraud outweigh the benefits. In addition, the Department of Homeland Security's Office of Inspector General recommends that FEMA increase its capacity, both through improved employee training and an improved web site, to find fraudulent or potentially fraudulent registrations as they are made instead of months later, also increasing the risk of committing the crime (DHS OIG 2006).

Conclusion

The features of the crimes of VCF and FEMA benefit fraud fit well with those of rational choice theory. VCF was a hard target and while its expected yield was high, the effort, skill and time required to commit the crime were large and because of the many steps involved, the chances of being caught were high. FEMA, on the other hand, was an easy target with an expected high and possibly repeated yield, there was little one needed in terms of effort and skill to commit the crime and the perceived chances of being caught were low.

Thinking of disaster fraud in this way, as well explained by rational choice theory, and examining where features of the theory reduced or induced fraud is instructive. The VCF provides a quality blueprint of how to distribute awards to those most devastated after a disaster. While the financial needs after a natural disaster such as Katrina may be more timely than those after a manmade disaster such as September 11 (and this is not a certainty), the same principles of checking between agencies such as the Social Security Administration and the Postal Service to verify claimants' information can be employed quickly enough for financial assistance to reach those who have been left in dire circumstances. It is imperative that FEMA and other disaster relief agencies make use of this cross checking and other best practices if they wish to avoid fraud on the scale seen after Katrina in the future. Fraud in the wake of disaster of any kind is a despicable crime because it makes those who have truly suffered and lost subject to unwarranted scrutiny, as well as to additional stress and hardship. Insight into this crime and how to stop it are just two more tools available to cope with the aftermath of a disaster and it is useful to supplement the arsenal as the possibility for disaster is ever present.

References

Associated Press. 2007. Woman sentenced in 9-11 fund fraud. June 14, 2007. Available online at: http://cms.firehouse.com/web/online/911/Woman-Sentenced-in-9-11-Fund-Fraud-/41$19352.

Calavita, K. and H. N. Pontell. 1993. Savings and loan fraud as organized crime: Toward a conceptual typology of corporate illegality. *Criminology* 31(4): 519–48.

Calavita, K. and H. N. Pontell. 1994. The state and white-collar crime: Saving the savings and loans. *Law & Society Review* 28(2): 297–324.

Calavita, K., R. Tillman and H. N. Pontell. 1997. The savings and loan debacle, financial crime, and the state. *Annual Review of Sociology* 23: 19–38.

Clarke, M. 1989. Insurance fraud. *The British Journal of Criminology* 29(1): 1–20.

Clarke, M. 1990. The control of insurance fraud. *The British Journal of Criminology* 30(1): 1–23.

Cornish, D. and R. Clarke. 1986. Crime as a rational choice. In *Criminological Theory: Past to Present*, eds. F. T. Cullen and R. Agnew, Los Angeles, CA: Roxbury Publishing Company, 278–83.

Cornish, D. and R. Clarke. 1987. Understanding crime displacement: An application of rational choice theory. *Criminology* 25(4): 933–47.

Cromwell, P., R. Dunham, R. Akers and L. Lanza-Kaduce. 1995. Routine activities and social control in the aftermath of a natural catastrophe. *European Journal on Criminal Policy and Research* 3(3): 56–69.

Davila, M., J. Marquart and J. Mullings. 2005. Beyond mother nature: Contractor fraud in the wake of natural disasters. *Deviant Behavior* 26: 271–93.

DHS OIG. 2006. A Performance Review of FEMA's Disaster Management Activities in Response to Hurricane Katrina. Report by the Department of Homeland Security's Office of Inspector General. Available online at: http://www.dhs.gov/interweb/assetlibrary/OIG_06-32_Mar06.pdf.

Erikson, K. T. 1976. *Everything In Its Path: Destruction of Community in the Buffalo Creek Flood*. New York: Simon and Schuster.

FBI. 2008. Hurricane Katrina/Rita information. Latest News available online at: http://www.fbi.gov/katrina.htm.

Frailing, K. and D. W. Harper. 2007. Crime and hurricanes in New Orleans. In *The Sociology of Katrina: Perspectives on a Modern Catastrophe*, eds. D. L. Brunsma, D. Overfelt and J. S. Picou, Lantham, MD: Rowman and Littlefield: 51–70.

FTC. 2006. Investigation of gasoline price manipulation and post-Katrina gasoline price increase. Available online at: http://www.ftc.gov/reports/060518 PublicGasolinePricesInvestigationReportFinal.pdf.

Gauthier, D. K. 2001. Professional lapses: Occupational deviance and neutralization techniques in veterinary medical practice. *Deviant Behavior* 22(6): 467–90.

Gottfredson, M. R. and T. Hirschi. 1990. A general theory of crime. In *Criminological Theory: Past to Present*, eds. F. T. Cullen and R. Agnew, Los Angeles, CA: Roxbury Publishing Company: 240–52.

Grasmick, H. G., C. R. Tittle, R. J. Bursik and B. J. Arneklev. 1993. Testing the core empirical implications of Gottfredson and Hirschi's general theory of crime. *Journal of Research in Crime and Delinquency* 30(1): 5–29.

Guerette, R. T., V. M. K. Stenius and J. M. McGloin. 2005. Understanding offense specialization and versatility: A reapplication of the rational choice perspective. *Journal of Criminal Justice* 33(1): 77–87.

Heininger, C. 2008. Mercer man admits largest ever 9/11 fund fraud. *The Star Leger*, January 31, 2008. Available online at: http://www.nj.com/news/index.ssf/2008/01/a_mercer_county_man_today.html.

Holtfreter, K. 2005. Is occupational fraud "typical" white-collar crime? A comparison of individual and organizational characteristics. *Journal of Criminal Justice* 33(4): 353–65.

Horney, J. and I. H. Marshall. 1992. Risk perceptions among serious offenders: The role of crime and punishment. *Criminology* 30(4): 575–94.

Ishiguro, Y. 1998. A Japanese national crime: The Korean massacre after the great Kanto earthquake of 1923. *Korea Journal* 38(4): 331–55.

Krause, J. H. 2001. Medical error as false claim. *American Journal of Law & Medicine* 27: 181–201.

Matsueda, R. L., D. A. Kreager and D. Huizinga. 2006. Deterring delinquents: A rational choice model of theft and violence. *American Sociological Review* 71(1): 95–122.

Market Watch. 2008. Vet pleads innocent in 9/11 fund fraud. November 4, 2008. Available online at: http://www.marketwatch.com/news/story/vet-pleads-innocent-911-fund/story.aspx?guid=%7BCE4C3DED-D9B2-4BD4-A937-F3FBEA0DBC26%7D.

McKeever, G. 1999. Detecting, prosecuting and punishing benefit fraud: The social security administration (fraud) act 1997. *Modern Law Review* 62(2): 261–70.

McKeever, G. 1999a. Fighting fraud: An evaluation of the government's social security fraud strategy. *Journal of Social Welfare and Family Law* 21(4): 357–71.

McKeever, G. 2003. Tackling benefit fraud. *Industrial Law Journal* 32(4): 326–31.

Morley, N. J., L. J. Ball and T. C. Ormerod. 2006. How the detection of insurance fraud succeeds and fails. *Psychology, Crime & Law* 12(2): 163–80.

Morris, C. 2002. *The San Francisco Calamity by Earthquake and Fire*. Urbana, IL: University of Illinois Press.

Nagin, D. S. and R. Paternoster. 1993. Enduring individual differences and rational choice theories of crime. *Law & Society Review* 27(3): 467–96.

Naylor, R. T. 2003. Towards a general theory of profit-driven crimes. *The British Journal of Criminology* 43: 81–101.

Neuman, S. 2009. Madoff sentenced to maximum 150 years in prison. *National Public Radio*, June 29. Available online at: http://www.npr.org/templates/story/story.php?storyId=106083649.

Paternoster, R. and S. Simpson. 1996. Sanction threats and appeals to morality: Testing a rational choice model of corporate crime. *Law & Society Review* 30(3): 549–83.

Rebellon, C. J. and I. Waldman. 2003. Deconstructing "force and fraud": An empirical assessment of the generality of crime. *Journal of Quantitative Criminology* 19(3): 303–31.

Siman, B. A. 1977. *Crime During Disaster.* University of Pennsylvania PhD diss. Ann Arbor, MI: University Microfilms International.

Sutherland, E. 1949. *White Collar Crime.* New York: Dryden.

Tennyson, S. 1997. Economic institutions and individual ethics: A study of consumer attitudes toward insurance fraud. *Journal of Economic Behavior & Organization* 32: 247–65.

Tillman, R. and H. Pontell. 1995. Organizations and fraud in the savings and loan industry. *Social Forces* 73(4): 1439–463.

Times Picayune archives. 2006. Staff graphic on looting statistics published online at www.nola.com on February 7, 2006.

Titus, R. M., F. Heinzelmann and J. M. Boyle. 1995. Victimization of persons by fraud. *Crime & Delinquency* 41(1): 54–72.

Titus, R. M. 2001. The victimology of fraud. Paper presented at the Restoration for Victims of Crime Conference in Melbourne, Australia.

Titus, R. M. and A. R. Gover. 2001. Personal fraud: The victims and the scams. In *Crime Prevention Studies: Special Issue on Repeat Victimization,* eds. R. Clarke, G. Farrell and K. Pease. Available online at: http://www.isrcl.org/Papers/titus.pdf.

Trahan, A., J. W. Marquart and J. M. Mullings. 2005. Fraud and the American Dream: Toward an understanding of fraud victimization. *Deviant Behavior* 26: 601–20.

U.S. Bureau of the Census. 2000. Government Printing Office.

U.S. House of Representatives. 2006. Waste, fraud and abuse in Hurricane Katrina contracts. Available online at: http://oversight.house.gov/documents/20060824110705-30132.pdf.

USAO/LAM. 2009. United States Attorney's Office, Middle District of Louisiana web site. District information published online at: www.usdoj.gov/usao/lam/about.html.

USAO/LAM. 2009a. United States Attorney's Office, Middle District of Louisiana web site. Press releases available online at: www.usdoj.gov/usao/lam/index.html.

USA Today. 2006. Hurricane Katrina statistics published online at: www.usatoday.com/weather/graphics/hurricane/hurricane2005/flash.htm.

USDOJ. 2002. First awards announced in 9/11 victim compensation fund. Department of Justice, August 22, 2002. Available online at: http://www.usdoj.gov/opa/pr/2002/August/02_civ_486.htm.

USDOJ. 2003. The September 11 victim compensation fund of 2001. Department of Justice Office of the Inspector General, October, 2003. Available online at: http://www.usdoj.gov/oig/reports/plus/a0401/final.pdf.

USDOJ. 2004. 9/11 victim compensation fund pays over $2.6 billion to date. Department of Justice, April 1, 2004. Available online at: http://www.usdoj.gov/opa/pr/2004/April/04_civ_207.htm.

USDOJ. 2007. Hurricane Katrina Fraud Task Force home page with links to the HKFTF Progress and Annual Reports available online at: www.usdoj.gov/katrina/Katrina_Fraud/.

Wright, B. R. E., A. Caspi, T. E. Moffitt and R. Paternoster. 2004. Does the perceived risk of punishment deter criminally prone individuals? Rational choice, self-control, and crime. *Journal of Research in Crime & Delinquency* 41(2): 180–213.

Zhou, D. 1997. *Disaster, Disorganization, and Crime.* University of Albany State University of New York PhD diss. Ann Arbor, MI: University Microfilms International.

Discussion Questions

1. What are some of the contexts in which the crime of fraud has been studied? Describe some of the research in these areas.
2. What are some of the theories of crime that have been used to explain fraud? What are some of the strengths and weaknesses of each of these theories?
3. Describe the process by which people could apply for and receive money from the Victim Compensation Fund (VCF) after the September 11 attacks. How many instances of fraud are known to have occurred against the VCF?
4. Describe the process by which people could apply for and receive money from the Federal Emergency Management Agency (FEMA) after Hurricane Katrina. How many instances of fraud are known to have occurred against FEMA?
5. What theory of crime can explain the difference in instances of fraud against the VCF and against FEMA? What are some potentially useful techniques to deter post-disaster fraudsters?

9

Changes in the Illegal Drug Market in New Orleans after Hurricane Katrina

By Patrick Walsh

Introduction

The metropolitan New Orleans area suffered a natural disaster unparalleled in the city's history with the landfall of Hurricane Katrina in August, 2005. The storm's impact resulted in the almost total evacuation of the city and the surrounding metropolitan area, involving approximately 1,000,000 people. Some New Orleans residents migrated to the four corners of the country (Los Angeles, Seattle, Boston and Miami), while approximately 250,000 moved just far enough west, 75 miles to Baton Rouge, to avoid the brunt of landfall (Thomas 2007, Bass 2008).

As a result of the damages and subsequent evacuation caused by Katrina, numerous changes were forced upon the government, citizenry, businesses, institutions, both formal and informal, and non-government organizations of the area, resulting in outcomes that often were neither expected nor desired. One informal institution that changed after the hurricane was that of the illegal drug markets. Illegal drug markets and New Orleans had been synonymous phrases for years in various mediums, including television news stories, print media, locally produced rap music and among area church officials, police and local citizens. Prior to the landfall of Hurricane Katrina, the New Orleans area had historically been challenged with numerous shootings and homicides related to its expansive illegal drug markets. In this chapter, I examine data from the year before the storm (2004) and the year after (2006). Both quantitative and qualitative findings indicate that the current metropolitan New Orleans illegal drug market has surpassed its pre-hurricane levels in terms of the amount of drugs seized in typical arrests, the amount of monies seized in those transactions, the adaptations of the business models and the socioeconomic characteristic of the people, both seller and purchaser, in the current marketplace. Information for this study was obtained from policing agencies, as well as the private sector.

Historical Perspective—Drugs, Crime and Criminal Justice Challenges

Extensive writings, both academic and journalistic, have been produced concerning the devastation wreaked upon the city of New Orleans. Much has been written on the crime related to Hurricane Katrina, including crime reported to have occurred in the days immediately after the storm, (Frailing and Harper 2007) and crime related to the diaspora (Bass 2008, Brezina and Kaufman 2008, Simon 2007). Other research (Berger 2007, Thornton and Voigt 2007, this volume) has been conducted on post-Katrina crime, focusing on the commonly accepted stages of disaster recovery (Briton 2007, Killian 2002, Neal 1997, Lystad 1995, Drabek 1986, National Governors Association 1979, Stoddard 1968, Powell, Rayner and Finesigner 1954, Powell, Rayner and Finesigner 1953, Powell 1954, Carr 1932).

Prior to Hurricane Katrina, New Orleans had been a city heavily impacted by crime and a reportedly dysfunctional criminal justice system that faced numerous internal and external challenges in the police department, district attorney's office and the criminal courts. Contrasted with the rapid assault on the city by Hurricane Katrina, New Orleans had been experiencing the "slow-motion disaster" (Draus 2009) of illegal drug usage and sales for years, if not decades. Policing efforts against the illegal drug market usually operationalized by the arrests of numerous persons for simple possession of narcotics necessitated responses from the district attorney's office and the criminal court system. Thusly, the majority of the city's available criminal justice budgetary resources were expended on non-felony charges often resulting in limited jail time for offenders. The Metropolitan Crime Commission (MCC, Inc.) reported "that only 3 percent or 1,977 of the 58,050 Orleans Parish arrests in 2007 have resulted in felony convictions, and less than 1 percent of the arrests resulted in a violent felony conviction" (2009: 1).

The city of New Orleans (Orleans Parish) has recorded over 200 homicides annually for the past 22 years, with the exceptions of 2008, with 179 murders, 2006 (the year following the diaspora caused by Hurricane Katrina) when 162 homicides were recorded and 1999, with 158 homicides. It has been anecdotally offered by law enforcement officials that the majority of crime in general and homicides specifically in New Orleans are related to the illegal drug markets, especially the distribution of crack cocaine (*USA Today* 2006). The Drug Policy Information Clearinghouse's New Orleans, LA Profile of Drug Indicators noted that "according to New Orleans homicide detectives, the number of murders believed to be motivated by illegal drugs, most notably crack cocaine and heroin, increased from 19 percent in 1998 to 37 percent in 2001" (Office of National Drug Control Policy (ONDCP) 2002).

For that same time period, the Orleans Parish Coroner's Office reported that of the homicides in 2001, "75 percent were drug related a decline from 83 percent in the first half of 2000" (NIDA 2001). Further, as noted by the National Drug Intelligence Center's Louisiana Drug Threat Assessment, "the New Orleans Police Department (NOPD) estimates that as many as 75 percent of homicides are drug-related" (NDIC 2002). This trend carried forward—the "Orleans Parish Coroner's Office reported 269 homicides in 2002, up from 215 in 2001 and 165 in 1999. Drug-related homicides increased to 80 percent in 2002, up from 50 percent in 2001" (NIDA 2003) and 75 percent of the city's 147 homicides from July 2004 to December 2004 were drug-related (NIDA 2005). This belief still holds true. After a two-day period in July 2007, when five persons were murdered, NOPD Deputy Police Superintendent Marlon Defillo noted that "many of the murders are driven either by the use of narcotics or the sale of narcotics, and as a result you start to have retributions and you start to have arguments" (WDSU 2007). All these data indicate that homicides and illegal drug distribution and use in New Orleans are closely related.

A limited overview of the pre-Hurricane Katrina New Orleans' illegal drug market is available from the National Institute of Justice's (NIJ) Arrestee Drug Abuse Monitoring (ADAM) program, which collected data from 2000 through 2003. Some of the relevant findings include: (1) New Orleans arrestees were highly likely (71 percent) to have positive drug tests at the time of their arrest and 37 percent were classified to be at risk of drug dependence (2) crack cocaine was the major hard drug used (by 40 percent of people), with the reported number of days of crack purchases in a month being 14 (3) marijuana usage was reported by 46 percent of the arrestees while heroin usage was reported by 15 percent of the arrestees and (4) the majority of illegal drug sales occurred at outdoor (street) locations.

Literature Review

As noted by Decker, Varano and Greene, "despite their rich theoretical and practical importance, criminologists have paid scant attention to the patterns of crime and the responses to crime during exceptional times" (2007: 89). The nexus of criminal activity during and after times of natural and manmade disasters has been documented in both academic literature and the mass media. In fact, it is a major focus of this volume and as such, the reader is encouraged to investigate the relevant chapters. However, limited research has been conducted on the impact of disasters on illegal drug markets, specifically as it relates to both the supply and usage. The September 11 World Trade Center attacks impacted the local illegal drug trade in three distinct ways, namely, street level (end-user) sales methods, availability and pricing. As reported by the ONDCP, policing challenges in the early days after the attacks led to more brazen open-air sales. One user commented that on "the day of the disaster, it was like a super-sale day." It was additionally reported that drug customers in parts of New York were seen lined up waiting to make purchases (ONDCP 2002a). Availability and pricing adaptations were also noted in New York after the attacks. The limited availability of quantities of desired drugs led to lesser amounts of narcotics being sold in "standard" packaging, resulting in a net price increase to the end-user. Additionally, to make up for limited quantities of available drugs, primarily cocaine and heroin, mid-level suppliers would "step on" their products, reducing their quality by mixing the drug with other, non-narcotic materials. It was surmised that the increased police surveillance of all varieties of traffic for terrorism prevention purposes impacted the flow of narcotics into the city. Similar availability, quality control and pricing issues were noted in other cities after the World Trade Center attacks, including Columbia, South Carolina, Denver, Colorado, Honolulu, Hawaii and Seattle, Washington (ONDCP 2002a). Two unintended consequences of law enforcement shifting to a more terrorism oriented paradigm were that street level violence related to drug distribution increased as police officers were redeployed to counterterrorism and homeland security operations from their usual patrol and narcotic units and that users unable to procure street narcotics for their addiction switched to abuse of prescription drugs or visited methadone clinics. The disruption in delivery of narcotics was generally resolved within several months as alternative delivery routes, including trains, buses, automobiles and human couriers, were developed.

New and Relapsed Users in the Post-Disaster Period

The emotional and psychological stress suffered by residents after a natural disaster has been well documented (Alexander 1990, Brooks and McKinlay 1992, Galea, Nandi and Vlahov 2005, Green and Lindy 1994, Kar 2006, Krug et al.. 1998, Krug et al.. 1999, Steefel 1993, Schuster et al. 2001, Williams 2002) and especially by Norris et al. (2002) in their meta-analysis of over 200 articles concerning over 60,000 individuals who had experienced 102 distinct disasters. Some research has even endorsed the acceptance of drug usage in post-disaster settings to assist victims of post traumatic stress disorder (PTSD). Johansen and Krebs (2009) have endorsed the administration of the MDMA, the pharmaceutical version of ecstasy, to traumatized disaster victims, specifically mentioning the victims of the London transportation attacks of July 7, 2005.

Prior research on manmade disasters and traumatic incidents, including incidents such as the 1979 Three Mile Island nuclear accident (Kasl, Chisholm and Eskenazi 1981), the 1987 sinking of the Herald of Free Enterprise ferry (Joseph et al. 1993, McKernan 2006), the 1988 Pan AM Flight 103 crash in Lockerbie, Scotland (Brooks and McKinlay 1992), the 1991 mass shooting at the Luby's restaurant in Killeen, Texas (North, Smith and Spitznagel 1997), the 1995 bombing of the Oklahoma City Alfred P. Murrah Federal Building (North et al. 1994, North, Nixon and Shariat 1999, Smith et al. 1999, Pfefferbaum and Doughty 2001, Pfefferbaum et al. 2002), the street violence in Northern Ireland (Loughrey et al. 1988), the 2001 World Trade Center attacks (Chemtob et al. 2009, DiMaggio, Galea and Guohoa 2009, Galea et al. 2002, Schuster et al. 2001, Factor et al. 2002, Weiss et al. 2002, Williams 2002, Vlahov et al. 2002, Vlahov et al. 2004, Deren et al. 2002, Boscarino et al. 2004, McKernan 2006) has yielded some contradictory results on substance abuse, but with the majority of the research indicating increases in post-disaster drug and alcohol abuse.

Similarly, research on natural disasters, including incidents such as the 1972 Buffalo Creek dam collapse (Gleser, Green and Wignet 1981, Green et al. 1992), the 1980 ash fall following the Mount Saint Helens eruption (Adams and Adams 1984), the 1989 landfall of Hurricane Hugo (McKernan 2006), the 1992 destruction by Hurricane Andrew (David et al. 1996, Norris et al. 1999), the 1995 Great Hanshin Earthquake in Japan (Shimizu et al. 2000), the March, 1998 sweep of F-3 and F-4 tornadoes in southern Minnesota (Schroeder and Polusny 2004), the 2003 Canberra, Australia bushfires (Parslow and Jorm 2006) and the 2003 Bam, Iran earthquakes (Movaghar et al. 2005) has yielded the same contradictory results on substance abuse with a similar bias towards increased usage.

According to the Substance Abuse and Mental Health Services Administration (SAMHSA) Disaster Technical Assistance Center, there are six mechanisms of increased substance abuse post disaster, namely: (1) some people in the general population increase substance abuse to cope with stress (2) some people near the border of substance abuse or dependence cross the line (3) some people in active addiction increase their use (4) some people in recovery experience relapse (5) some people experiencing PTSD or depressive symptoms increase use and (6) some people in other at-risk groups, such as first responders, increase their use (McKernan 2006: 10).

Labor Markets and Illegal Drug Usage

Prior research has confirmed the anecdotal belief that construction workers, including day laborers, use and abuse illegal narcotics primarily marijuana, cocaine and crystal methamphetamine. In the past few years, Australia has undergone an influx of young temporary workers and has noted a growing drug culture which has been identified among that group. Jill Rundle, director of the Australian Network of Alcohol and Other Drug Addictions, as well as Dave Noonan, National Secretary of the Construction, Forestry, Mining and Energy Union had both observed increases in narcotic use among this class. Rundle noted that, "just the increased amount of money impacts on people's capacity to buy drugs" (Australian Broadcasting Company 2008). SAMHSA's Office of Applied Sciences issued findings that indicated that certain occupational categories recorded higher than average illegal drug usage. Construction workers classified as "other" ranked highest at 17.3 percent, construction supervisors ranked second highest at 17.2 percent, followed by helpers and laborers, ranked fifth at 13.1 percent, janitors, ranked seventh at 13 percent and construction and other laborers at 12.8 percent (1996). A subsequent SAMHSA study found that 15.1 percent of construction workers were using illicit drugs, second to food service workers at 17.4 percent. The research also noted that substance abuse users had higher turnover rates, with 12.3 percent of substance-abusing full-time employees working for more than three employers in the past year, necessitating the need for more workers to be hired (2007).

The literature clearly indicates that several compounding effects of the hurricane, ranging from stress on victims to the influx of new persons to the metropolitan New Orleans area, among those newcomers construction workers laborers who are already prone to drug use, would result in at least the possibility of new customers to the drug market once the recovery of the area began.

Drug Markets in New Orleans Pre-Hurricane Katrina

As offered by Fitzgerald, "Drug markets are temporary and secondary in the sense that they only predominate because the conditions are not right for sustainable and legitimate markets to develop. Drug markets emerge from a social, economic, and political pathology" (2005: 564). The existence of the drug market was well known to the police and the community before the storm. Ray Nagin, mayor of New Orleans, in an interview shortly after the flooding of the city, voiced his concerns about the illegal drug markets in the context of the crime that was occurring in the city:

> And one of the things people … nobody's talked about this. Drugs flowed in and out of New Orleans and the surrounding metropolitan area so freely it was scary to me, and that's why we were having the escalation in murders. People don't want to talk about this, but I'm going to talk about it. You have drug addicts that are now walking around this city looking for a fix, and that's the reason why they were breaking in hospitals and drugstores. They're looking for something to take the edge off of their jones, if you will. And right now they don't have anything to take the edge off, and they've finally probably found guns. So what you see is drug-starving, crazy addicts, drug addicts, that are wreaking havoc. And we don't have the manpower to adequately deal with it. We can only target certain sections of the city, and form a perimeter around them, and hope to God that we're not overrun (WWL Radio 2005).

Contrary to the often seen gang model of drug distribution, the New Orleans market was more neighborhood centric, with sales territories being micro-geographically rooted. Violent disputes would erupt between small close-knitted groups, still generally contained within limited geographic areas. Anecdotally, it was reported that nationally organized gangs, such as the Bloods and the Crips failed in their attempts to encroach on the local drug market. The extremely splintered nature of the New Orleans drug market may explain the violence associated with distribution. The illegal drug market in New Orleans would be most identified with the "drug markets as effects of economic transition" model as offered by Fitzgerald (2005), Trocki (1999) and Keh (1996). This model offers a criminogenic underpinning, in contrast to that of a retreatist anomie market, rational market or driver of liberal market economics.

The structure of the illegal drug market post-Hurricane Katrina was impacted on multiple levels. Drug market participants were among the 80 percent of the population who fled the city as part of the mandatory evacuation in the hours before landfall, who relocated to the refuge of last resort, the Louisiana Superdome or who had to be rescued from rooftops and overpasses. Anecdotally it was reported that drug dealers were some of the last residents to leave; interviews conducted after the storm included reasons for the delay such as: "I knew the police were searching people going in the Dome or getting on buses," "People knew where I kept my stuff," "If I leave I may have to fight someone to get my spot back," and "I might get ahead by staying."

Methodology

Three distinct approaches were utilized in the study of illegal drug markets in New Orleans. A common challenge of illegal drug research has been the difficulty in constructing valid and reliable quantitative measures of the illegal drug market. While some research has utilized an index based on indirect proxies, such as drug arrests, drug related emergency room visits, drug deaths, arrestees testing positive for illegal drugs, mentions in newspapers and DEA drug busts (Baumer et al. 1998, Cork 1999, Grogger and Willis 2000, Ousey and Lee 2002, Ousey and Lee 2004, Fryer et al. 2005), other data sources were selected for this study, which were believed to be more indicative of changes in street-level drug distribution. Additionally, due to the operational challenges of the criminal justice system and other public sector institutions after the storm, e.g., hospitals, the coroner's office, treatment centers and mental health clinics, none could be assumed to be at maximum reporting efficiency.

The three-pronged research focus included interviews, police data and commercial sales and purchase records of retail merchandise associated with the usage of illegal narcotics. Similar to the ethnographic model used by Dunlap, Johnson and Morse (2007) interviews were conducted with persons involved in the New Orleans illegal drug market both before and after Hurricane Katrina. Available records of metropolitan New Orleans law enforcement agencies were reviewed for the amount of illegal drugs and cash seized in street level narcotic arrests. Narcotic seizures through interdiction efforts were not included in the analysis, as street level sales were the focus of the research. Lastly, commercial records, obtained through personal interviews and wholesaler and industry reports, as well as individual retailer purchase records were reviewed for the sales of three distinct items: blunts, crystal stemmed roses and metal tire gauges. All three items are often associated with the usage of marijuana and crack cocaine.

The research at hand therefore focused on several aspects of the street-level drug market, namely, the amount of cash being held by dealers, the amount of drugs being held by dealers and the amount of verifiable legitimate market goods that could be associated with the usage of certain illegal drugs. These quantifications were then compared and contrasted with anecdotal information gleaned from ethnographic interviews. As the central findings of the ethnographic interviews were generally consistent, for continuity purposes the comments of one interviewee (DD1) will be utilized in this chapter.

As noted by Booth (1999), researchers often face multiple methodological challenges when working with transient, hard-to-reach populations. These populations are often "invisible" and hidden from contact with researchers on any given day. Illegal drug markets have historically been disproportionately focused in areas of marginalized groups, often involving socioeconomically challenged persons and minority communities. Sampling methodologies need to accept that these populations may be geographically clustered in non-traditional residential settings (e.g., official homeless shelters, non-official homeless gathering points, street locations with no permanent or physical identification, vacant housing units and various short-stay places of accommodation). I believe employing mixed methodologies will overcome these challenges, increase the accuracy of my results and thereby increase their validity and value.

Results

My research focused on specific adaptations to the illegal drug market due to the impact of Hurricane Katrina, new dealers and distributors, upward mobility of established dealers and new customers (including both those new to drug usage in general and those previously purchasing from others) and how those adaptations impacted the daily operation of street-level drug sales.

Drug Distribution and Retail Markets

As noted earlier, I will utilize one ethnographic interviewee (DD1) as the representative voice of the total interviewed body. Interviewee DD1 primarily sold heroin but would handle other drugs as opportunities arose. He comes from a family of twelve siblings, four of whom have died due to their involvement with drugs. DD1 has a criminal history dating back to when he was ten years old, assisting one of his now deceased brothers with armed robberies. He offered that he and his brothers began to sell drugs strictly for monetary purposes. Their mother was only able to afford housing for the family in a two bedroom apartment in one of the city's housing projects and other kids laughed at the knock-off shoes and clothes he and his siblings wore.

The ethnographic interviews revealed a quasi-stable drug market in the New Orleans area before the storm. DD1 offered that the prior to the storm, crack cocaine and heroin were the primary drugs of the street level trade, with relatively stable packaging and pricing. Cocaine, primarily in the form of crack rocks, sold for $10 to $20, and heroin "foils" (approx. 0.1 grams of heroin) sold for $20 to $25. The club scene was more focused on alcohol, prescription drugs and the combination of the two. User participants in the market knew of probable sales locations and exhibited a qualified sense of loyalty. Similarly, seller participants had generally dedicated supply channels. Violence was primarily related to the lower level, in terms of purchase dollars per transaction, drug sales and robberies committed against and between dealers and users.

Mid-level dealer drug pricing, especially for cocaine, was relatively stable with an ounce of cocaine being purchased for $650–$900 and transportation fees, primarily from Houston, were assessed at a $1,000 per kilogram (just over 35 ounces). Purity was generally consistent throughout the area and users had little difficulty in finding either open-air or interior markets. Both long- and short-term relationships existed between participants throughout the transaction continuum. If a purchaser needed a supply of drugs and could not locate his or her standard supply sources, other intermediaries would offer to buy from their sources (with the seller's money) but would charge a tax or a fee for the service.

In the four years since the storm, DD1 stated that almost 50 percent of the people he was acquainted with in the distribution side of the illegal drug market are dead, 30 percent are in jail and 20 percent are still in the distribution market. He acknowledged that in the early days and weeks after the storm, prices rose rapidly as limited supplies were available. However, once the flow of people back into the city started, the availability issue resolved itself. He noted that some evacuees secured temporary new supply sources from their time spent in Houston and Atlanta. These new supply sources essentially removed one level of price increases from the wholesale price to the ultimate retail price. The removal of one pricing tier, especially if it meant the dealer could purchase their supply outright could increase the dealer's profit and status, moving them from an "hourly position" into lower management (Levitt and Venkatesh 1998). As reported by Caulkins et al., "Entrepreneurs who own the drugs they sell retain the largest share (about 50 percent). Independent consignment sellers retain less (about 25 percent). Consignment sellers who operate within fixed selling locations or "spots" retain still less (10 percent), and the sellers who were paid hourly to sell from spots retained the smallest proportion (3 percent)" (1998: 1). According to local policing sources those percentages, while somewhat dated, are relatively accurate in the metropolitan illegal drug market.

For the average purchases made by a mid- to small-level dealer, two and one half ounces of cocaine, the pre-Katrina price was $1,250 and during the first few weeks after the storm, the prices were stabilized at $1,475. Transportation and taxing charges would also apply. After the storm, some mid-level dealers became more chemically knowledgeable and also began to use inositol powder, which is available at vitamin retailers, to cut the product, reducing the purity while appearing to be of the appropriate size for the purchase price. This cutting process would produce further profits for the dealer, easing some of the price increase from the supply chain.

Lower level dealers would then generally retail the cocaine in quantities of 3.5 grams, being approximately one-eighth of an ounce, leading to the street term "eight ball." While street level pricing remained relatively consistent, the quality of the drug came into play. For small- to lower-level dealers to make their anticipated profits, cocaine would be water-whipped or soda-whipped, which is preparing the crack with more baking soda to add more air bubbles to the final product. This creates more rock size without having to include an equivalent amount of cocaine. The product would then be less effective than in the past. While the price remained constant, more quantity would need to be purchased for the desired effect.

DD1 reported that some new dealers entered the street level sales market after the storm. He offered that several types of new dealers appeared, namely: (1) former dealers who were forced to relocate within the city due to the dearth of residents/potential customers in the area they previously lived and sold in (2) new local dealers, mostly lower level user-dealers before the storm, who were local residents and entered the drug trade due to the influx of cash they acquired after the storm and (3) dealers new to the city who attempted to supplant former dealers from their dedicated sales location.

As expected by both the participants in the illegal drug trade and policing authorities, an increase in drug-related violence was observed. According to DD1, dealers returned to the city and their primary method of income sooner than did the majority of their customers, leading to an increased number of distributors having a smaller number of customers to sell to. DD1 offered that a potential customer who before the storm would travel three to five blocks to his source would pass up several other dealers before reaching his prior primary source. As entire sections of the city were still generally uninhabitable, including the now infamous Lower Ninth Ward, New Orleans East and other outlying sections, Central City, previously known for its violence, became the primary selling area, as it had not flooded. Between attrition by dealer-on-dealer assaults, the steady return of former customers and the influx of new customers, the violence stabilized to pre-Hurricane Katrina levels within a few months of the city being repopulated. Some established dealers retained their sales territory but improved their business operation as they had established wholesale contacts when temporarily displaced to other metropolitan areas, principally Houston and Atlanta.

New Customers

The demographics of customers changed after the storm as well, with four groups adding to the pre-Katrina base of customers already involved in the illegal drug market. These new groups included an influx of transient workers, volunteers and other wanting to assist in the recovery efforts, a criminal element moving into the area in order to take advantage of reduced policing capabilities and prior residents who began to use illegal drugs due to the stress of the storm, including relapsed users who returned to illegal drug usage after the storm. In the following section, I will focus on two types of new customers, namely, transient workers and relapsed users, in the reemergence of the New Orleans illegal drug market.

Influx of Transient Workers

While much of the research concerning New Orleans and Hurricane Katrina focused on the evacuation phase, either in the days before or after landfall, this study is also concerned with the recovery phase, specifically the influx of transient workers, needed for the massive cleaning and rebuilding efforts. Due to the massive destruction and damage caused by the winds and waters of the storm, it was clear that an unprecedented number of both skilled and unskilled workers would be needed in the area. A vast spectrum of workers sought employment in the metropolitan New Orleans area, from crews to gut houses and empty out formerly refrigerated warehouses to skilled trades people, i.e., electricians, sheetrock installers and carpenters. The population shift in New Orleans was quite dramatic, with migrant construction crews arriving in New Orleans within five days after Hurricane Katrina had passed. As noted by Margie McHugh, co-director of immigration policy at the Migration Policy Institute, "There's no place in the world like New Orleans in terms of how rapid the population change has been" (Gonzales 2008).

As noted earlier, there is both anecdotal and quantitative evidence linking persons involved in the construction trades with substance abuse. The influx of construction trade recovery workers was never officially quantified, especially concerning the number of migrant, undocumented workers. The number of undocumented workers who moved to the New Orleans metropolitan area has been estimated by various sources, including the NOPD, charitable organizations and governmental bodies, as ranging between 30,000 and 100,000. A study undertaken to measure HIV/STI risk behaviors by Latino migrant workers in New Orleans reported that in anonymous structured interviews "the majority drank alcohol in the past week (75.5 percent), and of those, 68.7 percent engaged in binge drinking. A lower percentage used marijuana (16.6 percent) and cocaine (5.5 percent) at least once in the prior week" (Kissinger et al. 2008).

Relapsed Customers

According to Calderon-Abbo, "It is not surprising that after Katrina there was an increased demand for mental health services in New Orleans. In January, 2007, the Substance Abuse and Mental Health Services Administration estimated that 25 to 30 percent of individuals in the affected area would have significant needs for mental health care and another 10 to 20 percent would have subclinical conditions that nevertheless would require care" (2008: 5).

The Louisiana area not only suffered the presumably stress-induced increase in substance abuse by new and former users, but the storm also effectively destroyed or shuttered numerous treatment facilities for substance abuse. According to McKernan (2006), all seven New Orleans opioid treatment centers were destroyed, along with 19 outpatient programs and 25 prevention programs. It was estimated that over one third of all treatment capacity was destroyed. Mental health services offered by the city government were still reported to be lacking and deficient in post-Katrina New Orleans in 2009 (GAO 2009, Hudson 2009). The challenge of the government in maintaining and supplying drug rehabilitation services, as well as other mental health services, combined with anecdotal reports of increased numbers of drug users supports the notion that more first-time and recently relapsed drug market customers had added to the ranks of previously existing customers.

The Effect on Daily Drug Operations

To measure the effect of the possible increase in customers and temporary decrease in dealer participants, this research attempts to quantify changes in daily drug distribution operations. The operational challenges of local law enforcement were evident after the storm as manpower deficiencies necessitated the redeployment of specialized narcotic unit officers to street patrol. It would be assumed that such a refocusing of policing efforts would produce two consequences, first a decrease in drug arrests accompanied by a corresponding decrease in the amount of illegal narcotics seized by local law enforcement and second, an increase in seizures by federal or state agencies.

The expected increase in federal seizures was noted. In ten months in 2006, the Drug Enforcement Agency (DEA) had confiscated over 2,600 pounds of cocaine, a 92 percent increase over the previous year and over 2,400 pounds of marijuana, a 406 percent increase over 2005. These increases in seizures involved the post-Katrina New Orleans population, estimated to be about half of the city's pre-Katrina population. By way of example, one DEA seizure involved 110 pounds of cocaine, 3,500 tablets of MDMA, five pounds of marijuana and weapons and cash, all of which was destined for New Orleans. The material was routed through Slidell, Louisiana from Houston, Texas. The seizure was the largest in New Orleans since Hurricane Katrina and the largest seizure ever in St. Tammany Parish, a suburb of New Orleans.

Review of official data and interviews with greater New Orleans metropolitan area policing authorities, including individual narcotic unit detectives revealed the following: (1) a net increase of 28 percent in street level drug arrests occurred in 2006 as compared to 2004, with an increase in adult arrests and a decrease in juvenile arrests (2) there was an increase in the cumulative amount of drugs seized from 2004 to 2006. There was a 236 percent increase in cannabis seizures, a 105 percent increase in heroin seizures, a 96 percent increase in cocaine seizures and a 17 percent increase in MDMA seizures and (3) a 176 percent increase in cash seizures, the money taken from drug distribution arrestees, from 2004 to 2006. Additionally, police officers revealed that suspects who in the past had been arrested with $50 to $100 now had $250 to $500 on their person at the time of arrest.

While some would argue the root cause of the increase in seizures was an increased effectiveness of local policing, I would proffer that it indicates an increased flow of illegal drugs into the area. The previously mentioned DEA drug seizure in Slidell, the largest ever in that community, involved evacuated New Orleans residents who had made drug contacts with suppliers in Houston. In contrast, numerous print and media articles belabored the manpower, morale and equipment challenges facing policing agencies after Katrina. In 2006, the New Orleans Police Department stated that their sworn manpower was currently 18 percent lower than pre-Katrina levels, down from 1,700 to 1,400. Additionally, the 1,400 includes officers unable to report to duty due to sick leave, vacations or administrative suspensions, reducing the numbers of officers on the street even further (Drew 2006). The effectiveness of those available police officers was further negatively impacted by the loss of equipment and specialized functions, i.e., the crime lab, patrol vehicles, SWAT entry shields, et cetera, all ruined by the flood waters (Sullivan 2006). National Guard troops were present but were assigned to patrol functions mostly in still-deserted sections of the city.

The final data source employed in this study is a review of the sales of three items that could legally be purchased in the greater New Orleans area but which are associated with the use of illegal drugs. These three items are blunts, crystal stemmed roses and metal tire gauges.

Blunts

The first data source of this type was sales records for blunts, a type of cigar. Blunts are named for their blunted tip and are easily identified by their small diameter. They are wider than a cigarillo but narrower than a corona. Blunts are often referred to as Phillies because they were originally manufactured in Philadelphia, but they are sold under multiple brand names, including Dutch Master, White Owl, El Producto, Swisher Sweets and Optimo.

Blunts are readily available at most convenience stores, corner grocery stores and gas stations. It has become widely known that many purchasers buy blunts to use in the smoking of marijuana. The tobacco product within the blunt is removed and replaced with marijuana. Anecdotal interviews with convenience store employees revealed that many, if not most, of the purchasers remove the tobacco product from the blunt before leaving the parking lot. The popularity of blunts has lead to the increase in the number of flavors, now including banana, berry, cognac, honey, mango, peach, pina colada, tequila and watermelon. While larger packs, including 5 packs, 10 packs and 50 pack "barrels" can be purchased, the typical sale, anecdotally estimated at 90 percent of total sales, is a single blunt. Flavored wraps, basically blunts that have already had the tobacco product removed, are also available to consumers.

As blunts are generally regarded as a legal delivery system for illegal drugs, their rate of sales can be used as a proxy for evidence of a change in illegal drug sales, primarily marijuana. In the years before Hurricane Katrina, industry publications and retailer purchase records indicated annual sales trends of four percent increases to three percent decreases. After controlling for the first several months subsequent to the storm and the diaspora it caused, annual sales of blunts, including flavored wraps, increased over 200 percent from 2004 to 2006. When further controlling for single blunt sales, generally costing from $1 to $1.25, the sales increase was over 300 percent. Retailers began to not only increase the amount of their general stock but began to carry multiple flavors to satisfy customer demand. The reduced number of stores was additionally controlled for, meaning that the sales increase was a true indication of more blunts being purchased, not just the same amount of blunts being sold from fewer locations.

Crystal Stemmed Roses

Commonly available in convenience stores and liquor stores, crystal stemmed roses, also known as rose tubes, are four-inch long glass tubes the width of a ballpoint pen, with a fake rose bud enclosed and capped off by cork on each end. They are presented as a novelty impulse purchase. Many customers who purchase the rose easily transform it into a crack pipe, a device designed to facilitate the smoking of a crack rock. Combined with a piece of brillo pad, which is employed as a screen at one end of the tube to hold the crack rock in place (as offered by one interviewee, "Ain't nothing ruins a crack smoke worse than getting a hot rock in your mouth") and any type of narrow push rod, the glass tube is available for use as a crack pipe and is referred to a "Chore Boy." The apparatus is generally legal to sell in many states, as long as the tube, brillo pad and push rod are not packaged together as a set or as long as the customer does not request a crack tube rather than a rose stem or rose tube. Some independent retailers continue to sell these sets even though have been determined to be illegal. Anecdotal interviews with some owners revealed two primary reasons for their actions, namely satisfying customer demand so the customer will purchase other items and enjoying the higher profit margin from sets, especially in stores that focus on "dollar customers," those seeking discount beer in single cans, off brand soft drinks, candy and cigarettes. For stores that do retail sets, they are usually kept below a sales counter and require a specific request to get one. They are usually sold for $5–$8.

Due to the more questionable intent of the crystal rose stems, I was unable to obtain the detailed sales record needed to complete this analysis. Some retailers would not disclose sales information for proprietary reasons and wholesaler records were not completely reliable as some retailers used secondary markets to purchase their supplies. Blunts, in contrast, are a regulated tobacco product and records are maintained according to state guidelines. Moreover, because some stores sold their rose tubes as illegal sets, they did not quantify their sales for legal reasons. However, through interviews with some national retail convenience store chains and some locally operated convenience stores, it appears that crystal tube sales have increased dramatically post-Hurricane Katrina, with some vendors noting that their sales have "more than doubled."

Metal Tire Gauges

Due to enhanced prosecution for the possession of drug paraphernalia—local judges were administering sentences of one to three years for possession of crack pipes, defined informally as devices which have no purpose other than the smoking of crack—many users had desisted from using readily identifiable crack pipes and began to employ items that would not be as readily identifiable. One such device was metal tire gauges, which upon removing the plastic stem and rinsing out the lubricating oil, functioned well as a crack rock delivery system. It was assumed that an increase in the sales of metal tire gauges could serve as a proxy for an indicator of increased crack usage.

Through the review of available wholesaler and retailer records, I was able to ascertain that from 2004 to 2006, there was a marked (58 percent) decrease in the sale of metal tire gauges. In further researching this unexpected sales decrease, it was discovered that it was due to the fact that most convenience stores and gas stations had stopped retailing the metal tire gauges because of the high incidences of theft of the item. Anecdotal interviews revealed that stores were purchasing large amounts of the items in early 2006 but limited, if any, sales of the item were being recorded through their point-of-sale (POS) registers, which automatically tracks sales of items by the universal pricing code (UPC). The majority of retailers began to offer a plastic-bodied tire gauge, which while functioning as well as the metal tire gauges for their intended purpose, could not function as a crack rock delivery system, as the plastic body would melt before the crack rock would be sufficiently heated.

Conclusion

The information obtained in this research indicates that the illegal drug markets in New Orleans expanded and reorganized, rather than disappeared, in New Orleans after Hurricane Katrina. While it would be generally assumed that an event of the magnitude of the evacuation caused by Katrina would be a crippling blow to the illegal drug markets, three data sources, namely, interviews, official records and merchant data, revealed that the storm actually produced better supply sources, lessened police attention and increased customer demand by returning customers, new customers and relapsed customers.

The pre-Katrina extent of the illegal drug market in New Orleans was evidenced in both the ADAM data of 2002 and 2003, as well as the number of drug arrests and drug-related homicides occurring in the city over the prior decade. The post-Katrina illegal drug market is evidenced by the amount of illegal drugs being seized, the marked increases in the paraphernalia retail market and drug-related homicides. In light of the fact that for months after the evacuation there were neither consistent supply lines, nor dealers nor customers, it is remarkable that the illegal drug market has recovered and grown they way it has. The population base, a number of private businesses and many government functions have yet to return to pre-Katrina strengths, even though many groups and organizations have received cash infusions from private charitable donations, insurance proceeds and federal programs and grants.

The illegal drug market has exhibited a resilience that few expected and offers policy implications for future events. While the reduction of crime in the first few months may have lulled the public in general, and law enforcement specifically, into believing that the evacuation rid the city of its crime problem, that belief was short-lived and short-sighted.

References

Adams, P. and G. Adams. 1984. Mount Saint Helens' ashfall: Evidence for a disaster stress reaction. *American Psychologist* 39: 252–60.

Alexander, D. 1990. Psychological intervention for victims and helpers after disasters. *British Journal of General Principle* 40: 345–48.

Australian Broadcasting Company. 2008. Drug use among construction workers rising: Union. Available online at: http://www.abc.net.au/news/stories/2008/04/03/2206890.htm.

Bass, L. 2008. A pooled-time series analysis of Hurricane Katrina evacuees and their effects on crime. Abstract available online at: http://www.mpsanet.org/Portals/0/mpsa-prog08.pdf.

Baumer, E., L. Lauritsen, R. Rosenfield and R. Wright. 1998. The influence of crack cocaine on robbery, burglary and homicide rates: A cross-city, longitudinal analysis. *Journal of Research in Crime and Delinquency* 33: 316–40.

Berger, D. 2007. Constructing crime, framing disaster: Hurricane Katrina, mass incarceration, and the crisis of journalistic authority. Paper presented at the annual meeting of the NCA Annual Convention, Chicago, IL. Available online at: http://www.allacademic.com/meta/p192592_index.html.

Booth, S. 1999. Researching health and homelessness: Methodological challenges for researchers working with a vulnerable, hard to reach, transient population. *Australian Journal of Primary Health* 5(3): 76–81.

Boscarino, J., Galea, S., Adams, R., Ahern, J., Resnick, H. and D. Vlahov. 2004. Mental health services and medication use in New York City after the September 11, 2001 Terrorist Attacks. *Psychiatric Services.*55: 274–83.

Brezina, T. and J. Kaufman. 2008. What really happened in New Orleans? Estimating the threat of violence during the Hurricane Katrina disaster. *Justice Quarterly* 25(4): 701–22.

Briton, N. 2007. Disaster in the South Pacific: Impact of the Tropical Cyclone Nomu on the Solomon Islands. *Disasters* 11(2): 120–33.

Brooks, N. and W. McKinlay. 1992. Mental health consequences of the Lockerbie Disaster. *Journal of Traumatic Stress* 5: 267–82.

Calderon-Abbo, J. 2008. The long road home: Rebuilding public inpatient psychiatric services in post-Katrina New Orleans. *Psychiatric Services* 59: 304–09.

Carr, L. 1932. Disaster and the sequence-pattern of social change. *American Journal of Sociology* 38(2): 207–18.

Caulkins, J. P., B. Johnson, A. Taylor and L. Taylor. 1998. What drug dealers tell us about their costs of doing business. Heinz Works paper 43. Available online at: http://repository.cmu.edu/heinzworks/43

Chemtob, C., Nomura, Y., Josephson, L., Adams, R. and L. Seder. 2009. Substance use and functional impairment among adolescents directly exposed to the 2001 World Trade Center Attacks. *Disaster* 33: 337–52.

Cork, Daniel. 1999. Examining space-time interaction in city-level homicide data: Crack markets and the diffusion of guns among youth. *Journal of Quantitative Criminology* 15: 379–406.

David, D., T. Mellman, L. Mendoza, R. Kulick-Bell, G. Ironson and N. Schneiderman, N. 1996. Psychiatric morbidity following Hurricane Andrew. *Journal of Traumatic Stress* 9: 607–12.

Decker, S., S. Varano and J. Greene. 2007. Routine crime in exceptional times: The impact of the 2002 Winter Olympics on citizen demand for police services. *Journal of Criminal Justice* 35: 89–101.

Deren, S., M. Shedlin, T. Hamilton and H. Hagan. 2002. Impact of the September 11th attacks in the city of New York on drug users: A preliminary assessment. *Journal of Urban Health* 79(3): 409–12.

DiMaggio, C., Galea, S. and L. Guohoa. 2009. Substance use and abuse in the aftermath of terrorism. A Bayesian meta-analysis. *Addiction* 104(6): 894–904.

Drabek, T. 1986. *Human System Responses to Disaster*. New York: Springer-Verlag.

Draus, P. 2009. Substance abuse and slow-motion disasters: The case of Detroit. *Sociological Quarterly* 50(2): 360–82.

Drew, C. 2006. Police struggles in New Orleans raise old fears. *The New York Times*, June 13.

Dunlap, E., B. Johnson and E. Morse. 2007. Illicit drug markets among New Orleans evacuees before and soon after Hurricane Katrina. *Journal of Drug Issues* 37(4): 981–1096.

Factor, S., Y. Wu, J. Monserrate, Y. Cuevas, S. Del Vecchio and D. Vlahov. 2002. Drug use frequency among street-recruited heroin and cocaine users in Harlem and the Bronx before and after September 11, 2001. *Journal of Urban Health* 79(3): 404–08.

Fitzgerald, J. 2005. Illegal drug markets in transitional economies. *Addiction Research and Theory* 13(6): 563–77.

Frailing, K. and D. H. Harper. 2007. Crime and hurricanes in New Orleans. In *The Sociology of Katrina: Perspectives on a Modern Catastrophe*, eds. D. L. Brunsma, D. Overfelt and J. S. Picou, Lanham, MD: Rowman and Littlefield: 51–68.

Fryer, R., P. Heaton, S. Levitt and K. Murphy. 2005. Measuring the impact of crack cocaine. NBER Working Paper No. W11318. Cambridge, MA: National Bureau of Economic Research.

Galea, S., Ahern, J., Resnick, H., Kilpatrick, D., Bucuvalas, M., Gold, J. and D. Vlahov, 2002. Psychological sequelae of the September 11 terrorist attacks in New York City. *New England Journal of Medicine* 346(13): 982–87.

Galea, S., Nandi, A. and D. Vlahov. 2005. The Epidemiology of Post-Traumatic Stress Disorder after Disasters. *Epidemiologic Reviews* 2005 27(1): 78–91.

Gleser, G., Green, B. and C. Wignet. 1981. *Prolonged psychosocial effects of disaster: Buffalo Creek*. San Diego: Academic Press.

Gonzales, J. 2008. Immigrants reshape post-disaster New Orleans: For New Orleans immigrants, pathway to American dream winds through a troubled city. *Associated Press*, December 23. Available online at: http://abcnews.go.com/US/wireStory?id=6518874.

Government Accounting Office (GAO). 2009. Hurricane Katrina: Barriers to mental health services for children persist in greater New Orleans, although federal grants are helping to address them. Statement of Cynthia A. Bascetta, Director Health Care. Testimony before the Ad Hoc Subcommittee on Disaster Recovery, Committee on Homeland Security and Governmental Affairs, U.S. Senate.

Green, B., J. Lindy, M. Grace and A. Leonard. 1992. Chronic posttraumatic stress disorder and diagnostic comorbidity in a disaster sample. *Journal of Nervous and Mental Disease* 180: 760–66.

Green, B. and J. Lindy. 1994. Posttraumatic stress disorder in victims of disasters. *Psychiatric Clinics of North America*17: 301–09.

Grogger, J. and M. Willis. 2000. The emergence of crack cocaine and the rise in urban crime rates. *Review of Economics and Statistics* 82: 519–29.

Hudson, A. 2009. Mental illness tidal wave swamps New Orleans. *The Washington Times*, August 4. Available online at: http://www.washingtontimes.com/news/2009/aug/04/mental-illness-tidal-wave/.

Johansen, P. and J. Krebs. 2009. How could MDMA (Ecstasy) help anxiety disorders? A neurological rationale. *Journal of Psychopharmacology*. 23(4): 389–91.

Joseph, S., W. Yule, R. Williams and P. Hodgkinson. 1993. Increased substance abuse in survivors of the Herald of Free Enterprise disaster. *British Journal of Medical Psychology*. 66: 185–91.

Kar, N. 2006. Psychosocial issues following a natural disaster in a developing country: A qualitative longitudinal observational study. *International Journal of Disaster Medicine* 4: 169–76.

Kasl, S., R. Chisholm and B. Eskenazi. 1981. The impact of the accident at Three Mile Island on the behavior and well-being of nuclear workers. *American Journal of Public Health* 71: 472–95.

Keh, D. 1996. Drug money in a changing world: Economic reform and criminal finance. United Nations Office for Drugs and Crime (UNODC).

Killian, L. 2002. An introduction to methodological problems of field studies in disasters. In *Methods of Disaster Research*, ed. R. Stallings, Philadelphia, PA: Xlibris Corporation, 49–93.

Kissinger, P. et al.. 2008. HIV/STI risk behaviors among Latino migrant workers in New Orleans post-Hurricane Katrina disaster. *Sexually Transmitted Diseases* 35(11): 924–29.

Krug, E. et al.. 1998. Suicide after natural disasters. *New England Journal of Medicine* 338(6): 373–78.

Krug, E. et al.. 1999. Retraction: Suicide after natural disasters. *New England Journal of Medicine* 340(2): 148.

Levitt, S. and S. Venkatesh. 1998. An economic analysis of a drug-selling gang's finances. NBER Working Paper No. W6592. Cambridge, MA: National Bureau of Economic Research.

Loughrey, G., P. Bell, M. Kee, R. Roddy and P. Curran. 1988. Posttraumatic stress disorder and civil violence in Northern Ireland. *British Journal of Psychiatry* 153: 554–60.

Lystad, M. 1995. Phases of disasters: The Missouri model. Rockville, MD: Center for Mental Health Services, U.S. Department of Health and Human Resources.

McKernan, B. 2006. Lessons learned from the 2005 Hurricane Katrina response. Substance and Abuse Mental Health Services Administration, U.S. Department of Health and Human Services.

Metropolitan Crime Commission, Inc. 2009. Orleans Parish criminal justice system accountability report Spring, 2009. Available online at: http://www.metropolitancrimecommis-sion.org/documents/NOCJSOversightProjectSpring2009Report.pdf.

Movaghar, A., R. Goodarzi, E. Izadian, M. Mohammadi, M. Hosseini and M. Vazirian. 2005. The impact of Bam Earthquake on substance users in the first 2 weeks: A rapid assessment. *Journal of Urban Health* 82(3): 370–77.

NDIC. 2002. Louisiana drug threat assessment. National Drug Intelligence Center, U.S. Department of Justice.

NIDA. 2001. Epidemiologic trends in drug abuse. Volume II: Proceedings of the community epidemiology work group. National Institute on Drug Abuse. Available online at: http://drugabuse.gov/PDF/CEWG/CEWG1201.pdf.

NIDA. 2003. Epidemiologic trends in drug abuse. Volume II: Proceedings of the community epidemiology work group. National Institute on Drug Abuse. Available online at: http://drugabuse.gov/PDF/CEWG/Vol2_603.pdf.

NIDA. 2005. Epidemiologic trends in drug abuse. Volume II: Proceedings of the community epidemiology work group. National Institute on Drug Abuse. Available online at: http://drugabuse.gov/PDF/CEWG/Vol2_105.pdf.

National Governors Association. 1979. Emergency preparedness project final report. Washington, D.C.: Government Printing Office.

Neal, D. 1997. Reconsidering the phases of disasters. *International Journal of Mass Emergencies and Disasters* 15(2): 239–64.

Norris, F., J. Perilla, J. Riad, K. Kaniasty and E. Lavizzo, E. 1999. Stability and change in stress, resources and psychological distress following natural disaster: Findings from Hurricane Andrew. *Anxiety, Stress, and Coping* 12: 363–96.

Norris, F., C. Byrne, E. Diaz and K. Kaniasty. 2002. 50,000 disaster victims speak: An empirical review of the empirical literature, 1981–2001. Unpublished technical report, National Center for PTSD. Hanover, NH: Dartmouth Medical School.

North, C., Smith, E and E. Spitznagel. 1994. Posttraumatic stress disorders in survivors of a mass shooting. *American Journal of Psychiatry.* 151: 82–88.

North, C., E. Smith and E. Spitznagel. 1997. One-year follow-up of survivors of a mass shooting. *American Journal of Psychiatry* 154(12): 1696–1702.

North, C., Nixon, S., Shariat, S., Mallonee, S., McMillen, C., Spitznagel, E. and E. Smith , 1999. Psychiatric disorders among survivors of the Oklahoma City bombing. *JAMA: Journal of the American Medical Association,* 282(8): 755–62.

Office of National Drug Control Policy. 2002. New Orleans, Louisiana profile of drug indicators. Rockville, MD: The Drug Policy Information Clearinghouse.

Office of National Drug Control Policy. 2002a. Pulse check: Trends in drug abuse, April 2002, Special topic: The impact of September 11. Available online at: http://www.ncjrs.gov/ondcppubs/publications/drugfact/pulse-chk/impact_of_sept11.pdf.

Ousey, G. and M. Lee. 2002. Examining the conditional nature of the illicit drug market-homicide relationship: A partial test of the theory of contingent causation. *Criminology* 40: 73–102.

Ousey, G. and M. Lee. 2004. Investigating the connections between race, illicit drug markets and lethal violence, 1984–1997. *Journal of Research in Crime and Delinquency* 41: 352–83.

Parslow, R. and A. Jorm. 2006. Tobacco use after experiencing a natural disaster: Analysis of a longitudinal study of 2,063 young adults. *Addiction* 101(7): 1044–1050.

Pfefferbaum, B. and D. Doughty. 2001. Increased alcohol use in a sample of Oklahoma City bombing victims. *Psychiatry* 64: 296–303.

Pfefferbaum, B., S. Vinckar, R. Trautman, S. Lensgraf, C. Reddy, N. Patel and A. Ford. 2002. The effect of loss and trauma on substance abuse behavior in individuals seeking support services after the 1995 Oklahoma City bombing. *Annals of Clinical Psychiatry* 14(2): 89–95.

Powell, J. 1954. Gaps and goals in disaster research. *Journal of Social Issues* 10(3): 26–41.

Powell, J., J. Rayner and J. Finesinger. 1953. Responses to disaster in American cultural groups. Paper presented at the Symposium on Stress, Army Medical Graduate School, Washington, D.C.

Powell, J., J. Rayner and J. Finesinger. 1954. An introduction to the natural history of disaster. Final contract report. Disaster Research Project, The Psychiatric Institute of the University of Maryland.

SAMHSA. 1996. Drug use among U.S. workers: Prevalence and trends by occupation and industry. Available online at: http://www.oas.samhsa.gov/work1996/toc.htm.

SAMHSA. 2007. Worker substance use, by industry category: The NSDUH report. Available online at: http://www.oas.samhsa.gov/2k7/industry/worker.htm.

Schroeder, J. and M. Polusny. 2004. Risk factors for adolescent alcohol use following a natural disaster. *Pre-hospital and Disaster Medicine* 19(1): 122–27.

Schuster, M., B. Stein, L. Jaycox, R. Collins, G. Marshall, M. Elliott, A. Zhou, A. Morrison and S. Berry. 2001. A national survey of stress reactions after the September 11, 2001 terrorist attacks. *New England Journal of Medicine* 347: 1507–1512.

Shimizu, S., K. Aso, T. Noda, S. Ryukie, Y. Kochi and N. Yamamto. 2000. Natural disasters and alcohol consumption in a cultural context: the Great Hanshin Earthquake in Japan. *Addiction.* 95: 529–36.

Simon, J. 2007. Wake of the flood: Crime, disaster, and the American risk imaginary after Katrina. Catastrophic Risks: Prevention, Compensation, and Recovery. *Issues in Legal Scholarship*, Article 4.

Smith, D., Christiansen, R. Vincent et al. 1999. Population effects of the bombing of Oklahoma City. *Journal of Oklahoma Medical Association* 92: 193–98.

Steefel, L. 1993. The World Trade Center disaster: Healing the unseen wounds. *Journal of Psychosocial Nursing and Mental Health* 31: 5–7.

Stoddard, E. 1968. *Conceptual Models of Human Behavior in Disasters.* El Paso, TX: Texas Western Press.

Sullivan, L. 2006. Crime wave surfaces in post-Katrina New Orleans. *National Public Radio*, August 12. Available online at: http://www.npr.org/templates/story/story.php?storyId=5640177.

Thomas, S. 2007. Lies, damn lies, and rumors: An analysis of collective efficacy, rumors and fear in the wake of Katrina. *Sociological Spectrum* 27: 679–703.

Thornton, W. and L. Voigt. 2007. Disaster rape: Vulnerability of women to sexual assaults during Hurricane Katrina. *Journal of Public Management and Social Policy* 13(2): 23–49.

Trocki, C. 1999. *Opium, Empire, and the Global Political Economy: A Study of the Asian Opium Trade.* London: Routledge

USA Today. 2006. NOPD News Release: Chief Riley says 70% of murders are drug-related. December 8.

Vlahov, D., Galea, S., Ahern, J., Boscarino, J., Bucuvalas, M., Gold, J. and Kilpatrick, D. 2002. Increased use of cigarettes, alcohol, and marijuana among Manhattan, New York residents after the September 11th terrorist attacks. *American Journal of Epidemiology* 155: 988–96.

Vlahov, D., S. Galea, J. Ahern, H. Resnik and D. Kilpatrick, D. 2004. Sustained increased consumption of cigarettes, alcohol, and marijuana among Manhattan residents after September 11, 2001. *American Journal of Public Health* 94: 253–54.

WDSU.com. 2007. Police: Drugs to blame for most killings, disputes with dealers, users causes city's violence. Available online at: http://www.wdsu.com/news/20007722/detail.html.

Weiss, L., A. Fabri, K. McCoy, P. Coffin, J. Netherland and R. Finkelstein. 2002. A vulnerable population in a time of crisis: drug users and the attacks on the World Trade Center. *Journal of Urban Health* 79(3): 392–403.

Williams, J. 2002. Depression, PTSD, substance abuse increase in the wake of the September 11 attacks. National Institute on Drug Abuse Research Findings 17(4).

WWL Radio. 2005. Unofficial Transcript of Mayor Ray Nagin interview with WWL news reporter Garland Robinette, September 1. Available online at: http://www.cnn.com/2005/US/09/02/nagin.transcript/.

Discussion Questions

1. Using specifics found in the chapter, describe the "slow-motion disaster" taking place in New Orleans before Hurricane Katrina.
2. What happened to the illegal drug market in the wake of the 9/11 disaster? How were street level methods, availability and pricing each affected?
3. Describe the three methods employed in this study. What is an advantage of using mixed methods?
4. Describe the condition of the New Orleans drug market before and after Katrina.
5. Research indicates that what groups made up the new drug market customers in New Orleans after the storm?
6. Besides law enforcement data, how else did the author determine that the drug market flourished in New Orleans after Katrina? Be specific about the objects of his investigation.

PART 3

THE CRIMINAL JUSTICE SYSTEM RESPONSE TO DISORDER AND DISASTER

10

INTRODUCTION

The chapters in this section provide examples of specific disasters as case studies in criminal justice response. Additionally, the United States' disaster response infrastructure comes under close scrutiny by practitioners and researchers.

The first chapter, *The Los Angeles Riot and the Criminal Justice Response*, provides a unique opportunity to see how the criminal justice system responds to a large scale riot for which actions of criminal justice system components, namely the Rodney King beating and the court trials that followed, were widely viewed as the precipitants.

This comprehensive review addresses what exactly is a riot, provides an historical treatment of the Rodney King affair and examines what the social science literature says about why riots happen, including a variety of theories that take into account the pre-conditions for riot, particularly in Los Angles. The chapter addresses the issues surrounding how the criminal justice system responded to the King beating and the riot and to the response of the black community in particular to the latter event. Finally, the authors raise the question of what should have been the criminal justice system's response and examine how future riot responses can be better handled.

The next chapter provides a more global perspective, with an examination of the Mumbai, India terrorist attack of 2008 and the criminal justice system's response to it. *The Mumbai Terrorist Attack and the Criminal Justice Response* opens with a discussion of the nature of terrorism and points out its long history as a violent method of advancing a political or cultural agenda by coercing or intimidating governments or societies. For example, the September 11, 2001 attacks were not targeted towards the specific victims working in the World Trade Center, the Pentagon or the passengers on the four aircraft. The deaths were incidental to the real target of the attack, namely American economic, military and political interests. Moreover, the attack demonstrated the reach of Islamic extremists, making it clear that the United States is no longer safe from terrorists. Similarly, the targets of the Mumbai attacks were the economic hub of India, places where foreigners were known to stay and Hindu/Muslim relations. These major terrorist attacks not only caused considerable damage to people and property, but changed each society in ways that can be unpleasant to contemplate.

After reviewing some of the disastrous consequences of terrorism, the authors focus on the Indian experience with terrorism, pointing out that except for Iraq, India has recorded the highest number of terror attacks and killings in the world. The different forms terrorism in India has taken has had disastrous consequences for many parts of the country.

The authors turn next to a detailed description of the Mumbai attacks, which occurred on November 26, 2008. One hundred sixty five people were killed during the attacks and an additional 304 were injured. Ten terrorists in five teams of two attacked five pre-selected sites, indiscriminately killing people with automatic weapons and explosives. Nine of the terrorists were killed in the attack, which lasted two days. Augmenting their description, the authors provide chilling first person accounts from survivors.

As in the case of September 11, there was credible intelligence about an impending attack on Mumbai. Even the United States had warned the Indian authorities about it, but there was little coordination between the two major Indian intelligence agencies or among them and the local police, so that intelligence was not acted upon. The chapter concludes with a discussion of the implications of the Mumbai attack for the criminal justice system and related agencies, calling attention to the need for disaster planning to include not only counterterrorism strategies but also longer term response measures, such as those which will be required for the resulting psychological stress, as well as the economic and financial disruptions.

The third chapter of this section, *The New Orleans Police Department's Response to Hurricane Katrina and Its Aftermath*, is an interview with Superintendent of Police for the City of New Orleans, Chief Warren J. Riley. Riley was Chief of Operations in New Orleans when Katrina struck. As such, he had responsibility for directing all operations by the department. The interview includes a discussion of issues facing the department in the aftermath of the storm, as well as the direct impact of the storm on the functioning of the criminal justice system. The system was essentially shut down for the next year, with 500 police officers either evacuated or quit, prisoners released and only 12 criminal trials conducted. However, law enforcement personnel in the form of National Guard troops and police officers from across the nation were in the city and New Orleans became as quiet as the fictional town of Mayberry. The tranquility of the immediate post-storm period was short lived. By 2006, murder rates quickly returned to pre-Katrina levels. The Chief voiced pessimism about policing "urban cities" because of the persistence of drug markets and the easy availability of guns. By 2007, NOPD was on the rebound with a steady stream of new recruits drawn by better salaries and progress in dealing with crime.

According to the Chief, Katrina had some important lessons for the department. Among these were planning for temporary housing, the need for responders to be equipped for extended emergency operations and the need for the National Guard to be on the ground *before the storm makes landfall.* Mental health issues of first responders need to be addressed and emergency planning needs to be constantly updated. Finally, the Chief discusses those lessons learned from Katrina that were applied to Gustav.

Colonel Terry Ebbert was Director of Homeland Security for the City of New Orleans when it was struck by Hurricane Katrina. His responsibilities included overall direction for police, fire, emergency medical services, emergency preparedness and criminal justice. Based on the Katrina experience, he raises a number of issues regarding reforming the way the nation responds to large scale disasters. Colonel Ebbert's principle thesis is that disasters place an exceptionally heavy burden of planning and response on local agencies that are usually stretched to their limits by day to day operations. Moreover, the resources needed to respond effectively are not owned locally, therefore, they may or may not be available as needed during a disaster.

This interview, entitled *The Heavy Lifting—Local Emergency Response Planning and Preparedness*, reveals a variety of issues that make effective response to disaster difficult. For example, Ebbert notes that there is a push to make local emergency response plans compliant with the Americans with Disabilities Act. It is difficult for local planners to do this because as mentioned they do not own the resources they have to plan with and they incur liability if the plan fails. No one wants this type of responsibility or liability. While the Stafford Act spells out how the government responds to disasters, it is problematic for Ebbert, who believes it does not differentiate enough between the response and recovery phases of disaster. For Ebbert, the response phase should be short, days at most, and has but three elements, namely, save lives, stabilize infrastructure and secure what property is left. Ebbert goes on to outline the main strategic issues in emergency planning and responding, including mission versus compliance organizations, logistical difficulties and command and coordination. He also notes the post-Katrina improvements made and challenges remaining.

In Katrina Berger's chapter, *National Emergency Preparedness and Response Plans: An Overview*, she closely scrutinizes the nation's homeland security infrastructure and response plans. Beginning with an explanation of the federal legal foundations for disaster relief, she moves on to explain the role and responsibilities of the Department of Homeland Security (DHS) and the role of the Federal Emergency Management Agency (FEMA). Next is an examination of the key policy documents that when implemented, animate the federal response to disasters and terrorism events.

A key part of the chapter is a discussion of how response and recovery assets are deployed to an area affected by a disaster. Particular attention is given to the role of FEMA's Specialized Response Teams. The discussion then turns to the deficiencies of core capabilities that were exposed by Hurricane Katrina and the reorganization and policy changes that have been implemented as a result of the Post-Katrina Emergency Management Reform Act. Finally, the chapter addresses some outstanding challenges to national preparedness. These challenges are seen as an evolving process that identifies the necessity for interagency coordination, adequate assessment systems and after-action reviews so that lessons learned can be immediately incorporated into action plans.

Readers of this section should find themselves more aware of the complexity and difficulty the various components of the criminal justice system face when responding to a disaster. They should also take away an understanding of issues central to emergency planning and homeland security. The most central issue concerns communication within agencies as well as between them. Each of the disasters discussed in this chapter at some point involved a communication failure or a failure to act on intelligence provided. Participants in and observers of the criminal justice system, emergency preparation and homeland security will find this information valuable as they are faced with future disasters, as with it they will be able to build on lessons learned in the past.

THE LOS ANGELES RIOT AND THE CRIMINAL JUSTICE RESPONSE

By Komanduri S. Murty and Julian B. Roebuck

What Is a Riot?

By way of definition, several elements are required for the crime of riot: (1) there must be at least three persons participating in public disorderly conduct with a common goal (2) there must be an unlawful assembly and overt acts committed without authority of law and (3) there must be the use of force and violence. In a few states, riots remain a common-law crime; however, most states have statutory enactments that define riotous behavior. Several statutory riotous crimes include inciting to riot, conspiracy to riot, failing to disperse when ordered to and failing to give assistance upon lawful order. Minor riots are usually classified as misdemeanors, however most jurisdictions provide for "aggravated riot," which is a felony. One or more felony offenses usually occur in riots: looting, vandalism, assault, arson, burglary, et cetera. The Federal Riot Act of 1968 made it a federal crime "to use any facility of interstate commerce to incite or engage in a riot" (Nolan and Nolan-Haley 1991, Quarantelli et al.. 1983). Though there are disagreements as to whether violent crowd behaviors are riots or rebellions, such actions challenge the legitimacy of existing law and social order and are usually behavioral responses to perceived injustices of one kind or another. Riots in the United States have not posed serious threats to governmental structure, but rather have declared political messages drawing attention to a particular issue, that is, when other means are deemed futile (Horton and Hunt 1964, Rosenthal 1969, Radelet 1986, Wall 1992). Regardless of precise definitions, many of the nation's most violent and destructive civil disorders have been called riots, as were the Los Angeles violent and collective protests in 1992.

The Rodney King Beating and Court Trials

On March 3, 1991, four Los Angeles Police Officers apprehended Rodney Glenn King, a black, 25 year old Los Angeles male motorist and two passengers in a high speed chase on the Foothill Freeway, after being pulled over in Lake View Terrace district. King was tackled, tasered and heavily beaten with clubs by the officers, who claimed that King violently resisted the arrest. The incident was captured on camcorder by an amateur photographer, Argentine George Holliday, from his apartment in the vicinity. The police officers claimed that King appeared to be under the influence of PCP and did not submit to lawful arrest procedures. In a later interview, King, who was on parole from prison on a robbery conviction and who had past convictions for assault, battery and robbery said that, being on parole, he feared apprehension and being returned to prison for parole violations.

The footage of police beatings of King while lying on the ground became a focal point for media and a rallying point for activists in Los Angeles and other places in the United States. The majority of the media coverage interpreted the incident as a shocking tragedy and accused the police of abusing their power. As a result, all four police officers were charged with assault and use of excessive force. Because of the wide publicity in the media, the trial was moved, at defense counsel request, from Los Angeles County to Simi Valley in neighboring Ventura County, a predominantly white and politically conservative city. The jury was drawn from the nearby San Fernando Valley, a predominantly white and Hispanic area and was comprised of ten whites, one Hispanic and one Asian. The prosecutor, Terry White, was black. On April 29, 1992, the seventh day of jury deliberations, the jury acquitted all four officers of assault and acquitted three of the four of using excessive force. Later the four police officers were tried again on violation of civil rights charges in a federal court and convicted; two were sent to prison.

The Los Angeles Riot: What and How?

The riot began in the evening of the first Simi Valley verdict at 3:15 p.m. local time on Wednesday, April 29, 1992, acquitting the four accused officers of the Los Angeles Police Department. It peaked in intensity over the next two days. Stores were openly looted, fires burned unabated as fire officials refused to send firemen into personal danger, violence was on the rise, the intersection of Florence and Normandie was completely looted, burned and destroyed, looters threw bricks to smash windows and Molotov cocktails to start fires, cars were torched to block intersections, others were carjacked and their drivers beaten and shots were fired at rescue personnel (see Appendix A at the end of this chapter for a chronological account of the riot events).

At approximately 6:45 p.m. on Wednesday, April 29, 1992, Reginald Oliver Denny, a white truck driver who stopped at a traffic light at the intersection of Florence and South Normandie Avenues, was dragged from his vehicle and severely beaten by a mob of local black residents as news helicopters hovered above, recording every blow, including a concrete fragment connecting with Denny's temple and a cinder block thrown at his head as he lay unconscious in the street. The police never appeared, having been ordered to withdraw for their own safety, although several assailants (the so-called L.A. Four) were later arrested and one, Damian Williams, was sent to prison. Instead, Denny was rescued, not by police officers, but by an unarmed, African-American civilian named Bobby Green Jr. who, seeing the assault live on television, rushed to the scene and drove Denny to the hospital using the victim's own truck, which carried 27 tons of sand. Denny had to undergo years of rehabilitative therapy and his speech and ability to walk were permanently damaged. Although several other motorists were brutally beaten by the same mob, Denny remains the best-known victim of the riot because of the live television coverage.

At the same intersection, just minutes after Denny was rescued, another beating was captured on video tape. Fidel Lopez, a self-employed construction worker and Guatemalan immigrant, was ripped from his truck and robbed of nearly $2,000. Damian Williams smashed his forehead open with a car stereo as another rioter attempted to slice his ear off. After Lopez lost consciousness, the crowd spray painted his chest, torso and genitals black. Reverend Bennie Newton, an African-American minister who ran an inner-city ministry for troubled youth, prevented others from beating Lopez by placing himself between Lopez and his attackers and shouting, "Kill him and you have to kill me, too." He was also instrumental in helping Lopez get medical aid by taking him to the hospital. Lopez survived the attack, undergoing extensive surgery to reattach his partially severed ear and months of recovery.

Organized law enforcement response effort, a curfew and deployment of the National Guard began to control the situation and eventually, United States Army soldiers and Marines were ordered to the city to quell disorder as well. Los Angeles Mayor Tom Bradley announced a dusk-to-dawn curfew on Thursday, April 30 at 12:15 a.m. and lifted it after six days, on Monday, May 4, 1992, as a sign of the official end of the riot. However, sporadic violence and crime lasted for a few days after the curfew. Federal troops remained on the scene until May 9, the state guard until May 14 and some soldiers until May 27, 1992. Fifty-three lives were lost with as many as 2,000 people injured. Estimates of the material losses vary between about $800 million and $1 billion. Approximately 3,600 fires were set, destroying 1,100 buildings, with fire calls coming once every minute at some points. Widespread looting also occurred. Stores owned by Korean and other Asian immigrants were widely targeted, although stores owned by whites and African-Americans were targeted by rioters as well. Many of the disturbances were concentrated in South Central Los Angeles, which was primarily composed of African-American and Hispanic residents. Approximately 51 percent of all riot arrestees and more than one third of those killed during the violence were Hispanic.

Why Do Riots Happen?
What Does the Literature Say?

The study of riots has been a specialty of students of collective behavior (Smelser 1963) and are couched in conflict theory (Ritzer 1992). Some researchers have concentrated on particular types of riots (Roebuck, Murty and Smith 1993, Abu-Loghod 2007). Since the 1960s, the riot literature has focused on examinations of collective disorders, with numerous studies on urban and campus crowd behaviors and disorders. Some of these, for example, the research conducted by the Disaster Research Center at the Ohio State University (Quarantelli and Dynes 1970) and the investigation of the Kerner Commission (1968) were broad comparative studies, while others have been case studies. Case studies usually characterize riots as unplanned, spontaneous, emotional, violent outbursts by frustrated participants, who envision no alternate measures to their plight. Most of these deal with the rioting of ethnic minorities in their own neighborhoods (Rosenthal 1969, Cohen 1970, Hacker 1970, Parmenter 1970, Singer and Osborn 1970, Cockburn 1991). Rainwater (1970) claimed that inner city riots are triggered by particular instances of police brutality and presaged by the heavy migration of blacks into white communities, resulting in cultural conflict and racial competition for jobs, as exemplified by the riots in Chicago in 1919, the Watts section of Los Angeles in 1965, Washington, D.C. in 1968 and Tulsa in 1968. In summing up the riot literature involving blacks prior to 1968, Tanowitz (1968) pointed out that their primary focus has been on: (1) selected accounts of previous riots (2) social tensions and frustrations generated by prejudice, discrimination and poverty and (3) weaknesses in the social control and law enforcement systems which gave way to violence.

The McCone Commission (1965), in an analysis of riots that occurred in black communities prior to 1965 in seven cities (New York, New York; Rochester, New York; Newark, New Jersey; Patterson, New Jersey; Elizabeth, New Jersey; Chicago,

Illinois; and Philadelphia, Pennsylvania), found several common community causes for these disturbances: unemployment, inadequate housing, poverty, ineffectual educational institutions, open hostility towards the police and a significant growth of the black populations. Studies of riots in other cities have found similar causes, for example, in the Detroit riot of 1967 (Nicholls 1968, Parmenter 1970, Kerner Commission 1968, Balbus 1973), in the Watts riot of 1965 (Glasgow 1980, Crump 1966, McCone Commission 1965, Sears and Tomlinson 1968, Cohen 1970, Bayard 1971, Hacker 1970, Kerner Commission 1968) and in the Miami riot of 1980 (Miami Herald 1980, 1991, Porter and Dunn 1984).

Riot Theories

Several riot theories have been developed ranging from the primitive nonsocial reaction theory, which argues that individuals in some crowds when frustrated act in a uniform subhuman, animalistic manner, that is, they either regress to a non-human level of behavior or were not properly socialized in the first place, to more sophisticated contextual, multicausal models. Some of the latter include tension-release explanations, convergence theory and an emergent norm theory (Quarantelli et al. 1983). Perhaps the frames of reference of the most empirical value focus on the facilitating elements of riot development that explain why riots occur in some settings and not in others (Myers 1997). Such elements include structural variables, e.g., rate of minority unemployment, size of minority population, rates of growth, income levels, housing conditions, integration of minority groups into local power structures (Spilerman 1976), social-psychological variables, e.g., relative deprivation, an intolerable gap between perceived reality and expectations (Leach, Iyer and Pedersen 2007, Olson, Roese and Meen 1995) and behavioral variables, e.g., interaction involving the exchange of information about events, grievances and adverse social conditions that evolve into collective protest ideologies, rumor behavior and precipitating events (Rosenfeld 1997, Snow and Oliver 1995, Tierney 1994, Turner 1994).

Natural Actor Studies

A few studies have utilized natural actors' first-hand reactions in the form of personal interview data by riot participants and observers. For example, Sears and McConahay (1967), utilizing interview materials from Tomlinson and TenHueten's 1965–66 database on the Watts riot (1970) identified two types of rioters: gladiators (active participants) and active spectators (those on the street in close proximity to the gladiators, the victims and the property being destroyed). Hacker (1970) ascertained from his own interview data among Watts riot community residents, following the riot, that the majority supported the disorders in retrospect. Most viewed the riot as a rebellious reaction to intolerable poverty, despair, racism and discrimination and as a symbolic message to the power structure. Participants reported to Hacker that their looting and violence was justified 'in an equitable cause," that they had developed a "collective identity" as a consequence of actions in the riot, that they had forced the nation to recognize their cause, that the riot had restored their feelings of self worth and that they had paved the way for others in the fight against injustice. None of those interviewed concluded that the riots were "bad" or "criminal."

In sum, the literature suggests that riots do not just happen by chance, but rather transpire in response to perceived injustices, isolation, economic deprivation, racial discrimination, police brutality, powerlessness and despair, that they are messages to the power structure to right existing wrongs and that they usually follow a precipitating incident. Riots in European countries by formerly colonized immigrant enclaves, Asians and Africans, seem to support these suggestions (Fukuda 2000, McMillan 1992).

What Were the Pre-Conditions in Los Angeles?

Many suspected that pre-conditions in Los Angeles such as demographics, economics, the political system, the long-standing perception that the Los Angeles Police Department (LAPD) routinely involved in racial profiling and used excessive force, et cetera led to the riot. Let us examine them in turn. Out of a total population of 523,000 people living in South Central Los Angeles (SCLA) in 1990, 56 percent were black, 30 percent of whom lived below the poverty line. Forty four percent of resident children lived in families below the poverty line (Senate Task Force 1992). Forty to 50 percent of all black men were unemployed (Waters 1992). The Los Angeles area lost 300,000 jobs between 1990 and 1992, which accounted for 60 percent of California's job loss during this period (Assembly Special Committee 1992). The LAPD consisted of 8,450 officers who served an area of 450 square miles, averaging two officers per 1,000 residents. The police employed a highly professional, specialized, mobile, reactive and aggressive type of operation, geared toward crime fighting and "rough justice" rather than toward a crime prevention approach. This paramilitary style, though apparently effective in one sense for the white community, isolated the department from the black community it served (Dunne 1991, 1991a, Morrow 1991).

Several investigative reporters note that the LAPD has treated black community members unequally, unjustly, brutally and without respect for the past two decades (Dunne 1991). Reported examples of this mistreatment include false "justifiable homicide reports" (Dunne 1991), forcible illegal entry into private dwellings without proper search warrants followed by destruction of private property (Braun 1991, 1991a, Domanic 1992), unjustified police raids in the black community involving massive unlawful arrests (Webster Commission 1992, Cooper 1992), roughing up arrestees and "rough justice" (Chavez 1991, Cockburn 1991, 1991a, 1992).

A *Los Angeles Times* report in 1991 revealed that one out of every four citizens polled said they had either seen or been involved in an incident involving the excessive use of force by LAPD officers (Rohrlich 1991). The Independent Commission (1991), in an investigation of all police complaints filed against the LAPD between 1986 and 1990, found that many involved charges of assault and aggravated racism, that out of 1,440 excessive force complaints, less than one percent of the officers charged were fired and that stiff penalties against police officers for using excessive force were rare. Finally, Dunne (1991a) and Barrett and Parrish (1991) along with other investigative reporters of the LAPD prior to the riot noted racial bias, the use of unnecessary force and a breakdown in departmental leadership. In brief, the police and black community members' relationships prior to the riot were characterized by tension, hostility and suspicion.

How Did the Criminal Justice System Respond to the King Beating and Los Angeles Riot?

Black Community Response

Before we visit this issue, it is instructive to examine how the black community in Los Angeles reacted to the riots. In a unique study by Murty, Roebuck and Armstrong (1994), 227 members of the SCLA community were interviewed about their feelings toward and participation in the riot. All interviewees were black, about just over half were men, about seventy percent were under 30 and earned less than $20,000 per year, three quarters were employed at least part time, about two thirds had not graduated from high school and about a quarter had been arrested before the riot.

When asked about the Rodney King beating, respondents expressed anger, sadness and fear. They were angry about the change of venue and outraged at the verdict of not guilty the four officers received, viewing it as a failure of the criminal justice system. Respondents felt an immediate overhaul of the police department was warranted, as was a change in criminal court proceedings, the firing of all officers related in any way to the King incident and the hiring of more black officers. Some respondents also expressed outrage and sadness at the Reginald Denny beating, though not as many as expressed these feelings about the Rodney King beating.

Though few respondents participated in the riot, almost all respondents did not feel as though the rioters deserved punishment and felt that the protests would result in positive changes for the city. In more detail, the 26 respondents who did participate in the riots differed significantly from the 201 who did not in the following ways: (1) riot participants were younger than non-participants (2) riot participants were more likely to be male than non-participants (3) riot participants had less education than non-participants (4) riot participants had a lower income level than non-participants and (5) riot participants had more arrests than non-participants.

The non participant group did not accept rioting as either a proper or moral means to effect social change. In fact, 25 percent of these non participants feared that the present or subsequent riot could result in a white backlash. Yet, in a contradictory fashion, 75 percent of the non participants reported that the rioters were justified in their actions. A large proportion understood the rioters' degree of frustration, hostility and violence, understood why they rioted and did not blame them for rioting and looting. Furthermore, most thought the riot would bring about positive change for the city.

The participants, on the other hand, fully embraced the riot and stated (in different ways) that they had been suffering and struggling under unequal and unjust social, economic and criminal justice conditions, including police brutality, for too long and without any noticeable improvement in their situations. They asserted that they had decided their views must be heard through and by force because other alternatives had failed. They claimed that the anger and dismay following the King beating and the ensuing not guilty verdict of the four white policemen triggered them to take violent action. According to them, the time had come to change things and their actions might make things better for themselves and other blacks in the future—"no justice no peace." In brief, they presented themselves as freedom fighters.

Though their reactions were sometimes mixed and contradictory, both participants and non-participants generally understood the functions of riot in promoting social change, even though rioting may not be viewed by respondents as the best way to bring about change. Differences in reactions were in degree rather than in kind. Justification of the riot was based on the failure of the criminal justice system to punish the men who beat Rodney King, thereby demonstrating racial injustice and the power structure's lack of concern for blacks in Los Angeles. Most, as good citizens, objected to riot in principle but concluded that collective violence pays off.

The remarks of most respondents about the Reginald Denny beating indicate a justification of an illegal terrorist-type act based on blind ethnic retribution. This beating also served as a symbolic message meant to intimidate a targeted institution, the criminal justice system, rather than the immediate victim. To the participants and their supporters, the Denny attack was a political act, not a crime, a rational response to the injustice of the criminal justice system. The same tactics were used in Denny's case as those employed against Rodney King. (A similar beating of a white male took place in Miami on May 28, 1993 following the not guilty verdict of police officer William Lozano in Orlando, Florida. The verdict was the second for Lozano, who on June 11, 1989 was convicted by a Miami jury of manslaughter in the deaths of two black motorcyclists. An Appeals Court subsequently granted Lozano a retrial in another city because it ruled that the Miami jurors in the first trial may have feared a riot if they acquitted Lozano. For more, see Williams 1993.)

Many respondents' reactions to the "parallel beatings" of King and Denny denote an attempt to "balance injustice in the absence of a balance of justice." This so-called balancing act indicates the willingness of some blacks to induce change in the criminal justice system by and through force. Actually, this balancing metaphor is specious. Though the beatings of King and Denny were both illegal and reprehensible, King was an offender resisting arrest, whereas Denny was an innocent motorist. Furthermore, under the rule of law, the commission of a crime to rectify another is flagrantly illegal. Such action often leads to backlash and the further escalation of violence.

Criminal Justice System Response

The policeone.com columnist Captain Greg Meyer (2007) gave the following account:

> In the middle of the night of March 3, 1991, King, a paroled robber, drove a vehicle at speeds over one hundred miles-per-hour on a Southern California freeway. He was pursued by California Highway Patrol officer who requested Los Angeles Police Department assistance when King exited the freeway and continued driving recklessly on surface streets. Once stopped, King's two passengers complied with police orders to get out of the car and submit to arrest. King eventually got out of the car and performed a bizarre "dance." He was sweating, laugh-

ing and talking irrationally, and many officers on the scene believed
he was on drugs, most likely PCP.

The sergeant on the scene ordered four officers to approach and hand-
cuff King, but King threw them off. The sergeant used a Taser electronic
gun device on King, who fell to the ground. At that moment, a bystander
across the street began videotaping the event. King rose to his feet and
charged an officer who delivered a baton blow to King's upper body
simultaneously with the sergeant's use of the Taser device again. King
fell to the ground and sustained an ugly facial wound. King repeatedly
attempted to regain his footing as two officers kicked and used police
batons on him for well over a minute as the amateur video camera
recorded the action.

Thus, King was hit by two high-voltage Tasers and then struck dozens of times
with metal batons and was kicked, while more than 20 police officers were
present and a police helicopter was hovering overhead, its floodlights illumi-
nating the scene. Attracting far more attention was the trial of the police officers directly involved in the beating (Cannon 1999). All four officers, Stacey
Koon, Laurence Powell, Timothy Wind and Theodore Brisenio, were charged
with assault by force and with unnecessarily beating a person under color of
authority. Koon and Powell were charged with submitting a false police report
and Koon was charged with being an accessory after the fact (Geller and Hemenway 1997: 164–65, 316–17). Nearly everyone—the public, journalists, lawyers
and the defendants—expected a guilty verdict on at least some of the charges.
Hence, news of the verdict of not guilty for all four officers acted like a shock
wave through the country and especially through SCLA. Koon admitted that
the arrest was undoubtedly brutal, but insisted that it followed procedure (Koon
1992: 25–52, see also Deitz 1996: 61–91). He rationalized police force options
in response to the suspect's behavior. He claimed that he "had been in charge
of the officers, but Rodney King had been in charge of the situation" (1992: 45).
This theme of King being "in charge" was used by the defense throughout the
trials and nicely captures the reinterpretation involved. Normally, "in charge"
implies having power or authority, which the police certainly had during the
arrest. By portraying King as being "in charge"—validly so, from the perspective of police use-of-force options—the responsibility for the beating was
attributed to King. More generally, the defense tried to make King the focus
of attention, not the police (Geller and Hemenway 1997: 186, Martin 2005).
Koon concluded from King's "buffed out appearance" that he was most likely
an ex-con who had been working out on prison weights and assumed therefore that he was a dangerous character. Finally, it was King's criminal history

that explained the decision of prosecutors to keep him off the witness stand. If King testified, defense attorneys would be allowed to present the jury with his record of arrests, a record that might influence their deliberations. In the initial Simi Valley trial, the jurors accepted the police side of the argument and found the four officers on trial not guilty (Osborne 1992). The police thus held King accountable for his own beating. Koon also blamed LAPD managers, especially Chief Daryl Gates, as self-interested bureaucrats who protected themselves at the expense of street cops (1992: 105–09).

At the end of March, 1991, Los Angeles police chief Gates formed a commission to investigate the beating. Mayor Tom Bradley formed one as well. By agreement of the two bodies, they combined to form the Christopher Commission, led by Warren Christopher (who would become Secretary of State the following year under President Bill Clinton), which carried out a thorough investigation in a matter of months, reporting in early July, 1991 (Cannon 1999). The commission did not examine the culpability of individual officers for the beating, which was a matter for the courts, but instead reported on systemic problems in the LAPD: the use of excessive force, racism and bias, police culture, recruitment and training, complaint systems and formal structures for control of the police department and its chief. The commission's report was seen by many as a largely sound and far-sighted document which, if its recommendations were implemented, would transform the police (Cannon 1999: 121–47). After release of the report, pressure mounted on Gates to resign. Eventually he announced he would step down in 1992. A year later, the four acquitted police officers faced a second trial on federal charges of violating Rodney King's civil rights. Stacey Koon and Laurence Powell were found guilty and received 30 month jail terms while Timothy Wind and Theodore Briseno were cleared. Rodney King won $3.8 million in damages from the city of Los Angeles. Over the years, he refrained from talking to the press about the incident or his troubles, with the exception of his appearance on two reality television shows about drug addiction and recovery.

As viewed by many in retrospect, the Los Angeles riots were the result of social neglect. Some reforms such as community policing were contemplated in Los Angeles but were never implemented due to underfunding. "The first problem," LAPD police chief Gates claimed, "is the need for more officers. But again, how much more can taxpayers be asked to pay?" (Gates and Shah 1992: 39). As a result, Los Angeles' police force was viewed at least by one expert as "the antithesis of community policing. The department was cool, aloof, disconnected from the community" (*Newsweek* 1992). Secondly, the leadership in both the city of Los Angeles and in the LAPD were totally unprepared for the riots in part because Mayor Bradley and Chief Gates were engaged in a personal feud and had not talked to each other for 13 months prior to riots (Mendel 1996, Rasmussen 1999). They both expected guilty verdicts, as did everyone else and therefore saw no reason for any contingency planning. When the verdicts were announced, Mayor Bradley left to attend a rally at a black church with the intention of launching Operation Cool Response, the brainchild of the Reverend Cecil Murray, which was designed to appeal to blacks to channel their frustration through conventional political means. Though the intention was to encourage non-violence, it came too late because the rioters were already taking to the streets. Cool Response should have been launched much earlier during the jury deliberations, which began on April 23. Thirdly, the LAPD was totally unprepared to face the rioters. Chief Gates, to his unprofessional credit, left his post to attend a political fund-raiser at the time the riots broke out. Most of the captains were away from their desks, on a three-day course outside Los Angeles. Shift changes in many divisions took place at 3:00 p.m., meaning just 838 officers were on duty when the verdicts were announced. Alas, these officers had no civil disturbance equipment, no reserve ammunition and no riot control plan. The only LAPD unit that had undergone minimal riot control training was the elite but small Metropolitan Division, which was asked to report to duty at 6 p.m., when the riots were already in full swing. Fourthly, standard procedures for riot control called for the cordoning off of the intersection with patrol cars. Properly equipped with riot gear and in sufficient strength, police would then lock arms and advance. Instead, at 5:45 p.m., the LAPD abandoned the intersection and the riots spread everywhere. Officers assembled at an emergency command post, where there were no televisions, no computers and only a few radios or telephones. Fifthly, the standard procedure also called for the implementation of the Mutual Aid system. However, because the LAPD failed to take any precautions against rioting, civilian officials panicked and overreacted. Mayor Bradley and the governor of California, Pete Wilson, circumvented the Mutual Aid system and called in military forces.

Lastly, as Rasmussen (1999) argued, soldiers did not necessarily represent the best response to this crisis. However, if soldiers were going to be employed at all, guardsmen were probably the soldiers best suited to this task because: (1) the initial 2,000 mobilized lived in the neighborhoods affected by the riots and were familiar with the terrain (2) many of these citizen soldiers held civilian jobs in law enforcement or related areas (3) the California National Guard has vast institutional experience responding to emergencies, such as fires or floods, always in aid of civilian law enforcement and (4) many of the older guardsmen had been deployed during the Watts riots of 1965 (Delk 1995, Schnaubelt 1997).

However, guardsmen were not given a chance to do their job. On May 1, 1992, the third day of rioting, President Bush authorized the deployment of regular Army troops and Marines and federalized the California National Guard. By the next day, 10,465 guardsmen, 2,023 Army soldiers and 1,508 Marines joined 1,717 other federal law enforcement officers in Los Angeles. There was no need for such a massive deployment of troops because the rioting was over after the first night, giving way to massive looting on the second day, with sporadic looting and violence on third day. By the time federal forces arrived in Los Angeles, the problem was not the restoration of order but the maintenance of order. Therefore, guardsmen, soldiers and Marines patrolled neighborhoods that were not yet affected by the violence as an effort to prevent the spread of the riots, protected shopping malls under threat of arson or looting, protected the post office when postal workers handed out welfare checks, escorted firefighters who went out on missions, directed traffic and accompanied police detectives as they recovered some of the loot. In essence, they performed all non-military missions for which they were not adequately trained.

In 1980, the Los Angeles city authorities created an Emergency Operations Plan, which called for an Emergency Operations Organization (EOO), headed by the mayor and with representatives from every major city agency. The EOO was supposed to plan for contingencies such as riots before they occurred and expected to assume command of operations once an emergency developed. Before and during the 1992 riots, the EOO "should have been the nerve center of the City's emergency response. In this case, however, the EOO was dysfunctional" (Webster Commission 1992, as quoted in Rasmussen 1999).

What Should Have Been the Criminal Justice System Response?

No one knows for sure. Several social scientists and criminal justice practitioners revisited the Los Angeles riot and underlying causes over the past one and a half decades and have offered some views. One thing that all agree on is that the Rodney King incident was a complex event open to many interpretations. As Cannon (1999) pointed out, one could see the 1992 Los Angeles riot as the fault of the jurors who failed to convict the officers at their first criminal trial, or the fault of rioters who were encouraged by inflammatory comments from the mayor of Los Angeles and then president George H. W. Bush, or the fault of the police, who ironically hesitated to use deadly force against the initial rioters, who were engaged in major race-based assaults against innocent people or of the police leaders who failed to organize a coherent response to suppress the riot. Martin (2005) indicated that the police officers should not have indulged themselves in certain unseemly practices such as cover-up, devaluation, reinterpretation, using official channels and intimidation, had they not wanted to invite a backfire effect. Barlow and Barlow (1993) recommended a cultural diversity awareness training for police officers and other criminal justice personnel as a way to maintain healthy police-community relations.

In its report, which was entitled City in Crisis and was sponsored by the Los Angeles Board of Police Commissioners, the Webster Commission (1992) found a general lack of emergency preparedness for civil disorder on the part of the city and the LAPD and a specific lack in the period before the Simi Valley verdict in the Rodney King case. The city and the LAPD each have designed general mechanisms to cope with some emergencies. However, none of their preparedness efforts have resulted in a meaningful plan for response to an emergency. Based on these findings, it was recommended that: (1) the LAPD adopt new priorities that place renewed emphasis on basic patrol duties (2) the Police Chief is urged to reallocate police officers away from special units and toward patrol assignments (3) the field command experience in patrol should become a primary criteria for advancement within the command ranks (4) more attention is to be paid to emergency response planning and training, not only within the police department, but also for the city as a whole (5) leaders of the city and the LAPD should be involved in training designed to enhance their crisis management experience and skills and (6) modernization of the communications system is essential to permit the city to conduct both normal and emergency operations, among other things.

Conclusion

There is no obvious way that the community can organize itself to prevent another riot from occurring (Cannon 1998), nor can the police department of Los Angeles, or for that matter any other city, adequately prepare itself to respond to such a riot. There are, however, some lessons to be learned from the Los Angeles experience as found in Rasmussen (1999). First, the time to think about public order emergencies is well before the riot begins, not as it happens. In Los Angeles, politicians failed to improve social conditions, which themselves were a factor in the Watts riots. Politicians and voters in Los Angeles failed to fund LAPD adequately for its equipment, training and personnel needs. The LAPD continued to operate without meaningful oversight and alienated the South Central community. To compound the problem, civilian officials gave little attention to what should happen if the violence broke out. When they saw the widespread riot, they resorted to the military and provided them little guidance. Second, the police must be trained and equipped to deal with disorders in a manner that does not worsen the situation. City management should recognize that policing is a labor-intensive activity and provide adequate funding for training, equipment and personnel. Third, police need to develop skills in public order management. For example, in some European nations, police meet and negotiate with protestors and demonstrators prior to an event and assist them with preparations for the march, discussing issues such as transportation, first aid and alternative routes. The attitude and behavior of the police have strong influence on the way citizens think of the social order under which they live. In Los Angeles, the police lost legitimacy in the eyes of minority. Civilian oversight might help but only if it is effectively implemented. In this case, the Los Angeles mayor is supposed to exercise control over the police, but as we know, he was not speaking with Chief Gates for over a year preceding the riot. Fourth, police must be held accountable to civilians on a regular basis by incorporating appropriate judicial review of the use of force and police misconduct when detected and/or alleged. In the two years prior to the Rodney King incident, LAPD officers had been taken to court in record numbers on charges of excessive use of force and the LAPD had paid astronomical sums in compensatory damages. Yet, this did not prompt any police re-evaluation of its conduct. Fifth, unless police earn the confidence of the minorities they are supposed to serve, a repetition of periodic outbursts of violence is likely. In order for the police to gain acceptance in a multiethnic and multicultural community, it is important to make the composition of the police force similar to the community. Sixth, the LAPD should move forward with implementing of community policing effectively, so that police officers on the beat become a constant presence in the local schools, parks and homeowners' and merchants' associations. Community policing has not only shown to be effective in fighting crime, but also provides a constant communication channel with the community. Finally, should the widespread civil disturbance become unmanageable to local police and calls for a need for military deployment arises, appropriate and socially acceptable procedures must be employed. Here, we may draw on the practices of other nations such as Austria, Spain and France, where a separate riot control police force is maintained. This national riot force can support and work in conjunction with the local police when needed as a part of a Mutual Aid plan. To ensure that such operations take place effectively and in a non-provocative manner, periodic joint exercises may be conducted and evaluated.

Even with all the above steps, we cannot expect a perfect society. Some sort of unrest on the part of community and some occasional wrongdoing on the part of police are likely to happen and many people understand that possibility. What is not permissible to the public is systemic wrongdoing and systematic use of excessive force on the part of police. They can certainly reduce the violence by focusing less on personal emotions and the victim's profile, including arrest records, and more on policies and procedures. In this case, all it took was one videotape and in our current technologically advanced and media-centric era, it should be anticipated that someone somewhere is watching and interested. Oral testimonies have less chance to stand alone as credible defense, even if they come from the mouth of a police officer.

Bernstein et al. (1982) used the concept of the "iron fist and velvet glove" to describe the contradictory nature of policing in a class society. The iron fist, or hard side of policing, is the capacity of the police to use force and developments, such as increasingly sophisticated technologies, that enhance that capacity. The velvet glove, or the softer side of policing, consists of efforts in the area of community pacification and programs that sell the police to the public. These two aspects of policing operate simultaneously, each supporting the other. Both are strategies of repression. Neither the obviously conservative interest in developing more effective strategies of control nor the liberal interest in seeking community input challenge structures of privilege and exploitation in the United States. Indeed, both support that structure "by making the system of repression that serves it more powerful or more palatable or both" (1982: 49).

Certainly, the police must maintain a good image in the community in order to minimize the risk that their actions will become a focal point or a precipitating event for a riot (Murty, Roebuck and Smith 1990). That said, we contend the overriding problem leading to riots is inherent in our socioeconomic class structure. We live in a capitalist welfare state differentiated by socioeconomic class, race, religious, special interest, regional and moralistic groupings. As with all western societies, those in the top classes (middle to upper) get more and live more affluently than those in the lower class. The problem is that there is a growing disparity between the rich and the poor in terms of what each group has and receives. The United States leads the Organization for Economic Cooperation and Development (OECD) countries in income and wealth inequality, poverty, crime, higher educational opportunity, hours worked and infant mortality (Madrick 2009, Hacker 1992, Delbanco 2007). The nexus of these social, political, economic and demographic factors may spur periodic communal dissatisfaction and outrage. Moreover, political exclusion cuts off channels for the redress of grievances, acting in concert with segregation, population change and economic competition to foster violence.

Appendix A

Chronological Account of the 1992 Los Angeles Riot Events

Wednesday, April 29, 1992

12:45 p.m.: Notice was given to the public that verdicts on the four police officer defendants would be announced in two hours.

3:10 p.m.: Verdicts were announced.

3:20 p.m.: Angry crowds gathered at Florence and Normandie, the spot where Rodney King was beaten.

4:00 p.m.: A black teenager beat a Korean store owner, was chased by police to Dalton and Florence Avenue and arrested. An angry crowd gathered to protest the arrest and was dispersed by the police.

4:15 p.m.: First looting occurred at Florence and Normandie Avenue.

5:00 p.m.: Chief Gates made this public announcement, "We are prepared for this."

5:45 p.m.: Rioters at Florence and Normandie Avenue attacked cars and motorists.

6:15 p.m.: Field Command Post established at 54th Street and Arlington Avenue (RTD Bus Yard).

6:45 p.m.: Reginald Denny was pulled out of his truck and beaten at Florence and Normandie Avenue by four black men.

7:00 p.m.: Protesters were reported to be smashing windows at Parker Center (LAPD Headquarters). Their cry was, "No justice, no peace."

8:00 p.m.: Governor Wilson announced that 2,000 National Guard Troops would be sent to Los Angeles.

8:45 p.m.: First report of wanton arson along Vermont Avenue.

10:00 p.m.: Protesters ransack City Hall, City Hall East and Los Angeles Mall.

11:00 p.m.: Chief Gates went to the 77th Division and ordered changes in deployment procedures.

Thursday, April 30, 1992

Midnight to 3:00 a.m.:   Three new fires per minute were reported.

12:10 a.m.: Governor Wilson declared a state of emergency.

2:55 p.m.: Transformers began exploding and darkened areas extended from Manchester to Vernon Avenue. At least 30 to 40 buildings were smoldering or actively burning. Stores were being entered and looted.

10:30 a.m.: Vons, a grocery store at 3rd Street and Vermont Avenue was looted. Nearby apartment building was burned. No police were present.

1:30 p.m.: First National Guard troops were deployed into South Central Los Angeles.

3:30 p.m.: Major structure fires occurred. The entire block at Pico and Alvarado was burning.

3:55 p.m.: Curfew, gasoline and ammunition restrictions were extended citywide until sunrise Friday, May 1.

10:00 p.m.: 12,700 customers, mostly in the South Central area, were without power.

Midnight: Death toll stood at 25, plus 572 injuries, 1,000 fires, 720 arrests and 30 active structure fires. 122 LAFD Fire Companies and 20 Rescue Ambulances committed.

Friday, May 1, 1992

12:01 a.m.: National Guard federalized.

5:01 a.m.: President Bush ordered 1,200 federal agents to assist in restoring order to Los Angeles.

9:00 a.m.: Mayor Bradley signed order extending curfew.

Early afternoon: Rodney King made conciliatory statement on television, "Can we all get along?"

Saturday, May 2, 1992

11:30 a.m.: Mayor Bradley announced a citywide curfew indefinitely.

5:15 p.m.: Mayor Bradley announced that Peter Uberroth would head the Rebuild L.A. effort. President Bush declared Los Angeles a disaster area.

Late p.m.: Television programming returned to normal, power lines were repaired and limited bus service was restored.

Sunday, May 3, 1992

9:55 p.m.: L.A. County Sheriff approved withdrawal of law enforcement mutual aid forces from Los Angeles

12:06 p.m.: California Highway Patrol (CHP) demobilized.

Monday, May 4, 1992

8:00 a.m.: Emergency Control Center was shut down.

10:40 a.m.: Curfew was lifted but ban on gasoline in containers and on alcohol remained.

11:50 a.m.: Agreement was made that federal law enforcement presence was no longer needed.

References

Abu-Loghod, J. L. 2007. *Race, Space, and Riots in Chicago, New York, and Los Angeles.* New York: Oxford University Press.

Assembly Special Committee Report. 1992. To rebuild is not enough: Final report and recommendations of the Assembly Special Committee on the Los Angeles crisis. Sacramento, CA: California Legislature State Capitol.

Balbus, I. D. 1973. *The Dialectics of Legal Repression.* New York: Russell Sage.

Barlow, D. and M. Barlow. 1993. Cultural diversity training in criminal justice: A progressive or conservative reform? *Social Justice* 20: 3–4.

Barrett, B. and D. Parrish. 1991. Few fired for excess force. *Los Angeles Times,* May 5: A13–14, B2–4.

Bayard, R. 1971. The Watts "manifesto" and The McCone report. In *Down The Line,* Chicago Quadrangle Books: 140–53.

Bernstein, S., T. Platt, J. Frappier, G. Ray, R. Schauffler, L. Trujillo, L. Cooper, E. Currie and S. Harring. 1982. *The Iron Fist and the Velvet Glove: An Analysis of the U.S. Police, 3rd ed.* Berkeley, California: Center for Research on Criminal Justice.

Bradley, N. 1992. Man charges police abuse triggered riot. *Wave Newspapers,* May 20.

Braun, S. 1991. Black men, LAPD: A mix of bitterness and suspicion. *Los Angeles Times,* December 16: C2–4.

Braun, S. 1991a. Violent police searches often yield fear, anger. *Los Angeles Times,* December 18: F1–3.

Cannon, L. 1998. PBS interview with Lou Cannon.

Cannon, L. 1999. *Official Negligence: How Rodney King and the Riots Changed Los Angeles and the LAPD.* Boulder, CO: Westview.

Chavez, S. 1991. King beating foretold a year of tumult and change. *Los Angeles Times,* December 28: B6–7.

Cockburn, A. 1991. Beat the devil. *The Nation,* April 15: 474–75.

Cockburn, A. 1991a. The war at home. *New Statesman & Society* 3: 14–15.

Cockburn, A. 1992. Symbolic injustice. *New Statesman & Society* 5: 18–19.

Cohen, N. (ed.) 1970. *The Los Angeles Riots: A Socio-Psychological Study.* New York: Praeger.

Cooper, M. 1992. L.A.'s state of siege. In *Inside the L.A. Riots: What Really Happened and Why It Will Happen Again,* ed. D. Hazen, New York: Institute for Alternative Journalism: 12–19.

Crump, S. 1966. *Black Riot in Los Angeles.* Los Angeles: Trans-Anglo Books.

Deitz, R. 1996. *Willful Injustice: A Post-O.J. Look at Rodney King, American Justice and Trial by Race.* Washington, D.C.: Regnery.

Delbanco, A. 2007. Scandals of higher education. *New York Review of Books* 54(5) March 29, 42–47.

Delk, J. D. 1995. *Fires and Furies: The L.A. Riots.* Palm Springs, CA: ETC Publications.

Domanick, J. 1992. Police power. In *Inside the L.A. Riots: What Really Happened and Why It Will Happen Again,* ed. D. Hazen, New York: Institute for Alternative Journalism: 21–23.

Dunne, J. G. 1991. Law & disorder in Los Angeles. *The New York Review of Books,* October 10: 23–29.

Dunne, J. G. 1991a. Law & disorder in Los Angeles: Part two. *The New York Review of Books,* October 24: 62–70.

Fukuda, C. M. 2000. Peace through nonviolent action: The East Timorese resistance movement's strategy for engagement. *Pacifica Review* 12(1): 17–31.

Gates, D. F. and D. K. Shah. 1992. *Chief: My Life in the LAPD.* New York: Bantam.

Geller, L. H. and P. Hemenway. 1997. *Last Chance for Justice: The Juror's Lonely Quest.* Dallas: NCDS Press.

Glasgow, D. A. 1980. *The Black Underclass.* San Francisco: Jossey-Bass.

Hacker, A. 1992. *Two Nations: Black and White, Separate, Hostile, Unequal.* Chicago: Charles Scribner's Sons.

Hacker, F. J. 1970. What the McCone Commission didn't see. In *Ghetto Revolts,* ed. P. H. Rossi, Chicago: Aldine: 47–52.

Hartman, A. 1992. A message from Los Angeles. *Social Work* 37: 291–92.

Horton, P. and C. Hunt. 1964. Collective Behavior, Social Movements, and Social Change. In *Sociology, 2nd ed.* New York: McGraw-Hill: 484–85.

Independent Commission. 1991. *Report of the Independent Commission on the Los Angeles Police Department.* Los Angeles.

Kerner Commission. 1968. *Report of the U.S. National Advisory Commission of Civil Disorders.* Washington, D.C.: U.S. Government Printing Office.

Koon, S. C. and R. Deitz. 1992. *Presumed Guilty: The Tragedy of the Rodney King Affair.* Washington, D.C.: Regnery.

Leach, C. W., A. Iyer and A. Pedersen. 2007. Angry opposition to government redress: When the structurally advantaged perceive themselves as relatively deprived. *British Journal of Social Psychology* 46: 191–204.

Lieberman, P. 1992. 51 percent of riot arrests were Latino, study says. *Los Angeles Times,* June 18, E8–10.

Madrick, J. 2009. *The Case for Big Government.* Princeton, New Jersey: Princeton University Press.

Martin, B. 2005. The beating of Rodney King: The dynamics of backfire. *Critical Criminology* 13(3): 307–26.

McCone Commission. 1965. Violence in the city: An end or a beginning? Los Angeles: State of California Governor's Commission on the Los Angeles (Watts) Riots.

McMillan, A. 1992. *Death in Dili*. Sydney, Australia: Hodder and Stoughton.

Mendel, W. M. 1996. *Combat in Cities: The LA Riots and Operation Rio*. Fort Leavenworth, KS: Foreign Military Studies Office: 5.

Meyer, G. 2007. Rodney King revisited. Available online at: http://www.police one.com/writers/columnists/greg-meyer/articles/1202607-Rodney-King-revisited/.

Miami Herald. 1980. Rage at verdict, May 20: A32.

Miami Herald. 1991. Cyclists' death termed a murder, December 27: B1.

Morrow, L. 1991. Rough justice. *Time*, April 1: 16–21.

Murty, K. S., J. B. Roebuck and J. D. Smith. 1990. The image of police in black Atlanta communities. *The Journal of Police Science and Administration* 17(4): 250–57.

Murty, K. S., J.B. Roebuck and G. R. Armstrong. 1994. The black community's reactions to the 1992 Los Angeles riot. *Deviant Behavior: An Interdisciplinary Journal* 15: 85–104.

Myers, D. J. 1997. Racial rioting in the 1960s: An event history analysis of local conditions. *American Sociological Review* 62: 94–112.

Newsweek. 1992. Blacks and cops: Up against the wall, May 11: 52–53.

Nicholls, J. F. 1968. *Statistical Report of the Civil Disorder Occurring in the City of Detroit July, 1967*. Detroit: Detroit Police Department.

Nolan, J. R. and J. M. Nolan-Haley. 1991. *Black's Law Dictionary*. St. Paul, MN: West Publishing.

Olson, J. M., N. J. Roese and J. Meen. 1995. The preconditions and consequences of relative deprivation: Two field studies. *Journal of Applied Social Psychology* 25: 944–94.

Osborne, D. M. 1992. Reaching for doubt. *The American Lawyer*: 62–69.

Parmenter, T. 1970. Breakdown in law and order. In *Ghetto Revolts*, ed. P. H. Rossi, Chicago: Aldine: 51–68.

Porter, B. and M. Dunn. 1984. *The Miami Riots of 1980: Crossing the Bounds*. Lexington, KY: Lexington Books.

Quarantelli, E. L., D. Wenger, D. Binder, L. W. Sherman and R. B. McKay. Riots. In *Encyclopedia of Criminal Justice, Vol. 4*, ed. S. H. Kadish, New York: The Free Press: 1379–98.

Quarantelli, E. L. and R. Dynes. 1970. Property norms and looting: Their patterns in community crises. *Phylon: The Atlanta University Review of Race and Culture* 31: 168–82.

Radelet, L. A. 1986. *The Police and the Community, 4th ed.* New York: Macmillan: 221–29.

Rainwater, L. 1970. Open letter on white justice and the riots. In *Ghetto Revolts,* ed. P. H. Rossi, Chicago: Aldine: 69–86.

Rasmussen, M. J. M. 1999. The military role in internal defense and security: Some problems: Occasional Paper #6. Monterey, CA: The Center For Civil-Military Relations Naval Postgraduate School. Available online at: http://www.ccmr.org/public/images/download/defense.pdf.

RAND. 1992. RAND news release, June 17, 1992. California: RAND Criminal Justice Research Program.

Ritzer, G. 1992. *Contemporary Sociological Theory, 3rd ed.* New York: McGraw-Hill: 123–32.

Roebuck, J. B., K. S. Murty and R. A. Smith. 1993. Marielitos, Cuban detainees and the Atlanta riot: A study in identity and stigma management. *Studies in Symbolic Interaction: A Research Annual* 14(2): 239–68.

Rohrlich, T. 1991. Majority says police brutality is common. *Los Angeles Times,* March 10: E7–8.

Rosenfeld, M. J. 1997. Celebration, politics, selective looting and riots: A micro level study of the Bulls riot of 1992 in Chicago. *Social Problems* 44(4): 483–502.

Rosenthal, R. A. 1969. *Riots?* Westport, CT: Pendulum Press.

Schnaubelt, C. M. 1997. Lessons in command and control from the Los Angeles riots. *Parameters* 27(2): 88–109. Available online at: http://carlisle-www.army.mil/usawc/Parameters/97summer/schnau.htm.

Scott, J. 1991. Violence born of the group. *Los Angeles Times,* March 28: E3–4.

Sears, D. O. and J. B. McConahay. 1967. *Los Angeles Riot Study: Riot Participation.* UCLA: Institute of Government and Public Affairs.

Sears, D. O. and T. M. Tomlinson. 1968. Riot ideology in Los Angeles: A study of Negro attitudes. *Social Science Quarterly* 49: 485–503.

Senate Task Force. 1992. New initiatives for a new Los Angeles: Final report and recommendations, Senate Task Force on a new Los Angeles. Los Angeles, December 9.

Singer, B. and R. W. Osborn. 1970. *Black Rioters.* Lexington, MA: D.C. Heath and Company.

Smelser, N. J. 1963. *Theory of Collective Behavior.* New York: Free Press.

Snow, D. A. and P. E. Oliver. 1995. Social movements and collective behavior: Social psychological dimensions and considerations. In *Sociological Perspectives on Social Psychology,* eds. K. S. Cook, G. A. Fine and J. S. House, Boston: Allyn and Bacon: 571–99.

Spilerman, S. 1976. Structural characteristics of cities and the severity of racial disorders. *American Sociological Review* 41: 771–93.

Tanowitz, M. 1968. *Social Control of Escalated Riots.* Chicago: University of Chicago Center for Policy Study.

Tierney, K. J. 1994. Property damage and violence: A collective behavior analysis. In *The Los Angeles Riots: Lessons for the Urban Future,* ed. M. Baldassare, Boulder, CO: Westview Press.

Tomas Rivera Center (TRC).1993. Latinos & the L.A. uprising. Los Angeles: Economics Department and International and Public Affairs Center, Occidental College.

Tomlinson, T. M. and D. L. TenHueten. 1970. Riot participation. In *The Los Angeles Riots,* ed. N. Cohen, New York: Praeger: 127–39.

Turner, R. H. 1994. Race riots past and present: A collective-cultural behavior approach. *Symbolic Interaction* 17: 309–324.

Vernon, R. 1993. *L.A. Justice.* Colorado Springs, CO: Focus on the Family Publishing.

Vold, G. and T. J. Bernard. 1986. *Theoretical Criminology, 3rd ed.* New York: Oxford University Press.

Wall, B. H. 1992. *The Rodney King Rebellion: A Psychopolitical Analysis of Racial Despair and Hope.* Chicago: African American Images.

Waters, M. 1992. Testimony before the Senate Banking Committee. In *Inside the L.A. Riots: What Really Happened and Why It Will Happen Again,* ed. D. Hazen, New York: Institute for Alternative Journalism: 26–27.

Webster Commission. 1992. The city in crisis: A report by the special advisor to the board of police commissions on the civil disorder in Los Angeles. Los Angeles, October 21.

Williams, M. 1993. Miami officer Lozano acquitted. *The Atlanta Journal Constitution,* May 29: A1, A6.

Worsnop, R. L. 1991. Police brutality. *Congressional Quarterly Researcher* 1(17): 633–56, September 6.

Discussion Questions

1. Describe the Rodney King events and how they led to the Los Angeles riots.
2. What was the criminal justice response to the riots? How could the response have been improved?
3. How can the police reduce the amount of force and the use of firearms in quelling riots?
4. How can the police detect sooner the signs of community unrest, hostility and anger which precede riots and utilize immediate preventive measures? For example, this may require the arrest of disorderly leaders.
5. How can the police gain the respect, cooperation and aid of the lower class?
6. How can a city meet the economic, educational and social needs of its underclass before riots are employed as a mechanism of social change?

THE MUMBAI TERRORIST ATTACK AND THE CRIMINAL JUSTICE RESPONSE

By Arvind Verma and Sabrina Medora

Introduction: The Nature of Terrorism

Terrorism is now a well-known phenomenon and almost every part of the world seems affected by it. Even though the 9/11 attacks were the first ones that really brought its horrors to television screens around the world in dramatic fashion, it is not a new form of violent crime, but one that has been witnessed since the beginning of recorded history. Although a universally accepted definition of this crime still remains elusive, terrorism is associated with violence being used to achieve political objectives. However, this perception can change when the terrorist emerges victorious and the action might then be designated as freedom struggle rather than a terroristic act. For example, the British described George Washington and his men as terrorists and now we recognize them as freedom fighters.

Nevertheless, some attempts at defining terrorism are noteworthy. The United States Department of Defense defines terrorism as "the calculated use of unlawful violence or threat of unlawful violence to inculcate fear; intended to coerce or to intimidate governments or societies in the pursuit of goals that are generally political, religious, or ideological" (2009). Interestingly, another unit of the U.S. government, the State Department, defines terrorism to be "premeditated, politically motivated violence perpetrated against noncombatant targets by subnational groups or clandestine agents, usually intended to influence an audience" (2004). The FBI takes its version from the Code of Federal Regulations, defining terrorism as "the unlawful use of force and violence against persons or property to intimidate or coerce a government, the civilian population, or any segment thereof, in furtherance of political or social objectives"

(C.F.R. 2008). The United Nations definition established in 1992 has wide acceptability among many nations: "Terrorism is an anxiety-inspiring method of repeated violent action, employed by (semi-) clandestine individual, group or state actors, for idiosyncratic, criminal or political reasons, whereby—in contrast to assassination—the direct targets of violence are not the main targets" (UN 1992). Yet it needs to be emphasized that all the United Nations' members have not been able to agree on a commonly accepted definition of the crime.

Whatever its definition, it is clear that the objective of the terrorists is to influence wider public opinion and to bring media attention to their act and perhaps to their cause. The September 11, 2001 attacks were not targeted towards the specific victims working in the World Trade Center or taking those fateful flights. It was an attack on American economic, military and political interests and a demonstration of the reach of Islamic extremists across geographies. The Mumbai incident too falls in the same category: an attack on the economic hub of India, an attack on selected targets where foreigners congregate and an attack that could cause communal disharmony between the Hindus and the Muslims. A major terrorist incident not only causes considerable damage to people and property but also scars the society for a long time. The disastrous consequences of any such terrorist incident have the potential of causing fissures in the society, promoting social conflict and above all exposing the limitations and hollowness of government agencies. An act of terrorism therefore achieves multiple objectives for the perpetrators who succeed spectacularly despite their limited resources. Terrorism is also a kind of psychological battle where terrorists choose their targets and victims with deliberation to maximize the impacts of their actions and to project their criminal behavior in terms of larger causes. In this chapter, we examine the catastrophic outcome of terrorism that has been going on in India for many years and in particular focus upon the Mumbai attack. We describe the resultant impact upon many individuals targeted by the terrorists and the social, economic and psychological outcomes of this dastardly attack. We argue that Indian authorities, including all government agencies, must take into account the disastrous consequence of terrorism and focus upon the widespread calamity that emanates from any incident as major as that seen in Mumbai.

Literature Review: The Disastrous Consequences of Terrorism

The disastrous consequences of terrorism have largely been examined in terms of security issues but it is clear that terrorism has a broader impact

(Clarke 2003). Destruction of physical infrastructure, disruption of communications and transport, resources needed to rebuild the damage to buildings and general rehabilitation all have direct and indirect economic costs that themselves have a significant and long-term impact. For example, the terrorist attack on Indian Parliament in December, 2002 was blamed on Pakistan-based terrorists acting in concert with its army and notorious spy agency, Inter-Services Intelligence (ISI). The Indian government ordered the mobilization of the Indian army for a retaliatory attack against terrorist training camps in Pakistan-occupied Kashmir. Pakistan responded with a large scale deployment of its own troops and threatened escalation of war to other frontiers. Apart from the serious threat of nuclear war that seemed real at the time, the mobilization of troops also resulted in considerable economic costs for the two countries. It took a year before the tensions simmered down. Similarly, the explosives attack on Sarojini market in Delhi (Unnithan, Sharma and Mehra 2005) and the planting of bombs on Mumbai's commuter trains (CNN 2006) also caused a large amount of economic loss to the nation and to individual businesses. Thissen (2004: 321) states that besides the consequences of the destruction of the transport infrastructure itself, increased security measures also lead to significant changes in the costs of transportation and thereby have cumulative economic effects. India has been forced to enhance security measures for the transport sector including railways, buses and of course the airways. Armed guards and metal detectors have been placed at every station and entry-exit points in major metropolitan areas, which is an additional economic cost of these public services.

The impact of terrorist attacks on individuals and their family members is of course immense. After the Oklahoma City federal building bombing in 1995, there were sharp increases in psychological distress (Benight et al. 2000). Shalev (1992) reports post traumatic stress disorder among injured survivors in a terrorist attack on a civilian bus. In a focus group survey, it was observed that among those only indirectly impacted, the 9/11 attack caused fear, stress anxiety and frustration and further caused the people to look inward and reassess their lives (Daw 2002). The September 11 attacks also led to changes in cultural values and cosmopolitanism. Olivas-Lujan, Harzing and McCoy (2002) report that among the students sampled, those traumatized by the terrorist attack changed their perceptions to place a lower value on variety, adventure and challenge and were more concerned about security and stability in their job search. An inevitable change emanating from the September 11 attacks is the hardening of attitudes toward minorities and immigrants. There were attacks on Arabs, Muslims and even Sikhs after 9/11 and Esses et al. (2002) report that attitudes against immigrants in the U.S. and Canada hardened. This change in attitude has serious consequences, as community life is adversely affected and social conflict increases. Of course, such terrorist incidents seriously upset routine functioning of organizations and their personnel. "It was impossible for firms to continue business as usual immediately following the attacks of the WTC given the loss of lives and destruction of physical plant" (Burke 2005: 635). After the Mumbai attack of November 26, 2008, Bantillo and Chakravarty (2008) found that "Indian business confidence has suffered a serious blow following coordinated terrorist attacks in the country's commercial capital Mumbai." As expected, the attacks also took a significant toll on the city's populous. Dr. Bhutani, a psychiatrist in Mumbai reported that "the 'horrendous pictures' have had the most terrible impact on youngsters from three to fourteen" (Krishnan 2008).

Even bureaucracies and political leadership are seriously affected and compromised by disasters following major terrorist attacks. For instance, the establishment of the Department of Homeland Security (DHS) in the wake of the 9/11 attacks led to turf wars among its various agencies, which included the Federal Emergency Management Agency (FEMA). These functional changes "fighting terrorism from a crime fighting mode, rather than viewing terrorism as another disaster agent, has resulted in a collapse of morale at FEMA and a diminished role" (Fischer 2005: 659). The Mumbai attack led to the resignation of the Home Minister Shivraj Patil from the Union Cabinet as well as that of the Chief Minister of Maharashtra, where Mumbai is located, for security lapses. The security agencies received considerable flak and underwent massive reorganization as a consequence of the attack.

A Brief Review of Terrorist Related Disaster in India

It may come as a surprise to readers that a recent report suggests that except for Iraq, India records the highest number of terrorist attacks and killings (Raghuraman 2007). India is situated in a geographical region where terror abounds. Pakistan to its northeast is an unstable country and home to some of the terrorist group al Qaeda. Pakistan has also been exporting terrorism to India's Kashmir region where in the last two decades almost 50,000 people have been killed in extremist related activities. In the 1980s, Pakistan was also promoting Sikh terrorists who caused mayhem in the Punjab region of India. To the east, Bangladesh is another unstable nation where radical Muslim groups are active and spreading their tentacles to India. Recently, in several bombings carried out in Indian cities, the perpetrators had links with groups in Bangladesh. Northeastern Indian states have also been victimized by the tribal group Naga and other separatists who have been operating since the 1960s. In central India, the left wing Maoist groups have caused widespread terror and prevented developmental activities in several regions.

The disastrous impact of terrorism in the northernmost Indian state of Jammu and Kashmir has been extremely severe and caused immense hardship to the people. Pakistan's adoption of a policy of a "thousand cuts" has seen its military agencies covertly engaged in promoting terrorist attacks on the Indian side of the border. Many tactics have been used to terrorize the population and promote disharmony among the people. In particular, the militants targeted the Hindu minority population and have carried out a form of ethnic cleansing, driving almost all the Hindus from Kashmir valley. More than 350,000 people of the minority community have had to flee their homes in the valley and today live as refugees in other parts of their own state and country (Kashmir Information Network 2009). These militants also burned down the Hazaratbal mosque that is considered sacred to the Muslims in order to provoke violent clashes. To combat the terrorist threats, the government has been forced to deploy army and paramilitary units in large numbers. The area is littered with check points and encounters with the terrorists in dense neighborhoods are not uncommon. Tourism, which is the mainstay of the state, has been significantly destroyed and violence has scarred the young who have seen nothing else in their lives.

Pakistan-inspired terrorism has had disastrous consequences in other parts of the country, as well. In 2001, one group hijacked an Indian Airlines plane from Kathmandu and forced the Indian government to release three hard core terrorists imprisoned in the country. None of these offenders have since been arrested, as they have found shelter in Pakistan. One of the people that the Indian government was forced to release in exchange for the passenger hostages was Masood Azhar, who was involved in the murder of journalist Daniel Pearl in 2002. Pakistan's use of covert forces and undeniable assistance to terrorist groups indulging in attacks on India has prevented normal relations between the two countries. Both nations have acquired nuclear arms and spend a significant portion of their budgets on military preparations. This clearly has adverse effect upon their economies and makes them unable to provide for their impoverished populations. Illiteracy, poor health infrastructure and malnourishment of a large segment of the people are some of the additional disastrous consequences of terrorism in the region.

The North Eastern (NE) region of India is another area affected by separatist groups that have indulged in terrorism. The Nagas and most recently radical Assamese groups have carried out attacks against military, police and civilian targets. NE is largely a region inhabited by indigenous people with a history of inter-ethnic rivalries. In small pockets, terrorist attacks on government establishments, police and army posts have occurred since the 1960s. Their targets were also people who did not support their cause and those who were aligned with the state. Terrorism in NE has continued for a long period of time and its disastrous impact is visible everywhere; NE states are lagging behind in economic development despite abundant natural resources. Widespread poverty, illiteracy and lack of employment opportunities are one end product of violent extremism flourishing in the region.

The terror tactics of various factions of radical leftwing groups that are seeking the overthrow of duly elected governments have potentially disastrous consequences. Inspired by Maoist ideology, they have targeted the well-off farmers, money-lenders and generally the bourgeoisie who have been dubbed exploiters of the working people. Around 1967, a powerful movement emerged at Naxalbari in West Bengal and Srikakulam in Andhra Pradesh (Dasgupta 1974) and these radical leftwing extremists have been known as "Naxalites" in common parlance ever since. The threat of these Naxalites spread even to the city of Calcutta in the beginning of the 1970s, where extortion from business people, kidnapping and rape of women, as well as destruction of property were some of the acts perpetuated in the name of overthrowing the state. A major consequence was the flight of capital and businesses from Calcutta, which had disastrous impact upon the economy of the region (Gupta 2004).

These radical communist groups are now active in the Indian states of Bihar, Orissa, Madhya Pradesh and Andhra Pradesh (AP). The region of Central India today is seriously affected by radical Maoist extremism. Naxalites have prevented development activities such as roads and communications, diminishing police capacity to make inroads into their domains. They have destroyed schools, communication towers, railway stations and mining roads so that there is little economic growth taking place. This region is one of the poorest in the country and the tribal people residing there are unable to take advantage of the natural resources such as minerals, forests and rivers that could spur economic development. Terrorism has destroyed normal life and many areas of the region are akin to a war scenario.

In many cases, terrorism that begins with the objective of confronting the state for specific grievances ends up bringing immeasurable disaster in the long run. Terrorism in Punjab began with the demand of Punjabi Suba, an autonomous region for the Sikhs, and quickly degenerated into crippling the state apparatus through targeted, violent attacks. The Sikh terrorists found it convenient to operate from Pakistan and carry out attacks on police as well as the civilian population across the international border. They planted bombs on buses, trains and exploded them in market areas to terrorize the population and cause a breakdown in normal life and routines. Prominent people including journalists and newspaper editors who dared to speak against them were murdered. Even family members of police and army personnel were killed to break the morale of government forces and cause panic in the society. These Sikh militants received considerable support, funds and material resources, not only from Pakistan but also from Sikh communities in England, Canada and the United States (Gill 1997). For nearly a decade, terrorism continued in Punjab and could only be crushed with a heavy handed police and army action (Joshi 1993). The Sikh terrorists carried out some spectacular attacks, such as the murder of Prime Minister Indira Gandhi in 1984, the bombing of an Air India plane traveling from Toronto in 1985 and the killing of the Chief Minister of Punjab in 1995. For nearly 10 years, Punjab burned fiercely and posed a severe threat to the integrity of the entire country. At present, Punjab is largely at peace and has recovered economically, but several militant groups are merely dormant and not totally vanquished, nor have the scars of old wounds disappeared.

There are a number of other extremist groups operating in different parts of India. The Liberation Tigers of Tamil Eelam (LTTE) operated against the Sri Lankan government but also maintained several cells in southern India, where they carried out operations against the Indian authorities. As may be remembered, LTTE killed Rajiv Gandhi, a former prime minister in a suicide attack in 1992. At present and in a disturbing trend, some disgruntled Muslims have formed a group called Student Islamic Movement of India (SIMI), who have carried out a number of terrorist attacks in the country. The radical Hindu group Bajrang Dal has also promoted a terrorist outfit called Abhinav Bharat, targeting Muslims. India faces a number of formidable terrorist challenges that all have potentially dangerous consequences for the country and its people.

The Mumbai Incident of November 26, 2008

Thanks to the prosecution evidence filed in court, the story of the terrorist attack is now known to the public (*The Hindu* 2009). The incident on November 26, 2008 resulted in the murder of 165 people, including security personnel and 26 foreigners, with 304 people seriously injured. The terrorists focused their attack on five principal places, namely the CST railway station, the Leopold Café, the Taj and Trident Oberoi Hotels and Nariman house, all situated within two square kilometers of the Gateway of India monument in south Mumbai. Altogether, 10 terrorists perpetrated the attacks. Nine were killed during the melee and one was captured by the Indian police. These terrorists were trained and armed by Laskhar-e-Taiba (LeT) in Muridke, Manshera and Muzaffrabad in Pakistan. LeT had selected 35 operatives who were given extensive arms and ammunition training and taught to be suicide attackers. Some of these attackers were diverted and sent to fight in Kashmir while a final group of 10 was selected to continue training near a hideout in Karachi. LeT leaders involved in training and preparations included Zaki-ur-Rehman Lakhvi, Abu Hamza, Mujjamil (alias Yusuf) and Abu Kaafa who were known to the intelligence agencies of many different countries. The reconstructed sequence of events suggests that these 10 operatives set sail on November 22 from Karachi and hijacked an Indian fishing boat called Kuber. They killed all the sailors except one who was forced to take the trawler to Mumbai harbor. Here, the terrorists got down into two rubber dinghies about a nautical mile off the coast and killed the remaining sailor before setting sail again. However, in their haste, they left behind the GPS instrument that they were using for navigation. On the evening of November 26, they slipped into Mumbai harbor near the Gateway of India, split into groups and took taxis to their assigned destinations. They planted improvised explosive devices (IEDs) in these taxis, which later exploded and killed the drivers. Around 9:20 p.m., Ajmal Kasab, the terrorist captured by the police, and his leader Ismail Khan reached the Central Railway station where they fired their AK-47 assault rifles indiscriminately, killing 58 and injuring 104 people. They were engaged by police personnel, but managed to kill three senior officers and steal their vehicle. However, they were intercepted and engaged by the local police, who managed to kill Ismail and capture Ajmal Kasab alive. Most of the information about the attacks has come from the interrogation of this terrorist. The other groups attacked their targets, killing indiscriminately in a similar manner. One group lobbed grenades at Leopold Café and then came back again to kill anyone they could see alive. This group then moved to a neighboring locality known as Nariman house, which provides Jewish community living in Mumbai. Two groups stationed themselves at the Taj and Trident hotels, killing the guests and staff and setting fire to various parts of the buildings. It took almost two days before commandos and other security forces could corner and kill them in close combat encounters within the buildings' premises.

These days were filled with terror for the residents of and visitors to Mumbai and their horror was captured live by a host of television and other media that covered the attacks and engagement by security forces. This was a serious lapse, as the attack orchestrators could watch the live coverage and constantly inform the terrorists about police action and guide them in their attacks using satellite phones. This information enabled the terrorists to take defensive positions and locate and kill people hiding in different parts of the hotel. Commandos were air dropped onto the Nariman house by helicopter, which was shown live. The coverage alerted the two attackers to kill their hostages in a gruesome manner before they could be killed by the commandos. The mayhem in south Mumbai and the transmission of this terrifying experience to a global audience might have further encouraged the terrorists, as it brought attention to their group and its capacity to cripple a major metropolitan city of India.

The disastrous consequences of this terrorist attack were widely evident. The destruction of property including that of the old heritage tomb at the Taj Hotel was only a minor casualty of this attack, but a significant one. Ratan Tata, the Chiarman of Taj Hotels said, "I was truly emotionally overcome when I saw this old, venerable, rather beautiful building going up in flames, and I kept hearing the grenades or explosives going on inside" (Zakaria 2008). The disruption to road transport, railways and even pedestrian traffic in a major metropolitan region affected millions of commuters. In the ensuing attack, the apprehension of family members and relatives about their dear ones caught in the midst of the attack can only be imagined. As news of killing spread across the city, nation and world, the plight of grieving relatives and horrors of surviving the attack is difficult to describe. The emergency services, particularly ambulance and paramedic services in India are in a deplorable state. The inability of the government to come to the aid of the citizens for hours can only suggest the calamity that engulfed Mumbai residents over those fateful days.

We have some eyewitness accounts and personal narratives that vividly describe these horrendous moments. We will call one of these people X. X was having dinner with his wife at the Taj Harbour restaurant on the evening of November 26, when they heard what sounded like a heavy tray smashing to the ground followed by 20 or 30 similar sounds. Realizing that there were gunmen next door, they crouched behind tables to hide. A courageous staff motioned that it was safe to run to the stairwell and to another part of the building. They made it in time but after they climbed the stairs, terrorists came into the Harbour Bar, shot everyone who was there and executed those next door at the Golden Dragon restaurant. The staff there was equally brave, locking their patrons into a basement wine cellar to protect them. But the terrorists managed to break through and lob in grenades that killed everyone in the basement. X and his wife took refuge in the kitchen of another restaurant, Wasabi, and using text messaging, came to realize the extent of the ongoing terrorist attack on Mumbai. They hid in this area for some time, blocking the door with heavy tables. The terrorist followed them and banged at the door, but not hearing any sound from inside, gave up. Later, the Taj staff escorted X and his wife to another part of the hotel called Chambers, where almost 250 guests were assembled. Their safety was short lived as a thoughtless leader appearing on television announced that many dignitaries and foreigners were safe in the Chambers region of Taj Hotel. This information was communicated by the Pakistan-based orchestrators to the attackers at the Taj, who then went down to search for this room. There were several grenade attacks but the terrorists could not reach the Chambers. However, knowing that the terrorists were targeting foreigners, X separated from his wife, who was of Indian origin, in order to maximize the chance of survival of at least one family member. X hid in a toilet while his wife went with other people to another part of the hotel. X describes his experience in following words:

> I cannot even begin to explain the level of adrenaline running through my system at this point. It was this hyper-aware state where every sound, every smell, every piece of information was ultra-acute, analyzed and processed so that we could make the best decisions and maximize the odds of survival. Was the fire above us life-threatening? What floor was it on? Were the commandos near us, or were they terrorists? Why is it so quiet? Did the commandos survive? If the terrorists come into the bathroom and to the door, when they fire in, how can I make my body as small as possible? If Y [hiding with X in the toilet] gets killed before me in this situation, how can I throw his body on mine to barricade the door? If the Indian commandos liberate the rest in the other room, how will they know where I am? Do the terrorists have suicide vests? Will the roof stand? How can I make sure the FBI knows where I am? When is it safe to stand up and attempt to urinate? (Pollack 2008).

For hours, people were clinging to one another, hiding behind furniture and barely moving. Bullets were flying everywhere as commandos engaged the terrorists who too were running from room to room. Many people who tried to leave via the fire escape were shot and killed by the terrorists, as were the staff members trying to protect their guests. X states further:

> The 10 minutes around 2:30 a.m. were the most frightening. Rather than the back-and-forth of gunfire, we just heard single, punctuated shots. We later learned that the terrorists went along a different corridor of The Chambers, room by room, and systematically executed everyone: women, elderly, Muslims, Hindus, foreigners. Everyone was in deep prayer and most had accepted that their lives were likely

over. It was terrorism in its purest form. No one was spared. The next five hours were filled with the sounds of an intense grenade/gun battle between the Indian commandos and the terrorists. It was fought in darkness; each side was trying to outflank the other (Pollack 2008).

An elderly person, Y, had a horrendous experience of being shot and left for dead by the terrorists. He was in a large room when the terrorists forced their way in and rounded up the approximately 20 people hiding there, taking them to the 18th floor of the hotel. All the people were lined against the wall and the terrorists opened fire simultaneously. Y had the presence to duck and fall to the floor, getting hit by a bullet that grazed his neck. Other bodies fell on top of him and sheltered him as the terrorists fired another series of bullets intended to kill everyone. Y describes the scene as follows:

Bent almost in double, crushed by the weight of the bodies above him, and suffocating in the torrent of blood rushing down on him from the various bodies I held on for 10 minutes while the terrorists left the area. When I finally had the courage to wiggle my arms I found that there were four other survivors in the room. We communicated to each other by touch as we were too afraid to make a sound. I moved just enough to allow myself room to breathe and then lay still. We passed over 12 hours lying still in the heap of bodies too afraid to move. We constantly heard gunfire and hand grenades going off in the other parts of the hotel but lay still fearing that any noise would bring the terrorists back. After approximately 12 hours, the terrorists returned with a camera and flashlight and joked and laughed as they filmed what they thought was a pile of dead bodies. They then moved to the landing below to set up more explosives at which I ran away towards the roof to escape (*The Beehive* 2008).

Another person going through the same experience was traumatized so badly that he still suffers from the memory of the attack. His wife states, "His wounds have been treated but he is suffering severe emotional trauma. There are days when he refuses to eat or even drink. Naturally, he no longer has his job. He does not speak except for occasional screaming incoherently. He does not sleep at night and suffers from extreme cases of frequent panic attacks. He has not left his house since he returned from the hospital" (*The Beehive* 2008).

The comparatively short lived attack on the Leopold Café was equally frightening for the guests partying there that evening. Eric, a member of the staff at Leopold Café, was present during the attacks. His usual job was to greet guests outside the café, but he had taken a short break to sit with some friends at a table on one side of the café. At about 9:30 p.m., he noticed two men wearing heavy backpacks standing around outside Leopold's talking on the phone. He thought nothing of it. Approximately seven minutes later, he got up from his table to go to the cash counter, at which time the men strolled in and threw two grenades. One exploded, one did not. Amidst the confusion, the men began to fire at random, killing both customers and staff alike. Abruptly, the shooting stopped and the two men walked out. Everyone seemed to think the ordeal was over and the uninjured were trying desperately to help those who were shot. A mere three minutes later, the gunmen entered once again and resumed firing. Eric ran toward the back exit, followed by two of his fellow workers, who were both shot. Both collapsed, bleeding profusely. The terrorists soon followed and killed both the waiters. Eric ran for his life and a bullet grazed the right side of his head, causing him to bleed but leaving no permanent damage. Eric ran to Gokuldas Tejpal (GT) Hospital, calling his family along the way and telling them to meet him there. (GT Hospital has a link to Cama Hospital, which was also later attacked by the terrorists.) Eric and his family hid in one of the X-ray rooms for over an hour but managed to leave and go home by 4 a.m. Eric confided that the terrorists looked like they were on drugs. They wore calm expressions and were very methodical in their attack. There were some evening classes going on the first floor of a building opposite the café. A child stuck his head out to view the commotion and one of the terrorists shot him point blank in the head. Eric described that he could have been shot thrice, once at the entrance (but fate had it so that he was seated at a table), once at his table where his friends were grievously injured (but fate intervened again and sent him to the cash counter) and finally when the terrorists followed him and the waiters and shot them to death outside the café. He added, "The city runs on faith" (personal communication).

The city residents who were not directly victimized were nonetheless traumatized. One resident describes the aftermath in the following words:

> Yes I do but life goes on and people have short memories. Initially I was very shaky and did not want to go out to restaurants but slowly that changed. Life goes on but it could have been any of us at these places that night. Even now when I enter a hotel and I go through the security check my mind does go back to that night but I also know that if there was another attack today, these security checks will show up useless. What can one security guard with a metal detector do, when confronted with men with automatic guns? I still haven't gone to the Taj for a meal to date (personal communication).

Describing her losses, she added:

Yohann [her son] lost a batch mate [Uday Singh Kang, whose father is the general manager of the Taj Hotel]. I lost someone whose child and Yohann were in nursery and cathedral school together and we would meet often in school. She was wonderfully funny, outspoken and had a sunny disposition. I still find it hard to believe that she is gone. She and her husband were killed that night and left behind two young daughters. Mehmood [her husband] lost a school friend whose son is in Yohann's class at school. Our friend Chef Rego [the executive chef of the Taj] lost his son, who was a chef in the Bombay Hotel. I don't think life in Mumbai will ever be the same and I now do not like going to hotels and cinemas, any place where there isn't a quick way to exit. We went to Frangipani [the restaurant at the Oberoi Hotel] last week. I was uncomfortable because they have closed the restaurant entrance so you have to enter the hotel lobby and go down a flight of stairs. Can you imagine what would happen if there is a second attack? The people in Frangipani and India Jones restaurants will be sitting ducks because they will not be able to exit the hotel (personal communication).

The attacks negatively impacted the Indian economy, which compounded by the global economic meltdown, faced tremendous challenges for several months after. However, the Indian economy appears to be coming out of the slump as of mid-2009. Nevertheless, there is a growing realization that the failure to manage the immediate as well as the wide-ranging consequences of the terrorist attack brought about a greater disaster, which itself was compounded by a lack of planning and coordination among state agencies. Many injured and even the dead were sent from one hospital to another in the absence of orders detailing where each case would be handled. In one instance 10 foreigners, traumatized by the siege at the Taj Hotel, were taken to the Azad Maidan police station but were turned away, as the policeman in charge there stated he had no orders to record foreigners' statements. A civic hospital doctor stated that the failure to manage the disaster was a bigger tragedy than the attacks and that many lives may have been lost due to gross negligence and lack of coordination (personal communication). Mumbai lacked a disaster plan and all concerned agencies were caught napping when the attack took place. This lack of planning was evident in the use of municipal hospitals for both treating the injured and handling the dead bodies. For example, JJ Hospital was so overrun with those in need of medical attention that it affected the provision of medical assistance when urgently required. A doctor assisting the injured said "A Briton who was shot at Leopold was saved only because he was rushed to a private hospital. Had he been sent to an overburdened public hospital with inadequate staff, he would have bled to death in the huge pool of patients, each of who needed immediate attention" (Iyer 2008).

Response of Criminal Justice and Related Agencies

In its paper on the Mumbai attack, RAND (2009) has identified a number of lapses by Indian security agencies that we summarize here. First, there was credible intelligence about this impending attack on Mumbai and on the Taj Hotel in particular, with terrorists coming by way of Arabian Sea. Even the United States had warned the Indian authorities about this impending attack, but it seems that there was little coordination among the two major intelligence agencies, Research and Analysis Wing (RAW) and the Intelligence Bureau (IB), nor was there coordination with local police. Indian intelligence had picked up some chatter about preparations for this attack, but this was not adequately shared with the local police or with the coastal guards. The attack exposed the considerable limitations in maritime surveillance and the failure of the Indian navy and coast guards that enabled the terrorists to reach Mumbai harbor without detection. The biggest limitation was the poor quality of local police forces that had few modern weapons and virtually no training to combat the terrorists. As RAND (2009: 9) reports "Although the force has the ability to fend off common criminals, it is completely lacking in training to deal with a well orchestrated terrorist attack." Moreover, the sole commando unit trained to combat terrorists, the National Security Guards (NSG) was based in Delhi and took almost 15 hours to arrive at Mumbai and begin containing the terrorists. The Marine commandos were also called to help quell the attack, but there were multiple command centers and little evidence of coordination among the variety of forces engaged in action.

The logistic and organizational problems plaguing the Indian police authorities were completely exposed in this attack. The police failed to establish a command center to coordinate the counterattack. This meant that there was no one to guide the various police units involved in the combat. Furthermore, the absence of a control room meant that the media reported everything going on in the combat zone. Various television channels continued to show all police action live and as mentioned, this information was being observed by the attack orchestrators who used the information to guide the terrorists in their attacks. As the evidence presented in the courts reveals, the orchestrators not only provided information to the terrorists about the commandos moving in, but also about where the important guests were hiding in the hotel and instructed them to kill the hostages in advance of police action.

These orchestrators further instructed the terrorists to set fire to the hotels from within, which aggravated the problems. Like the police services, the firefighters were untrained and could not coordinate their action. Fires burned for long hours before they could be contained. There were inadequate ambulance services and many of the injured were shifted to the emergency rooms by family, friends or passersby. This was particularly disastrous at the railway station where almost 60 people had been gunned down and their bodies were lying unclaimed for hours. The breakdown in the communication systems, cordoning off of roads and disruption in railway trains all meant that thousands of people were dislocated, stranded and seemingly lost for many hours. The impact on their families and relatives can only be imagined. Many victims were young children who found themselves alone with the dead bodies of their parents or guardians. In some cases, it would take days before their acute traumatization ended and they could be comforted by their other relatives.

Conclusion

The Mumbai terrorist attack of 2008 brought into clear relief the dangerous consequences of terrorist attacks and how even a small group of perpetrators can cause mayhem in any modern metropolitan city. Just 10 terrorists armed with automatic weapons and grenades were able to bring a major financial and business center of the nation to a grinding halt. Apart from the economic blow to the country, this attack also revealed how large scale a disaster results from terrorism. Not only were a large number of people killed and injured, but thousands were adversely affected by this attack. For days, people were traumatized, not knowing if they or their loved ones were safe. Any terrorist incident in a modern city can cripple the transport system, disrupt the communication channels and give rise to virulent rumors that can affect millions of people. Furthermore, the ubiquitous media coverage meant that the widespread impact of terror was felt continuously. In Mumbai, not only were a number of foreigners deliberately targeted and killed, but the television coverage of the events was broadcast across the globe. The impact of the attacks was consequently worldwide.

The lessons of Mumbai are beginning to emerge for criminal justice and related agencies. Terrorism is no more merely a matter of combat and security. Terrorist incidents have wide-ranging effects that can turn disastrous for a vast multitude of people. The police need to think about many related issues other than simply battling the terrorists and apprehending them and they need to begin their planning during times of relative calm. In more detail, they need to plan for disruptions in communications and transport, for rumor mongering and for the provision of emergency services, all simultaneously. Moreover, careful consideration must also be given to the media's access to the terrorist attack as it is happening. A task so massive is going to require interagency cooperation, the groundwork for which needs to be laid long before the attack. The immediate impacts of a terrorist attack, those to which police, military, emergency and transportation services respond, are not the only ones that will need responses. Long-term impacts on individuals such as psychological distress, trauma and emotional problems that affect the young and the old must also be considered in disaster planning, as should economic and financial disruptions. Businesses are hurt and industries close down as a result of terrorist attacks, which aggravate unemployment problems and contribute to a subsequent loss of morale. Perhaps the greatest loss of all, people begin to question the ability of the government to ensure their safety and this loss of faith has long-term consequences for democratic functioning and governance of the nation. It is time that criminal justice and related agencies begin thinking about these issues and developing effective strategies to combat the terrorists before they strike. Unfortunately, the next attack cannot be discounted and may already be in the planning stage.

References

Bantillo, P. and M. Chakravarty. 2008. Mumbai attacks hit business confidence. *ICIS News* November 27. Available online at: http://www.icis.com/Articles/2008/11/27/9174934/mumbai-attacks-hit-business-confidence.html.

Beehive, The. 2008. A 26/11 survivor story from the front lines of Mumbai/Bombay India. December 5. Available online at: http://beehive135.blogspot.com/2008/12/2611-survivor-story-from-front-lines-of.html.

Benight, C. C., R. W. Freyaldenhoven, J. Hughes, J. M. Ruiz and T. A. Zoschke. 2000. Coping, self-efficacy, and psychological distress following the Oklahoma City bombing. *Journal of Applied Social Psychology* 30: 1331–44.

Burke, R. J. 2005. Effects of 9/11 on individuals and organizations: Down but not out! *Disaster and Management* 14(5): 629–38.

C.F.R. 2008. Code of Federal Regulations. 28 C.F.R. Section 0.85. Available online at: http://frwebgate.access.gpo.gov/cgi-bin/get-cfr.cgi.

Clarke, L. 2003. Terrorism and disaster: New threats, new ideas. *International Journal of Public Opinion Research* 17: 131–32.

CNN. 2006. At least 174 killed in Indian train blasts. *CNN*, July 11. Available online at: http://www.cnn.com/2006/WORLD/asiapcf/07/11/mumbai.blasts/index.html.

Dasgupta, B. 1974. *The Naxalite Movement.* Centre for the Study of Developing Societies, No.1. Bombay: Allied Publishers.

Daw, J. 2002. 'Window to self-discovery' opened after Sept. 11. *Monitor on Psychology* 33(3): 15.

DOD. 2009. Department of Defense Dictionary of Military Terms. Available online at: http://www.dtic.mil/doctrine/jel/doddict/.

Esses, V. M., J. F. Dovidio and G. Hodson. 2002. Public attitudes toward immigration in the United States and Canada in response to the September 11 2001 attack on America. *Analysis of Social Issues and Public Policy* 2: 69–85.

Fischer, H. W. 2005. The danger in over-reacting to terrorism: Has the U.S. embarked upon a road that should have remained less traveled? *Disaster and Management* 14(5): 657–65.

Gill, K. P. S. 1997. *Punjab: The Knights of Falsehood.* Delhi: Har-Anand Publications.

Gupta, R. K. 2004. *The Crimson Agenda: Maoist Protest and Terror.* Delhi: Wordsmiths.

Hindu, The. 2009. Mumbai attack final form. Available online at: http://www.hindu.com/nic/mumbai-terror-attack-final-form.pdf.

Iyer, M. 2008 Disaster that struck after 26/11 massacre *Times of India*, December 10.

Joshi, M. 1993. Combating terrorism in Punjab: Indian democracy in crisis *Conflict Studies No. 261*, London Research Institute for the Study of Conflict and Terrorism.

Kashmir Information Network 2009. Atrocities in Kashmir. Available online at: http://www.kashmir-information.com/atrocities/index.html.

Krishnan, M. 2008. Traumatic impact of Mumbai attack. *Deutsche Welle*, December 5. Available online at: http://www2.dw-world.de/southasia/South_ Asia/1.234699.1.html.

Olivas-Lujan, M. R., A. W. Harzing and S. McCoy. 2004. September 11, 2001: Two quasi-experiments on the influence of threats on cultural values and cosmopolitanism. *International Journal of Cross-Cultural Management* 4: 211–28.

Pollack, M. 2008. Heroes at the Taj. *Forbes*. Available online at: http://www.forbes.com/2008/12/01/mumbai-terror-taj-oped-cx_mp_1201 pollack.html.

Raghuraman, S. 2007. India loses maximum lives to terror except Iraq. *Times of India*, August 27.

RAND. 2009. Occasional Paper: The lessons of Mumbai. Available online at: http://www.rand.org/pubs/occasional_papers/2009/RAND_OP249.pdf.

Shalev, A. Y. 1992. Posttraumatic stress disorder among injured survivors of a terrorist attack. *The Journal of Nervous and Mental Disease* 180: 505–9.

Thissen, M. 2004. Indirect economic effects of a terrorist attack on transport infrastructure. *Disaster Prevention and Management* 13(4): 315–22.

U.S. State Department. 2004. Patterns of global terrorism 2003. Available online at: http://www.state.gov/documents/organization/31932.pdf.

United Nations. 1992. Definitions of terrorism. Available online at: http://web.archive.org/web/20070129121539/http://www.unodc.org/unodc/terro rism_definitions.html.

Unnithan, S., A. Sharma and P. Mehra. 2005. Terror in Delhi. *India Today*, November 14. Available online at: http://www.india-today.com/itoday/ 20051114/cover.html.

Zakaria, F. 2008. GPS transcript: Taj Hotel owner speaks to CNN. *CNN*, November 30. Available online at: http://www.cnn.com/2008/WORLD/ asiapcf/ 11/30/gps.transcript.tata/index.html.

Discussion Questions

1. What are some of the definitions of terrorism that have been proposed? How are they similar to and different from one another?
2. What were the Mumbai attacks designed to do? In your estimation, did they accomplish those goals?
3. What are some of the economic costs of terrorism? What are some of the deleterious effects of terrorist attacks on victims and families?
4. Describe some of previous terrorist attacks in India and their effects on the Indian people.
5. Provide an account of the Mumbai terrorist attack of November 26, 2008. What are the main sources of information about the planning and execution of the attack?
6. Do you believe the media coverage of the attack exacerbated them? Give evidence for your answer.
7. What were the limitations of criminal justice and related agencies that hampered their ability to effectively respond to the attacks? How might these agencies overcome these limitations for the future?

THE NEW ORLEANS POLICE DEPARTMENT DURING HURRICANE KATRINA—LESSONS LEARNED: AN INTERVIEW WITH SUPERINTENDENT OF POLICE, WARREN J. RILEY

By Dee Wood Harper[1]

Introduction

Warren J. Riley was appointed Interim Superintendent on September 27, 2005, 28 days after Hurricane Katrina. He was officially sworn in as Superintendent of Police on November 24, 2005. During the storm, he served as Chief of Operations from a command post in the French Quarter. Superintendent Riley is a 26-year veteran of the New Orleans Police Department. Prior to his appointment as Superintendent, he served as the Deputy Superintendent, the number two position in the Department, and as the Chief Operations Officer. As the Chief Operations Officer, Riley commanded all field and investigative units in the New Orleans Police Department which comprised 17 Divisions and over 1,700 commissioned members. Prior to being the Chief Operations Officer, he was the Assistant Superintendent in command of the Policy, Planning, and Training Bureau.

---

1. The material preceding the interview and portions of the interview itself was drawn from the NOPD website that recounts the history of the department. The Lessons Learned section near the end of this chapter is drawn from a paper I co-authored with Warren Riley and presented at the American Society of Criminology meeting in St. Louis, Missouri in 2008.

Superintendent Riley holds a Masters of Arts in Criminal Justice from Southern University of New Orleans. He has attended the Senior Management Institute for Police Executives at Harvard's Kennedy School of Government, and has taken courses in Advanced Police Administration, Criminal Justice Administration, Criminal Justice Human Resource Management, Statistics, Legal Ethics in Law Enforcement and Community Policing and Transnational Crime. He is also involved in several professional organizations and community groups such as the Police Executive Research Forum (PERF), the International Association of Chiefs of Police (IACP), The National Organization of Black Law Enforcement Executives (NOBLE), criminal justice advisor to the Louisiana University Violence Intervention Team, vice president of the High Intensity Drug Trafficking Area (HIDTA) and a Member of the State of Louisiana Drug Policy Board. The transcribed interview with Chief Riley from 2007 appears below. D. H. are the interviewer's initials.

Interview[2]

D. H.:   Tell me a little more about you.

Riley: I graduated from Booker T. Washington High School and grew up in what is the 6th Police District, otherwise known as Central City, an area of widespread poverty and crime. I joined the police department when I was 21 years of age. When I was first eligible to take the sergeant's exam, I decided to take it but didn't take it seriously. I really didn't put any effort into preparing for it until two weeks before the examination was scheduled. When I took the exam, there were 50 slots and I was the 49th; I was promoted to sergeant. Following that, each time a promotion exam was available or came up, which doesn't come up with any regularity in New Orleans, I would take it. The next exam came up for lieutenant. I took that exam and passed with pretty high scores. I then took the captain's exam when it first came up and was promoted to captain. During the same period of time, I was also a part-time college student.

D. H.:   What surprised you about your career development?

Riley: I was kind of surprised that I passed the sergeant's exam the first time around and was able to advance quickly.

---

2. At the time of the interview, the Chief occupied an 8'x 8' office in a trailer along with his staff in a storage yard owned by the city. Headquarters were flooded and would not be reopened until the following year.

D. H.:   Tell me about your personal policing philosophy. What do you think
          is the role of police in society?

Riley: The role of the police, of course, is to protect the residents, serve the
          citizenry, and to fight crime; however, I also believe that police lead-
          ers must be concerned with what works in police organizations and what
          doesn't work. Continuous reassessment of the internal functioning of
          the department is critical. The police also have problems with their
          public image.

D. H.:   Let's go ahead and talk about the recruitment and retention right now.

Riley: The real problem with recruiting and retaining police, particularly recruiting,
          is the police's image in the community. Police do not have a good image.
          Most people have a fairly negative assessment of what police do, and I
          feel like part of problem is the responsibility of the media. I have a for-
          mula, the "5-50 Rule." When a police officer does something good for a
          citizen, that citizen will probably relay it to five people. If the officer does
          something a citizen perceives as bad or unfair, then that will be passed
          to 50 people. That seems to be the operative ratio—five if you do some-
          thing good and fifty if you do something bad. So the result is that the po-
          lice do not have the most favorable image in the community. This in
          itself does not help in recruiting and retention. This department has
          made some major strides post-Katrina with regard to recruiting and re-
          taining police officers. This year alone, salaries were increased across the
          board by better than 20 percent. And that new recruits, after their first
          year, will be making $35,000 a year. After three years, they readily can
          advance to $55,000. A policy is now in place to raise salaries over the
          next three years by five percent per year if people stay after they receive
          their training. New Orleans Police Department is considerably more
          competitive vis-à-vis federal agencies and other police departments. This
          will help with the retention issue that we have had in the past. The res-
          idency requirement to live in the city has been relaxed so that New Or-
          leans police officers can now live all over the region, all over the state, without
          any penalty. Moreover, the New Orleans Police and Justice Foundation
          have assisted in obtaining loans and helping with down payments in
          order to get housing for officers. Housing has been a serious problem
          in the post-Katrina era but this program has largely ameliorated it.

D. H.:   What level of effectiveness would you describe your police depart-
          ment at the present time?

Riley: Very candidly, about 65 percent effective. The reason why the de-
          partment is functioning at 65 percent effectiveness is that the depart-
          ment still has a shortage of police officers, something to the tune of
          300 short. In 2006, there were times when there were no more than

700 police officers available which works out to be, in some incidences, 200 officers available on any given shift [three eight-hour shifts]. The reason for that, of course, was that under normal circumstances, 40 to 60 officers are out on some type of leave. During 2006, this was not uncommon, and of course in the aftermath of the hurricane in the last quarter of 2005, the department had between 120 to 140 officers at any given time out sick or on leave for a variety of different reasons.

D. H.:   Tell me about your department's experience with undocumented aliens in the New Orleans region since the storm.

Riley: More often than not, the undocumented people have been victims of crimes, not perpetrators. There have been a few minor incidents. The city has the largest number of people here from Mexico, Portugal, and from Russia. A few Russians have been involved in prostitution, but for the most part their involvement in crime locally is largely by being victims of crime, unfortunately.

D. H.:   Tell me about the impact of the storm on the police.[3]

Riley: The storm, of course, had a comprehensive impact. Between 70 and 80 percent of the city was inundated by flood water. This event was unique in the history of the United States, an event where roughly a half million people were evacuated. This city was virtually shut down for four weeks. There was no electricity, no water, and no communication system. It could not have been more totally destroyed had it been hit by a bomb. There were tragically almost 2,000 people who lost their lives.

D. H.:   Tell me how the police department responded to the storm, focusing first on each division of the department.

Riley: With the threat of Hurricane Katrina and as Deputy Superintendent/Chief of Operations, I began assisting in the planning and preparation for the Department's response. On Saturday, August 27, 2005 at approximately 7:30 a.m., I received a call from Colonel Terry Ebbert, the director of Homeland Security and Public Safety for the City of New Orleans, requesting that I meet him at City Hall as soon as possible. When I arrived at City Hall, I met Ebbert, Superintendent of Police Edwin Compass, and Deputy Superintendent Steven Nicholas. At that meeting, we were advised that Hurricane Katrina would impact New Orleans in a drastic way. After a brief conversation with Ebbert, an immediate Command Staff meeting was called. The command staff in-

---

3. The balance of our interview, and in fact most of our discussion, centered on the impact of the hurricane and the collapse of the levee system in New Orleans that led to the city being inundated.

cludes every commander and most of the assistant commanders of each division, district, and major units within the New Orleans Police Department. The Command Staff was advised that Hurricane Katrina was expected to be a very severe storm, Category 3 or 4, and the City of New Orleans would possibly be in the direct path of the storm and could, in fact, sustain substantial wind damage and street flooding.

The Emergency Preparedness Plan, outlining the requirements, duties, and responsibilities of each respective Bureau Chief and major command within the Department was reviewed prior to the first meeting with the departmental commanders. A summary outline was provided to commanders during the 10:00 a.m. briefing on Saturday, August 27th. Their principal duties and requirements were discussed at that time. All Commanders were instructed first and foremost to ensure that their officers provide for the safety of their families, and then be prepared for storm duty by 4:00 p.m. on Sunday, August 28th. Vehicles were to be fueled and a limited number of vehicles were to remain in service. The remainder of the fleet was to be stored in prearranged, designated locations where commanders felt they would be safe and easily accessible. Those commanders who believed that they did not have, within their geographic districts, suitable parking facilities, were instructed to place the vehicles in one of two designated parking garages near the Louisiana Superdome. The Department's own limited number of full-size SUVs remained in service.

I continued communications with all of the various commanders, assuring that all necessary actions were being taken in preparation for the storm. Later that day, Mayor C. Ray Nagin announced a mandatory evacuation of all New Orleans citizens.

The Commander of the Traffic Division was instructed to begin preparations to man traffic contra-flow positions to facilitate the evacuation of New Orleans. Beginning Saturday, August 27th at 5:00 p.m., members of the division were deployed to the contra-flow positions. This plan was worked out in conjunction with the Louisiana State Police, St. Tammany Sheriff's Office, and the State Department of Transportation. Due to the intensity of the prevailing winds, they had to discontinue operations on Sunday, August 28th at 4:00 p.m. and relocate to the driveway of Harrah's Casino located in the Central Business District [CBD] near the river.

The responsibility of the New Orleans Police Department was to traverse all areas of the city with marked units, lights and sirens on, announcing through their public address systems that there was a mandatory evacuation—that all citizens must leave—must evacuate the City of New Orleans. This effort continued until storm winds reached 50–55 mph at which time all officers were directed to relocate to their pre-staged locations to weather the storm.

Before Katrina made landfall, members of the Dive Team/Bomb Squad were pre-deployed with boats to different sectors of the city. Then when numerous areas were cut off by water, these members co-ordinated the deployment of over one thousand first responders, who were either assigned to rescue operations or to a district for supple-mental support. In the meantime, the Emergency Evacuation Shelter Command was activated Sunday afternoon in the Superdome. Under the command of a Deputy Superintendent the following units had the mission of crowd control in support of Louisiana National Guard troops and the delivery of law enforcement and security services. By night-time, as the storm struck New Orleans, the Superdome staff estimated the number of evacuees in the Superdome to be approximately 12,000.

On Sunday night, August 28th, Deputy Superintendent Steven Nicholas and I reported to Police Headquarters. We prepared to weather the storm with our staffs, all essential communications personnel, re-cruits, and other units, as well as civilian employees and family mem-bers. Strong storm winds began to roll in about 5:30am Monday, causing the windows to start leaking and then the ceiling tiles began to fall. At that point, many moved from the offices into the hallways.

At about 7:00 a.m., I went down to the Communication Section on the second floor to contact various commanders and get a status report. When I walked in, almost every dispatcher and 911 operators were crying. When I questioned one of the supervisors what was going on, she stated, "You have to listen in on the calls." I was given a head-set. At that point, no one knew only moments earlier, the Industrial Canal levee breached with an almost two hundred yard opening and water was pouring into the Lower 9th Ward. As I listened, I heard panicking mothers, fathers, husbands, wives and children desperately pleading and begging for help. They were asking if there were boats or helicopters available; they had water rising in their homes.[4]

The calls came in as the streets flooded from west to east. Dis-patchers and 911 operators heard the desperate pleas for help, but

---

4. When the water hit the Lower 9th Ward, it rose from nothing to as high as 14 feet within 23 minutes and covered almost 4.2 square miles. The Department had over 600 calls to 911 in less than 30 minutes.

were powerless to assist. They could not dispatch officers because the weather conditions were too dangerous. The city still had sustained winds in excess of 100 mph. Pursuant to the Emergency Preparedness Plan, we could not respond to emergency calls once sustained winds are greater than 55 mph.

Around 9:30 a.m., the levees in Lakeview breached and more desperate calls came from citizens trapped in their homes. Later that morning, the water overtopped the levees in Eastern New Orleans and then the London Avenue Canal breached.

The water was now rising around Police Headquarters, flooding the basement and first floor to a level that required evacuation of the facility. Chief Nicholas and I went to the foot of Canal Street at Harrah's Casino and located members of the Traffic Division. We then established a field command post under the protected overhang at Harrah's, due to its central location, high ground, protection from elements, and access to generator power and lighting. Morning briefings began to be held at Harrah's daily with the command staff.

The remaining staff at Police Headquarters was ultimately evacuated by boat to the nearby Broad Street overpass. I was finally able to convince the driver of a school bus, who was taking people off the overpass, to bring them to the 4th Police District. They then assisted the members of the 4th Police District in trying to re-establish calls for service and to combat the continuous problem of looting within certain areas.

Operations Bureau staff members reported to work prior to the impact of Hurricane Katrina to assist in the planning and preparation for the Department's response. After riding out the storm in Police Headquarters and being evacuated by boat to the Broad Street Overpass the following morning, they were immediately assigned to assist in patrols to prevent looting along the Canal Street corridor. They later assisted at the New Orleans Convention Center and with the United States Coast Guard in rescue operations in the St. Bernard Housing Development. After completing these critical duties, they were then assigned to support the NOPD Command Post which was set up at Harrah's Casino at the foot of Canal Street.

Public Affairs staff members were initially assigned to coordinate press conferences with the news media. During the course of Katrina's aftermath, those duties changed and the commander and officers engaged in a myriad of assignments including rescue operations, security relief at the Louisiana Superdome for the exhausted NOPD officers, traveled in helicopters in an effort to help coordinate how and where to launch rescue boats, as well as assisting the military in their efforts to coordinate with NOPD officers. This Division was also responsible for releasing information regarding what was going on in the City of New Orleans.

Technical and Support Bureau assisted in the evacuation of Police Headquarters on Tuesday August 30th. They then secured the multi-million dollar resources contained within the building and the hundreds of vehicles parked in the garage. In the days immediately following, their responsibility was to the area bordered by Canal Boulevard, Poydras Street, Jefferson Davis Parkway and Loyola Avenue, distributing food and water to the civilians who were trapped in their residences and government buildings. Later, they assisted in rescue. Also, personnel assigned to the Inspections Division prior to and during Hurricane Katrina provided coverage at the Louisiana Superdome and the Morial Convention Center.

The 911 Communications Division reported before the storm to work their positions and received countless telephone calls requesting rescue from high winds and rising water. The stress of not being able to send help to desperate people was overwhelming. Rising water forced the 911 Center and the Electronics Section, who were also on stand-by in Headquarters, to have to be evacuated by boats to the Broad Street overpass and eventually evacuated to the Convention Center, Hilton Hotel, and Sheraton Hotel. Another Communications Center was established in City Hall, at that time located in the Royal Sonesta and Hyatt Hotels.

Members of Juvenile Division also had to be evacuated by boat to the Broad Street overpass and were then taken to the W Hotel. Later, they relocated to the O. Perry Walker High School on the West Bank to provide security and staff a distribution center to handle food and supplies donated from various charitable organizations.

As Hurricane Katrina approached, members of the Evidence and Property Division took measures to secure and move as much evidence as possible. Commissioned members and civilians worked together in futile attempts to stop the rising water. After evacuating headquarters, all personnel relocated to the 8th Police District [located in the French Quarter] and assisted with security and patrols which kept looting and destruction to a minimum in that district.

Members of Records and Information Systems department were stationed at Headquarters to back-up, power down, and secure critical technology infrastructure in order to minimize data and server equipment losses while ensuring systems remained operable for as long as possible before the storm. After they were evacuated, the entire contingent also joined the members of the 8th Police District in protecting the French Quarter.

Members of the Scientific Criminal Investigation Division had many assignments, all targeting safety for citizens. Some members patrolled Canal Street, the Convention Center, and the CBD; others assisted in search and rescue with other units, while others worked in the Superdome assisting elderly citizens who needed medical care.

Members of the Public Integrity Bureau [PIB] worked with the Marksville Louisiana National Guard Engineers Unit on their high water vehicles from dawn to dusk in all areas of the city providing rescue services to both officers and citizens trapped by the flooding. One squad of PIB officers, who became trapped by high water in Methodist Hospital on Jefferson Davis Parkway in the 7th Police District, organized a helicopter rescue for the patients, doctors and themselves.

Members of the Research and Planning Division and Homeland Security Division staffed the Emergency Operations Center located on the ninth floor of City Hall in the first days of Hurricane Katrina. They assisted other city, state, and federal agencies with hundreds of emergency requests. When the radio and 911 systems failed, they monitored the mutual aid radio channel 24 hours a day. They also worked on other emergency projects.

The members of Public Housing Community Oriented Policing Squad [COPS] remained at their pre-assigned static positions and evacuated over 700 elderly and handicapped residents and their families from Guste Homes. They were joined with the officers assigned to the District Attorney's Office who helped them rescue several police families and numerous other citizens trapped by high flood waters in the American Can Condominiums and other areas. Simultaneously, other members relocated and continued joint rescue efforts in the 7th and 9th Wards. They then were forced to relocate to the 4th Police District where half of the members were assigned patrol duties, and the other half was assigned to the newly formed anti-looting squad.

Personnel of Special Operations Tactical and members of the Narcotics/Vice Crimes/Asset Forfeiture unit conducted the first organized rescue effort in the city. Working around the clock, these officers conducted rescue in the lower 9th Ward, New Orleans East, and Lakeview. These rescue efforts saved thousands of lives in the early aftermath of Katrina. Then Tactical officers began conducting SWAT operations in the Fischer Housing Development and the Morial Convention Center. The Narcotics officers, with FEMA and Fire Department Urban Search and Rescues, engaged in a citywide secondary rescue/human remains recovery operation. Several members continued to work with the New Orleans Fire Department and cadaver dog teams from throughout the United States in an enhanced human remains recovery operation.

In preparation for Hurricane Katrina, members of the Mounted Unit evacuated all of their horses to the Washington Parish Fairgrounds in Franklinton, Louisiana to insure their safety. Members of the K-9 Unit made vigilant patrols until Katrina's sustained winds reached 60 plus miles per hour. When the winds subsided, they began making arrests of looters in convenience stores and other businesses in the CBD and Warehouse District. Returning members of the Mounted Unit joined the K-9 members and were deployed with the Tactical/SWAT teams responding to sniper incidents, building searches, and armed subjects in vehicles.

D. H.:   Now tell me what the police in each of the city's eight police districts responded to the storm.[5]

Riley: The 1st Police District became known as Fort Apache for refusing to relinquish their post during and in the aftermath of Hurricane Katrina. They engaged in rescue operations throughout Treme, Central City and Esplanade Ridge. These officers additionally created a secure northern front for the Vieux Carre, supporting the successful preservation of the city's crown jewel.

The 2nd Police District was literally cut off from all other parts of the city without radio or telephone communication. They rescued the residents of Carrollton, Pigeon Town, Gert Town, and Back-A-Town, an area of heavy flooding, and many 2nd Police District officers had to be rescued. In Baptist, Touro and Memorial Hospitals, patients were carried up fire escapes to heliports or down to waiting boats.

As the winds of the hurricane continued to increase, 3rd Police District personnel were still patrolling and evacuating citizens to the Superdome. When the 3rd Police District area completely flooded, the officers were relocated to the Convention Center by boat. They assisted with stranded evacuees and patrolled the areas for looting and other crimes.

Members of the 4th Police District (the unflooded West Bank of the city) continued answering calls for service until they were forced to seek cover in the Crescent City Connection Building (located under the west bank approach to the Mississippi River bridge). When they

---

5. For those readers unfamiliar with the layout of police districts in the city of New Orleans, they may find the map in Figure 13.1 near the end of this chapter helpful.

were able, they re-established calls for service and by using personal generators at a commercial gas station, were able to fuel police vehicles from all parts of the city. Additionally, they provided essential supplies for their district and other districts and divisions throughout the Department. Even though this part of the city was not flooded, it was dangerous and chaotic. One police officer in the 4th District suffered a gunshot wound to the head when he confronted a band of looters in a convenience store.

In the 5th Police District, which includes the 9th Ward and the Lower 9th below the Industrial Canal, most of which was eventually under water, rank and officers conducted rescue throughout their area until it was no longer possible to reach stranded residents. They then took shelter in the Bywater Hospital and found 40 plus bed-ridden patients and 20 plus on respirators who had not been evacuated. These patients had to be carried down three flights of stairs and evacuated by wading through contaminated water. The thousands of citizens, who had opted to ride it out and could walk or swim to Poland and St. Claude, were transported to the Superdome and hospitals. As the Bywater operation concluded, the officers shifted from evacuating desperate citizens to looting suppression on Canal Street and providing security for the hotels. The Sheraton Hotel had over 1,000 tourists and citizens needing to be evacuated and officers escorted buses in and out of the city.

The 6th Police District [Central City] officers and rank spent the night of August 28th through August 29th in the station. As the eye of the storm passed, several officers retrieved a front-end loader from a construction site near the station and cleared the streets of large trees and other storm debris. This allowed the men and women of the 6th Police District to retrieve their patrol cars which had been safely stored in a multi-level parking garage and resume patrol duties as well as answer calls for service. Several officers, using their own personal watercraft, were instrumental in rescuing several hundred citizens from flooded areas of the 6th Police District and also Lakeview and Gentilly. They set up a food distribution site on vacant land next to the Wal-Mart store and began distributing the food and water.

Members of the 7th Police District [eastern New Orleans] deployed to several high-rise buildings in the district but shortly found themselves trapped in over ten feet of water. The 7th Police District suffered almost total flooding apart from Hayne Boulevard, which runs parallel the levee along Lake Pontchartrain. Some officers were able to swim from the buildings and found boats with which to rescue other officers trapped on their rooftops. All rescued officers assembled at

Chef Menteur Highway and Read Road where they established a command post at the Crystal Palace Reception Hall. They then were able to rescue several thousand citizens plus the infirmed from neighboring hospitals and hospice homes and transport them safely to the Convention Center.

The men and women of the 8th Police District performed valiantly during Hurricane Katrina. Many officers did not know the location of family members or the condition of their own residences; knowing they were responsible for the survival of the historic French Quarter and the CBD, they worked long hours under extreme conditions to keep the looting and destruction to a minimum. A huge concern was the threat of fire, as the French Quarter has been destroyed almost entirely on two occasions since New Orleans was founded.

Many Reserve officers remained in the city, and following the landfall of Hurricane Katrina, they immediately began assisting with district patrol and rescue operations. Members of the Reserve Division are unpaid volunteers, and without regard for their own personal safety and responsibilities, gave of their time and persevered when our city needed them the most.

D. H.: What about the Superdome?

Riley: All officers assigned to the Superdome worked under profoundly difficult and challenging conditions for some 180 continuous hours. The living conditions in the Superdome caused many evacuees to become apprehensive and fearful for their health and safety. Evacuee restlessness and the inability to effectively cope with primitive conditions made it difficult to effectively police the crowd and provide for the safety of all evacuees. Finally, the Superdome Evacuation Shelter was deactivated on Saturday, September 3rd. The evacuation plan consisted of moving evacuees through the New Orleans Centre and the Hyatt Hotel to Loyola Avenue where they were to board buses. NOPD personnel were posted in both buildings to assist evacuees along the established evacuation route through these structures. Through much of the evacuation operation, buses were not consistent and the police control of crowd behavior and temperament depended largely on the continuous availability of evacuation buses. Evacuation continued around the clock. Late on the night of Saturday, September 3rd, NOPD and the Louisiana National Guard personnel had completed the safe transport of all evacuees. Estimates by Superdome staff placed the number of evacuees transported to safe locations to be between 32,000 and 35,000.

D. H.: Let's talk about the impact of Katrina on the functioning of the criminal justice system after the storm.

Riley: The criminal justice system was essentially shut down. The prison was flooded; we had no place to put people who had been arrested. Five hundred police officers were lost to the impact of the storm; they were either evacuated or quit, many of whom never returned. Of course, there are a few returning now that are being reinstated but a large percentage of those officers lived in areas of the city that were inundated. They were in the Gentilly area principally, but also in New Orleans East. Many of these officers lost everything; something like 70 to 80 percent of all police personnel lost their homes to the storm.

Also, the city had something like twenty-three criminal court judges. They operated out of two court rooms that were on loan from the federal government in the federal court house. During 2006, these judges conducted only twelve trials! Ordinarily, there can be twelve trials a week. But for the whole year, there were only twelve trials. The judiciary was essentially shut down.

The prisoners were evacuated from Orleans Parish Prison and assigned to lock-ups all over the state of Louisiana. Because the evidence room at the court house was inundated and essentially destroyed [records of all the arrests that had been made], 3,000 prisoners were released back onto the streets of New Orleans. Imagine, 3,000 prisoners! This, perhaps, accounted for the rather rapid uptick in the problem of violent crime in the city in 2006. Releasing 3,000 prisoners who had been arrested but not convicted would probably leave them with the sense that perhaps the criminal justice system doesn't work. It was not working was the fact of the matter. In the diaspora, some of our criminal element was evacuated just like everyone else, and some ended up in Houston.

In New Orleans, we have something called a 701 release. After 60 days, if a person has not been indicted with a crime, they must be released. On the streets of New Orleans we have something known as 701 murder, which means you serve 60 days for a murder, and then you get out.

The Houston Police Department called and asked, "What in the world is this '701 murder?'" The reason it came up was some New Orleans evacuees were imprisoned in Houston and were not talking. They would say, "I don't need to talk because I am going to be out in 60 days." And the Houston police told them, "This doesn't work over here, buddy. You are in jail and you are going to stay here until you go to trial." So it came as a shock for some of our locals who were jailed in Houston.

D. H.: Can you describe what New Orleans was like after the National Guard and other police departments from across the nation arrived?

Riley: When the federal presence arrived, along with police officers and other emergency personnel from all over the United States, we then had a substantial population of law enforcement in the city. During this period of time, I described this city, as far as crime was concerned, as Mayberry [a small, bucolic rural community made famous in a 1960s television situation comedy *The Andy Griffith Show*]. In other words, there was virtually no violent crime going on. However, the main crime issue during this period, especially the period of the 21 days when the city was flooded, was looting, looting, looting, and more looting. Practically every house in Lakeview, Gentilly, and New Orleans East that had a second story was looted. You have to remember for those people who voluntarily evacuated before the storm struck, they thought they were only going to be gone for a couple of days so they did not exercise any additional kinds of security; they simply left and of course locked their houses, but that didn't deter the looters. Every house that had a second floor, the second floor was looted in those areas of the city that were impacted by the flooding. So looting was a big issue; it was the main crime.

D. H.:   During this period of time, what were the main policing issues?

Riley: The main policing issue was, and still is, having enough police officers to put on the streets to deploy. Even at this time, the department is still roughly 300 officers short of what is needed to effectively police the city even with its reduced population. Remember, the city is still the same size geographically. While the department still has a personnel shortage, it is gradually being rectified by the increase in pay, benefits, and the overall competitive salaries.

D. H.:   In 2006, the rate of murder in the city returned to pretty strong levels. What transpired to bring this about? What specifically are the policing challenges in dealing with this problem?

Riley: Following Katrina, something like 3,000 prisoners were released from jail. They didn't go to trial; they were just cut loose. Putting that many criminals back on the streets with the disruption of neighborhoods and the disruption of normal flow of drug dealing activities brought about significant numbers of drug feuds. Battles over turf erupted. Something like 85 percent of the homicides in New Orleans during 2006 and so far in 2007, are drug, retaliatory and gang related.

New Orleans does not have gangs in any sort of traditional sense that you find, for example, on the West Coast or other large metropolitan areas in the country. Locally, they are small groups of five or six people that are centered in neighborhoods that come together to deal drugs and for other kinds of mischief. These neighborhood groups are playing a major role in the lethal violence of the city along with the drug trafficking. Another thing that has transpired is that while they were evacuated, this criminal element, or, as I refer to them, the "thug element," made contacts and have maintained contacts in Houston, Atlanta and elsewhere. So if they get accused of a crime here, they simply say they were in Houston, and "if you doubt that call this person and they'll verify that I was there." They now have a built-in cover for practically all of their criminal activity by claiming that they were not in town when it occurred. There is a good bit of back and forth between here and Houston, here and Atlanta, and here and other locales outside of New Orleans where people evacuated.

D. H.:   Research indicates that random stops have proven effective in reducing murder by taking weapons off the streets. Yet the police are being criticized because innocent people feel inconvenienced by this strategy and because a lot of citations are written for motor vehicle violations.

Riley: The Department plans to continue doing it; it is very effective. We actually made an arrest on an outstanding warrant for a murder that was committed in 1979. This individual that had a warrant out for his arrest had left the city, moved elsewhere, and came back just to visit relatives and was arrested. We have plans to continue using road blocks. The police are actually picking up, targeting, and retrieving weapons, and there is also a federal charge if a felon is found in possession of a firearm. If they are caught, they do federal time.

D. H.:   The eastern part of the city that suffered the most comprehensive damage from the storm has recently become a hot spot for lethal violence. It is also an area in which the police patrol has been supplemented by the National Guard.

Riley: This hot spot sort of flared up over night. I have deployed a 32-person strike force that is essentially saturating the area. We also have available to us one of the two SWAT teams. We are taking a very aggressive approach to deal with these murders out in the eastern part of the city. Two of the incidents are triple murders. One of these involved a home invasion. It is pretty certain the other was drug related. A third person was killed, an innocent bystander, apparently. There was also a high profile invasion of a police officer's home where the officer was seriously wounded and subsequently died and his wife was also shot. [The police have a suspect in this case and, at this writing, have made an arrest.]

D. H.: What do you see in the future as far as policing New Orleans is concerned?[6]

Riley: I am very pessimistic about the future of these urban cities and their ability to deal with the crime rate. What we need to do, besides talking about murder rates, is to talk about the "thug rate." Those "urban cities" have these groups of "thugs." It is very, very difficult to deal with this except with aggressive policing, making arrests, and so forth.

D. H.: Two of the most criminogenic neighborhoods in New Orleans for at least 30 years are in Central City, the area where you grew up. How do you account for this long tradition of violent crime in this area?

Riley: Those areas in the city have historically been retail drug operations going all the way back certainly through the heroin era and up to the present time; that would be the 1970s to the present time.[7] I am very much in favor of controlling at least automatic weapons. We have to get those off the street. There is no reason for the Tac 9, AK-47, and weapons like that being available. We need to stop the availability of those kinds of weapons. The other things we can deal with, but those are outrageous. I am very much in favor of controlling those on the streets.

D. H.: In October and November 2007, it seems the Department was really on the rebound. What is bringing this about?

Riley: We are making substantial progress on a number of operational recommendations made by the consulting group Brown Group International (BGI), a firm hired by the New Orleans Police and Justice Foundation and some business leaders to develop ways to improve the Department. The areas recommended for change include: recruiting, training, technology, crime prevention and crisis intervention. In these areas the department is working toward higher levels of functionality and accountability. We know that to have greater public trust and respect, we must continually improve every facet of our operations, and that's what we are working towards with this strategic plan as our guideline.

---

6. With this question, Chief Riley began to talk about and use the expression "urban cities." He ran off a list of these, and what he meant by "urban cities" are those cities that have majority black populations.

7. This took the Chief into a discussion of the problem of guns.

The Department has a 25 member task force of officers to analyze and implements the BGI plan's specific 375 action proposals and tasks. The task has been organized into specific categories where members can devote their individual attention to improvement in areas within their field of expertise. The task force meets regularly to report on progress and to work out inter-departmental issues. Presently, we are making progress on change initiatives in improving the crime lab, fleet management and internal communications.

D. H.:   It also appears that the Department is making significant strides in dealing with crime in the city.

Riley: In October and November the Department cleared 43 murders. Of the 15 murders committed in November, 11 have been cleared by arrests. For the year so far our clearance rate is 51 percent for murders, low by national standards, but improving. Our rape clearance rate of 72 percent is above the national percentage.

The deployment of tactical units in hot spots has been effective in stopping criminal activity. Also, there has been an upswing in the willingness of the community to assist the police by providing tips about criminals and criminal activity. One part of the city that was seriously damaged by the hurricane was experiencing home invasion robberies and theft of building materials such as copper plumbing; we are bringing this under control with concentrated patrol and arrests. Another area of the city was being plagued by a pair of spree robbers. Street robberies were occurring almost nightly. We deployed a tactical squad to the area and caught them in the act and effected an arrest on the first night we deployed.

Lessons Learned

Remember that 80 percent of the city was flooded meaning that approximately 80 percent of first responders were instantly homeless. These circumstances require that our plan include providing housing for personnel and that our rapid response team be equipped for extended emergency operations under harsh conditions.

Rapid response teams from outside of the city were, of course, needed and welcomed. However, to be most effective, they must be self-sufficient. Moreover, sending personnel just to send them may not be helpful. Outside agencies must provide what we ask for, not what looks good. For example, are prison buses needed, are booking officers needed, are correction units needed, search and rescue, are other vehicles and boats needed? Response teams must be self-sustaining, with adequate equipment, food and water, sleeping bags, et cetera, for a minimum of seven days.

Outside agency support that was desperately needed in the immediate aftermath of the storm did not arrive in any significant numbers until the fifth day after the storm. During this time, NOPD was mainly involved in search and rescue and patrolling the Central Business District and the French Quarter, as was mentioned earlier.

One extremely important issue in the immediate aftermath of the storm was mental health challenges faced by police officers as well as the city generally. Officers were experiencing a great deal of stress and anxiety. There were almost no hospital beds or medical staff on the ground, no mental health case workers and with the destruction of some of the homeless shelters, a substantial increase in the homeless population on the streets. In the months following Katrina, mental health calls for service averaged 200 per month compared to 40 per month before the storm.

The city lost all psychiatric beds, all outpatient clinics and 85 percent of local psychiatrists. NOPD continued to serve the chronically mentally ill by transporting them to hospital emergency departments in neighboring parishes on a rotation basis so as to not overburden any one hospital. Tragically, two officers were murdered by individuals with apparent chronic mental illnesses.

In summary, it is critical to have and constantly update an Emergency Operations Plan for both common and uncommon events. The failure of the levee system following Katrina was a catastrophic event, but the plan must anticipate this type of event. The plan must also dictate which personnel are essential to emergency operations. This is important in order to document cost. Finally, training must be mandatory and ongoing for all personnel, sworn and civilian. In a disaster such as Katrina, essential government personnel eventually included payroll clerks, financial administrators, city attorneys, civilian NOPD administrators, other city department heads such as finance and civil service, court employees and sanitation workers.

Postscript (June 2009)

Almost three years to the day after New Orleans was struck by Katrina, it was struck by Hurricane Gustav, which made landfall on September 1, 2008. A comprehensive evacuation of the city and the region was ordered and carried out. Many people were apprehensive about leaving the city because of their memory of the extensive looting that occurred in the wake of Hurricane Katrina. Property was protected more effectively during Gustav because the National Guard was deployed before the storm hit and not five days afterward, as was the case with Katrina. Louisiana National Guard troops and vehicles were stationed at all pharmacies and other commercial locations that were thought to be potential looting targets. Police were deployed to every major intersection throughout the city from the time the evacuation was ordered until citizens were allowed to return.

The highly visible police and National Guard presence served as an effective deterrent. Moreover, their effectiveness during the storm in protecting private property won the admiration and respect of many citizens. However, shortly after midnight on January 1, 2009 a squad of plainclothes police officers patrolling Treme, a neighborhood bordering the French Quarter to the northwest, after hearing gunshots in the area, surrounded a suspicious vehicle with an occupant in the driver's seat. What happened in the next few minutes has set the police department back in terms of winning the support of the community.

A young man without a police record who was living in Houston and had returned to visit his family the previous day was sitting in the car. The police squad, operating a robbery prevention detail in the area, heard gunshots and descended on the area in two unmarked cars flashing blue dashboard lights. What happened next was only witnessed by the police because the suspect in the car did not survive. According to the police on the scene, he fired his handgun from inside the car, jumped out and began to run and was killed in a volley with most of the entrance wounds in his back.

While the officers involved have been found by the internal police investigation to have acted appropriately, the incident is still under investigation by Federal authorities. This incident has not helped to improve the image of the police or to gain the support of the community in fighting violent crime, to say the least. Even after all the improvements cited in the above interview have been instituted, in 2008, New Orleans remained the murder capital of the country.

Figure 13.1 A Map of New Orleans Police Districts

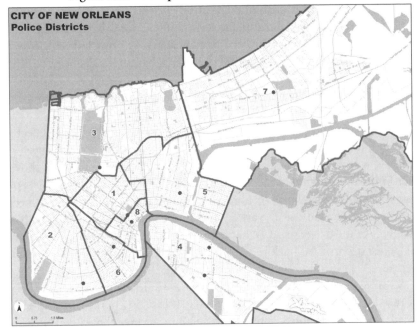

Reprinted with permission of the New Orleans Police Department.

Discussion Questions

1. Describe problems with NOPD recruitment and retention at the time of the interview and steps taken to overcome them.
2. When did Chief Riley and the NOPD begin planning for Hurricane Katrina? What were the first and most important instructions for commanders to follow?
3. What was NOPD's primary responsibility from August 27 through August 28, before Katrina made landfall?
4. Why couldn't police officers be dispatched to help those in the lower 9th Ward being inundated with water from the Industrial Canal on August 29th?
5. Though each division of the Department had prescribed duties before Katrina's arrival, what duties they generally end up performing instead? How were rescue and anti-looting operations carried out when New Orleans was underwater?
6. Describe the state of the New Orleans criminal justice system in the immediate aftermath of Katrina.
7. What was the main crime in New Orleans after the National Guard and members of other police forces arrived? How and where was this crime being committed?
8. What does Chief Riley say was responsible for the high murder rate in New Orleans in 2006?
9. What does Chief Riley think accounts for the sustained high crime rate in areas such as Central City and what could be done to combat this problem?
10. What steps have resulted in the rebound of the NOPD and its ability to deal with crime? What has detracted from it?
11. What are the most important lessons learned for law enforcement from Katrina?

The Heavy Lifting—Local Emergency Response Planning and Preparedness: An Interview with Colonel Terry Ebbert

By Dee Wood Harper and Kelly Frailing[1]

Introduction

Colonel Terry Ebbert, United States Marine Corps Retired, founded Ebbert & Associates to provide consulting, planning, training and education in all aspects of emergency preparedness, public safety, disaster management and security matters. Colonel Ebbert is the former Director of Homeland Security for the City of New Orleans. In this role, he was responsible for the administration and leadership for all public safety agencies, which included police, fire, emergency medical services (EMS), emergency preparedness and criminal justice organizations. He served as the Incident Commander and coordinated all local, state and federal responses to New Orleans in the aftermath of Hurricane Katrina.

Colonel Ebbert's views on the Katrina experience have been documented in extensive federal testimony, books, articles, television broadcasts, lectures and personal sessions with the White House and Department of Homeland Security. His input has been taken into consideration in the creation of national reforms for emergency planning and operations. For his service during

---

1. The material preceding the interview was drawn from the Ebbert & Associates website. The questions for the interview were drawn from a PowerPoint presentation by Colonel Ebbert entitled The Heavy Lifting.

the disaster, he received the United States Coast Guard Public Service Award, The Louisiana Legion of Merit and the American Spirit Gold Medallion.

Colonel Ebbert's previous positions have included serving as the Director of the New Orleans Police Foundation and as the Director of Security for the National Strategic Petroleum Reserve. In addition, Colonel Ebbert completed a distinguished career in the United States Marine Corps where he held nuclear security positions and served as Security Office for the United States Pacific Fleet. Other assignments included serving as the Military Secretary to the Commandant of the Marine Corps and as Commanding Officer of The Basic School for Marine Officers. He is the recipient of the Navy Cross, the nation's second highest award for valor for leadership actions in the Republic of Vietnam. The transcribed interview with Colonel Ebbert from 2009 appears below. D. H. are the interviewer's initials.

Interview[2]

D. H.: The best place to start is to ask you to tell me a little bit about your background—where did you grow up, what drew you to the military, how did the course of your career in the Marines progress, how did you get interested in homeland security?

Ebbert: At my age, that's going back a long way. I was born and raised in the greater Chicago area. My dad was a high school football coach/athletic director, but I spent all my summers in central Illinois where my mother is from and all of her family members are farmers. I stayed at her brother's house and he was a World War II Marine. As I was growing up, he was always talking about the Marine Corps. My dad had served in the Army in World War II so I had always looked at the military as something that I wanted to look into. When I went to Southern Illinois on a wrestling scholarship, I had two or three fraternity brothers who were either Marine Reserves or Marine PLCs [Platoon Leaders Class]. I signed up, graduated, and became an officer. I attended the Basic School, as well as the airborne and ranger school and then transferred to the West Coast. In the early years of the Vietnam War, I divided my time between serving as second lieutenant and captain, and moving in and out of Vietnam where I was a platoon commander, patrol leader and a company commander. After that, I had multiple assignments and multiple tours in various places and that included a

---

2. The interview was conducted in Colonel Ebbert's office in the Central Business District of New Orleans.

lot of teaching. I served as a commanding officer of a Marine detachment on a cruiser for 30 months, which got me my first security-related position. I was the nuclear security officer for the war heads we were carrying on board. Later in my career, I had a tour as the Security Officer for The Pacific Fleet. I had responsibility for all the port police departments and for all land-based ports throughout the Pacific, as well as security responsibility for over 250 ships. When I retired [from the Marines], I came to Louisiana and went to work as the Head of Security and Emergency Preparedness for the Strategic Petroleum Reserve, which got me involved with about 46 different law enforcement agencies between New Orleans and Freeport, Texas. I received a very good foundation by dealing with the first responder agencies because, of course, at all of our sites, we had major security and disaster planning. Then I moved into the police foundation. After 9/11, I became the Director of Homeland Security for the city of New Orleans and was responsible for the police department, the fire department, EMS, and the Office of Emergency Preparedness. Now I'm in business with a partner and several strategic partners involved in emergency preparedness planning.

D. H.: You recently referred to emergency planning at the local level as the "heavy lifting." What did you mean by that?

Ebbert: Well, I think that the current national model is based upon all emergencies being local until the locality expends 100 percent of its resources, then state resources are used, and once the state can no longer provide what's needed, emergency response moves to the federal support level. All planning is done locally, in the areas that have the least capacity and capability. It's very hard for a local area to control its destiny when all the resources it will need in a major disaster are owned by state and federal agencies. You may have a detailed plan, but it's a problem when you don't know the details of state and federal plans. The issue relates to large scale emergencies that go across state boundaries and affect multiple parishes/counties: everybody needs equipment, people, resources and capacity. At the local level responders don't know if supplies will be available because they don't own the resources. Most of the published plans are written, and the onus of the liability of the performance is based upon, the local emergency planners and those agencies at the bottom. When you look at the United States today, you will not find an urban area in America that has more police officers, firefighters and EMS workers than they need to get through today. When there is no emergency, they are barely manned to handle routine requirements, and many of them don't even have enough to do that. Local first responders are already dealing with the day-to-day routine, providing first response capability in urban America. It's a stretch to get through the normal day. You can't expect that a local organization is going to draft a plan which will enable them to manage a response of something that can be 6, 8, 10, 12 or 20 times larger than their normal organization. After being in the bulls eye myself, and taking a hit, I think it's a heavy burden to put on the shoulders of local agencies. That's what I am talking about. It's pretty heavy lifting at the local level to be able to manage, plan for, train and ultimately be held responsible for all levels of capability.

D. H.:   That sort of leads into my next question which is what is meant by capability-based training?

Ebbert: I don't think that any local agency can write a good plan and provide resources that it doesn't own. I can plan for the city of New Orleans based upon how much I have in the way of people, equipment, capacity and capability. When I start going with my plan and say, "Well, I need buses, planes, trains, people, National Guard, et cetera," I am stretching my capabilities. I don't really own those agencies, and I am dependent upon them to respond to my plan. My question remains how do I write a plan that responds to my current capability and my local needs, when in fact a major incident takes those resources away and I must spread them further? Consequently, I have written a plan that needs X amount of capacity that I don't own and on game day, the resources are not there. I am going to be held responsible and my plan will be the one that is criticized because the plans that people see and read, as well as those that are widely published, are local plans. I won't see a written federal plan. Once you start planning beyond your capabilities, it becomes somewhat a figment of your imagination that you can pull off some of this response.

D. H.:   That idea is sort of unnerving in a way, to know that we can be hit with another type of storm like Katrina and in fact, there's no national plan in place. Can you respond to that?

Ebbert: I'll give you a good example. One of the toughest conversations I have had over the past 20 years was with the Justice Department's Assistant Attorney General of the United States, who came down [to New Orleans] a couple years ago and said, "Terry, we're going to update our federal court order to include the requirement that all of your emergency plans have to be sent for approval to the Justice Department to ensure that they are ADA [Americans with Disabilities Act] compliant." This again gets back to the capability issues. I said, "Well I can't do that. I don't own buses. I don't own planes. I don't own any of these resources." When someone is lifted out of his/her wheelchair and is put on a bus that is not configured to his/her needs, and rides for 12 hours to get to Shreveport during the evacuation, if he/she ends up with back problems, I am going to be held liable because she needed to be sitting in her wheelchair. This was a long and difficult conversation. They were going to enter the federal court system and demand that we do this. I don't have the ADA-capable equipment, so how do I plan for something I don't have and then be held responsible? The next planners, who are at the local level in a major capacity during a disaster, are not going to be sitting before the Congress; they are going to be sitting in front of the Justice Department trying to stay out of federal prison for negligence. Emergency planners at the local level don't have the capacity to meet all of these requirements, yet must draft these plans. The disabled people are our most at-risk people. To take care of these citizens, you have to work with agencies that have the capability/capacity and team them. I asked where else they wanted to review the ADA-compliant plans and the Feds told me they were starting in New Orleans. No one else, not [Mayors] Bloomberg in New York or Daly in Chicago, is going to agree with being held responsible for a law they can't physically comply with. The Justice Department is establishing requirements that I don't have the capability or the capacity to comply with. I am forced to draft plans that state I am going to be in 100 percent compliance, but if I fail, the after-action report will state, "Well, it was your order. This is what your plan stated, and you didn't execute it so you're liable." In the end, I said [to the Justice Department] that basically I didn't want to go to court over this. I told them, "I need your input and your resources and your expertise to learn how to take care of ADA citizens," so we signed an agreement to work together for the benefit of all citizens and they would provide input and expert advice to our plans. In drafting our plans, we would take those suggestions into consideration, given our resources and our capabilities. That's how tough it is at the local planner level since Katrina. We have had an increase in the number of federal laws which our plans must comply with, for which we will be held accountable.

D. H.:   Can you talk more about that?

Ebbert: New Orleans was sued for taking weapons away from people during the Katrina emergency. Well, now I have a distinct new law that says, "Thou shall not take a weapon away from any citizen once the declaration [of emergency] is signed." But, I am also responsible for evacuating these people. You know they can't get on a plane or train with a gun. So which law do you want me to follow? In the end, the federal government is not going to tell me which conflicting law to follow because that makes them complicit and they don't want to be held responsible. The federal government does not want to be held responsible for anything in the aftermath of these catastrophes. They are catastrophes by definition and this is my interpretation: They are classified as catastrophes because the resources needed to deal with the situations are not great enough to handle the problems, and this creates major emergencies. If you will not have the capacity to deal with it, then it becomes an emergency. You have a system where local planners know they can't handle anything much beyond day-to-day requirements and yet in a real catastrophe, they have to fail twice in order to get federal help. Current plans are built around limited local capacity and capability.

D. H.:   Well, we have been talking locally. There is an expression out there, the "National Response Framework." What does that mean in this context?

Ebbert: In 2005, we had a National Response Plan. It didn't work very well, and it needed a lot of improvement, so two years ago we spent millions of dollars cleaning it up. We re-published it and, low and behold, it comes out as a National Response Framework. Now ask me why it's called a framework and I will tell you it's called a framework because plans assign responsibilities. A framework is like a college professor teaching a class with a book: a framework is not a plan. Taking a class doesn't assign a student any responsibility. A plan says that a certain agency is responsible for doing a particular task; this agency is responsible for doing that. A framework says this is how you ought to do it. At the time in which our framework was written, the people who had responsibility in the federal government were not willing—or didn't have the fortitude—to call it a plan. The framework is a framework, not a plan with delegated responsibilities. Now, the current administration is trying to improve it and, I think, put some meat to it. I do not think that framework is strong enough language. Framework is a classroom instruction. What we need is a national response plan.[3]

D. H.:   One question just occurred to me, which we probably need to address, is the Stafford Act.[4] What's wrong with it and from a local perspective, what needs to be done to make it work?

Ebbert: Well, I think you need laws which make sense to everybody up and down the line, and I believe there is not enough distinction in the Stafford

---

3. The National Response Plan and National Response Framework are covered in some detail elsewhere in this volume.

4. The Stafford Act is a federal law designed to make orderly and systematic the distribution of federal resources to state and local levels during an emergency or disaster.

Act between preparation and response, which involves the immediate hours and days after a disaster. My definition of a response is a little bit different than the federal government's. Not a lot, but I believe response is just three things: saving lives, stabilizing the infrastructure and providing and re-establishing security for what's left. Until you do those three things, you can't even talk about the complexities of recovery. I believe the United States needs to have a Stafford Act or a law that says this recovery is sunk cost. We're not going back to try to figure out who was on overtime the day after a disaster. That's just absolutely ludicrous. What we need to do is have an emergency declaration and come up with a specified time at which the initial response should be finished. It should be hours, or days at the maximum, when you have saved all the lives you are going to save (and you have gotten them out of the fire, or the flood or off the rooftop), the damage to your infrastructure is stabilized, and there is somebody providing security for the area. The problem is that the Stafford Act doesn't adequately address the hours and initial days, immediately after the incident. I believe that Congress should set aside money for federal, state and local agencies to respond during those hours and days. That is, they [agencies] don't have to come back and justify their response to the federal government. That's a sunk cost. At a future date and time is when you have time to start development of project worksheets. I think there needs to be a better separation of response and recovery operations.

D. H.: Can you talk about what you consider to be the main national strategic issues regarding emergency planning at the national level?

Ebbert: I think we have several. Some are philosophical and some of them more concrete. I think the first one is that as a nation, we haven't yet figured out the difference between mission-driven organizations and compliance-driven organizations. Mission-driven organizations are organizations can be given a mission in two or three sentences and then can deploy millions of dollars of equipment, thousands of people. There is the Department of Defense, National Guard, law enforcement, fire, EMS. All of these are mission-driven organizations that don't need thousands of pages of policies and procedures on how to carry out missions. When we talk in the aftermath of a disaster, you have to respond during a response phase with mission-driven organizations. You don't know what's out there, but must go forward and do what you can within the capacity and capability of your organization. Compliance organizations are different by nature. They are comprised of different people, and there's a different risk avoidance culture; they don't operate like mission-driven risk management organizations. They don't ever want to be held responsible. They draft thousands of pages of policies and procedures, written by attorneys, to ensure that in the aftermath of a disaster, they are not responsible. I was asked during my Congressional testimony to define a mission-driven organization. I can tell you that on the Friday following the storm, the Commanding General of the 82nd Airborne found me and said, "I am not working for anybody. I'm not working for the National Guard. I'm not working for the governor. I am working for you. I've got 6,000 airborne troops who are going to be on the ground in four hours. What do you want me to do with them?" And I said, "Split your troops up by eight. We are going to provide you escorts out to the eight police districts. Your airborne troops will operate in support of the captain in that district who will maintain all law enforcement responsibility." He turned around and said, "I got it. Ok, that's how we are going to deploy. The mission is to save lives, protect property, and do the right thing. Move out." That's mission-driven: doing the right thing within the capacity that an agency has. Now, the opposite of that was getting a phone call on the Wednesday night after the storm from a state trooper located up Interstate 10 by LaPlace,[5] saying he'd been on scene for four hours with 200 buses. He was watching a safety inspector with a tread depth gauge checking tread depth of the tires on every vehicle before sending them in. That's compliance! That's compliance-driven! That's the contract mentality! This mentality is driven by risk avoidance. Someone is applying these rules in an emergency situation and I think that those issues are compliance issues that a risk manager should be able to override in a situation in which lives are at stake. When people and lives are at stake, you've got to go with a mission-driven organization that can respond. They must manage risk, as it is impossible to avoid risk.

D. H.:   So mission-driven versus compliance-driven organizations is the first issue. What's the second?

Ebbert: That's the first philosophical issue. The second issue is that emergencies and disasters are nothing more than logistical wars. Wars that move massive amounts of stuff and people in and out of areas do something. How we as a nation, in today's world, think we can do that with no universal logistics system is crazy. Now Wal-Mart has a logistics system. Home Depot has a logistics system. We fight mili-

---

5. LaPlace is located about 25 miles west of New Orleans.

tary wars. We can manage an individual piece of equipment halfway around the world using 18 and 19 year olds. We have the most complex equipment, and we keep it running because we have a logistics system that tracks everything. Our current federal government does not have that required integrated system at the local, state or federal levels. I believe that on the non-military side, you must develop software that's in every EOC [Emergency Operations Center] in America, and it must be the same software. It would enable the local level Incident Commander to make a request and know what happens to that request. Currently, all you do is make a request. You don't know who is fielding the request, when it's coming, who has been tasked to deliver it or how to coordinate delivery. This capability doesn't currently exist. In today's world, when we have these very sophisticated systems available, why are we afraid? We know how to do it, but I believe we are afraid to designate one piece of integrated software to run it all. Nobody wants to deal with deciding whose software is going to be used. The heart and soul of response is the logistics system that can track all requirements. In a major disaster, the President of the United States ought to be able to call his department heads in there and say, "Ok, what and how much has been requested to support this disaster?" If you have 20,000 requests and you have filled 18,000, you are doing a good job. That is when the President can really say you are doing a good job, Brownie. But if you have 20,000 requests and you have filled 200, then that allows someone in a senior federal position to say, "In 45 minutes we are going to reconvene. I want to know what the hell you are doing about this. This is not satisfactory." Currently there's no capacity to visualize the total logistics picture. In this web-based world, not being able to come up with a product that allows the Commander in Chief, or the Secretary of Homeland Security, to look at one source and get a common operating picture is criminal. Leadership at every level must know how the response is going and should be able to drill down to any specific request.

D. H.: So the unfulfilled need for much improved and an easily accessible logistics system is the second issue. What's the third?

Ebbert: The third issue is tied to the first one. Recently, you saw the military and Congress going around and around again. Who is in charge during a catastrophic response? Who is going to run this show? How are we going to do it? What sort of organization will be utilized? How do you provide command and control for a major disaster that crosses multiple political entities? My issue with this challenge is with the civilian side of the government, not the Department of Defense. We have an Incident Commander who is in the bulls eye. He or she is the one who is in the fight, and he or she wears the title of commander and has the responsibility to direct things to happen. The next person who has "commander" in their title and makes final decisions regarding the resources of people and equipment is the Commander in Chief. There is command at the local level, but the next person who is the commander is the President on the civilian side. You can't have that. Today, every person between those levels is a coordinator. Every agency has coordinators. You see it in every other word in the framework: coordination, coordination, coordination. How do you coordinate if you've got a situation where requirements are greater than available resources? I am down in New Orleans and say I need 10 lifesaving widgets. (Of course without a logistics system, I wouldn't know where the widgets were located, but let's just assume I do.) At the same time, my neighbors over in Mississippi and Mobile have the same problem and each one of them is asking for the same 10 widgets. We now have multiple requests coming from three states. Local agencies are making requests to the state and the state is making requests to a federal coordinating agency. The problem begins when the coordinating agency responds and says there are only 10 available. The situation now exists where 30 widgets have been requested, but there are only 10 available. Somebody must come back and say, "Terry, you don't get any. I sent them to Mobile. I decided that I can save more lives by sending these lifesaving widgets to Mobile." You cannot coordinate that! That is a decision and a command! Coordination will not work in this situation. How do you develop this command authority? Many models exist, but what we need is a system. In a disaster where there is not enough local capacity, and there are multiple political agencies, multiple states, multiple local entities all pumping requests up the line, somebody has to have the authority to make decisions and direct federal resources. Someone has to have the authority to make critical decisions. Our current system is fundamentally flawed. We value coordination over command, compliance over mission and risk avoidance over risk management.

D. H.: One other thing related to logistics is communication. Is there any sort of thinking about how is that supposed to occur? I'm thinking too on a very local level where we didn't have methods to communicate with each other here for the first week after Katrina. What's being done?

Ebbert: The challenge of interoperability communication is huge. One of the positive products of the Katrina aftermath, for those of us who live in New Orleans, is that we created one of the best interoperable radio systems in America. There are very few regional systems elsewhere that are close to it. We have four parishes, and really it's grown to six parishes and the state on one 800/700 MHZ Project 25 Compliant radio system. We have interoperable capacity. To make this system work we need a very detailed, very complex and very extensive interoperability plan. Before Katrina, each agency owned its own frequencies and separate radio system. No agency owns the new radio system. Nobody! The integrated regional radio system is a joint venture, and we formed a governing body to make all management decisions. Each agency still owns some of the operational pieces. You, as a sheriff, still have your portion of the system and you control whether you want to let me in or not. But in an emergency, all agencies can talk without any operational boundaries. Interoperability is something we need to continue to push. The nation realizes it is desperately in need of universal first responder communication interoperability. It's a huge, huge deal. We are talking about hundreds of millions of dollars across America to make that happen. The technology exists and the money can be found, but the political will to work together is lacking.

D. H.: What about New Orleans' capability now to handle an event similar to Katrina? Are we better prepared?

Ebbert: If we weren't better prepared, then I think we all ought to pack it in. I think the outcome of Katrina has produced some positive improvements. We have a much improved communication system. We have much better training, education, planning and exercise programs. We have the advantage of strong regional and state support. Everybody now realizes that the only place we can find parish boundaries is on a map. The Urban Area Security Initiative and the new memorandums of understanding [MOUs] between agencies have enabled us to increase our capacity.

D. H.: What are some lingering challenges?

Ebbert: There are still challenges. The area for which I have great concern relates to the disabled, elderly, poor, sick non-hospitalized citizens. In preparation for Gustav last year it cost the government $100 million dollars to move about 9,000 such citizens. How many times can you continue to move this dependent population at $100 million per evacuation? It's a great strain and you'll lose several of them any time you undertake this operation. We have to look critically and create an internal capacity to properly and safely shelter these citizens. There is local capability to do it in this city. When you make that decision, you harden, identify and equip a facility. We should develop a capacity to take 20,000 pre-registered [disabled and infirm] people. You don't take people off the street! New Orleans has over 20,000 people pre-registered this year. Such a program would move these citizens to a multi-use facility that, unless you need it for an emergency, has another function. This program would be safer, cheaper and more effective. If we have another disaster the size of Katrina, our plans would ensure that this facility is linked to transportation and next to the river. This would allow for safe and orderly after-storm evacuation by ship. This city will not survive as the entity we know unless we demonstrate to the world that we know how to manage storms. Ordering mandatory evacuation for every Gulf storm is not the answer.

D. H.:   Can you talk more about our shelter and transportation needs in the event of a disaster?

Ebbert: Our success as a city—our vision—has got to be that New Orleans is the one place in America that can demonstrate that our government and citizens can manage storms. We can't avoid them. Managing storms and protecting lives means taking care of those people least capable of taking care of themselves. We must have a better plan than simply putting them on buses and shipping them to nowhere. I think the whole national/regional sheltering plan needs a very hard look. We need to look at FEMA regions. States are currently responsible for sheltering their own people. This creates a situation that causes planners in southeast Louisiana to ship thousands of people hundreds of miles to Shreveport, rather than 30 miles to Mississippi. This makes no sense at all and is not an efficient system. Louisiana is not a separate country. We need to look at regional sheltering plans. We ought to be looking at Base Realignment and Closure [BRAC] military base closings. These bases have capacity that could be utilized to shelter. We are going to have a major evacuation, one of these years, without any notice. A hurricane you know is coming, but terrorist or nuclear/biological events you don't. The potential problem is not only Mother Nature, but also human nature. We need to have regional sheltering and transportation plans. We know that someday there is going to be a bad earthquake in California. Where are you going to take millions of people? What's the plan? How are you going to get them there? On buses that are underneath the rubble? If the nation does not plan for shelters, we can't come up with a matching transportation plan. We will continue to struggle. Transportation is a difficult challenge, yet I have seen very little emphasis to push for development of national and regional plans. The Secretary of Transportation ought to be the guy that is responsible for creating a national transportation plan. I've learned more about railroads—more than I ever wanted to know—and the only thing I can say is that the descendants of rail-road barons are alive and well today, protecting their turf. We have a thousand rules, regulations and laws about driving an Amtrak train down a freight rail line and we haven't got laws that allow for the mod-ification of extensive regulations in the event of an emergency. Think about it. You have an agency in your own town that can't figure out how to cross railroad and streetcar tracks[6] and is then faced with the task of moving a million people. These agencies refuse to realize the problems they create. We need to really look at this compliance men-tality if we are going to take care of our citizens.

D. H.:   What's your assessment of how New Orleans responded to Gustav?

Ebbert: The city did a very good job. Evacuating the city is very costly process. We are doing a better job at being able to predict hurricanes and I think the better we get at that, the easier it becomes to make deci-sions. To execute evacuation, for the people who don't travel well, you need to start the process when hurricanes are 120 hours away from local landfall and when they are on the other side of Florida or the other side of Cuba. I don't believe that we can attempt to empty south-east Louisiana every time a storm enters the Gulf. The reason it is nec-essary to start the evacuation process so far in advance is not because of the people who are evacuating by cars, but to assist the citizens that need help leaving. We must develop a plan to either shelter those in-dividuals here or in a shelter nearby. This would enable evacuation calls to be made only 50 hours out and would reduce the total num-ber of mandatory evacuations. This is still two days before landfall. That's a lot of time, but not enough when you have to move planes, trains and buses. An additional problem is the limited number of available buses needed to evacuate large portions of the Gulf Coast at the same time. The same buses that Houston contracted, we con-tracted. Mobile did, too. During Gustav, when the state called for their buses, they were not available. This plan would work if the only city being evacuated was New Orleans. It doesn't work well if you are trying to evacuate hundreds of miles of coastline. I think it is essen-tial that we learn how to take the most elderly, at-risk citizens and care for them without moving them to another city every time a storm comes.

D. H.:   Yeah, if you go back and look at the demographics of people who per-ished during Katrina, they are almost all over 70.

---

6. Here Colonel Ebbert is speaking of recent plans and problems with reinstalling street-car tracks in New Orleans.

Ebbert: Absolutely. Elderly citizens are the most vulnerable segment of the population.

D. H.: You covered just about everything we had questions for. There are two last questions that I wanted to ask you about that we haven't touched on. What are Title 10 Forces and how are they to be used in homeland security?

Ebbert: That's a great question, and it's being debated. Title 10 are your active duty forces in the Department of Defense. Title 32 Forces are your National Guard forces. While they are working in their normal role for the state's governor, National Guard forces are not federalized. The National Guard forces deployed in Afghanistan today are federalized, so Title 10 rules apply to them. We must consider these differences in planning military support for disasters. By law, the Defense Department's Title 10 Forces cannot work under civilian control. They can only work under the control of the Department of Defense [DOD]; by law, they cannot participate in law enforcement operations. They are military war fighting forces, not law enforcement forces. When Title 10 forces are deployed in support of disaster operations, they must work within a command structure that allows them to perform within their capacity, but in accordance with the established laws of our nation. The active duty forces have tremendous capacity and capability to help in an emergency. We should not have to sit and argue for five days, as we did during Katrina, over rules concerning how to employ forces and who's working for whom. We must have these procedures well documented. These well structured plans will ensure missions and command structures are fully understood by both military and civilian organizations. This detailed planning allows for immediate execution once a mission has been assigned. I don't believe in taking control away from local entities or governors, but there are a lot of different models that work. Our problem is that we haven't had the people in Washington with enough desire to work together to come up with a suitable solution. To leave the armed forces of America on the sideline while citizens of our own country suffer is inexcusable. There are ways of utilizing active duty forces without breaking the law; the United States Northern Command has a major role to play in this. I don't believe that NorthCom [United States Northern Command] should be in charge of local emergencies as some people are proposing. I think they should be available to perform functions in all emergencies, when they are requested by the proper agencies. They can provide their equipment, their helicopters, their trucks, their manpower. The military is a powerful security force and providing security is not law enforcement, as long as the correct mission is directed. We've got thousands of people in this city carrying weapons today that perform private security functions, but have no law enforcement capacity. Currently we have politicians unwilling to admit that it's all right to have active duty troops in this town to perform security functions. I think it's cowardly to continue to find excuses as to why we cannot have detailed plans and command relationships that would allow for the immediate utilization of DOD forces when citizens are at risk.

D. H.: Can you react to the following quote? And this is your quote as a matter of fact. "It is distressing that this country continues to put their trust for disaster management in the hands of the fearful senior public officials who operationally hide behind the protective cloak of compliance, risk avoidance, and feel good coordination. We remain at risk until we find tough mission-driven decision leaders, who are willing to accept the responsibility for timely hard decisions—regardless of organizational or personal liability." Can you also provide a few examples of leaders who you think fit this description of tough, mission-driven and willing to accept responsibility?

Ebbert: Well I think that's a lot of what we have talked about so far. I just believe that as a nation, we first have to come up with an organization that allows us to use the capabilities we have at the local, state and federal levels. We then must develop a plan, not a framework, and then train in accordance with the plan. We have agencies that fit perfectly. We have the National Guard in every state, but it doesn't do a lot of good for governors to have National Guard forces responsible for state emergencies running up and down 14,000 foot mountains in Afghanistan. In fact, war is not their primary mission. Currently, the government does not have enough guts to say we should create a sufficient number of Title 10 Forces to fight wars, and use National Guard forces for what they are really designed to do. We are fighting a war on the cheap by using the National Guard. Your National Guard forces can't be automatically given primary responsibility for state disasters because they may not be available to the affected area. We must ensure that a permanent trained command and control agency exists to run any emergency in any state. You have Guard forces. You have the United States Coast Guard, which is a military organization external to the Department of Defense, and thus not constrained by any rules or regulations of command and control. It is led by officers, who by nature through their careers, have dealt with industry and political leadership, and do so on a daily basis. The Coast Guard is the organization that interfaces with every element of the civilian community, whether it is an oil spill, an accident or a natural disaster. These folks spend their careers growing up interfacing with law enforcement, business and political leadership. I think by nature those organizations, like the Coast Guard, are the mission-driven organizations. FEMA is not mission-driven but compliance-driven, with thousands of rules in place to ensure that nobody, except the local agencies, is held responsible. If we continue to think that we can assemble a group of contractors who do not know each other's names and place them under one roof in the middle of a maelstrom and expect to efficiently provide command, control and direction, we're doomed to failure. The military spends years working together, and it's still difficult in a joint environment of putting the Army, Navy, Air Force and Marines all together. Even they struggle, and those officers have spent years in school trying to figure out how to make all that work. The idea on the civilian side—that you can hire a bunch of contractors and expect them to handle major disasters—is a fallacious argument.

D. H.:   So what can be done?

Ebbert: We have capacity. We can create another response organization as we have done in law enforcement with the FBI national S.W.A.T. team. We can create a National Command and Control team that's self-contained. We would need to fully equip and train them, and pay them enough money so they are not fly-fishing in Montana when they are needed. They must be available within a short response time, and they respond to any area in the United States. It would be a full time job. Every day that they are not deployed, which is 99 percent of the time, they would be training with every major community in the country. They would know the mayor of New Orleans and state governors. When they arrive, they would not take command away from other officials. They would arrive and say, "Mr. Mayor, we are here. We know your systems are down and we will provide everything needed to your staff. We will provide you the link to all federal resources through our fully trained staff and, oh by the way, we will give you our best advice in all areas of your operation. Mr. Mayor, you make the call, but this is what is available." The local leadership retains control, but is provided with the means to execute orders, as well as advice and required capacity.

The last thing I would like to say is that this is a Jeffersonian democracy: elected officials at the lowest levels run local agencies. They obtained that job because they had one more vote than their opponent. They may, and in most cases may not have, any idea of what their responsibilities are during emergencies. We have created the National Incident Management System [NIMS], which is very positive and a great step forward. We are spending millions of dollars training first responders, but what is lacking is the law that says, "Mayor, Governor, within 30 days of election, you are assigned a seat at the Emergency Management Institute. You are required to be there, with none of your staff, and you are going to sit there for five days and learn about your responsibility according to NIMS. You will learn where you fit, what you are responsible for and what you are not responsible for. When you go back and your emergency management staff, or your chief of police, comes in and says this is what you ought to be doing, you'll understand why." We should pass a law that requires the training of senior elected officials so that they will understand their roles in emergency operations. They would be more sensitive to their organizations, and their capacity and training, if they understood their personal responsibilities.

D. H.: It strikes me too that perhaps they can use training in public relations.

Ebbert: All of that is important, but if senior elected officials don't know what to do and have not been trained, they may have to get up in front of the public and say, "I don't know what the hell is going on. There is chaos all around me." They need to know everyone's roles before they can talk the language. Do we have three or four star generals in charge of the Marine Corps who we enlisted last week? No, it has taken them 35 years to learn their jobs. We have a false expectation that elected officials know how to manage disasters. It's clear, without getting into politics, that most of them don't know the first thing about these responsibilities, and we need to train them. We train everybody else, why not senior elected officials? In the end, if the trained governor or mayor wants to override his first responders and say, "Well, you work for me and I am telling you what to do," at least he would understand the impact of those decisions.

D. H.: Politicians, of course, have a lot of ego, and they have to do what they have to do.

Ebbert: Well that's true, but all great generals have a lot of ego too.

D. H.: One thing on reflecting on the Katrina experience. My impression is that the Coast Guard did a pretty good job with what they had to work with, but they didn't get a lot of recognition for it.

Ebbert: We had two outstanding admirals down here. I was in a meeting the Tuesday after the storm and it was chaos. We had multiple federal officials arriving and we were over at the Superdome trying to hold a meeting. You had people running around asking your name, federal guys asking who are you, what's your job. This went on for about 10 minutes until Admiral Robert Duncan, stood up and said, "I don't know what's going on here. I don't have any more time to spend in this meeting. I have a rescue mission to complete. I am out of here and I am not coming back." He walks out and 2,500 flights later, he parks his airplanes. Mission complete! That's what mission-driven organizations do. The Coast Guard knew how to do it, and they did it. Admiral Duncan didn't ask any questions: he knew what his job was, he knew what his capability was, so he went and did it. He didn't sit in a meeting trying to figure out all this bureaucratic stuff. The Coast Guard is an incredibly capable organization, and it is part of the Department of Homeland Security. I don't understand why we wouldn't look at the Coast Guard as an initial response agency and designate, even pre-designate, various admirals to take the lead on major responses. The Coast Guard knows all sides of the street, military, civilian, law enforcement, business, politics and public affairs. I think they have underutilized potential. We would need to expand their capability, their people and their equipment. We are spending a lot of money today. I think we should be spending more on the Coast Guard. They should be the heart of our response system. This is why I say it's not priority. We are going to spend $3 billion for Cash for Clunkers, but we don't have a well defined, trained and equipped command and control system to manage and save the lives of civilians in the United States in the next emergency. It's disgraceful.

D. H.:   As a parting shot, can you please give some concrete ideas about how we might overcome some of these frustrating divisions between local, state, regional and national responses?

Ebbert: Let's take hurricanes for example. What about a ship designed for response? It has food and water, electrical generation capacity, diesel fuel, gas, and the ability to sleep and care for people. You can deploy such a ship at the beginning of hurricane season and when a tropical storm gets close, you locate the ship behind the storm and follow the storm ashore. There are a couple of common things about hurricanes: they all come from the water and the only time they hurt anything is when they hit urban areas. If they hit King Ranch outside Corpus Christi, I guess you would have some cows in trouble, but you wouldn't have a large population in trouble. All of the urban areas located on the coast have a port facility in common. After the storm passes, everyone comes out of their foxhole and the first thing they see is the recovery ship. They have instant communications, medical supplies, water, electrical power, food and fuel. The local Incident Commander would have all those resources the instant the ship arrives. I do not understand why we resist studying this potential capability. We spend tens of millions of dollars trying to stage and pre-stage supplies in multiple places. You don't need water and food anywhere except at the impacted area. The same concept of mobile logistics holds true with trains and other transportation. Why don't we shrink the amount of supplies, but load them on something that can respond where it is needed? FEMA has not been willing to open up the discussion on any of those ideas, even though it is clear that we need to rethink these logistical issues.

D. H.: That idea is probably too good. It makes too much sense.

Ebbert: But we want to spend $100 million evacuating 9,000 people every time a storm enters the Gulf.

D. H.: What we need to do is have a big contract planning for that, the Recovery Ship coming in after a storm.

Ebbert: There are a lot of things we could do. I think we are blessed to have a good head of FEMA. [Craig] Fugate is a professional. Now we will have to see if this administration likes him in the first emergency. He is going to make some tough calls and has a proven track record of making the right ones regardless of the politics involved. I think we are lucky in that regard. This does not change my opinion that FEMA should not be in charge of those first few hours. That's asking a lot from a compliance-driven organization. That's just my opinion.

D. H.: Well, I think always we seem to react. We never seem to plan ahead. It's always a reaction to events. It takes another event to get us to move. I don't know what it's going to take for something like that.

Discussion Questions

1. What are the difficulties of doing emergency planning at the local level?

2. What is meant by capability based planning?

3. Describe the differences between the National Response Plan and the National Response Framework.

4. What are the three elements of Colonel Ebbert's response stage of a disaster? How long should the response phase last?

5. Describe the differences between mission-driven and compliance-driven organizations and give examples of each. Which ones are more useful in a disaster and why?

6. How does not having a nationwide, centralized way to manage requests for resources hinder disaster response?

7. Describe the differences between command and coordination in terms of disaster response. What is problematic about the present organization of disaster response?

8. What are some positive outcomes for New Orleans' emergency response planning resulting from Hurricane Katrina?

9. Why is having a regional shelter and transportation plan so important and why is it so challenging? Provide some detail in your answer, especially on the elderly and infirm.

10. What are Title 10 Forces and Title 32 Forces and how might each be utilized in disaster response?

11. How can we better coordinate our response to a disaster? Be specific about the roles various organizations and agencies might take, especially the Coast Guard and the National Guard. Also discuss the possibility of a dedicated disaster response team.

15

NATIONAL EMERGENCY PREPAREDNESS AND RESPONSE PLANS: AN OVERVIEW

By Katrina Workman Berger

Introduction

This chapter will examine the roles that the Department of Homeland Security (DHS) and the Federal Emergency Management Agency (FEMA) play in developing and administering the United States' national emergency preparedness and response plans. Key policy documents relating to emergency response will be discussed along with an explanation of how FEMA deploys response and recovery assets following catastrophic incidents. Additionally, an overview of Mission Assignments and Emergency Support Functions will be provided. While recent catastrophic events such as Hurricane Katrina have shed light on a number of deficiencies in the United States' emergency preparedness and response plans, significant progress has been made in the past several years to address these deficiencies and take the necessary corrective actions to make these plans stronger and more effective.

The Role of DHS and FEMA in Disaster Preparedness and Response

Disaster Relief Act of 1974

Congress passed the Disaster Relief Act of 1974 (Public Law 93-288) after a series of devastating tornado outbreaks hit six Midwestern states. The Act established the processes by which the President of the United States could make disaster declarations which would trigger a state and federally coordinated relief effort. In 1979, President Jimmy Carter created the Federal Emergency Management Agency (FEMA) by Executive Order. Until that time, disaster response was handled by more than 100 agencies across state and federal government. The creation of FEMA centralized the coordination of disaster response activities into one cabinet-level agency.

The Stafford Act

By the 1980s, Congress had become concerned with the President's use of disaster declarations for non-natural disasters such as Carter's use of the Disaster Relief Act to manage the Three Mile Island accident and also the influx of Cuban refugees into Florida (Moss and Shellhamer 2007: 11). In response to these concerns, Congress amended the Disaster Relief Act of 1974 in 1988 and renamed it the Robert T. Stafford Disaster Relief and Emergency Assistance Act (The Stafford Act, codified at 42 USC § 5121 et. seq.). The Stafford Act created the system which is in place today whereby the President can declare a national emergency, which triggers financial and physical assistance to state, local and tribal governments through FEMA (Government Accountability Office (GAO)-07-1142-T 2007: 7). The Stafford Act imposed limits on what would qualify for a declaration of a disaster and thereby trigger large scale federal disaster assistance. Major disasters which would trigger federal assistance were limited to any natural catastrophe and also any fire, flood or explosion regardless of cause (Moss and Shelhamer 2007: 12). FEMA was designated as the federal government entity responsible for administering the Stafford Act (GAO-07-1141T 2007: 7).

National Strategy for Homeland Security: The Creation of the Department of Homeland Security

The September 11, 2001 terrorist attacks shifted the emphasis of disaster response to terrorist activity and away from its previous focus, which had been natural disasters. This new emphasis shifted new power and roles to law enforcement agencies and to the military (Pampel 2008: 35). In July 2002, President George W. Bush issued the National Strategy for Homeland Security. As part of the National Strategy, President Bush signed the Homeland Security Act in November 2002. The purpose of the Act was to increase homeland security after the terrorist attacks of September 11, 2001. This Act centralized the core leadership of many of the homeland security-related functions and activities under a single federal department, namely the Department of Homeland Security

(DHS).[1] DHS is responsible for various national security related functions such as preventing terrorists from entering the United States, protecting the United States' land, sea and air transportation systems, preventing terrorist attacks utilizing chemical, biological, radiological and nuclear weapons and enforcing the United States' immigration and customs laws. Several large federal government agencies with homeland security and border enforcement-related functions were absorbed into DHS. The major agencies making up DHS include the United States Coast Guard, which is responsible for protecting the United States' waterways and ports, Immigration and Customs Enforcement, which is the investigative branch of DHS, Customs and Border Protection, which inspects passengers, vehicles and cargo entering or leaving the United States, the Secret Service, which is responsible for protecting the President, Vice President and other high ranking government officials as well as conducting investigations relating to counterfeiting and financial violations and FEMA, which plans for and coordinates response efforts following disasters and catastrophic incidents.

The Role of FEMA

FEMA is the federal government entity responsible for coordinating the federal government's response and recovery efforts following a major disaster or catastrophic incident. Following a declaration by the President, FEMA can dispatch personnel and resources to aid in response and recovery efforts following a natural disaster or major emergency incident (FEMA 2007: 1). FEMA is assisted by other federal agencies in response and recovery efforts and works with state and local governments as well as private non-governmental relief agencies and organizations.

Critics claimed that the overriding concern with terrorism weakened FEMA's ability to respond to natural disasters. Critics further argued that it was a mistake to move FEMA into DHS because the new Department would be concentrating exclusively on terrorism whereas FEMA had much broader goals, including natural disaster response, which was more civilian-oriented and not focused predominately on a law enforcement and military response. The U.S. GAO also noted its concerns stating in a June 2003 report that the shifting of FEMA's resources from natural disasters to manmade disasters such as terrorism was problematic. The GAO felt that FEMA could become overwhelmed by the additional homeland security demands with the increased emphasis on the response to terrorism (Pampel 2008: 43).

---

1. Readers unfamiliar with the structure of DHS or of FEMA should consult the organizational charts at the end of this chapter.

Additionally, moving FEMA into DHS created another bureaucratic layer in disaster response. It further confused the responsibility regarding primary leadership roles in the response to a disaster or other significant incident, as both the Secretary of DHS and the Director of FEMA had major roles (Pampel 2008: 43). U.S. emergency management experts were troubled by the decline of FEMA as it was absorbed into DHS; the added layers of bureaucracy could adversely impact FEMA's ability to effectively and rapidly respond to disasters (Tierney 2006: 407).

The move to DHS also impacted FEMA's funding. FEMA now had to compete with all of the other DHS components in the newly created Department for funding and oftentimes it came up short (Pampel 2008: 42). DHS viewed FEMA as its piggy bank, at one point taking $10 million of FEMA's $20 million Flood Mitigation Fund and using the money to brand DHS as a distinct department (Cooper and Block 2006: 84).

Key Policy Documents

There are several controlling documents which have been issued by DHS defining national roles and responsibilities and also capabilities for emergency preparedness and response. The key policy documents are the National Response Plan, the National Incident Management System, the National Response Framework and the National Preparedness Guidelines.

The National Response Plan

The National Response Plan (NRP) is an approach to the management of a domestic incident including guidance for the prevention, preparation, response and recovery (NRP 2004: 2). It is a comprehensive plan which provides structure and various mechanisms for policy, procedures and operational coordination at the national level for the management of domestic incidents (NRP 2004: 1). The NRP describes national capabilities and resources and establishes roles and responsibilities as well as operational procedures and protocols that should be followed by participants in a national recovery effort (NRP 2004: 2). It is a very complex and detailed document and requires significant experience with incident response and management to be used effectively (Pampel 2008: 44).

The National Incident Management System and the Incident Command System

In November 2004, a new framework for the NRP was announced by DHS and the document was subsequently revised again in 2006. The enhanced NRP outlined general strategies dealing with response. First, it set forth the procedure for the declaration of an Incident of National Significance. Such a declaration would give the Secretary of DHS the authority to assume management of a multi-agency national response and recovery action. Second, the NRP stated that a declaration of an Incident of National Significance would trigger the establishment of the National Incident Management System (NIMS) which sets out the procedures, duties and guidelines for each participant in the response and recovery action (Pampel 2008: 44). Under NIMS, the Incident Command System (ICS) is utilized as the management structure to oversee, direct and coordinate the response and recovery action (Pampel 2008: 44). The NRP holds that ICS, which relies on command and control principles, is the preferred organizational structure for managing disasters (Tierney 2006: 409).

The National Response Framework

The National Response Framework (NRF) was the successor document to the NRP. It became effective in March, 2008 and was intended to be a comprehensive structure providing guidance and various performance goals to be utilized in the development and ongoing evolution of an effective national preparedness and response system (GAO-08-868-T 2008: 8). The NRF is a guide to how the country conducts response activities to catastrophic incidents. It was developed to be a flexible and adaptable guide which aligns key roles and responsibilities of responders and links all levels of government, including nongovernmental and private sector stakeholders and participants, in a response and recovery effort (NRF 2008: i).

The Catastrophic Incident Annex and Supplement

The NRF also includes the Catastrophic Incident Annex and Supplement, which describes proactive, accelerated national response plans for catastrophic incidents (GAO-08-868-T 2008: 8). It also provides further clarification of the roles and responsibilities of the various participating agencies and entities involved in large scale response and recovery actions. It reiterates that all incidents should be handled at the lowest possible level of response, meaning that the responsibility for responding to both natural and manmade disaster incidents begins at the local level, with the individuals and public officials in the immediate town, city or county impacted by the incident (NRF 2008: 15). State governments should supplement and facilitate local efforts in response activities before, during and after catastrophic incidents (NRF 2008: 21). If state capabilities are insufficient, then a request for federal assistance, including a Stafford Act Presidential declaration of an emergency if applicable, should be made and at that time the federal government becomes engaged and utilizes the NRF to involve all necessary federal department and agency capabilities to organize and deploy a federal response in coordination with all response partners and stakeholders (NRF 2008: 24). The specific agencies deployed to render assistance are determined by the type of assistance that is needed. Examples of specific types of duties and the responsible agencies will be discussed below with Mission Assignments and Emergency Support Functions.

The National Preparedness Guidelines

Another key policy document issued by DHS is the National Preparedness Guidelines (NPG). DHS developed the NPG utilizing 15 emergency scenarios which were designed to illustrate the realistic scope and magnitude of these incidents and identify the necessary capabilities to carry out an effective response and recovery action (GAO-07-1142T 2007: 23). The 15 scenarios include various types of terrorist incidents such as attacks by an improvised nuclear device, aerosol anthrax, nerve agent, blister agent, improvised explosive device, radiological dispersal device and cyber attack (NPG 2007: 31). Additionally, natural disasters and other emergency incidents are included in the scenarios, such as major hurricanes and earthquakes, an outbreak of pandemic influenza, plague, or foreign animal disease, a toxic chemical spill and a chlorine tank explosion (NPG 2007: 31).

Homeland Security Presidential Directives

In addition to these policy documents, there are over 20 Homeland Security Presidential Directives (HSPDs) which further define the roles and responsibilities of DHS as well as various other federal agencies in their efforts to prepare for and respond to terrorist attacks, natural disasters and other emergency incidents (GAO-08-868-T 2008: 5). HSPD-5, issued in February, 2003, designated the Secretary of Homeland Security as the principal official for domestic incident management and the person who would be responsible for coordinating the federal government's resources to be utilized during the response and recovery efforts relating to any type of disaster or emergency incident (GAO-08-868-T 2008: 5). HSPD-8, which was issued in December 2003, called for the creation of new national goals and performance measures. As part of this, standards were to be developed which would assess the nation's overall preparedness and capabilities.

Under HSPD-8, it was non-FEMA components which carried out the elements of national preparedness. This changed in July 2005, when the Secretary of Homeland Security separated preparedness functions, including planning, training and funding, into a new DHS Directorate for Preparedness. FEMA became a separate component which was responsible for response and recovery only (GAO-09-369 2009: 20). Critics argued that splitting emergency planning and training from FEMA was a mistake. This action created a new and separate division which lacked critical knowledge and experience with disaster response and recovery duties, which remained with FEMA (Pampel 2008: 43). This organizational change was later reversed in October 2006, under the Post-Katrina Emergency Management Reform Act, which restored most of the preparedness functions back to FEMA (GAO-09-369 2009: 20). Hurricane Katrina, including deficiencies in the response, lessons learned and the Post-Katrina Emergency Management Reform Act itself will be discussed further below.

Deployment of Response/Recovery Assets: Mission Assignments, Emergency Support Function and Specialized Response Teams

Mission Assignments

FEMA Mission Assignments are designed to coordinate immediate, short term emergency deployment of federal resources to assist with urgent disaster-related needs (GAO-08-868T 2008: 13). The concept of Mission Assignments, including their issuance, management and close-out procedures was formalized during Hurricane Andrew in 1992. Since that time, Mission Assignments have become the accepted system to direct and reimburse federal agencies for emergency missions during catastrophic response and recovery efforts. These Mission Assignments outline specific activities that will be carried out by various federal agencies and organizations, under FEMA's direction, to assist state and local jurisdictions in response and recovery efforts following a catastrophic disaster or other emergency incident (GAO-09-369 2009: 27). It is important to note that FEMA is not the provider of emergency support following a catastrophic incident; instead FEMA tasks other agencies to carry out specific tasks or assignments and coordinate the overall response effort. Mission Assignments are for emergency work only and are not to be used to complete long term restorative work or as part of long term studies. Mission Assignments outline the pre-arranged deployment plan for a wide variety of services including law enforcement support, health equipment, medical teams and military equipment to support state and local jurisdictions following emergency incidents (GAO-08-868-T 2008: 13). Examples of Mission Assignments that have been used during response efforts to recent catastrophic hurricanes include the U.S. Army Corps of Engineers being tasked to provide emergency power to hospitals and other critical facilities and the United States Coast Guard being tasked to provide emergency transportation to search and rescue teams being deployed to disaster sites.

Signatory federal departments and agencies of the NRP include the following: the Department of Homeland Security, Department of Justice, Department of Defense, Department of Transportation, Department of Energy, Department of Commerce, Department of Labor, Department of State, Department of Treasury, Central Intelligence Agency, Environmental Protection Agency, Federal Bureau of Investigation, Nuclear Regulatory Commission and the National Aeronautics and Space Administration. In addition, several non-governmental organizations (NGOs) which are active in disaster response and recovery are also signatories to the NRP. These signatory NGOs include the American Red Cross, the Corporation for National and Community Service and the National Voluntary Organizations Active in Disaster. Federal government departments and component agencies who are signatories under the NRP can be called on by FEMA to deploy personnel and resources to support a Mission Assignment and provide assistance as part of an Emergency Support Function in a disaster response effort (FEMA 2007: 1).

Emergency Support Functions

Emergency Support Function (ESF) is defined as a grouping of certain government and private sector capabilities into an organizational structure for the purpose of providing support, resources and services following a disaster or other catastrophic incident (NRP 2004: 10). FEMA is able to direct a full or partial activation of the ESF structure as needed to respond to actual or potential incidents of national significance (NRP 2004: 11).

The ESFs provide a structure for the coordination of various agencies to support a Federal response to a catastrophic incident. There are 15 ESFs in the NRF and they are known as the ESF Annexes. These ESFs cover response functions such as Public Safety and Security (ESF 13) and Public Health and Medical Services (ESF 8). Each ESF has a primary agency which has certain resources and capabilities that render it as a sort of expert in that particular field. The primary agency for a particular ESF has certain authorities and responsibilities in its response and is assisted by various support agencies in executing the mission assignment of the particular ESF. For example, after a major hurricane, it is likely that FEMA would deploy agencies to support an ESF 6 Mission: Mass Care, Emergency Assistance, Housing and Human Services to provide assistance to those whose homes were destroyed by the hurricane. Pursuant to the ESF Annexes, the scope of this particular ESF is to assist in providing mass care, emergency assistance, disaster housing and related human services; the primary agency for this ESF is DHS/FEMA and the various supporting agencies include the Department of Health and Human Services, the Department of Housing and Urban Development, the Department of Labor and the Department of Justice. In large-scale catastrophic incidents, it is common for a number of ESFs to be activated with a large number of agency personnel and assets deployed as part of these ESFs.

FEMA's Specialized Response Teams

FEMA has also structured a number of specialized response teams which can be dispatched to assist with disaster response as part of a mission assignment or ESF deployment. The Emergency Response Teams-National (ERT-Ns) are dispatched by FEMA to respond to major disasters or incidents designated as having national significance. The ERT-Ns are responsible for coordinating disaster response activity including the deployment of national response assets. These teams are also responsible for providing situational awareness and facilitating the flow of information to DHS (FEMA 2007: 2).

The Emergency Response Teams-Advanced (ERT-As) can be deployed during the early stages of an emergency incident to work directly with the impacted state or local entity to assess the damage impact and begin the coordination of the response effort. The Federal Incident Response Support Teams (FIRSTs) are a forward component of the ERT-As and are responsible for providing core on-site federal management support to the local incident commander in the earliest stages following a disaster (FEMA 2007: 2).

The Hurricane Liaison Team (HLT) is a small team designed to enhance the response and recovery efforts following hurricanes. These teams facilitate and coordinate the flow of information between federal, state and local officials, the National Hurricane Center and the National Oceanic and Atmospheric Administration. The Urban Search and Rescue Task Forces (US&Rs) are specialized teams deployed to assist state and local governments in rescue efforts following structural collapse or other rescue missions (FEMA 2007: 3).

FEMA also has Mobile Emergency Response Support (MERS) teams which can provide mobile telecommunication capabilities, as well as logistics and operational power and support to sustain the on-site management response activities following a disaster (FEMA 2007: 3).

Hurricane Katrina and Deficiencies Relating to Core Capabilities

The response to Hurricane Katrina which made landfall in August 2005, along the Louisiana-Mississippi gulf coast failed at all levels of government. The response effort raised grave concerns regarding the government's ability to respond effectively to catastrophic disasters and major emergency incidents (Pampel 2008: 45). After-action critiques of actions at the local, state and federal levels revealed many deficiencies in basic elements of preparation for natural disasters, or other emergency incidents, as well as the response to and recovery from such incidents (GAO-07-1142-T 2007: 8). Many critical capabilities that were needed to respond to and recover from a natural disaster were found to be severely lacking. Two fundamental areas which needed improvement were situational awareness/assessment and emergency communications (GAO-07-835T 2007: 13).

Situational Awareness/Assessment

The lack of situational awareness was a significant problem in the immediate aftermath of Hurricane Katrina. DHS officials located in Washington, D.C. were unable to get accurate information and assessments regarding the situation and conditions in New Orleans, information and assessments which they needed in order to make effective decisions regarding the response effort (Pampel 2008: 51). To address this problem, FEMA has developed the concept of deployable incident management teams which will act as a forward federal presence in a future incident response. These incident management teams will conduct an initial assessment and provide immediate situational awareness for the decision-making officials who are likely not on scene. They will also provide initial support to the state and local jurisdiction and work on establishing a unified incident command structure at the scene of the incident (GAO-07-835T 2007: 14).

Emergency Communications and Interoperability

In the area of emergency communications, it is critical that communications systems first be operable but secondly have interoperability so that all participants—law enforcement agencies at all levels, public safety agencies and service agencies—can communicate in real time. Following Hurricane Katrina, there was a complete failure of the communications infrastructure in the area impacted by the storm. Responders were left without a reliable network to use in the coordination of emergency response operations (The Federal Response 2006: 31). The State of Louisiana's 800 MHz radio system ceased functioning and was not repaired for several days; this radio system was the core component of mutual aid communications. The response effort was severely impacted by the complete lack of ability for first responders to communicate via telephone or radio for days after Hurricane Katrina made landfall. FEMA had pre-deployed two of its five MERS detachments to the gulf coast area immediately after Hurricane Katrina made landfall. These MERS detachments are comprised of vehicles and personnel trained to provide mobile communications, operational support and power generation assets to support the federal, state and local response efforts (The Federal Response 2006: 44). However, three additional MERS were available outside the disaster zone; FEMA failed to deploy them in a timely enough fashion to provide assistance with the communications breakdown, even after recognizing that the two pre-positioned detachments were not going to be adequate in a disaster of Hurricane Katrina's magnitude.

DHS's Office for Interoperability and Compatibility (OIC) was created in 2004 specifically to address these types of problems. The purpose of the OIC was to strengthen and integrate emergency communications interoperability efforts. OIC created Project SAFECOM, which is a program responsible for the development of systems and procedures designed to improve interoperability (GAO-07-835T 2007: 30). However, issues still persist with interoperability in general and the SAFECOM program in particular. SAFECOM has made only limited progress in the improvement of interoperability at all levels of government. Even though $12.5 billion was awarded in grants to state and local jurisdictions between 2003 and 2005 for interoperability enhancements to their communications systems, federal government agencies were not addressed at all and received no funding to enhance their communications systems to achieve interoperability, despite the large role they play in disaster response (GAO-07-301 2007: 16). Additionally, a GAO audit of SAFECOM's effectiveness reviewed four states and a number of selected local jurisdictions and found the program to be lacking. Officials interviewed for the audit reported to the GAO that

SAFECOM's tools and planning assistance were not helpful to them. Some were unaware that the program even existed. GAO linked SAFECOM's ineffectiveness to poor program management and inadequate performance measures (GAO-07-835T: 32). The bottom line is that a lot of work remains to be done in the field of interoperability for emergency communications.

Post-Katrina Emergency Management Reform Act

Congress passed the Post-Katrina Emergency Management Reform Act (Post-Katrina Act) in October, 2006, in response to the catastrophic 2005 hurricane season. The Act was designed to address problems and deficiencies identified during the response to Hurricane Katrina. The Post-Katrina Act made organizational changes in DHS and consolidated the emergency preparedness and response functions within FEMA. Under the Act, FEMA was given primary responsibility for the coordination and implementation of the core elements of the nation's federal emergency preparation and response plans (GAO-08-868T 2008: 2). FEMA emerged as a distinct entity within DHS under the Act and ten regional FEMA offices were established in the following cities: Boston, Massachusetts; New York, New York; Philadelphia, Pennsylvania; Atlanta, Georgia; Chicago, Illinois; Denton, Texas; Kansas City, Missouri; Denver, Colorado; San Francisco, California; and Bothell, Washington.

While these were positive aspects to the re-organization, there were also negative elements which continued to have an adverse impact on FEMA's effectiveness and ability to plan for and lead a response effort. One result of the re-organization was that FEMA inherited preparedness programs, including parts of a comprehensive assessment system, which had been created and carried out by other DHS components that had less experience in the area than did FEMA personnel. Additionally, the organizational changes in FEMA have resulted in a large turnover of staff and a severe loss of personnel with corporate knowledge and practical experience with previous disaster planning, response and recovery efforts (GAO-09-369 2009: 20).

DHS re-organized pursuant to the Post-Katrina Act, with the changes becoming effective March 31, 2007. The new national preparedness directorate was included in FEMA and consolidated existing FEMA programs' preparedness assets as well as assets from legacy Preparedness Directorate programs. Functions relating to preparedness doctrine, planning and policy were consolidated under FEMA (GAO-07-835T 2007: 19). Additionally, the re-organization established the National Integration Center, which was responsible for the ongoing management of NIMS and the NRP and was also charged with insuring that training and exercise activities followed these documents' directives (GAO-07-1142T 2007: 10).

Although there is still work to be done, the Post-Katrina Act has been successful in further enhancing the country's emergency preparedness response plans and strategies and has strengthened the identification of leadership roles and responsibilities in catastrophic incidents (GAO-07-1142T 2007: 22).

Exercises and Training

One of the requirements under the Post-Katrina Act involves exercises and training. FEMA was mandated to design exercises that would test the United States' emergency preparedness system and capabilities. Exercises are a critical component of the national emergency preparedness system, as they afford the opportunity to test the existing capabilities against the desired target capabilities (GAO-09-369 2009: 34). By doing so, the exercises would provide validation that the policies and procedures in place under the emergency preparedness system are effective (GAO-09-369 2009: 34). Exercises allow emergency preparedness plans and capabilities to be tested in a risk-free environment; deficiencies can be identified and corrective actions taken to improve proficiency (GAO-09-369 2009: 5). Exercises are designed to involve participation at various levels. Some are designed to address responses at the local and state level, for example, a localized chemical spill. Other national level, or Tier 1, exercises involve scenarios with a more national impact such as the response to a large-scale terrorist attack and are designed to include broader participation by all appropriate federal departments and agencies as well as regional participation by the applicable state, local and non-governmental organizations.

Hurricane Pam Exercise

An example of an emergency preparedness exercise is the Hurricane Pam exercise which FEMA sponsored in July 2004 (prior to Hurricane Katrina). The goal of the exercise, which itself was an eerie portent of Katrina, was to predict damage and plan a course of action to respond if a severe hurricane hit New Orleans or the southeast portion of Louisiana. The scenario consisted of a Category 3 Hurricane with sustained winds of 120 mph, 20 inches of rain and the evacuation of more than one million residents from 13 parishes in southeast Louisiana, including the New Orleans area. Over 250 emergency preparedness officials from 50 parish (county), state, federal and volunteer organizations participated in the eight-day tabletop exercise. However, even though Hurricane Pam was a worst case scenario disaster simulation, it was never imagined that the flood control system for the city of New Orleans would completely collapse (Cooper and Block 2006: 22). In fact, only a few scenarios used in the Hurricane Pam simulation mentioned the possibility that the levees could be breached. Additionally, lessons learned in the Hurricane Pam simulation were not implemented as part of the real-life response to Hurricane Katrina. The Hurricane Pam simulation recommended that Louisiana would require 69 water truckloads, 69 ice truckloads, 34 food truckloads, 28 trucks full of tarps and 10,000 sets of bedding for the aftermath of a severe hurricane. However, on the Sunday before Hurricane Katrina made landfall, FEMA only had 30 trucks of water, 17 trucks of ice, 15 trucks of meals, six truckloads of tarps and one truck of blankets in the area. In addition, the Hurricane Pam scenario predicted that due to the large indigent population in New Orleans, only a third of the people would evacuate because over 100,000 residents lived in households which did not own a car (Hurricane Pam 2005). Despite this prediction, no adequate plan was developed to address the evacuation or sheltering of these residents who did not have the means to leave the city on their own. This lapse became glaringly apparent a year after the Pam simulation when, in the aftermath of Hurricane Katrina, thousands of New Orleans residents who did not have the means to evacuate the city were stranded at the Louisiana Superdome and Morial Convention Center.

Deficiencies in the Exercise Program and Applicable FEMA Databases

FEMA is required under the Post-Katrina Act to assess performance and take corrective actions following the completion of training exercises. However, FEMA has not been able to meet this requirement because the states do not consistently follow up on the status of corrective actions taken. Moreover, the after-action reports that are submitted do not consistently provide time frames for the implementation of corrective actions (GAO-09-369 2009: 10). The lack of procedures makes it very problematic for FEMA to verify if any corrective actions are even carried out.

Part of the procedural problem is that the databases FEMA utilizes to measure the effectiveness of the National Exercise Plan contain incomplete data. One of the stated performance measures of the National Exercise Program is the number of DHS-funded exercises conducted each year. States are required to use the National Exercise Schedule (NEXS) system to schedule their exercises.

However, the states are failing to enter all exercises conducted in the database and they are not consistently following up with after-action reports and verification of corrective actions taken (GAO-09-369 2009: 49). In order to have valid exercises which provide an accurate assessment of the country's capabilities and operating procedures, the exercises must be realistic, involve key players and be designed to truly stress the system. Following the exercise, there should also be a critical assessment of the performance and outcomes of the exercise and lessons learned should be implemented as part of the follow-up and corrective action taken (GAO-07-1142T 2007: 29).

The Secure Portal is another database FEMA uses to assess states' compliance with exercise requirements. States receiving federal grant funding to support their exercise are required to enter their after-action reports in the Secure Portal. However, this is not consistently completed and FEMA lacks adequate procedures to track and verify that these reports are entered timely, if at all (GAO-09-369 2009: 50).

The Corrective Action Program (CAP) system is a third database used by FEMA to measure compliance with the National Exercise Program. Users of the CAP system can enter, track and analyze corrective actions and improvement plans developed from exercises and training, as well as from actual incidents. The problem with this system is that the federal agencies participating in exercises are encouraged but not required to use this system. After-action reports and verification of corrective actions are not consistently entered in the CAP system (GAO-09-369 2009: 51). Without the ability to track corrective actions, the information in these databases is incomplete and thereby adversely impacts FEMA's ability to effectively measure the progress being made by the National Exercise Program (GAO-09-369 2009: 10).

One inherent problem with the National Exercise Program is that there is always a degree of artificiality no matter how well the exercises are designed. It is very difficult, if not impossible, to design an exercise that simulates real-world conditions following a catastrophic disaster. Additionally, it is difficult to design a valid exercise to test a plan when there is not a firm plan in place to start with (GAO-09-369 2009: 46). Key planning documents are still lacking in the nation's emergency preparedness strategy, making it extremely difficult to design valid exercises, which in turn adversely impacts FEMA's ability to meet its testing requirements and improve from results of the tests.

Significant Progress

With all that being said, FEMA has made significant progress since 2007 in the implementation and development of the National Exercise Plan and also in the area of tracking corrective actions (GAO-09-369 2009: 9). FEMA's National Exercise Division is a component of FEMA's National Integration Center. This Division is responsible for leading and coordinating all activities relating to exercises dealing with preparedness, response and recovery. FEMA has developed an implementation plan with specific requirements for exercises that will involve the participation of various federal agencies (GAO-09-369 2009: 9–10). However, the development and implementation of a National Exercise Program is very difficult; a huge coordination effort is necessary due to the large number of agencies and organizations involved in national emergency preparedness and response. Also, there is no procedure in place outlining how FEMA is to work with other federal agencies and FEMA has no authority to force other federal agencies to comply with its exercise programs. This is an issue that will need to be addressed at the Congressional level if federal agencies are to be mandated to comply with FEMA directives. At the state level, FEMA can link exercise compliance requirements to its grant programs (GAO-09-369 2009: 34). However, FEMA still lacks procedures to effectively monitor states' compliance with the National Exercise Program. Specifically, there are no procedures in place to insure that the required after-action reports are prepared following exercises and no tracking procedures to insure that corrective actions have been implemented (GAO-09-369 2009: 38).

Outstanding Challenges with National Preparedness/Response Plans

Interagency Coordination

If we are to enjoy long term success in the realm of national preparedness and response, it is critical that FEMA coordinate with the various stakeholders involved, including federal and non-federal agencies and non-governmental organizations. This coordination should focus on the development of response plans, exercises and assessments and work towards integrating those elements into a comprehensive approach aimed at national preparedness (GAO-09-369 2009: 70). FEMA does recognize the necessity to coordinate with stakeholders at all levels to ensure that their views and ideas are incorporated into the development and implementation of a comprehensive system to assess national preparedness. However, any such large scale coordination is very time consuming and can oftentimes take much longer than expected, thereby resulting in missed deadlines and other delays (GAO-09-369 2009: 58). For example, non-federal stakeholders were included in the initial revision process of the

NRF. However, those stakeholders were not provided the first full revision draft and were not asked for additional comments and suggestions (GAO-08-868T 2008: 8). Instead, a closed internal federal review was conducted. This was not in accordance with the Post-Katrina Act's requirements of the establishment of a National Advisory Council which would incorporate non-federal stakeholders' input and recommendations into the revision process of the document (GAO-08-868T 2008: 9). However, the time involved to re-engage the large number of non-federal stakeholders in the revision process was prohibitive and would have resulted in further delays in the completion of the document.

The Need for an Assessment System

A significant problem in the national preparedness plan is the lack of an adequate system to assess the country's overall preparedness and response capabilities (GAO-08-868T 2008: 15). FEMA has developed a project management plan for completing a comprehensive assessment system. This comprehensive assessment system is scheduled for completion by 2010. However, the plan does not identify the program elements that are necessary to complete the system. Missing elements include the establishment of milestones and the identification of risks necessary to measure capability levels for response (GAO-09-369 2009: 11). Other problems with the management plan that may impact FEMA's ability to meet its 2010 deadline for completion of the comprehensive assessment system include the lack of specific actions as to how preparedness information will be integrated into the system and also a general lack of risk assessment information that can be included in the system (GAO-09-369 2009: 61). Additionally, DHS has not completed a full inventory of the federal response capabilities. Challenges in coordinating with other stakeholders as well as difficulties in obtaining necessary data are other factors adversely impacting FEMA's ability to develop and implement a comprehensive assessment system for national preparedness.

The Need to Complete and Integrate Policies and Response Plans

An effective disaster response plan is contingent upon having well-trained leaders and responders. However, until FEMA completes all outstanding policies and plans relating to disaster preparedness and response and assessment thereof, it is impossible to provide effective training on the applicable policies and plans (GAO-09-369 2009: 28). While FEMA and various other federal entities have completed the majority of the critical policies, especially those defining the roles and responsibilities of the participants in emergency preparedness and response, 68 percent of the plans to implement these polices remain incomplete (GAO-09-369 2009: 9). While a program management plan is critical for the implementation of these policies, FEMA has yet to develop and implement a comprehensive plan which outlines the development and integration of core policies and procedures defining the planning process for emergency preparedness and response as well as defining the roles and responsibilities of the participants in these processes (GAO-09-369 2009: 23).

FEMA has made strides in the completion of some policies. For example, in December 2008, DHS issued the revised NIMS which provided further clarification regarding the roles and responsibilities of participants during a multiagency response. However, other policies which are just as important remain incomplete, such as the four Partner Guides to the NRF which are to provide descriptions of the key roles and responsibilities of the specific federal, state, local and private non-governmental organizations involved in disaster preparedness and response under the NRF (GAO-09-369 2009: 25). Additionally, progress has been made toward addressing deficiencies relating to Mission Assignments. In 2008, FEMA completed a Mission Assignment Catalog which defined the roles and responsibilities of 31 federal agencies in 236 pre-scripted mission assignments, ranging from deployments following a natural disaster to a terrorist attack in a major U.S. city (GAO-09-369 2009: 27). While additional work remains to be completed, these pre-scripted scenarios provide a useful road map to be used in a response and recovery effort.

Another serious problem FEMA faces is its inability to determine whether other entities are on schedule with their own policy development and planning requirements. Without having this information, FEMA cannot determine how to integrate these outstanding pieces into the overall comprehensive policy and plan (GAO-09-369 2009: 33). FEMA has great obstacles to face in the effective development of a national preparedness plan which integrates all elements, including those from other entities. First, the sheer number of agencies and organizations involved in national preparedness and response and the complexity of the activities involved creates a daunting task (GAO-09-369 2009: 19). Dealing with such a large number of participants and stakeholders demands extensive coordination. Additionally, each agency or entity has varying procedures and work patterns which creates additional challenges in implementing any planning, training or other activity relating to national preparedness or response. There also remains a lack of communication among all of the participating agencies and stakeholders, due primarily to the large number of participants involved (GAO-09-369 2009: 19). Another major obstacle facing FEMA is the organizational and staffing changes it has suffered, first when being incorporated in DHS and then again with departmental re-organizations following the enactment of the Post-Katrina Act (GAO-09-369 2009: 20). Each of these re-organizations has resulted in setbacks to the agency, from which it has taken time to recover.

Conclusion

The United States' response plans and strategies have been modified over the past several decades following catastrophic incidents or natural disasters which have had a broad impact on the country. Large-scale federal department re-or-ganizations including the creation of DHS and several re-organizations of FEMA have been executed with the long-term goal of increasing homeland security and strengthening the country's response plans for catastrophic incidents and disasters. As response and recovery efforts for specific catastrophic incidents are critiqued, modifications are made to existing response plans and strategies in hopes that the country will be better prepared and able to launch a more effective response and recovery effort following the next catastrophic incident.

This is an evolving process and even though significant progress has been made, there is still much work that needs to be done. Progress has been made in the development and integration of response plans which more specifically define and clarify the roles and responsibilities of the key stakeholders and participants in response efforts, but there are still outstanding policies and procedures that need to be developed and then incorporated into the overall national strategy and response plan. The United States still lacks emergency communication interoperability for responders, which was a huge problem in the recovery efforts following Hurricane Katrina. Progress is being made but full interoperability has not yet been achieved. Additionally, the U.S. is still lacking an adequate system to assess its overall preparedness and response capabilities.

As the country works to further strengthen its emergency response plans, it is imperative that there be cooperation and coordination between all participants at the local, state, federal and non-governmental levels. Realistic training and exercise must continue, along with critiques and after-action assessments in order that lessons learned can be incorporated into future plans to help strengthen response and recovery efforts. While DHS and FEMA remain at the forefront of these efforts, it is the responsibility of all stakeholders to work together to accomplish the goal of insuring that our country is prepared to respond effectively to the next catastrophic incident.

References

Cooper, C. and R. Block. 2006. *Disaster: Hurricane Katrina and the Failure of Homeland Security*. New York: Henry Holt & Co.

Department of Homeland Security. 2004. *National Response Plan*. Washington, D.C.

Department of Homeland Security. 2007. *National Preparedness Guidelines*. Washington, D.C.

Department of Homeland Security. 2008. *National Response Framework*. Washington, D.C.

The Federal Response to Hurricane Katrina: Lessons Learned. 2006. Available online at: http://georgewbush-whitehouse.archives.gov/reports/katrina-lessons-learned/.

FEMA. 2007. *FEMA Disaster Response Assets and Enhancements*. Washington, D.C.

Hurricane Pam. 2005. Available online at: http://www.globalsecurity.org/security/ops/hurricane-pam.htm.

Moss, M. and C. Shelhamer. 2007. *The Stafford Act: Priorities for Reform*. New York: New York University.

Pampel, F. C. 2008. *Library in a Book: Disaster Response*. New York: Facts on File, Inc.

Tierney, K. J. 2006. Recent developments in U.S. homeland security policies and their implications for the management of extreme events. In *Handbook of Disaster Research*, eds. H. Rodriguez, E.L. Quarantelli and R.R. Dynes, New York: Springer.

U.S. Government Accountability Office. 2007. *Homeland Security: Observations on DHS and FEMA efforts to Prepare for and Respond to Major and Catastrophic Disasters and Address Related Recommendations and Legislation*. GAO-07-835T. Washington, D.C.: May 15.

U.S. Government Accountability Office. 2007. *Homeland Security: Observations on DHS and FEMA Efforts to Prepare for and Respond to Major Catastrophic Disasters and Address Related Recommendations and Legislation*. GAO-07-1142T. Washington, D.C.: July 31.

U.S. Government Accountability Office. 2008. *Homeland Security: Observations on DHS: Preparedness for Catastrophic Disasters*. GAO-08-868T. Washington, D.C.: June 11.

U.S. Government Accountability Office. 2009. *FEMA has Made Progress, but Needs to Complete and Integrate Planning, Exercise, and Assessment Efforts*. GAO-09-369: Washington, D.C.: May 7.

Figure 15.1 Organizational Chart of DHS

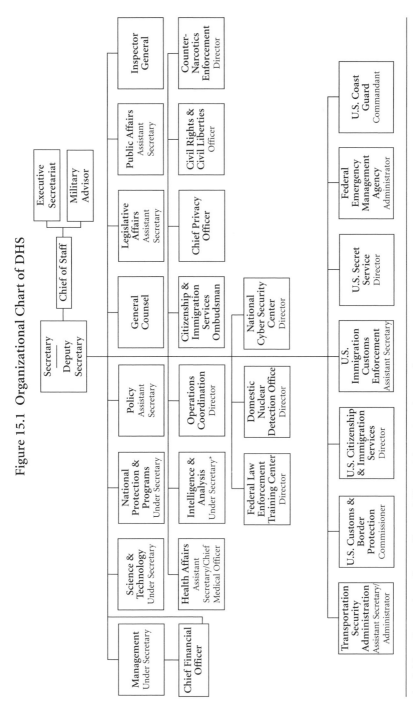

Available online at: http://www.dhs.gov/xlibrary/photos/orgchart-web.png.

Figure 15.2 Organizational Chart of FEMA

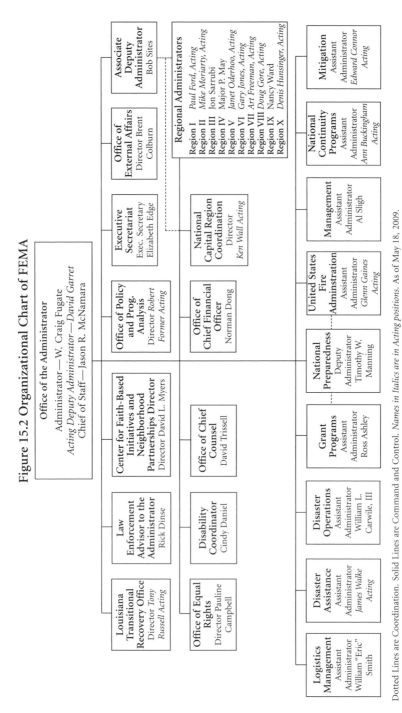

Dotted Lines are Coordination. Solid Lines are Command and Control. *Names in Italics are in Acting positions.* As of May 18, 2009.

Available online at: http://www.fema.gov/pdf/about/org_chart.pdf.

Discussion Questions

1. What is the Stafford Act? What is its role in emergency preparedness?
2. How did disaster response planning change after 9/11?
3. What is FEMA's role in disaster preparedness?
4. What are some criticisms of FEMA's location within DHS? Be specific.
5. Describe the NRP, NRF, NIMS and NPG and how they interrelate.
6. What was the consequence of HSPD-8 as it related to FEMA? How did critics view this change?
7. Discuss the purpose of a Mission Assignment. Provide an example of a Mission Assignment that FEMA may task following a natural disaster such as a Category 5 hurricane.
8. What are the specialized response teams that FEMA operates and what are the tasks of each?
9. Describe the changes brought about by the Post-Katrina Emergency Management Reform Act. Why was this Act necessary in the first place?
10. What is Hurricane Pam? What are the still-unresolved problems with FEMA's exercise and training protocol?
11. What are some of the challenges of true interagency coordination?

16

WHERE SHOULD WE GO FROM HERE? THEORETICAL AND POLICY IMPLICATIONS

By Kelly Frailing and Dee Wood Harper

Introduction

It strikes us that the bromide, it is not a question of will it happen, but when, applies not just to the ubiquity of disaster but also to the presence of crime related to the disaster occurring before, during and after the event. The idea that an event is a disaster only if there is not adequate preparation for it is also relevant here. To avoid the criminal consequences of disaster requires adequate preparation beginning with the recognition that various crimes do in fact occur before and during a disaster and its aftermath.

"Those who cannot remember the past are condemned to repeat it" (Santayana 1905: 284). With this in mind, our book opened with an historical perspective on crime and disaster. Beginning with an attempt to clarify what exactly constitutes a disaster, we examined many historic examples of disasters and the crimes that were linked to these events. As a final note, we examined an event that changed forever the way we define disaster—the terrorist attack on the World Trade Center and on Washington, D.C. on September 11, 2001. All of these historic disasters have implications for avoiding the condemnation of repeating them. We are of course more aware of what was not done that could have been done to avoid the terrible tragedy of 9/11. Federal law enforcement failed in a number of ways, not the least of which was the failure of interagency communication.

To make sense out of any patterns of human conduct requires us to develop a theoretical framework that helps us to organize the more salient dimensions of what is taking place. Therefore, what we are trying to accomplish with this work is to suggest some of the theoretical issues that must be addressed in developing a criminology of disaster. Thornton and Voigt do just this by proposing a typology of crime in disaster in the second chapter of Part I. Their chapter is a distillation of the research literature on phases of disaster which is linked with observations about why and what types of criminal activity emerge during each phase, using crime that occurred during the Katrina Disaster to illustrate. This chapter provides the theoretical lenses through which we subsequently look at the crimes occurring in conjunction with and the criminal justice system's responses to disaster. Moreover, it makes clear that the disaster-crime linkage needs more theoretically informed research, beginning with a clear conceptualization of what a disaster is.

The third chapter in Part 1 also examines different types of disaster and uses the 1989 *Exxon Valdez* oil spill to illustrate how a disaster may be viewed as a crime. Of critical importance in developing this thesis are the consequences of litigation to the individuals and communities that were directly affected. The slow pace of litigation has seen at least 20 percent of those directly affected die off, while those still alive are re-victimized by the long, drawn out nature of the process, never experiencing a full recovery from the disaster. Clearly, disasters, as the *Exxon Valdez* oil spill illustrates, can have exceptionally long term consequences. At this writing, 20 years later, some litigation in this case remains unsettled.

Our intention in Part 1 of the book was to call attention to the need to historically contextualize disaster and to demonstrate that while disaster takes many forms, there are commonalities, particularly in the area of criminal behavior that lend themselves to developing a generalized response. To begin with, while it goes against our desire to believe the good in people far outweighs the bad, we still must recognize that there are people who will take advantage of a breakdown in the normal routines of life to take advantage of others or to enrich themselves.

Following Katrina, a local priest paraphrasing on the United Negro College Fund slogan, "a mind is a terrible thing to waste" (UNCF 1972) was reputed to have said, "a disaster is a terrible thing to waste." We assume that he meant the event was an opportunity to do good things or to bring about positive change. On the other hand, he could also have meant that the disruption and disorder caused by disaster was an opening to enrich oneself at the expense of others. This seems to be the case for people who steal, rape, rob and commit fraud as well as other crimes, opportunities for which the disruption of the storm provided.

In Parts 2 and 3 of the book, authors highlighted the occurrence of different crimes in the wake of disaster and the criminal justice response to various disasters. We conclude this chapter with the recommendations that we see as stemming from each authors' treatment of these events. Astute readers should observe that these recommendations are repeated in some cases and overlap in others, providing a full range of policy suggestions for disaster response improvement, especially as they relate to crime and criminal justice. It is important to remember that our book is not intended to be comprehensive in its coverage of disasters or the criminal justice system response to them. Rather, we intended to develop a thesis that crime does in fact emerge and evolve in the various stages of disaster and the criminal justice system must do the same in order to effectively react to and contain it.

Policy Recommendations

Fear, Prosocial Behavior and Looting

The starkest difference between Katrina and Gustav in terms of property crime in New Orleans was the guardianship in place after the latter storm. National Guard troops were on the scene before Gustav made landfall and were stationed all over the city, especially at commercial locations. This guardianship is an absolute necessity when a major storm threatens the city. It puts people more at ease to leave when an evacuation has been called. It also frees up police and other first responders to attend to emergent situations in which lives are in danger of being lost. Emergency response plans should make sure that the need for guardianship is widely known and planned for. In the longer term, improving socioeconomic conditions in the city will reduce looting. An investment in improving schools and recruiting business to New Orleans will, over time, aid in the stability that itself aids in disaster recovery.

Disaster Rape: Vulnerability of Women to Sexual Assaults During Hurricane Katrina

This chapter revealed that rape occurs in each phase of a disaster, from warning to reconstruction. One of the difficulties in measuring the occurrence of rape after a disaster is an inability to report it where it occurred. In the case of New Orleans, this was due to the complete absence of the criminal justice system in the wake of Katrina. A mechanism to report rapes that occurred in the disaster-impacted area in the cities to which victims evacuated must be implemented. Jurisdictional concerns should be set aside during the disaster's aftermath so that victims can pursue legal action. Bringing criminal justice system attention to rapes is also a public safety issue, in that pursuit and prosecution can begin, as can warnings to the public. More generally speaking, the unique needs of women in disasters need to be addressed. These needs include emergency preparation on the part of women's services so that disruption of them is limited.

Fraud Following the September 11, 2001 and Hurricane Katrina Disasters

To reduce federal benefit fraud in the wake of disaster, it is necessary to harden the target of federal benefits. To do this, agencies responsible for distributing the benefits must work together to ensure that those applying for them are entitled to them. In the case of Hurricane Katrina, these agencies should have been FEMA, the United States Post Office and the Social Security Administration. Working together, these agencies could have confirmed addresses and Social Security numbers before FEMA distributed benefits. This would have reduced some of the fraud which occurred in the storm's wake. Of course, time is of the essence when emergency relief is needed. However, it would almost certainly be less costly to incorporate a system that provided instant checks of applicants' details than to pursue and prosecute fraud claims years after the fact. To do so would also improve FEMA's reputation among disaster victims.

Changes in the Illegal Drug Market in New Orleans after Hurricane Katrina

The biggest revelation of this chapter is that even in the face of a hugely destructive disaster such as Hurricane Katrina, illegal drug markets reorganized and continue to flourish. This information, that there will be new suppliers, new connections among dealers and suppliers as a result of the evacuation, new dealers and new users as a result of storm-related stress and the influx of people to the disaster area to assist in the recovery, should aid law enforcement in preparing a response. Executing an effective response should help to quell the violence associated with the reorganization of these illegal drug markets. Also of note from this chapter is the unique methodology employed. It should assist researchers in using their own creative methods for studying illegal phenomena.

The Los Angeles Riot and the Criminal Justice Response

The precipitating factors of the 1992 Los Angeles riots were many, among them the socioeconomic conditions in South Central Los Angeles, where minority residents lived in poverty, underfunding for community policing, which jeopardized relations between citizens and law enforcement, a general lack of emergency preparedness on the part of the Los Angeles Police Department and an ineffective use of the National Guard to quell the riots. Lessons learned from the riots included preparing for civil disturbances in advance, not at the time they occur, and being able to respond to them in a way that does not worsen them, obtaining sufficient funding for police operations, including community policing, which can improve relations among law enforcement and the citizenry, improving social conditions, as socioeconomic stability decreases participation in riots and if they are required, the effective use of military troops.

The Mumbai Terrorist Attack and the Criminal Justice Response

The lessons of Mumbai for the criminal justice system are just now coming into focus. The police need to plan for disruptions in communications and transport, for rumor mongering and for the provision of emergency services, all simultaneously. They need to do this well in advance of an attack. Particular consideration should be given to the media's role during an attack and whether limits should be set on the information that is disseminated. Responding effectively to a terror attack like Mumbai requires interagency cooperation. The groundwork for this cooperation needs to be laid long before the attack so that effective planning for both the immediate and longer term impacts can occur. If this coordination and planning is not done and the recommended improvements to police and intelligence coordination, to police training, equipment and command center creation, to fire department training and coordination and to the ambulance service do not occur, people may begin to lose faith in the ability of the government to ensure their safety. This loss of faith would have long-term consequences for democratic functioning and governance of the nation. Criminal justice and related agencies need to consider these issues and develop effective strategies to combat terrorists before they strike.

The New Orleans' Police Department's Response to Hurricane Katrina and Its Aftermath

Police Chief Riley's recommendations for improving disaster response come from his experience during Hurricane Katrina and are focused on law enforcement. First, undamaged housing must be available for police and related first responders in the disaster area so they may stay and continue to execute their post-disaster duties. They must also be equipped for an extended stay in an area that may have no functioning infrastructure. The National Guard needs to be on the ground before the disaster strikes so that troops may immediately aid in meeting the basic needs of survivors and in restoring law and order. Mental health services must be available for those first responders facing unprecedented tragedy. During non-disaster periods, emergency plans must be constantly updated, with essential personnel identified, and training for response must be ongoing. Finally, to retain police force members so that they are available for disaster response, salaries and benefits must be competitive.

The Heavy Lifting—Local Emergency Response Planning and Preparedness

The main point Colonel Ebbert made in his interview had to do with local level planning for emergencies and disasters. Local level planners do not have ownership of the resources they will need in the case of a disaster, so they either have to plan without these resources or plan with them, thereby risking blame if these resources are rendered unavailable. The focus on planning at the local level has to be augmented by state, regional and national planning so it is clear what resources are available to whom and under what circumstances. These plans must be coordinated and involve as many mission driven agencies as possible, for those are the ones most prepared to react in an emergency, especially during the crucial response phase. Based on his experience in Hurricane Katrina, Ebbert also advocates for the creation of regional transportation and shelter plans. These would be especially useful in evacuating the elderly and other vulnerable citizens so that they can be out of harm's way when a disaster strikes. Having them safely sheltered also frees up first responders to attend to other emergent needs.

National Emergency Preparedness and Response Plans: An Overview

The overview of DHS and FEMA in this chapter notes several places where improvements in disaster preparedness can be made. Moving FEMA into DHS after the 9/11 attacks stripped it of most of its ability to effectively respond to a large-scale disaster and this was partially remedied by the Post-Katrina Emergency Reform Act. The Act consolidated emergency planning, preparedness and response functions within FEMA, making it a distinct DHS entity. However, challenges remain, principal among them the incomplete databases used in preparedness assessments. This incomplete information hampers the ability to take corrective steps after each training exercise designed to assess readiness and thereby hampers actual disaster preparation. There is also still no procedure in place for how FEMA is supposed to work with other agencies, nor does FEMA have any authority to compel compliance from those agencies. The sheer number of agencies involved complicates FEMA's ability to complete outstanding disaster preparedness and response policies and plans. Until it does so, however, it will be impossible for FEMA to provide effective training for responding to the next disaster.

In summary, it is clear that disasters only occur when they have not been adequately planned for. The same can be said for crime in the context of disaster—it would not occur or would occur less frequently if adequate safeguards were in place. Our goal for this book has been to stimulate thinking about the interconnections of crime and criminal justice in the context of disaster, an issue often overlooked by those responsible for disaster planning. While our work is not comprehensive either in the enumeration of all forms of disaster, the crimes that occur or the criminal justice system's responses, the examples provided should call attention to the problem and suggest some of the policy responses that might be appropriate.

Implications for a Criminology of Disaster

The issue of crime in the context of disaster has been largely overlooked by disaster researchers on the one hand and criminologists on the other. Only in the post-9/11 era and with the 24/7 news cycle have we become more aware of disasters around the globe, whether they are natural, man-made or perpetrated. With each disaster, horrible enough in its own right, comes the even darker prospect of criminal activity. Whether the criminal activity was the cause of the disaster or is the result of people taking advantage of it to exploit those who have been disadvantaged by the disruption is, as we have demonstrated in this volume, not an uncommon feature of disasters and their aftermath. We believe these facts call for a more systematic examination of crime in the context of disaster. To this end, there are a number of research issues that must be addressed.

First, we believe that fear plays a significant role in people's behavior in disasters. Some disasters engender fear more than others. Our national terrorism policy, at least that we are aware of, seems to be driven by creating fear with constant reminders of threat levels and suspicious behavior in airports. The rituals of airport security, presumptively designed to allay our fears, do not seem to accomplish the task. Fear drives decision-making. Take for example an impending hurricane: Do I evacuate or stay? If I evacuate, will my property be safe from looting? If I stay, will I be in danger of marauding thieves, not to mention the physical consequences of a terrible hurricane? This linkage between fear and behavior in the context of disaster has not been systematically addressed in the disaster research literature or in criminology. A related line of research should look at the role of rumor in supporting and perpetuating fear. There were many unsubstantiated rumors that were passed on as truth by the media and other responsible people during the Katrina Disaster, as well as during other catastrophic events.

Second, we know from our research that the social and economic conditions of a disaster zone can engender varying degrees of antisocial behavior. Looting of non-survival merchandise and of homes in the aftermath of Katrina was widespread and carried out by people not subjected to significant guardianship who defined the situation as an opportunity to enrich themselves. At the time of the storm, New Orleans had over 27 percent of its population living in poverty and another fourth of the population near poverty. The economic circumstances of the city over the previous forty years had effectively set the stage for the high levels of property crime observed after Katrina. South Central Los Angeles exhibited similar circumstances that contributed to the riots there in 1992.

Third, we need to address the issue of interpersonal victimization in disaster. What is it about a disaster that compels some people to personally take advantage of other people's vulnerability? We know, for example that rapes occurred in every phase of the Katrina disaster. What are the dynamics of offender/victim interaction that lead to sexual attacks in the various phases of a disaster?

Fourth, fraud is a serious issue for agencies responsible for the distribution of benefits following disasters. Research questions that need to be addressed center on offender motivation and the degree to which responsible agencies exercise reasonable processes of distributing resources so as not to create circumstances that allow for fraud, but at the same time distributing those resources in a timely fashion. In the chapter on disaster fraud in this volume, the author contrasts 9/11 and Katrina processes and found less fraud in the former than the latter. The primary difference was that the 9/11 process required a qualifying process that was considerably more challenging than Katrina's process.

A fifth area of inquiry has to do with how illegal activities disrupted by disaster, even by a disaster as hugely destructive as Katrina, manage to reorganize and continue to flourish. This raises some important research questions in the area of criminal organizational development and change. In the chapter on illegal drug markets in New Orleans after Hurricane Katrina, we learned that the drug trade never really died off and dealers were quite resourceful in supplying their customers and in developing new markets. Of course the attendant violence associated with the drug trade returned and in 2006, with the population of the city of New Orleans reduced by almost a third, the high murder rate gave the city the dubious title of "Murder Capital of the United States".

A criminology of disaster by necessity must be cross-cultural and transnational in orientation. Disasters are world-wide phenomena and are uniformly feared, yet they often have different cultural meanings. In Western cultures, for example, there are few instances of people resorting to suicide attacks, yet it is a not at all uncommon tactic in the Middle East. Understanding cultural differences in the perpetuation of violence (in the case of suicide attackers, what are the underlying cultural and religious reasons for taking one's life and the lives of others) and what it means to the victims is an important step toward developing a comparative approach to crime and disaster.

Finally, the governmental and organizational response to disaster raises myriad research questions concerning organizational development and change in response to crime in disaster. All of the selections in Part 3 of this book pointed to a variety of organizational flaws and failures or lack of preparation in dealing with the exigencies confronted as a result of the disaster and its aftermath. The lack of interagency communication and coordination and how to overcome this glaring weakness in disaster response is a common theme in all the selections. The importance of planning and the sharing of plans at each level of government was also emphasized. Yet while plans were in place they never seemed to be adequate for the task at hand. The impact of crime can be minimized when adequate plans are in place to deal with it.

References

Santayana, G. 1095. *Life of Reason: Reason in Common Sense.* New York: Charles Scribner's Sons.

UNCF. 1972. United Negro College Fund. Available online at: http://www.ad council.org/default.aspx?id=134.

About the Authors

Katrina Workman Berger is currently the Deputy Special Agent in Charge for the Department of Homeland Security Immigration and Customs Enforcement (DHS/ICE) Office of Investigations in New Orleans, Louisiana. She received her Bachelor of Arts degree from the Virginia Polytechnic Institute and State University in 1989, her Juris Doctorate from Shepard Broad Law School, Nova Southeastern University in 1993 and then a Master of Criminal Justice from Loyola University New Orleans. In 2006, she was a recipient of the Secretary of Department of Homeland Security's Gold Medal Award, the Department's highest award, in recognition of her outstanding leadership and service during the Hurricane Katrina response effort. Ms. Berger co-authored and presented a paper entitled Relevant Law and Empirical Research on Profiling in Law Enforcement in the United States at the 2007 International Police Executive Symposium in Dubai, U.A.E.

Clifton Bryant is Professor Emeritus of Sociology at Virginia Tech University, where he served from 1972-2007. His teaching and research specialty areas include the sociology of deviant behavior, death and dying, military sociology and the sociology of work and occupations. During his 47-year career, he enjoyed faculty status at six U.S. colleges and universities and two Southeast Asian universities. He served as president of the Southern Sociological Society and the Mid-South Sociological Association. He has received several awards for distinction, including placement on the Southern Sociological Society's Roll of Honor, as well as a number of teaching awards. In addition to founding *Deviant Behavior*, he has served on the editorial boards of a number of notable journals. Professor Bryant has authored dozens of reference books, books and journal articles, including those published in *Social Forces*, *Society*, *Sociological Inquiry*, *Sociology and Social Research*, *Rural Sociology*, *Sociological Forum*, *American Journal of Public Health* and *Deviant Behavior*.

Kelly Frailing received her Bachelor of Arts in Psychology from Grinnell College and her Master of Criminal Justice from Loyola University New Orleans. She is currently a Ph.D. student at the University of Cambridge Institute of Criminology. She is studying various aspects of mental health courts, including referrals, service utilization, outcomes and participant and staff perceptions. Her research in this area has appeared in the *Cambridge Student Law Review* and in *Per Incuriam*. She is also interested in disaster and crime and her research in this area has appeared in the *American Journal of Economics and Sociology*, the *Natural Hazards Observer* and in the book *The Sociology of Katrina: Perspectives on a Modern Catastrophe*. She has made numerous conference presentations on both of these topics.

Duane A. Gill is Professor and Head of Sociology at Oklahoma State University. He is part of a research team that has been investigating the human impacts of the 1989 *Exxon Valdez* Oil Spill in Alaska through a series of longitudinal studies. He was also part of a research team that examined the community impacts of the 2004 *Selendang Ayu* shipwreck and oil spill in the Aleutian Islands and the 2007 *Cosco Busan* oil spill in San Francisco. He also collaborated on several studies of Hurricane Katrina and organized and led a Katrina Summit that brought together national and local disaster scholars to discuss research needs and approaches to the disaster. He served as guest editor for special Katrina issues of *Sociological Spectrum* and the *Journal of Public Management and Social Policy*.

Dee Wood Harper, Jr. is professor of sociology and criminal justice at Loyola University in New Orleans. His scholarly research, spanning over 40 years, has been wide ranging, addressing issues in gerontology, the sociology of education, the epidemiology of addiction, the sociology of tourism and crime and, more recently, the death penalty and violent crime and deviance. His research has appeared in the *American Journal of Sociology*, *Sociological Spectrum*, *Annals of Tourism Research*, *International Journal of Law and Information Technology*, *Artificial Intelligence and Applications*, *Criminal Justice Review*, *Homicide Studies*, *Deviant Behavior* and the *American Journal of Sociology and Economics*.

Sabrina Medora is currently a junior at Indiana University, majoring in criminal justice. She plans to attend law school and become a criminal lawyer. Having lived in India for majority of her life, she has witnessed the terrifying impact terrorism can have on a country. She believes that creating awareness will ultimately result in a greater strength and unity, not just between countries that have been affected, but among those who can empathize and help fight against the evil phenomenon. As one who lost several friends and loved ones in the Mumbai attacks, she hopes their memories will live on and greater awareness will prevent further deaths.

Komanduri S. Murty, Professor and Coordinator of Sociology Program at Fort Valley State University, is the author or co-author of five books and more than 60 chapters and articles, which have appeared in numerous books and journals, including the *Encyclopedia of American Prisons*, *Encyclopedia of Anthropology*, *En-*

cyclopedia of Great Black Migration, Intimate Violence, Criminal Justice Review, The Status of Black Atlanta, Studies in Symbolic Interactionism, Deviant Behavior, International Journal of Comparative and Applied Criminal Justice, Journal of Police Science Administration, Journal of Social and Behavioral Sciences and *Victimology.* Dr. Murty has presented more than 90 articles at national and international professional meetings. He served as professor and chairman of criminal justice and sociology for 25 years at Clark Atlanta University, where he received the 2005 Aldridge McMillan award for Outstanding Overall Achievement.

J. Steven Picou is currently Professor of Sociology at the University of South Alabama (Mobile). Professor Picou's teaching and research interests include environmental sociology, disasters, risk and applied sociology. He has published numerous articles in these areas, the most recent appearing in *The Journal of Applied Social Science, Humboldt Journal of Social Relations, Sociological Inquiry, Social Forces, Environment and Behavior* and *Law and Policy*. In 2001, Professor Picou was awarded the Distinguished Contribution Award by the Environment and Technology section of the American Sociological Association for his basic and applied research activities in Alaskan fishing communities. In 2008, he was the recipient of the William Foote Whyte Distinguished Career Award given by the Sociological Practice and Public Policy Section of the American Sociological Association. He is a co-editor and contributor to *The Sociology of Katrina: Perspectives on a Modern Catastrophe,* published by Rowman and Littlefield. Professor Picou is presently directing research projects on community recovery from Hurricane Katrina and from the *Exxon Valdez* oil spill.

Liesel Ashley Ritchie is the Assistant Director for Research at the University of Colorado's Natural Hazards Center. Her research on the 1989 *Exxon Valdez* oil spill (EVOS) examines the relationship between technological disasters and social capital, as well as social impacts associated with protracted EVOS-related litigation. Other projects with which she has been recently involved include a study of disaster preparedness among community-based organizations in San Francisco and research on tsunami awareness and preparedness in various U.S. coastal states. Dr. Ritchie spearheaded the development of the American Evaluation Association's interest group on Disaster and Emergency Management Evaluation. She has served as guest editor for two disaster-related journal issues: *New Directions for Evaluation* and the *Journal of Public Management and Social Policy*.

Julian B. Roebuck is an internationally known criminologist and retired professor from Clark Atlanta and Mississippi State Universities. He is the author or co-author of over a dozen books on a wide range of subjects, including the seminal work, *Criminal Typology, The Etiology of Alcoholism, Rendezvous, The*

Southern Subculture of Drinking and Driving, The Southern Redneck and *Deviance and Crime in Colleges and Universities: What Goes on in the Halls of Ivy.* He has had an abiding interest in the study of collective behavior and riots, with articles on the subject published in *Studies in Symbolic Interaction, Deviant Behavior* and *The Journal of Police Science and Administration.* Dr. Roebuck was the founding president of the Mid-South Sociological Society. He was also a case worker with the U.S. Bureau of Prisons and the District of Columbia Department of Corrections.

William E. Thornton is Professor of Sociology and Chair of the Department of Criminal Justice at Loyola University New Orleans. His teaching has covered a wide range of undergraduate and graduate courses and topics in the disciplines of sociology, criminal justice, criminology and security. He is a forensic criminologist specializing in crime foreseeability, crime prevention, premises security litigation and security assessment. He is author and co-author of several books, chapters, articles and other materials in the fields of criminology, juvenile delinquency, security and social justice. He is currently conducting research on the physical and social aspects of disasters in relation to different types of criminal activity including violent, property and white collar crimes. His most recent research involves the analysis of Latino homicides and robberies in post-Katrina New Orleans and the adjoining region, as well as the impact that these crimes have on migrant worker populations.

Arvind Verma has been a member in the Indian Police Service and has served for many years in the State of Bihar, holding several senior level positions in the organization. His first degree was in Engineering Mathematics from the Indian Institute of Technology in Kanpur and he earned his doctoral degree in Criminology from Simon Fraser University in Canada. He has served as the Managing Editor of *Police Practice and Research: An International Journal* and he has also been an advisor to the Bureau of Police Research and Development in India. His current research interests are in data analysis and visualization, criminal justice in India and comparative policing. His recent publications include the books *Understanding the Police in India* and *The Indian Police: A Critical Review,* as well as a number of journal articles. He is currently on the faculty of the Department of Criminal Justice at Indiana University-Bloomington.

Lydia Voigt is a professor of sociology and holds the Joseph H. Fichter, S.J., Distinguished Professorship in the Social Sciences at Loyola University New Orleans. She is currently serving as Loyola's Senior Vice Provost for Academic Affairs. Her scholarship and teaching have covered a wide range of topics, such as international criminology and juvenile delinquency, the restorative justice movement, the history of violence, homicide trends in New Orleans, integrated homicide-suicide theories and typologies and evaluating security in premises liability lawsuits. She has authored or co-authored numerous books, monographs, book chapters, journal articles and reviews. She is currently collaborating on a research project examining human rights violations during the Katrina Disaster and also on a book on the history of homicide in New Orleans.

Patrick H. Walsh is an assistant professor of criminal justice at Loyola University New Orleans. He received his Ph.D. in criminal justice from the University of Southern Mississippi. He worked for many years as a loss prevention specialist for a major convenience store corporation. His primary research focus is on planning and the role of rational choice in the commission of both property and violent crime. He has presented his research on the reestablishment of illegal drug markets after Hurricane Katrina both nationally and internationally, most recently at the European Society of Criminology meeting. He is presently co-authoring a paper on armed robbery for a forthcoming handbook on deviance.

Index

Pages with tables or figures are in bold font. Case names and book titles are in italic font.